TWAYNE'S INTERNATIONAL HISTORY SERIES

Akira Iriye, editor
Harvard University

FRANCE AND THE UNITED STATES

The Cold Alliance Since World War II

Frank Costigliola
University of Rhode Island

TWAYNE PUBLISHERS • NEW YORK

MAXWELL MACMILLAN CANADA • TORONTO
MAXWELL MACMILLAN INTERNATIONAL • NEW YORK OXFORD SINGAPORE SYDNEY

Twayne Publishers
Macmillan Publishing Company
866 Third Avenue
New York, New York 10022

Maxwell Macmillan Canada, Inc.
1200 Eglinton Avenue East
Suite 200
Don Mills, Ontario M3C 3N1

Macmillan Publishing Company is part of the Maxwell Communication Group of Companies.

Printed in the United States of America

Library of Congress Cataloging-in-Publication Data

Costigliola, Frank, 1946–
    France and the United States : the cold alliance since World War
II / Frank Costigliola.
        p.   cm. — (Twayne's international history series ; no. 9)
    Includes bibliographical references and index.
    ISBN 0-8057-7902-7. — ISBN 0-8057-9205-8
    1. United States—Foreign relations—France.   2. France—Foreign
relations—United States.   3. United States—Foreign
relations—1945–1989.   4. France—Foreign relations—1945–
I. Title. II. Series.
E183.8.F8C68 1992
327.73044—dc20   91-41179
                                                                            CIP

The paper used in this publication meets the minimum requirements
of American National Standard for Information Sciences—Permanence
of Paper for Printed Library Materials. ANSI Z3948-1984. ∞™

10 9 8 7 6 5 4 3 2 1

For Molly Hite

CONTENTS

ILLUSTRATIONS

ABBREVIATIONS

AFL	American Federation of Labor
CAP	Common Agricultural Policy
CCF	Congress for Cultural Freedom
CERES	Center for Socialist Study, Research, and Education
CFR	Council on Foreign Relations
CGT	Confédération Générale du Travail
CIO	Congress of Industrial Organizations
CSCE	Conference on Security and Cooperation in Europe
EC	European Community
EEC	European Economic Community
EDC	European Defense Community
EPU	European Political Union
FFI	French Forces of the Interior
FLN	National Liberation Front (Algeria)
FO	Force Ouvrière
GATT	General Agreement on Tariffs and Trade
IMF	International Monetary Fund
INF	Intermediate Range Nuclear Force
MLF	Multilateral Force
NATO	North Atlantic Treaty Organization
NSC	National Security Council
NEP	New Economic Policy

PCF	Communist Party of France
PS	Socialist Party
SACEUR	Supreme Allied Commander in Europe
SDI	Strategic Defense Initiative
SDR	Special Drawing Right
USIA	United States Information Agency
USIS	United States Information Service
WEU	Western European Union

FOREWORD

Twayne's International History Series seeks to publish reliable and readable accounts of post-World War II international affairs. Today, nearly fifty years after the end of the war, the time seems opportune for a critical assessment of world affairs in the second half of the twentieth century. What themes and trends have characterized international relations since 1945? How have they evolved and changed? What connections have developed between international and domestic affairs? How have states and peoples defined and pursued their objectives, and what have they contributed to the world at large? How have conceptions of warfare and visions of peace changed?

These questions must be addressed if one is to arrive at an understanding of the contemporary world that is both international—with an awareness of the linkages among different parts of the world—and historical—with a keen sense of what the immediate past has brought to human civilization. Hence Twayne's *International History* Series. It is hoped that the volumes in this series will help the reader to explore important events and decisions since 1945 and to develop the global awareness and historical sensitivity required for confronting today's problems.

The first volumes in the series examine the United States' relations with other countries, groups of countries, or regions. The focus on the United States is justified in part because of the nation's predominant position in postwar international relations, and also because far more extensive documentation is available on American foreign affairs than is the case with other countries. The series addresses not only those interested in international relations, but also those studying America's and other countries' histories, who will find here useful guides and fresh insights into the recent past. Now more than ever it is imperative to understand the linkages between national and international history.

In this volume, Professor Costigliola, author of a pathbreaking book on U.S.-European relations after the First World War, offers a comprehensive and stimulating account of U.S.-French relations after the Second. Like the earlier work, this book examines economic, cultural, and psychological aspects, as well as strategic and political considerations, of the relationship between the United States and its oldest ally. Indeed, the author shows that the less tangible aspects of the relationship—the two peoples' images of each other, their leaders' mutual likes and dislikes, the pervasive influence of American material and popular culture in France, and the French intellectuals' changing perceptions of the United States—are particularly important for understanding U.S.-French relations since 1945. The period began in less than auspicious circumstances, with a France trying to rediscover its greatness after having succumbed to German aggression without a long struggle, and with an America positioning itself to function as the new superpower, having shouldered the primary responsibility for the defeat of Germany. How the French sought to redefine their destiny in Europe and in the world, how the Americans sometimes supported and sometimes stood in the way of such an effort, and how this binational drama was intimately linked to the turbulent political and economic changes of the postwar world—all these and many other themes are examined with a richness of detail and in a lively prose. The author has made extensive use of archival as well as printed documents. A product of several years' research and writing, the book deserves to be extensively read by all who would ponder the meaning of international affairs during the last half-century.

Akira Iriye

PREFACE

"Those damn French!" exploded President Dwight D. Eisenhower in 1954 when, once again, France appeared to be complicating the carrying out of U.S. foreign policy.[1] Nearly every U.S. president since Franklin D. Roosevelt has experienced similar exasperation with "those damn French," and for many American policymakers and citizens such epithets evoke stereotypes of an ally needlessly stubborn or vacillating, proud, independent, and other-minded.

This study questions those stereotypes by analyzing U.S.-French relations from a perspective that takes seriously the perceived national interests of both France and the United States. More than any other Western ally, France has challenged American foreign policy by maintaining a coherent, often distinctly French global view and policy. Despite such self-direction, however, France has often lacked the necessary national power and international backing to carry out its ambitions. And Paris has consistently appreciated the value of an alliance with Washington to help contain the Soviet Union and Germany. The United States and France, then, have remained allies that are often coldly apart because of policy differences.

Yet such differences and U.S. perceptions of French intransigence do not alone explain American exasperation with the French. Despite the ritual rhetoric about partnership and consultation that has filled countless communiqués issued after meetings between U.S. and Western European leaders, Washington has most often monopolized or at least dominated serious decision making within the alliance. While the United States has assumed that such predominance is the superpower's prerogative, France has pressed, annoyingly from an American perspective, for an influential voice for itself. By illuminating America's relationship with the European ally that has most often thought otherwise than Washington, this study casts light on the shape of the Western alliance as a whole, particularly by showing how the United States has expected its allies to be followers and how the alliance has largely failed to fulfill its democratic rhetoric about partnership and shared decision making.

The United States has had historic difficulties with alliances. In desperate need for aid during the American Revolution, the United States contracted an "entangling alliance" with France in 1778—and chafed almost at once at the limits that the French tried to put on the Americans' unbounded ambitions. Even before the United States officially broke free of the French tie in 1801, the new nation had on its own negotiated the triumphant peace settlement with Great Britain in 1783, and George Washington had warned his fellow Americans against further binding alliances in the farewell address of 1796. Thereafter the United States maintained not an isolationist foreign policy but rather a unilateral one. Washington officials insistently steered their own course, even in 1823, when London sought American cooperation to guarantee Latin America's newly won independence from Spain and in 1919–21, when the United States emerged from World War I as the globe's most powerful nation. In a wracking postwar domestic debate, the United States decided, in effect, not to restrict its options by joining the League of Nations but rather to continue exercising power independently and unilaterally. Not until after 1945, when the United States wielded overwhelming military, political, economic, and cultural predominance in the world and faced a perceived serious threat from the Soviet Union and communist ideology, did the Americans again contract an entangling alliance, this time with France and the other nations of NATO.

In terms of constraints on U.S. freedom of action, there was no great shift from America's acting alone before World War II and America's operating as the leader of an alliance system after the late 1940s. The United States made, largely on its own, the West's major decisions about war and peace in the various conflicts, crises, and accords of the cold war and about intervention in the third world. Americans usually set the agenda, the language, and the outcome of debates within the alliance. There were occasions when U.S. officials did genuinely consult with the European allies, instead of simply informing them of American decisions, but most often they did so with the like-minded British or Germans rather than with the "damn French," who tended to have their own perspective and agenda.

America's past difficulty in sharing decisions and in accommodating sharply different points of view within the framework of an alliance has become a crucial problem of the 1990s. In a figurative sense the Atlantic Ocean is widening. The economic rivalry between the European Community (E.C.) and the United States has intensified, and their differences over the third world continue. America has apparently too little money to play a leading role in rebuilding the economies of Eastern Europe. If relations between the West and the republics of the Soviet Union continue to improve, the reduction in tensions will eliminate many of the common security concerns that have bound Western Europe to the United States. If the fractured Soviet Union becomes chaotic, or if Moscow shifts back to policies of repression at home and toughness abroad, as was threatened by the abortive coup of August 1991, Western worries about security will intensify. That development would restore some authority to NATO and to the United States, but even in a new cold war Germany and France, leading the E.C., might decide to pursue their own accommodation with their giant eastern neighbor. At the present conjuncture Washington no longer can pursue a largely unilateral foreign policy and expect its allies to follow along dutifully. If the Western alliance is to endure into the future, Americans must become more willing to engage in multilateral decision making and to accept the restraints imposed by genuine partnership.

In writing this book I have incurred many debts both professional and personal. The National Endowment for the Humanities, the Lyndon B. Johnson Foundation, and the University of Rhode Island Alumni Association have provided generous financial support. George Ball, McGeorge Bundy, C. Douglas Dillon, and Bertrand Goldschmidt graciously took time out of their busy schedules to grant me interviews. The University of Rhode Island library team, particularly Vicki Burnett, Marie Rudd, Mimi Keefe, Dusty Haller, Deborah Mongeau, and Pamela Stoddard, were enormously helpful. I also wish to thank the staff of Olin Library at Cornell University, especially Fred Muratori, and the staff of the Rockefeller Library at Brown. Sally Marks at the National Archives, Ron Whalen at the John F. Kennedy Presidential Library, David Humphrey at the Lyndon B. Johnson Presidential Library, and the reference persons at Yale's Sterling Library, Princeton's Mudd Library, and the British Public Record Office also provided essential assistance. The personnel at the excellent Bibliothèque de Documentation Internationale Contemporaine in Nanterre, particularly Sonia Combe, were friendly and efficient, as were those at the Bibliothèque Nationale. I owe a special debt to Detlef Junker, Manfred Berg, and the staff at the Universität Heidelberg library.

I deeply appreciate the care with which Tom Paterson, Sally Marks, Pierre Mélandri, Stanley Hoffmann, Doug Little, and Michael Meimeth have read drafts of this study and suggested changes. In terms of this book and in many other matters, I continue to benefit from the special friendship, advice, and example of Walter LaFeber. Akira Iriye offered me the opportunity to participate in the Twayne International History Series, and his helpful criticism has been valuable. I am grateful for the patience and encouragement of Twayne editors Meghan Wander, Carol Chin, Barbara Sutton, and Jacob Conrad. Gino Silvestri has helped with every phase of this project. Other URI colleagues, especially Sharon Strom, Jim Findlay, Joel Cohen, Terri Murphy, Shaun Marmon, and Maury Klein have provided cheer and assistance. I thank Steven Sapp for sharing with me his own work on U.S.–French relations. Arnold Offner and Tom Paterson also contributed documents from their research. Mike Hogan and Irwin Wall were very kind to let me read early drafts of their excellent books. I owe special thanks to Robert Brigham and Jeff Mead. I continue to rely on the emotional support of Umberto, Nancy, and Charles Costigliola. My daughters Jennifer and Molly Amanda had the good sense not to let my work on this book slow them down too much.

My greatest debt is to Molly Hite, who has read with sharp intelligence every sentence of this book, who has listened with good humor to innumerable promises that I would finish the project "in two more weeks," and who remains my partner in life and scholarship.

Ithaca, New York   Frank Costigliola

INTRODUCTION

NO "SAVAGE GODDESS": THE STATUE OF LIBERTY, THE UNITED STATES, AND FRANCE

The Statue of Liberty was unveiled on 28 October 1886 to a crowd of diverse New Yorkers and French dignitaries who cherished a common allegiance to the ideal of liberty and an often conflicting understanding of what "liberty" meant. The French creators of the sculpture intended their work to become a giant beacon of liberty pointed across the Atlantic that would strengthen republican government in France, mobilize U.S. support for regaining Alsace-Lorraine, and stimulate French-American business and political ties. Yet once set upon its pedestal in New York harbor, *Liberty, Enlightening the World*, as its sculptors named it, became almost completely Americanized, an internationally-recognized symbol of U.S. power and concerns. After 1886 *Liberty* had no great impact on domestic French politics. And although Americans appreciated the gift of the statue, they did not respond with quickened interest in either the lost French provinces or in French products.

The failure of the statue to influence U.S.-French ties in the way that some in France had hoped points to some recurring patterns in the relationship between the two nations, themes particularly important in the half-century after 1940. Although France and the United States were allies for most of the period since 1940 and shared many general concerns, the two nations often had conflicting perspectives and agendas. More than any other ally, France attempted to maintain a foreign policy at least partially independent of the United States. The French doggedly pursued this autonomy for reasons of

1

pride and national interests and, in so doing, set off disputes with the Americans. Far stronger than France, the United States usually assumed that it could set basic policy for all its allies, including the French. Imbued with a sense of America's mission to the world—a faith symbolized by the Statue of Liberty—Americans often found it difficult to accept that the French had legitimate national interests and perspectives significantly different from those of the United States. This difficulty sometimes led Americans to interpret French disputes with the United States or dissimilarities in national style and values as evidence of French inferiority. Particularly from 1940 to 1958, Americans often stereotyped France as pathological or as negatively feminine. The latter image was not dispelled by France's gift of the Statue of Liberty.

Shortly before leaving for the United States in 1871 to generate support for his grand plan, *Liberty*'s sculptor, Frédéric-Auguste Bartholdi, paid an anguished farewell to his native Colmar in Alsace. Along with Lorraine, Alsace had just fallen to German control after France's humiliating defeat in Emperor Napoleon III's disastrous war against Prussia. Bartholdi longed to see these provinces returned to France and imperial France become a republic. He shared these aspirations with Edouard-René Lefebvre de Laboulaye, a prominent French jurist. Bartholdi and Laboulaye planned to spotlight their republican cause with a huge metal sculpture, dedicated to liberty and erected in New York harbor. Bartholdi and Laboulaye agreed that by "trying to glorify the republic and liberty over there, [we] shall await the day when they may be found here with us."[1]

As would many French citizens in the twentieth century, Bartholdi and Laboulaye looked to America for aid in combating foreign enemies and domestic opponents. At times, such as in the first years of World War I and World War II, the United States responded coolly to French pleas for help. In other instances, such as later on in World War II and during the cold war, Washington used the opportunity to impose an American agenda on the dependent nation. Whether Americans assisted France or ignored it, however, they often incurred resentment from the proud French, who had to struggle to get the American help they needed while still retaining their independence.

The United States figured prominently in France's efforts to maintain both its international autonomy and its domestic liberty. President Charles de Gaulle's complaint that it was troublesome governing a nation with over 300 cheeses reflects a history of internal divisions. The huge figure of *Liberty* was in many respects an attempt to address, if not to heal, one of the most important of these splits. In the early 1870s the French divided over what form of government should replace Napoleon III's discredited empire. As moderate republicans, Laboulaye and Bartholdi designed their statue to counter both the monarchists on their right, who decried all liberty, and the radicals on their left, who saw liberty in terms of the extreme phase of the 1789 French Revolution and the just-crushed Paris Commune.

In March 1871, when the French imperial government fled Paris before the invading Germans, the socialist Communards, many of them women, set up a radical, working-class government in the capital city. American ambassador Elihu Washburne commented that "there never was such a 'hell upon earth' " as the Paris Commune. "Violence, blackguardism, vulgarity, indecency were everywhere. They called it fun," he wrote indignantly.[2] Like many in America, the *Providence Journal* condemned France's "irrepressible passion for insurrection and for street barricades"; the French mob had "prostitut[ed]" the very words *republic* and *liberty*.[3] In May French troops bloodily smashed the experiment. Tens of thousands of slain Communards were buried in mass graves dug hastily in Paris's elegant public parks. Horrified, Americans contrasted France's turmoil with their happier tradition of stable, moderate republicanism. The *California Daily Alta* commented, "Nothing, apparently, can be done in France without force. . . . No one thinks of solving the problem by free discussion in the press and public meetings."[4]

To Americans the Paris Commune appeared to be another cycle in France's wild swings from anarchy to despotism. When the French Revolution first erupted in 1789, Americans flattered themselves that France was following the path blazed by their own revolution. But in the early 1790s the French Revolution became far more radical than the model of 1776. As the guillotine devoured both nobles and discredited revolutionary heroes, Americans recoiled with disgust. In 1889, the centennial of the French Revolution and of the U.S. Constitution, future president Woodrow Wilson commented that "one hundred years ago we gained, and Europe lost, self-command and self-possession."[5] Similarly, after 1940 anxious Americans would worry that France might slip into right-wing dictatorship, fall under Communist control, or sink into chaos with its weak parliamentary governments. France often appeared as a precariously perched domino, its people peculiarly susceptible to instability, license, and excess, all corollaries of what seemed a French perversion of the notion of liberty.

In the 1870s Laboulaye, Bartholdi, and others who determined to create a moderate French republic also felt uncomfortable with their nation's tradition of turbulence. They hoped to copy America's apparent success in melding republican government and stability. Their political cast helped shape the Statue of Liberty. Giving liberty the form of a stately woman fit the evolving esthetic and political ideal of many middle-class Europeans and Americans. In the late nineteenth century writers and illustrators often portrayed "safe" nationalism—that is, respectable, bourgeois, rational patriotic sentiment—as a chaste, modest woman. Thus "Marianne," the French national symbol, evolved in pictures and sculpture from her French Revolutionary incarnation as a young, active, sexually desirable single woman to the self-controlled, dignified matron of post-Commune France. Laboulaye had a definite political message in mind when he described the Statue of Liberty as no half-naked "savage goddess," but rather as a calm, heavily clad figure who could inspire reason and order. This image of liberty had "nothing revolutionary in it," he insisted.[6] Indeed, this reformed goddess embodied a femininity carefully distinguished from the characteristics Americans feared most in the French: emotionalism, excess, extremes of behavior. If the new, improved *Liberty* was still female, she had become nearer to the American ideal of a suitable consort.

In the late nineteenth and twentieth centuries Americans often viewed the French in gendered terms, but their stereotype differed from Bartholdi's stately lady. Instead Americans, particularly from 1940 to 1958, referred to the French in ways that suggested a flighty, not-so-capable female: emotional, hypersensitive, frivolous, impractical, unrestrained, too concerned with food, drink, fashion, art, and love. Meanwhile Americans usually cast themselves in a "masculine" mode—rational, calm, pragmatic, and efficient.

In 1953 *Life* magazine, whose publisher Henry Luce had close ties with leading American politicians and whose photographs did much to shape the perceptions of the American public when television was yet in its infancy, criticized France's "impossible political habits" in terms which suggested that the French were too feminized to govern themselves properly or to understand the seriousness of the cold war. The *Life* editorial personified the French government as "a big can-can chorus," as the singer "Edith Piaf" doing "a sob ballad," and as the sultry actress "Zsa Zsa Gabor . . . slipping a billion dollar bill into her stocking"—cadged from a gullible W. C. Fields, here playing the U.S. government. Although almost all of France's politicans were in fact men, they lacked, in *Life*'s view, the requisite manly virtues of courage and seriousness. To the sensible American man-in-the-street, the French parliament appeared as a stage show, "a rollicking bedroom farce involving Marianne—the beautiful girl who symbolizes the Republic—and the prime minister and cabinet members, who rush around and hide behind and under things when there's another knock on the door." The knocks came from Uncle Sam, trying to mobilize the French for the cold war, "which demands everybody's first attention." "Logic is a French specialty," *Life* acknowledged. But French intellectuals, then predominantly leftist, appeared to many Americans as dogmatic and otherworldly, enamored of a false Communist paradise, and too spiteful to acknowledge America's sacrifices on behalf of the Free World. French thinkers often "pictured the U.S. government as dominated by gangsters and Coca-Cola millionaires," *Life* complained. For the *Life* editors and for many Americans, such imagery reinforced beliefs that it was almost impossible "to make sense of French politics" and that the United States justifiably could ignore or run roughshod over French objections to American policies.[7] The key point here is that French national interests, politics, customs, values, and lifestyles often differed from those of the United States; and Americans, who had the upper hand in the relationship, often interpreted those differences as evidence of French inferiority—as negatively feminine or pathological.

Such coding of the French as feminine diminished sharply after 1958, when patriarchal de Gaulle came to power and replaced the weak, diffused parliamentary government of the Fourth Republic with the strong, executive-dominated regime of the Fifth Republic. Yet Americans still often saw the French as pathological, particularly when de Gaulle stubbornly opposed Washington's policies. Americans had a long history of distrust for the political judgment of the French. At the unveiling in 1886, one of the Americans thanking the French for their gift noted that the Statue of Liberty represented values with only a "precarious" hold in France: "On our shores, and under the tendency of a race less theoretic, less excitable, and less impatient than the French people, has been realized . . . the most successful and most hopeful of all . . . social systems."[8] Particularly after World War II, American foreign policy seemed predicated on the model of "Father Knows Best." This bias reinforced the tendency of American policymakers to dismiss or take less seriously French viewpoints and concerns.

If this feminized France remained untrustworthy in American eyes, however, it also remained attractive. Although Americans often disregarded or trivialized what the French had to say, many liked spending time in their country. In his masterpiece *The Education of Henry Adams*, Adams described with ironic wit how he "squandered" much of 1860 in Paris. He "had wanted no French influence in his education. He disapproved of France . . . he disliked most the French mind. . . . France was not serious, and he was not serious in going there. . . . sincerely disapproving [of the French] he felt at liberty to enjoy to the full everything he disapproved." "Several thousand" other Americans delighted in similar disdain, Adams observed.[9] Those many Americans savoring France—pioneers of the millions of U.S. tourists in the twentieth century—also boosted the French economy.

French backers of the Statue of Liberty hoped to change the image of a "not serious" country. In particular, they wanted to build markets for French business and generate sympathy for conquered Alsace-Lorraine. Premier Jules Ferry, architect of the Third Republic's overseas expansion, had the French government assume responsibility for completing the statue and delivering it to New York. Engineered by Gustave Eiffel, the superbly crafted figure advertised France's metallurgical industry and general technical know-how. Americans heartily embraced this business spirit. "We welcome you in the name of commerce—commerce that lights the torch and the flames of liberty, and is the pioneer of civilization," declared an American spokesman at the October 1886 inauguration.[10] The sculpture remained a potent business icon. Exactly a century later, similar hymns to commerce accompanied the celebration of the statue's refurbishing. Large American corporations raised the money for the restoration and reopening of the statue and, by means of the televised hoopla, profited from the advertising rewards.

But despite French hopes, *Liberty* did not transform France into a consort stable and attractive enough to lure increased American business. In the five years after 1886 French sales to the United States actually dropped by 9.1 percent as compared to the five years before the gift of the statue. Meanwhile, total European exports to the United States rose by 9.2 percent over the same period. In the twentieth century France ran a persistent trade deficit with the United States, and its business with America lagged behind other trade partners, notably Germany. In 1956, for example, France sold $236 million to the United States and bought $562 million. France's total U.S. trade amounted to only 62 percent of that of West Germany. By 1986, in contrast, America's gaping trade deficit enabled even France to run a trade surplus with the profligate Americans. French sales to the United States reached $10.1 billion, while French purchases totaled $7.2 billion. Yet France's total U.S. trade had sunk to 48 percent of that of West Germany.[11] U.S.-French trade ties remained important but not central to either nation. Indeed, the two countries often quarreled over Paris's efforts to resist U.S. commercial expansion. (Similarly, the number of French immigrants to the United States—and their clout in American politics—remained small compared to other European nations.)

Nor did the gift of the statue bring about the American partnership some French sought. For example, Ferdinand de Lesseps, who had built the Suez Canal and sought to repeat that success in Panama, tried using the Statue of Liberty as a lever to reduce Washington's opposition to a French canal in America's backyard. But while President Grover Cleveland warmly applauded de Lesseps's speech at the 1886 inauguration, he remained cool to the Frenchman's plan in Panama. This refusal proved typical. In the century after 1886 the United States would restrict France's overseas dominion, at first in the Western Hemisphere, where Washington increasingly held sway, and after 1945 in Asia and Africa, where Americans came to see French imperialism as backward and destabilizing. If the gift of the statue did help improve France's image in the United States in the late nineteenth century, a time when Americans began to worry about German militarism, Americans refused until World War I to take up Paris's cause in Alsace Lorraine. Even when France and the United States became military allies, the two nations resisted each other's viewpoints. The United States rescued France from Germany in two world wars—tardily, the French complained. And after both conflicts, Washington brushed aside Paris's objections and rebuilt a powerful Germany.

American dominance of the U.S.-French relationship after 1886 was illustrated by changes in the statue's symbolic meaning. Though Bartholdi and Laboulaye had planned a monument erected in New York harbor that would face eastward with a specific political message for France, the United States quickly naturalized the Statue of Liberty, as it did so many immigrants with foreign agendas.

Rival U.S. groups struggled to make the Americanized icon their own. Bartholdi, though he had lined up many wealthy backers for the massive pedestal on which the statue would stand, failed to secure all of the requisite $300,000—not a huge sum among robber barons and tycoons. Newspaper publisher Joseph Pulitzer raised the remaining $100,000 by printing in the *New York World* the names of all donors, including schoolchildren who gave their pennies.

Despite their contributions, average Americans had to watch from the shore or from boats as political dignitaries, wealthy businessmen, and members of New York society monopolized the dedication ceremonies on Bedloe's Island that rainy day. President Cleveland and other representatives of the elite claimed the colossal sculpture as an emblem for the existing capitalist, democratic order—superior both to "kings and armies" and to "anarchists and bombs," they claimed. This was a pointed remark, for the statue celebration took place while the nation's attention was riveted on the Haymarket trial in Chicago. Eight anarchists stood accused of murder after several police officers had been killed by a bomb, thrown by someone at a Haymarket protest rally. The Chicago anarchists defined their goal as "liberty"; *Harper's Weekly* countered with a Thomas Nast cartoon captioned "Liberty Is Not Anarchy," depicting the statue crushing eight anarchists in her left hand. [12]

Denied permission to attend the ceremonies on Bedloe's Island, some 200 woman suffragists chartered a boat and "without asking anybody's leave took up one of the most favorable positions for viewing," the *New York Times* reported. In the only protest demonstration at the inauguration, the suffragists criticized the "delightful inconsistency . . . in erecting a Statue of Liberty embodied as a woman in a land where no woman has political liberty. [13]

Another feminist, Emma Lazarus, penned what became the most popular interpretation of the statue, "The New Colossus," with its famous lines, "Give me your tired, your poor, / Your huddled masses yearning to breathe free." But Lazarus's sonnet ignored Bartholdi and Laboulaye's vision of a beacon to light France's liberty. The sculpture became instead the torch welcoming immigrants fleeing from the travails and indignities of inadequate motherlands. Even after the United States in the 1920s partly closed its door to alien, huddled masses, the statue continued to symbolize America's global superiority—in freedom and in power. Liberty's French antecedents became a nearly forgotten historical footnote. [14]

The history of the statue highlights major themes in U.S.-French affairs since 1940. France and the United States have been close, but have rarely seen things the same way. With their different perspectives and interests, the two nations have had difficulty understanding each other. The American tendency to belittle French concerns and the mutual resentment arising from French dependence on U.S. assistance have often chilled their relations. Although they have been allies for a half-century, theirs has most often been a cold alliance.

Chapter 1

THE DIFFICULT BRIDE:
DE GAULLE, ROOSEVELT, AND WORLD WAR II

On 6 June 1945, exactly a year after the first U.S. soldiers stormed ashore at Normandy to liberate France from the Nazis, French soldiers threatened to fire upon American troops. At issue was French occupation of border areas in the Italian Alps, in violation of orders from Supreme Allied Commander Dwight D. Eisenhower. Although President Harry S. Truman forced French General Charles de Gaulle to back off without shots being fired, this incident—not the first time the Americans and French used or threatened force against each other—illustrated the often stormy relationship between France and the United States during World War II. Although grateful to the United States for its help, the proud French chafed at their dependence on the powerful, self-assured Americans.

The two nations emerged from the war as allies; yet they had not fought the same war. Their experiences diverged from the start of the conflict. In 1939–40 France appealed desperately for aid while America refused to fight in Europe's war. The sudden French collapse in June 1940 jolted President Franklin D. Roosevelt into realizing that America might have to enter the war to stop the German steamroller. France's shocking breakup also seared into American minds a long-lived image of French weakness. For almost two decades after 1940 Americans would tend to view France as a nation bankrupt—in morality, politics, and military power. Roosevelt and others belittled France's wartime effort to regain its sovereignty, pride, and empire. U.S. officials often judged French political ambitions as petty, dangerous, and

8

implicitly feminine intrigues that could only confuse the essential wartime issues. Americans viewed their own aims as embodying universal precepts that would benefit all nations, including selfish France. Since the time of the Puritans, Americans had prided themselves as a chosen people, uniquely gifted to guide and in effect husband other nations. In Roosevelt this messianism reinforced another American tradition, opposition to European imperialism. FDR breezily assumed that with France prostrate, he had become custodian of France's future and its empire.

The French saw all this differently. America's new global ambitions appeared to them as just the latest example of a predominant state exercising its superior power. For the French, American talk about the welfare of mankind only demonstrated the Yankees' capacity for self-delusion. Such censure offended Americans.

U.S. leaders found particularly irritating criticism from General de Gaulle, leader of the resisting Free French. A fiercely patriotic military officer who had pleaded in vain for the French Army to reorient its strategy around the tank and other modern weapons, de Gaulle escaped to London in June 1940. In radio broadcasts to occupied France, this defiant nationalist rejected the notion of French defeat and dependence. France had lost the battle of 1940, but not the war, he insisted; France would remain a great power and keep its empire. De Gaulle understood that perception shaped political reality, whether in occupied France or in the councils of his allies. Therefore, the frailty of France and of the Free French movement made the general even more concerned with issues of honor, form, and prerogative. De Gaulle's insistent demands and imperial demeanor drove Roosevelt to mock him, only to heighten the general's haughtiness.

In contrast to the tension with de Gaulle, Roosevelt and British prime minister Winston Churchill enjoyed warm personal ties, which probably eased Anglo-American disputes. Many of these differences came over the fate of France. Churchill, though he often found de Gaulle grating, appreciated the general's leonine effort to protect France and its empire. In the postwar world, Great Britain would need a strong France to help counterbalance Soviet and American influence in Europe. At times, wartime French and British imperial interests collided, as in Lebanon and Syria. But in the larger picture a strong French empire helped buffer the British empire from assertive nationalists and Americans, Churchill calculated. Roosevelt believed he had the backing of Soviet leader Joseph Stalin in reforming postwar France and peeling off part of its empire. Yet in 1944 Roosevelt's rising fear of revolution forced him to curb his anticolonial enthusiasm and reconsider Churchill's scheme for restoring France and its empire.

Roosevelt and de Gaulle emerged from different backgrounds, with different views of the world. FDR came from a wealthy family that had traveled often to Europe. As president he still retained some of the French and German he had learned as a boy. FDR's knowledge of France's history remained scanty, but what he did know gave him little confidence in that nation's stability or democracy. Before the war, he bluntly told de Gaulle, he had been unable sometimes to recall the name of the current French leader.[1] In contrast to his meager knowledge of history, FDR the avid sailor, navalist, and stamp collector possessed a detailed grasp of geography. When he mapped global strategy during the war years, France figured in his calculations as the mistress of territories that it had not governed fairly in the past, that it could not defend in the present war, and that had become vital for America's worldwide position in the future.

De Gaulle saw this all differently. Unlike the American, he was a military man. His background was far less cosmopolitan than Roosevelt's, and he lacked FDR's insight that colonial empires were becoming an anachronism. De Gaulle viewed the French empire not as a hodgepodge of territories at America's disposal but as a security for France's future world power. The empire testified to the glory of France. The volatile French people had to believe in this grandeur, de Gaulle emphasized. If they lost faith, they would neither make the sacrifices necessary to uphold French greatness nor moderate the internal divisions that threatened it.

Both leaders condemned the French disease of weak, revolving-door parliamentary government. The general sought remedy in a stronger executive branch and in a revived sense of national pride. The president feared the general would try to go further. De Gaulle would either become another Napoleon, destroying French democracy and threatening American interests, or he would plunge France into civil war. Although the general did possess messianic tendencies, he had too good a sense of history to think he could govern modern France as Napoleon had done.

In contrast to Roosevelt's primarily geopolitical view of France, de Gaulle analyzed America's wartime policy from a historical perspective. Having grown to world power by conquering a near continent, the United States "no longer had within herself sufficient scope for her energies," the general perceived. With its "messianic impulse" and "instinct for domination" the United States saw the war as a new frontier, an opportunity to create a Pax Americana.[2] Such ambitions, he feared, clashed with the goal of restoring France's greatness. Despite this rivalry, de Gaulle realized he had to make some accommodation to America's overwhelming might. Upon hearing of Japan's 7 December 1941 attack on Pearl Harbor, he concluded that regardless of the fighting ahead, "this war is over. Nothing can resist the power of American industry."[3]

French and U.S. perspectives on the war grew further apart after Pearl Harbor. By the time the United States started fighting, most of the French (unlike de Gaulle) had stopped. Americans viewed the war as a black-and-white struggle; many French saw it as a gray one. Although the Germans acted worse, both warring sides abused France, many patriots concluded. Unlike America, France suffered battlefield damage and heavy Allied bombing.

While World War II helped homogenize the American people, it aggravated divisions among the French. The French population fractured into collaborators and resisters, into Vichyites, Communists, Gaullists, and the indifferent. Frightened of the French left, many conservatives accepted Germany's occupation and welcomed its war against the Soviet Union as safeguards against revolution. Marshal Philippe Pétain, head of state in the collaborationist Vichy regime, and General de Gaulle denounced each other and disagreed on much. Yet they concurred that what remained of France's sovereignty and empire lay threatened by the Americans and British as well as the Germans. Pétain tried to play the Americans off against the Germans while minimizing the encroachments of both sides. De Gaulle also disputed what he regarded as America's trampling on French sovereignty in metropolitan France and in the empire. Both French leaders tried to revive the national power crushed by Germany.

When German armies roared into the French capital on 14 June 1940, they were met by William C. Bullitt, U.S. ambassador to France and provisional mayor of Paris. Descended from a wealthy Philadelphia family that spoke French at the dinner table, and voted most brilliant in his class at Yale, Bullitt had become Woodrow Wilson's emissary to Vladimir Lenin at age 28. When Wilson rejected the accord Bullitt negotiated with Lenin, the fiery young diplomat resigned and helped kill the Versailles Treaty with damaging testimony before the U.S. Senate. Bullitt then moved to France, wrote a bestselling novel, and married Louise Bryant, widow of John Reed. In 1933 he became the first U.S. ambassador to the Soviet Union, having shed Bryant and acquired the friendship of FDR. Disappointment with his reception and diplomacy in Moscow embittered Bullitt about communism and the Soviet Union.

In 1936 he rejoiced when Roosevelt named him ambassador to France. "Bullitt was closer than anyone in the diplomatic service to the President," noted a top FDR adviser.[4] The French appreciated the ambassador as a link to Roosevelt and as an elegant host. The emissary rented a luxurious chateau and bragged to FDR: "I even had it stipulated in the lease that I can swim in all the lake[s] . . . and can place an American Indian canoe on the great waterway." The president bantered back that Bullitt reportedly was "negotiating with the French Government for . . . Versailles."[5] The ambassador hired a superb chef, stocked the cellar with 18,000 bottles of the best wines, and charmed French leaders. His dinner table became a meeting place for top politicians, particularly Premier Edouard Daladier and his successor, Paul Reynaud. The premier once jokingly asked Bullitt to serve as French ambassador to Washington. "Bullitt practically sleeps with the French cabinet," observed one American official.[6]

With the ambassador's prodding, FDR in late 1938 approved French purchase (at first covert) of America's most advanced warplanes. By 1940 the

French had contracted to buy $425 million of U.S. aircraft. This infusion of cash enabled American firms to quadruple their plane production capacity. For France the deal ended less happily; only 10 percent of the planes had been delivered when the Germans struck on 10 May 1940.[7]

With the Nazi onslaught, Bullitt tried fervently to mobilize the Roosevelt administration behind France, but without great success. He endorsed French pleas to purchase American destroyers, and he angered FDR by nearly ordering him to dispatch the Atlantic fleet to the Mediterranean. He sympathized with Reynaud's desperate request for a U.S. declaration of war on Germany. The ambassador urged an immediate transfer to France of squadrons of warplanes; the U.S. Army could replace the aircraft with those coming off the production lines. FDR did send some planes, but he said no to Bullitt's other pleas. In response to Reynaud's cry for military help, FDR would only praise France's "magnificent resistance" and advise that the French get their fleet out of the Axis's reach. The United States was not committed "to the slightest military activities in support of the Allies," Roosevelt reminded Churchill as France collapsed. Facing strong antiwar sentiment in Congress and in the country, Roosevelt would not go out on a shaky political limb.[8]

Bullitt proved readier to take a risk. When the French government and most other diplomats fled Paris in advance of the onrushing Germans, he decided to stay. Alluding to the Paris Commune of 1871, Bullitt convinced himself that "the moment the French Government leaves Paris the Communists . . . will seize the city, and will be permitted to murder, loot and burn for several days."[9] Against this imagined slaughter he marshaled 12 tommy guns, ordered at his own expense. As Bullitt had hoped, the departing government asked him to oversee the transition to German occupation and appointed him provisional mayor. Glorying in the drama of the moment, the ambassador cabled Washington, "It will mean something always to the French . . . to remember that we do not leave though others do, . . . J'y suis J'y reste."[10] For de Gaulle, the diplomat's decision not to accompany the French government meant something quite different, "that the United States no longer had much use for France."[11] Bullitt probably felt some disappointment when the transition to German occupation proved orderly, with no Communist revolt. Secretary of State Cordell Hull certainly felt disappointed, for the headstrong diplomat had ignored his pleas to accompany the fleeing French government and to try to persuade it to continue the war from North Africa.[12]

Bullitt's overeager heroics point up some important themes in U.S.-French relations. Fearful of French radicalism, Americans tended to exaggerate its strength and aggressiveness. They were also inclined to overestimate the extent to which a U.S. representative, despite the power of his country and his personality, could shape French events and policy. Finally, Americans underestimated the advantages many French saw in a European bloc, whether it was under German tutelage during the war or, far more preferable, under French direction in the postwar era.

For most Americans June 1940 meant that France was probably finished as a great power and that the war against Hitler would take longer than they had expected. For many French, particularly those who formed the Vichy government, the defeat signaled an opportunity to remake France and a quick end to war. As their armies crumbled, most French turned to the father figure of Marshal Philippe Pétain, an 86-year-old hero of World War I. Like many, Pétain held in contempt the unstable governments of the Third Republic, especially the Popular Front, which in the 1930s had tried to institute social and economic reforms. Echoing a sentiment common in France and out, Pétain blamed the 1940 disaster on the softening of the nation's moral and patriotic fiber. Although the defeat was explainable in classic military terms, many critics preferred scapegoats. Socialist teachers in the schools, Pétain once told Bullitt, had destroyed the "fighting spirit" of young army officers. The defeat, the discrediting of the Third Republic, and the dramatic lesson of German efficiency all argued for remaking French society along more disciplined lines. In place of the republic's "liberty, fraternity, and equality," Pétain's Vichy state offered "work, family, and country."[13]

After the Germans occupied Paris, Bullitt caught up with the French government at Vichy. He reported that the new leaders, principally Pétain, Admiral François Darlan, and Pierre Laval, stood eager to collaborate with Germany and to remake France. Determined to "cut loose" from the republican past, these men hoped "that France may become Germany's favorite province—a new *Gau* which will develop into a new Gaul," Bullitt observed.[14] For the Vichy leaders, the sooner the war ended and the worse England was defeated, the better. Germany would satisfy itself with booty from England, and, the happy scenario went, France would join the Reich in rebuilding Europe. With its superior intelligence and civilization, France would eventually command this new order. Most French shared what then seemed like a sensible view: Germany had apparently won the war; defeated France should try to learn from its mistakes and work with the new reality to build a viable future; America lay far away and had given little aid; Great Britain would probably soon surrender and had refused to commit its air force to defend France. From the French perspective, the British had compounded the treachery on 3 July 1940 when they sank French naval ships anchored at Mers el-Kébir, Algeria, with the loss of many sailors.

Bullitt's reaction to this new mentality and leadership set the pattern for relations between the United States and Vichy France. He judged the French worldview of 1940—so different from the American perspective—not as adjustment to harsh reality but as evidence of "mental disorder." Although put off by outgoing president Albert Lebrun's "nervous excitement" and Darlan's "smile" at the thought of England's defeat, Bullitt found Pétain "calm, serious and . . . great."[15] Thus began the American romance with the octogenarian general. The United States courted Pétain as the Vichy leader who, because of his stubborn patriotism and substantial popular support, seemed the strongest resistant to German demands for the French fleet and colonies. Although Pétain valued U.S. friendship as a counterweight to the Axis, he pursued collaboration with the Nazis to build a new Europe. He tried to resist encroachments from both sides and dreamed of mediating a compromise peace. The Americans seriously underestimated Pétain's readiness to work with Germany. Thus they mistook Vichy's efforts at collaboration as resulting from Nazi pressure or as the elderly man's associates working behind his back.

Americans cultivated one such associate, Admiral François Darlan, hoping he would keep the French navy out of Axis hands. American suspicions that he would surrender the French navy insulted Darlan. In the armistice Germany had recognized French control of the fleet, the admiral explained. And, he insisted, if the Germans tried to seize any ships, the officers on board had orders to sink them. (Despite persistent American doubts, the French would carry out those orders in November 1942.) Bullitt remained skeptical. In the first months after June 1940 Americans assumed that Vichy lacked any independence whatsoever. "The fleet could not be more securely in Germany's hands than it is now," Secretary of State Hull fumed at Gaston Henry-Haye, the Vichy ambassador.[16]

After France's collapse, jittery Washington officials wondered where the seemingly unstoppable Nazis would strike next. If France could not safeguard such strategic colonies as Dakar, at the westernmost tip of Africa, and Martinique, in the West Indies, U.S. security stood imperiled. Crusty Henry L. Stimson, the protégé of Theodore Roosevelt whom FDR had just appointed secretary of war, took seriously rumors that the Germans planned to make Dakar into an airbase from which to invade South America and "get to us by December." The president approved Churchill's and de Gaulle's plan to rally Dakar to the Free French side with a patriotic appeal, backed by naval force. Because this was de Gaulle's first military action since leaving France in June 1940, the general, as well as his prestige, sailed with the expedition. It proved a disaster, with the pro-Vichy colonial government left unpersuaded by either de Gaulle's appeal or the naval guns. This confirmed FDR's already low estimate of de Gaulle. Stimson concluded from Dakar that the navy's plan to take Martinique by force would "provoke a bloody conflict" with the Vichy French.[17]

By late 1940 Washington concluded that Vichy still held on to a precarious semi-independence. Close relations with the collaborationists seemed the safest path to protecting American interests. Although no longer in the administration, Bullitt had pointed the way on 1 July with his overdrawn distinction between the craven collaborators and the honorable Pétain.

Cooperation with Vichy became part of a mix of policies that the United States devised to deal with the territories of France. Americans assumed that defeat had destroyed the unity and sovereignty of the French empire. They applied different policies toward different colonies, each suited to the power realities of that particular area. For example, Washington insisted on U.S. military predominance at Martinique, chafed at Japanese control of Indochina, collided with the Free French masters of nickel-rich New Caledonia, commenced trade with North Africa, and courted the regime at Vichy. Washington's preference for dealing with local authorities fit its wartime needs, but it frustrated the efforts of French leaders, whether Vichyite or Gaullist, to defend the sovereignty and interests of France as a whole. French legitimacy had passed intact to his organization upon Pétain's surrender, de Gaulle protested.

This argument made little impression on Admiral William Leahy, who became the U.S. ambassador to Vichy. His credentials as an anti-Communist conservative, a naval officer, and FDR's close friend signaled Washington's resolve to cultivate Pétain and keep the French fleet and empire out of Axis hands. The Americans also wooed the governor of North Africa, General Maxime Weygand. Like Pétain, Weygand appeared to Washington as a doughty hero from the last war who had counseled surrender in June but who now seemed resistant to German demands. If French cooperation with Germany did not go beyond the Armistice agreement, Washington would give valuable aid to Vichy France, Hull promised. FDR sent Pétain warm, personal letters, and American officials even helped Weygand get tires for his Lockheed plane.

Suffering from German confiscation and the British blockade, France soon grew short on supplies. After heated negotiations with London, the State Department poked a hole in the British blockade. The United States began food relief for children (primarily condensed milk and vitamins) in unoccupied France and trade with North Africa. Such aid fit the American practice, honed in the 1920s, of pursuing political ends with economic means. Sentimentalism had little to do with food relief, Washington officials explained. The aid won the United States influence with French public opinion, Americans believed, and that prestige would help sway Pétain. The aid agreement required Vichy authorities to publicize that the relief came from the United States and to promise not to reexport supplies to the occupied zone or to other territory controlled by the Axis. To guarantee that promise, the United States obtained Vichy's permission to send several special vice-consuls to North Africa. Besides inspecting the movement of goods in and out of this strategic region, these agents or "spies," as Leahy called them, reported on military matters to the War and Navy departments and tried to rally support for a future Allied invasion. Although aid yielded intelligence and influence, it failed to win significant military advantage. Washington's lavish attention to

Weygand aroused German suspicions, which led Vichy to dismiss him. American frustration was complete when Weygand, still loyal to Pétain, refused to cooperate with American planning for the invasion of Vichy-held North Africa.[18]

The Vichy policy also disappointed Americans by failing to limit French cooperation with Germany. This failure stemmed from a fundamental miscalculation about the relationship between Vichy and Germany. Pétain, Laval, and Darlan remained French patriots, deeply loyal to France. Despite serious political differences, they agreed that a German victory seemed inevitable, and that France had to end the 70-year feud with its powerful neighbor. Although Vichy leaders valued American support, that did not deter them from actively seeking a deal with Germany. They proposed collaboration in return for an easing of the armistice, a revival of sovereignty, and a secure place in the new European order. In mid-1941 Darlan offered the Germans extensive military rights in the empire, including an eventual submarine base at Dakar. In October, as German armies swept through the Soviet Union, the French offered Hitler help, including volunteer troops. Although some German officials welcomed these proposals from a "budding ally," Adolf Hitler, unwilling to lift his boot from the French neck, said no. Even as Hitler spurned French advances, Americans deluded themselves that their courtship was keeping Vichy free from the German grasp.[19]

Americans believed that wooing Pétain required keeping de Gaulle at arm's length. The hatred between the two generals ran as deep as their past friendship. In World War I Pétain had cited Captain de Gaulle for extraordinary bravery and afterward had taken him as a protégé. De Gaulle named his son after the older man, to whom he had dedicated his 1938 book *France and Its Army*. Soon after, conflicting ambitions and military doctrines cooled their relations. The final rupture came in June 1940 when de Gaulle, in London, denounced Vichy as a German puppet state. Pétain declared him a traitor, condemned to death. De Gaulle's rebellion helped the marshal win concessions from the Germans. Yet Pétain felt betrayed by the "viper that he had warmed in his bosom."[20]

Leahy shared the marshal's distaste for de Gaulle and his followers. The Free French lacked "stability, intelligence, and popular standing," Leahy concluded.[21] FDR considered de Gaulle just another French general, hardly a compliment after June 1940. The State Department decided that the Free French could not "inspir[e]" resistance since it had "no outstanding men with qualities of leadership and initiative."[22] French emigrés in the United States and in Great Britain squabbled over de Gaulle's leadership and other issues, encouraging Americans to dismiss them all as vainglorious talkers.

American officials held various images of de Gaulle, most of them negative. They falsely labeled the petulant general an English puppet who would deliver postwar France into a British-led bloc. Americans also saw de Gaulle as an undependable, power-hungry rebel who would not wait for postwar elections before assuming power. Leahy referred to the general's "radical" followers and lumped together Gaullist and Communist elements in the internal French resistance. Bullitt claimed that Stalin and de Gaulle had made a deal. At times FDR and Hull spoke of de Gaulle as a fascist. However Americans characterized the general's ideology, they did not trust him as being safely democratic. De Gaulle appeared dangerously uncontrollable because he insisted on his own wartime program and priorities. Vichy did too, but Washington found that less exasperating—the poor marshal, after all, had only limited control over his subordinates and independence from the Germans.

The St. Pierre and Miquelon affair of December 1941 aggravated American distrust of de Gaulle's autonomy. A small but strategic archipelago off the coast of Newfoundland, St. Pierre and Miquelon remained under Vichy control. The islands possessed a powerful shortwave radio transmitter. This posed the potential danger that Germans or Nazi sympathizers could report the location of Allied shipping to German submarines.

When the Free French seized the islands despite American opposition, the incident exploded into what the journalist Walter Lippmann termed a diplomatic Pearl Harbor. Coming just two weeks after the real event, the controversy underscored Washington's determination to favor Vichy over the Free French. This marked the first wartime occasion that Americans and Free French threatened to fire on each other.[23]

The affair directed the U.S. public's attention to an embarrassing contradiction. In the Atlantic Charter of August 1941 FDR had stressed the enemy's absolute evil and the Allies' high principles, yet here was the administration cozying to a regime subservient to the Germans while spurning a movement wanting to fight them. The American people failed to grasp—or to agree with—the administration's Vichy policy. In August 1941, 58 percent of the public had seen Vichy as "helping Hitler"; only 17 percent had found Vichy neutral or aiding the British. A month later, 74 percent of Americans had favored giving war materials to the Free French.[24] The St. Pierre and Miquelon incident strengthened support for de Gaulle among the American public.

The crisis erupted while Churchill and FDR conferred in Washington on wartime strategy. A short while earlier the president had reaffirmed his commitment to the status quo in France's Western Hemisphere possessions. In mid-December de Gaulle seemingly acquiesced when the Roosevelt administration vetoed his plan to have Admiral Émile Muselier rally St. Pierre and Miquelon to the Free French. The administration also denied Muselier's request to visit Washington. Instead, Roosevelt asked the Canadians to take over the radio station, using "force" if necessary. This violation of French sovereignty contradicted the pledge to Pétain, and it infuriated de Gaulle. When the general learned of Roosevelt's plan, he ordered Muselier to seize the islands regardless of U.S. objections. The admiral did so, and the next day inhabitants voted overwhelming approval of the Free French takeover.

A raging Hull interrupted his Christmas to denounce the Free French invasion and publicly demand restoration of the islands to Vichy control. Famous for his Tennessee hill temper, Hull did not soon calm down. To the British ambassador he compared Muselier's action with German and Japanese aggression. When FDR at first made light of the affair, Hull threatened to resign. The secretary exploded that now the volatile French would start fighting over their other colonies, or Vichy might allow the Germans to take North Africa. Despite his fury with the Free French, Hull warned Vichy ambassador Gaston Henry-Haye to drop any idea of retaking the islands by force. Henry-Haye's angry response "about French sovereignty" could just as easily have come from de Gaulle.[25] FDR warned Churchill that the United States might "force" the Free French out of the islands. When a British official conveyed this threat to de Gaulle, the audacious general warned that his people would "fire" on the invading Americans. De Gaulle understood the public uproar that would follow a U.S. attack on the Free French. "I have confidence in the democracies," he smiled at the British official.[26]

The St. Pierre and Miquelon incident deepened divisions all around. Eager to placate his new ally, Churchill echoed FDR's line, only to meet protest from Anthony Eden of the Foreign Office, who viewed de Gaulle as a savior for the strong France that Britain would need after the war. The Free French also split. To the American consul, Admiral Muselier denounced de Gaulle as "a dictator" and explained that "his wife was a descendant of Lafayette" and that he wanted to cooperate with America. Still, despite his distaste for de Gaulle, he would "fight to the last man" to hold the islands.

The American public applauded the intrepid Free French, whose victory stood out from the string of military disasters at Pearl Harbor, Wake Island, and elsewhere. Popular protest blew up when Hull condemned the takeover by the "so-called Free French ships." Letters and telegrams bombarded the "so-called Secretary of State" at the "so-called State Department." Although a majority of newspapers eventually rallied behind the administration, many of the more liberal publications remained critical. When 55 prominent American literary and academic figures, including Carl Sandburg and Helen Keller, cabled a protest to the president, State Department analysts lumped the signers with "Marxian revolutionaries." Once again de Gaulle meant trouble, U.S. officials concluded.[27] Public criticism of the administration's policy toward France sharpened after November 1942, when the American army stormed ashore in North Africa, only to uphold the leadership of that ardent German collaborator Admiral Darlan.

The politics of the North African invasion, code-named Torch, followed familiar tenets in U.S.-French relations. The Darlan deal flowed from the logic of Washington's policy toward Vichy. Pétain's orders to fight the invaders expressed the French impulse to resist encroachments, whether from the Allies or the Axis. Darlan's counterorders to cease resistance demonstrated the stronger impulse among Vichyites to defend French interests through collaboration with the predominant power. FDR's insistence on excluding de Gaulle deepened the gulf between the general and the United States. Operation Torch illustrated America's local-authorities doctrine and U.S. insensitivity to French sovereignty. Finally, the invasion and its aftermath demonstrated the Americans' tendency to assume they knew what the French wanted and the perils that ensued when they were wrong.[28]

Ironically, it was FDR, the master politician, who especially misjudged French politics. Much of the blame probably lay with Leahy, who as ambassador assumed he knew what the "inarticulate" French public wanted and believed—that is, to have the United States protect French interests and direct the war. When Leahy left Vichy to become FDR's chief of staff, he took with him these assumptions. Leahy's advice reinforced the president's sense that he could act as the trustee of French sovereignty. Shortly before leaving Vichy, Leahy reiterated the tenets of U.S. policy toward bankrupt France. America's supreme task in fighting for "our civilization" outweighed any "sympathy" for France, he asserted. In this titanic struggle, "the pride or sensibilities of defeated France in Madagascar, in Indo-China, or elsewhere" mattered little. France could neither help the Allies nor "assist . . . itself." Therefore "French territory [should] be utilized by the Allies wherever it promises advantage." Despite Vichy's objections, "French public opinion"— Leahy's silent majority—would "cheer us on," he declared.[29]

On 8 November 1942 the Americans and British "utilized" North Africa by invading it in Operation Torch.[30] Rejecting the advice of the War Department, which favored a cross-Channel invasion of France, Roosevelt in July 1942 accepted Churchill's plan of attacking the Germans in Libya from French North Africa. In choosing North Africa, FDR and Leahy expected that despite Pétain's pledge to resist any invader, American troops could wade ashore virtually unopposed. This rosy scenario rested on assurances from Robert Murphy, the State Department official in North Africa, that economic aid and intrigue by the "vice-consuls" had won over the population. To soften Pétain's resistance, FDR sent a personal letter, whose first draft began, "My dear old friend."[31] In order to secure French North Africa as quickly as possible, Washington planned to work with any cooperative Vichy officials on the scene.

François Darlan, commander in chief of Vichy armed forces and former deputy premier, appealed as a candidate who might deliver the French fleet. The diminutive admiral ("Popeye" in Leahy's correspondence) was ambitious, patriotic, and untroubled by political principles. He stood ready to ally with the Germans if they lifted the conqueror's yoke. Yet Darlan also told Leahy: "When you have 3,000 tanks, 6,000 planes and 500,000 men to bring to Marseilles, let me know. Then we shall welcome you."[32] Murphy maintained close contact with Darlan through an intermediary in North Africa, Admiral Raymond Fenard. "Mr. Murphy dined at my house on an average, I believe, of once a month. . . . I am sure you don't think we talked about moonlight," Fenard later recounted.[33] Darlan appeared to be a willing ally, but a slippery one. Far different from this intriguer was the Americans' first choice, the heroic but politically inept General Henri Giraud. Giraud had escaped from the Germans in World War I and again in April 1942. Murphy met with him at Vichy. Giraud agreed to help in North Africa if the Americans gave him the military command and excluded the British and the Gaullists. The United States had no intention of agreeing to the first two demands, but Murphy masked the disagreement. Giraud appealed to the Roosevelt administration as a safe, middle-of-the-road French leader, in between the quasi-Nazi Vichyites and the "radical" Gaullists. Like many such compromise figures, however, Giraud commanded neither a coherent political program nor popular appeal.

FDR had assumed that the French would not oppose an invasion of North Africa. He also expected that Giraud would attract a following, eclipsing de Gaulle's Free French. Both beliefs proved to be wishful thinking. The Vichy French fought hard against the invading Americans, as Pétain had warned. Even de Gaulle, who soon endorsed Operation Torch, was initially belligerent: "Well, I hope the people of Vichy throw them into the sea. You can't break into France and get away with it."[34] Meanwhile Giraud, who had been spirited away by submarine to Gibraltar, refused to leave that fortress. He demanded the military command of Allied forces in North Africa, as he believed Murphy had promised. Vichy troops continued shooting at Americans.

Then a happy "coincidence" occurred. Darlan was in Algiers visiting his polio-stricken son—and negotiating with Murphy. On 17 October 1942 FDR had ordered Murphy to try to strike a deal with Darlan. Such an accord would be insurance in case the Giraud option failed. "Popeye's" stature grew when Americans saw that Vichy commanders ignored proclamations issued in Giraud's name, while obeying those of Darlan, the marshal's representative. As American soldiers fought their way into Algiers, Darlan ordered Vichy forces to cease fire. The Americans then negotiated several agreements with Darlan, accepting him as the local civilian authority in North Africa. When Giraud finally arrived, the general became commander of French forces.

With the Allies now in North Africa, Hitler decided to occupy the rest of France. Vichy broke relations with the United States. Darlan had jumped to the American side, but he proved unable to deliver the fleet, still at Toulon. "Merde!" replied the fleet commander when Darlan ordered an escape to the Allies.[35] As the Germans approached, French sailors scuttled their ships. The French navy would fall neither to the Germans nor to the Allies.

Public outcry in the United States and Great Britain against this latest deal with those who dealt with Hitler grew louder than the uproar over St. Pierre and Miquelon. Beating a tactical retreat, FDR issued a brief explanation that repeated the word "temporary" five times. He justified the interim deal as necessary to save soldiers' lives. In fact, however, as Eisenhower reminded Washington, the arrangement was not temporary. Nor did it save many lives, since the ceasefire preceded the approval of Darlan's political authority.

The Darlan deal illustrates the ease with which the Roosevelt administration dismissed French sovereignty. Building up Pétain made sense only so long as the marshal cooperated. Now that he had resisted the American invasion, Hull considered Vichy a cipher and not at all representative of the French people. FDR believed the United States enjoyed in North Africa the unlimited rights of a conqueror. Accordingly, he demanded that the Darlan arrangement be called a "joint announcement" rather than an "agreement," because the latter implied a contract and hence mutual obligations. The document actually read like a surrender statement. Its emphasis on "complete control . . . both civil and military" highlighted a contradiction in U.S. policy. The president claimed the United States wanted to win the war as rapidly as possible.[36] Hence Washington approached issues from a purely "military" perspective—in contrast to de Gaulle's "political" emphasis on French sovereignty or dignity. Yet as Eisenhower complained, Washington's opposition to French control of liberated territory burdened him with civil responsibilities. Eisenhower, in need of French cooperation in North Africa, worried that acting like a conqueror might lead to renewed fighting or passive resistance. How could he handle that and also fight the Germans? Despite FDR's attitude of conqueror, Eisenhower tried to act as liberator, sharing power and publicly understating French armed opposition.

In the last two months of 1942 cooperation with Darlan grew particularly close. Stimson found the admiral "very useful."[37] Murphy grew fond of him. Darlan's worry over his son's polio touched FDR, who arranged treatment at Warm Springs, Georgia. Even Churchill warmed to Darlan, to de Gaulle's disgust. When Darlan was assassinated on Christmas Day, the Roosevelt administration reacted with "horror," Stimson recorded.[38] Although evidence never indicated that the assassin was other than a lone French royalist, Roosevelt officials shared popular suspicion that de Gaulle's organization was involved somehow. FDR abruptly canceled the general's planned trip to Washington.

Operation Torch had worsened the already poisoned relations with what Hull called those "polecats," the Free French. In an angry debate at the State Department, de Gaulle's emissaries disputed FDR's claim to supreme power in North Africa. De Gaulle "was brim full of bitterness," one of his deputies warned the department. When the general and FDR met, "there would be a very violent scene."[39] De Gaulle's criticism of Operation Torch underscored the basic issue of Europe's growing dependence on the United States. He tried to shame London for allowing Washington to run the show, a complaint he would repeat for the next quarter century. "I cannot understand how you British can stand aside so completely in an undertaking that is of such primary concern to Europe," he scolded Churchill and Eden.[40]

Another fundamental matter was the ideological split among the Allies. De Gaulle understood that Hitler's war had forced a shotgun wedding between the Soviet Union and the West. The great issue of who would dominate postwar France and Europe remained undecided. When the military war ended, the ideological battle would resume, de Gaulle emphasized. If the French concluded that the West meant to liberate them by imposing the likes of Darlan, they would turn to the Soviet Union and communism, he warned Churchill curtly. Here de Gaulle rang the alarm that in 1944–45 forced the Americans to ease their opposition to him. Communist takeover of France was a real possibility, de Gaulle stressed. And he stood out as the best protection against it.

From Darlan's death in December 1942 to D-Day in June 1944, this ideological clash remained submerged by the war with Hitler and the struggle between de Gaulle and Giraud. The generals' competition reflected basic divisions within France and among the Allies. The rivalry also demonstrated the sharp limits to Roosevelt's power, even as he led the world's mightiest nation. Roosevelt sorely underestimated the forces against him. After Darlan's death, he ordered Eisenhower simply to "appoint" Giraud as successor if the French put forth anyone else.

In January 1943 FDR met Churchill at Casablanca. Basking in the warm North African sun, the president proposed to the British leader a marriage to end the rivalry between the two French generals. "We'll call Giraud the bridegroom, and I'll produce him from Algiers," he said gaily, "and you get the bride, de Gaulle, down from London, and we'll have a shotgun wedding." Ever dutiful, Giraud arrived, assuring FDR that his concerns lay not with politics, but with weapons for the French North African army. De Gaulle, however, became insulted at the idea of foreigners summoning him to meet another French leader on French soil. A few weeks earlier, Giraud had rejected de Gaulle's proposal for a private meeting. Now de Gaulle refused to come to Casablanca. Enjoying Churchill's embarrassment, FDR ribbed, "Where is the bride?" Not tiring of the joke, he cabled Hull: "We delivered our bridegroom, General Giraud, who was most cooperative on the impending marriage. . . . However . . . the temperamental lady DeGaulle . . . has got quite snooty . . . and is showing no intention of getting into bed with Giraud."[41]

The metaphor was telling. Roosevelt saw himself as a lord of France's destiny, as a seigneurial matchmaker. He coded de Gaulle as the difficult bride who did not understand France's true interests and Giraud as the tractable and hence suitable surrogate who would take care of the lord's concerns. In London, Eden translated Churchill's cables of rage into a renewed invitation to the haughty Frenchman. Under pressure from his advisers and realizing that he had made his point, de Gaulle consented to go to Casablanca. Besides, it would be his first meeting with Roosevelt, and the supremely confident general hoped to impress the president.

Tense circumstances marked the meeting. The general stalked into the president's headquarters, freshly insulted by the swarm of American military guards in French Casablanca. One shudders at what his reaction might have been had he noticed what FDR's adviser Harry Hopkins detected behind the curtain in the meeting room: Secret Service guards "all armed to the teeth, with, perhaps, a dozen tommy-guns" aimed at de Gaulle. They could not take any chances on anything happening to the president, the guards told a startled Hopkins.[42] Yet the Secret Service had not deployed such armament during FDR's earlier conference with Giraud. Reportedly, FDR tried to set the austere general at ease by calling him by his first name. Each man wanted to charm the other even though their perspectives and policies remained sharply divergent. France had become "a little child unable to look out for . . . itself"; it needed a "trustee," FDR told the proud Frenchman.[43] De Gaulle rejected the plea to join Giraud's group. He did offer to make Giraud commander in chief of French forces, but only if Giraud would join de Gaulle's group which had renamed itself the Fighting French. Despite their differences, FDR and de Gaulle parted on friendly terms.

Soon after, Giraud, backed by the Americans and British, turned down de Gaulle's deal. With the French generals at loggerheads, Roosevelt pressed for at least a public display of friendship, to quiet criticism back home. Thus the famous photograph, staged for the press, of Giraud and de Gaulle stiffly shaking hands before the beaming president. Both FDR and de Gaulle had a history of winning others with the force of their personalities. Each came away from Casablanca hoping he had swayed the other. The next months disappointed both of them.

In June 1943 the organizations of Giraud and de Gaulle united, but FDR soon soured on the outcome. The two generals became copresidents of the French Committee of National Liberation (FCNL), with seven members divided between the two factions. Giraud, who often signed documents without reading them, sat as the lamb in the lions' den. De Gaulle immediately broadened the committee to 14, now with a majority of his supporters. In November Giraud signed the ordinance abolishing the copresidency, but remained commander in chief until de Gaulle eased him out of that post in April 1944. As Roosevelt remarked, "He was not a very bright old gentleman."[44]

Unlike de Gaulle, Giraud lacked a cogent vision for France's future. Giraud believed that French revival required only order and discipline. With far keener insight, de Gaulle saw the yearning among many French—both Communists and non-Communists—for revitalizing change. De Gaulle reached out to these patriots, and their support helped him triumph over American opposition. Many French mocked Giraud as an "American valet" whom they blamed for slights to the nation's sovereignty, like being shut out of Anglo-American armistice negotiations with Italy. Even Washington viewed Giraud as just the local authority in North Africa, and not a very impressive one.

"He'll be a dud as an administrator," the president had predicted.[45] FDR did not regard this as a handicap, since he wanted Americans to run the show.

De Gaulle rejected such client status. Although dependent on British money and facilities since June 1940, de Gaulle made sure to bite the hand that fed him, thus infuriating the prime minister, whom Roosevelt mocked for being unable to control the unruly "problem child." Caught between FDR, who opposed de Gaulle's movement, and Eden, who favored it, Churchill swung from pride in his paternity to rage at this prodigal son. From the British de Gaulle received only intermittent support and from the Americans even less respect than Giraud. But because he made respect for France his first policy, de Gaulle became the symbol of France reborn. De Gaulle's triumph over the hapless Giraud seemed inevitable.

FDR's opposition persisted nonetheless. The "first" reason to break with him, FDR cabled Churchill on 17 June 1943, was because "he has proven to be unreliable, unco-operative, and disloyal"—in short, independent.[46] Stimson feared that this "unstable . . . character . . . might actually get up a fight between his troops and ours."[47]

Yet however much Americans raged, they found themselves bound to the difficult general, particularly as D-Day approached. One tie was de Gaulle's popularity among the American and British publics. The Roosevelt administration tried to cool this ardor by planting in the press stories about de Gaulle's alleged fascism, citing the Gestapo tactics of his secret police. Some Free French organizations did act brutally against French dissidents. Yet the heavy-handed campaign backfired when many newspapers criticized Washington's anti–de Gaulle stance. Churchill had his own spats with the general, and he tried to accommodate FDR's viewpoint. But the feisty prime minister could not ignore the depth of Gaullist sentiment in Great Britian. More importantly, he wanted a strong France and a viable French empire to back British policy after the war. Under pressure from Eden and Parliament, he agreed in August 1943 to grant the FCNL limited, de facto status as a quasi-government. Hoping that committee would destroy itself, Hull would not go even that far.

In contrast, Stalin acted far more generously when he recognized the Free French. After all, de Gaulle was no thorn in his side. Meanwhile de Gaulle cast an eye toward Moscow, commenting, in remarks that reached the State Department, that in the future he would align France with the Soviet Union or even Germany.

By early 1944 the sour relations with the Free French worried U.S. military officials planning the June invasion of France. Throughout 1943 Eisenhower had tried to moderate what he called the "dictatorial" edicts coming from Washington and to work with the Free French on a practical basis. Eisenhower respected de Gaulle's growing influence with the resistance movement in France. In December 1943 Stimson's assistant John J. McCloy argued that

Generals Charles de Gaulle and Henri Giraud shake hands as Franklin D. Roosevelt requested them, but the two Frenchman remain far apart. *Courtesy of AP/Wide World Photos*

only the FCNL could help win over the French people "when we first invade France."[48] Stimson became a convert for two reasons: de Gaulle's status with the French resistance and the wily general's new willingness to cooperate. De Gaulle is "eating out of Eisenhower's hand," Stimson remarked. "De Gaulle was now more amenable than Giraud," Stimson told Hull, who also began to change his mind.[49] The two Cabinet officials did not go as far as McCloy, who urged outright recognition of the FCNL as the French government. Even Stimson wanted cooperation with the committee only on a local, temporary basis, waiting for a possible "better" group to arise. Although military concerns led the War Department to rethink policy, most State Department experts still nurtured their political distaste for "this French Adolf." In January 1944 one State analyst drafted an 18-page memorandum detailing why "this Government lack[s] confidence in General de Gaulle."[50]

Running deeper than the State Department's dislike for the general, FDR's opposition stemmed from his ambition to shape France's future. This aspiration reflected both self-interest and idealism, not a surprising blend considering Roosevelt's previous service under Woodrow Wilson, whose Fourteen Points had aimed for a similar goal in World War I. France would not need its own central government when it was liberated, or for months afterward, he argued. Of course, without such a government, France could not oppose his plans. Refusing to discuss the FCNL's proposals for governance after D-Day, FDR planned a military regime with Eisenhower's appointing French and American administrators. A two-month crash program in Charlottesville turned out "60-day marvels"—Americans supposedly trained to govern temporarily as French prefects.[51]

No one could predict what kind of government France would choose after the war, FDR liked to say. Then, like Leahy, who presumed to know what the "inarticulate" French masses thought, the president went on to prescribe the kind of government France needed—one modeled on the United States. As France's trustee, Roosevelt would preserve its options for the future by preventing de Gaulle's committee from exercising sovereignty in the present. Roosevelt's logic recalled the thinking of Woodrow Wilson who had also assumed that the president of the U.S. knew what was best for countries such as France and could deliver it—both shaky suppositions. Roosevelt made them shakier by keeping such advisers as Leahy, the former ambassador to Vichy, who suggested Pétain as the best leader for France after the D-Day invasion.

Stimson saw "unrealities" in the president's assumptions. A tough-minded former governor of the Philippines and a former negotiator in Nicaragua to prepare elections after a U.S. military intervention, Stimson distrusted and disliked de Gaulle. Yet he realized that France was no banana republic. "America cannot supervise the elections of a great country like France," he told FDR, and trying to do so would "permanently alienate" its friendship. Advised by Leahy that liberated France would likely undergo a revolution, the president fretted that U.S. troops would have to restore order. Stimson found "far fetched" the idea that the United States held responsibility for France's future. "She has had many revolutions before now," he reminded Roosevelt, and she should be allowed to settle any future ones herself.[52]

While trying to protect France from itself, FDR contemplated clipping its territory. He suggested the idea of "Wallonia," a new European state to include Belgium, Alsace-Lorraine, and part of northern France. Roosevelt also planned to lop off part of France's overseas empire. This ambition set him at odds with the French, the British, and his own State Department. Yet FDR had a clearer vision of the future. Unlike others, he perceived that rising nationalism would sweep away the old colonial empires. If the U.S. embraced this change, it could help stabilize the emerging nations and encourage them to develop along proper democratic and capitalist lines, Roosevelt believed.

Alongside this enlightened self-interest in decolonization there arose FDR's ambition to take over French territory for strategic bases. In March 1944 FDR outlined these thoughts to Edwin Wilson, Murphy's successor as representative to the Free French. Wilson argued the State Department view that postwar European stability required a strong France. This in turn meant restoring the French empire. Roosevelt pointed to the large map of the world in his office. Since Dakar stood so close to South America, he planned a "naval and air base . . . policed not by the French whom he did not want there, but by . . . the United States and Brazil." Sovereignty—more precisely, what remained of it—could stay with France. Again on New Caledonia in the South Pacific, Australia and New Zealand would police a base. Convinced that recovery from June 1940 would take decades, FDR discounted French participation in the postwar global security system.

Finally, Roosevelt pointed on the map to French-dominated Indochina, the area "most likely to cause difficulties." This understatement reflected the controversy that had already arisen over that territory's future "France has milked it for one hundred years," FDR asserted. He wanted an international trusteeship to prepare Indochina for independence in several decades. With France shut out, the United States, Great Britain, China, and the Philippines would supervise the colony's political and economic development.[53] This plan met fierce opposition from the French, from the British (who feared the precedent for their own empire), and from the State Department, which wanted a strong France to help balance Soviet influence in postwar Europe. Moreover, it assumed cooperation with the Chinese leader Chiang Kai-shek, an increasingly shaky ally. In the last year of his life the president slowly retreated from the the trusteeship plan, but he still had designs on French territory.

In late 1944 FDR ordered the Navy to occupy Clipperton Island, a French territory 2,000 miles west of the Panama Canal. This grab sparked a controversy that underscored the Americans' cavalier attitude toward French sovereignty, their suspicion of Anglo-French collaboration, and the jockeying for postwar advantage. FDR had fished off the uninhabited island. He valued its strategic location along the approach to the Panama Canal and across a projected British civil air route from England to the southwest Pacific. When the British sent a survey expedition to Clipperton in 1944, Roosevelt directed the navy to install a weather and radio station there. Citing alleged Japanese activity nearby, the navy forbade trespass by the French or anyone else. Meanwhile, FDR told George Messersmith, ambassador to Mexico, to urge Mexico City to revive its claim to Clipperton, which it had formally ceded to France in 1931. If Mexico obtained the island, the United States would sign a 99-year lease for a base.

The French grew alarmed, but lacked naval and air power in the area. French officials in Mexico nonetheless chartered a boat, explaining that the vessel and crew would investigate the possibilities of a shark-fishing industry based at Clipperton, where sharks allegedly had vitamin-rich livers of extraordinary size. Not buying this "fishy" story, Messersmith, on orders from the navy, persuaded the Mexican government to stop the French-chartered ship from leaving port.[54] Tempers flared. The French minister and his wife "were just as fanatic as de Gaulle," Messersmith reported, "and I think they hate our guts."[55] When the French made a formal protest in early 1945, the State Department worried that Roosevelt's grab for the island could blow up into an armed confrontation. "This is very humiliating to us," a French official pleaded with Americans.[56] A few weeks before he died on 12 April 1945, FDR came around to the State Department's position that it would be easier to get concessions from the French than from the Mexicans. "Mexico, morally, owes us nothing on this war," the Secretary of State reminded him; "France will."[57]

U.S.-French conflict over colonies and other matters complicated Eisenhower's work as he planned the invasion of Normandy on 6 June 1944. Before Normandy, quarrels with de Gaulle over St. Pierre or over Giraud remained side issues; as D-Day approached, such squabbles moved to center stage.

De Gaulle benefited from a contradiction of U.S. policy. Washington wanted to keep de Gaulle on a short leash—and the French Communists on an even shorter one. Yet Eisenhower needed help from the powerful French resistance, dominated by de Gaulle and the Communists. Fearing leaks to the Germans, Roosevelt and Churchill closed the French out of the detailed planning for the invasion. This stymied Eisenhower's work with General Pierre Koenig, whom de Gaulle had named commander of the resistance French Forces of the Interior (FFI). Meanwhile, Roosevelt planned a military government for France similar to the regime imposed on defeated Italy. He said no to Churchill's and Eisenhower's plea for an accord with de Gaulle on regulating civil affairs in liberated France. "It is very difficult to cut the French out of the liberation of France," an exasperated Churchill exclaimed.[58]

Once again FDR underestimated de Gaulle's political genius. Although the Allies shut the wily general out of the final planning for D-Day, they needed help from his FFI. Playing with a strong hand, the FCNL on 26 May declared itself the "Provisional Government of the French Republic." Full recognition by Washington or London now "interests us very little," de Gaulle airily declared; "the essential point is our recognition by the French people."[59]

The Communists, whose prominence in the resistance had won them enormous popular support, became the key to the ambitious general's rise to power. They stood out as de Gaulle's chief domestic rivals, and they scared the Americans and others into eventually accepting him. With the war still to be won, the Communists acknowledged the general's leadership. But what would happen once the Allies pushed the Germans out of France? As D-Day approached, de Gaulle planned for this contingency. He designated trusted administrators to take over each liberated district swiftly, thus outflanking both the Communists and the Charlottesville "60-day marvels."

Meanwhile, in occupied France people viewed the war through a lens different from that of Americans. After Germany extended its occupation to all of France in November 1942, Pétain and Laval clung to their tattered remnant of a government. Pétain still dreamed of a French-mediated end to the war. Like many compatriots, he feared that an Allied invasion would mean bloodshed and revolution, with Germans fighting Americans and Communists struggling to gain power.

Particularly frightening was Allied bombing. "What sense do these idiotic destructions make?" asked the anguished writer André Gide.[60] Pope Pius XII endorsed a protest by French priests against the "indiscriminate" bombing.[61] The Americans hoped their daylight, "precision" assault on German facilities in France minimized civilian casualties. But only one bomb in five landed within a thousand feet of its target, U.S. officials later concluded. American broadcasts warned the French to evacuate areas within two kilometers of war plants. Through accident or carelessness, U.S. bombs fell on other innocents. After the war, the U.S. government estimated that 12,000 civilians died from pre-D-Day bombing of western Europe. This destruction sparked vehement protest from even pro-Ally French. Shortly before D-Day, U.S. and British military leaders debated whether to unleash an all-out air attack on key French rail yards—most situated in densely populated areas. Churchill shrank from the prospect of "French slaughters." Roosevelt worried about "alleviating adverse French opinion" but endorsed Eisenhower's view of the attacks as a military necessity.[62] As a token gesture FDR suggested adding a Frenchman to the target committee.

Anger at Allied bombing helped keep the numbers in the resistance low. After the war the French cultivated a legend of glorious, nationwide opposition to the Germans. Yet before D-Day only 2 percent of adults risked their lives to become active in the resistance. In 1943–44 about as many French helped the Germans put down resistance "disorder" as participated in combating the occupiers. Both Germans and Americans remarked on the political apathy in France. Most French wanted to be rid of the Germans, but not at the cost of war or revolution. After D-Day the veteran dealer Laval played his last card by trying to install former premier Edouard Herriot as head of a transitional government. Although the Americans despised Laval, some evidence indicates that Allen W. Dulles of the Office of Strategic Services (forerunner of the CIA) supported the scheme. The Germans' arrest of Herriot scotched the plan, but Americans still sympathized with Pétain.[63] In concert with Leahy, Stimson and Army Chief of Staff George C. Marshall sought to prevent "the French radicals [from] executing Pétain."[64]

In this swirl of conflict and deceit, de Gaulle became the indispensable man. Like the Americans and conservative French, he opposed revolution. Only the stubborn general, the symbol of France reborn, could unleash the resistance against the Germans while reining in its revolutionary potential. As de Gaulle had expected, the Americans and British turned to him shortly before D-Day. On 4 June Eisenhower informed the Frenchman of instructions from Washington. Eisenhower would issue a proclamation to the French people, asking them to obey the Anglo-American liberators—while making no mention of de Gaulle or of the French provisional government. The U.S. Army had printed more than a million leaflets with this message, which it would drop over France on D-Day. Eisenhower asked de Gaulle to broadcast an endorsement of Allied rule.

The proud general angrily refused. He stormed that the Allies were invading France without acknowledging his government and without an agreement on civil administration, but with what he termed "counterfeit" francs in their pockets.[65] (Unlike Holland or Belgium, where the United States planned to use the native currency, for France the United States had printed special francs, designed personally by FDR. As Hull admitted, the power to issue currency was the litmus test of sovereignty.) De Gaulle remained defiant. Wage war with your fake currency, he raged at Churchill. "He's a nut," Roosevelt concluded.[66] "This supposed ally . . . has virtually stabbed our troops in the back," Stimson fumed. He had to be "beat[en] out of his . . . intransigence."[67]

Meanwhile, on the morning of 6 June, 4,000 ships, 14,000 airplanes, and 175,000 troops assaulted the Normandy beaches in the D-Day invasion. In this greatest amphibious landing in history the Allies met fierce resistance, particularly at Omaha Beach. The Americans alone suffered 100,000 casualties in the first month of fighting.

Later on D-Day, de Gaulle did make a broadcast endorsing the invasion—but he told the people to obey the French government. He said nothing about the Allies or the provisional status of the FCNL government. Despite the fireworks, the conflict over government became a moot issue. With his hands full fighting the Germans, Eisenhower soon turned most civilian matters over to the French provisional government. As the leader of the resistance, de

Gaulle became more useful with the Allied thrust into France. That made it difficult to "beat" him, so FDR tried charm when the general in July 1944 made his long-deferred trip to Washington.

In planning the visit, administration officials grew nervous about the Frenchman's popularity among the American people. He "will be lionized here," Stimson feared.[68] To "prevent de Gaulle from gaining a public ovation," the War and State departments planned an agenda packed with discussions, leaving little time for "a parade through the country." McCloy "stir[red] up publicity against de Gaulle" by planting hostile stories in the American press, Stimson noted with satisfaction.[69]

These efforts failed. When the general stopped off in New York, a large crowd greeted him as a hero. De Gaulle's press conference made a highly favorable impression on reporters. Countering his reputation as an arrogant dictator, this gifted, smiling actor projected himself as a modest public servant. Even Hull found him more reasonable. After de Gaulle's departure from the United States, Roosevelt, under heavy pressure from the War and Treasury departments, publicly accepted the FCNL as the de facto authority for the civil administration of France. A small step toward official recognition, this decision was one the president believed he could reverse once a more amenable leader surfaced in France. (Finally on 23 October 1944 FDR reluctantly granted the FCNL full recognition as the government of France.)

As at Casablanca, deep differences divided Roosevelt and de Gaulle when they met at the White House. The Frenchman later recalled how FDR, "this seducer," sketched plans for a postwar world order centered on Washington. The United States, the Soviet Union, Great Britain, and China—with France excluded—would establish a "permanent system of intervention . . . [to] settle the world's problems." With China and Great Britain dependent on American aid, with Soviet ambitions confined to Eastern Europe, and with U.S. bases around the world, the United States would, de Gaulle realized, dominate the system. Decolonization, encouraged by Washington, would further expand its influence. The United States was "already trying to rule the world," he told a Free French official.[70]

France had little importance in Roosevelt's order. FDR could not forget that France had governed itself poorly in the 1930s and had collapsed in 1940. That proud nation had forfeited its status as a great power, and Roosevelt saw little reason to restore it. Revolution would wrack postwar France, he predicted.

De Gaulle shared Roosevelt's view of the dismal past, but he burned with a bright view of France's future. He disputed the president's cavalier dismissal of Europe: the east abandoned to Soviet domination, and the west written off as a ruin. With France at the lead, western Europe still held great promise, the general insisted. FDR's plan for France would "impose . . . the psychology of the vanquished" and cripple recovery.[71] Postwar France could not act as a great power unless it emerged from the war with a victor's

General Dwight D. Eisenhower had to endure the many complaints of de Gaulle because the French general enjoyed broad support among the public in France, the United States, and Great Britain and because he remained the key to controlling the Communists in the Resistance movement. *Courtesy of the National Archives*

psychology, de Gaulle emphasized. He had to breathe new life into French pride. Accordingly, the general worked feverishly to maximize the role of France in Germany's defeat—and, more important, the perception of that role. De Gaulle viewed the remaining battles of the war as opportunities to revive French prestige and power. Two obstacles stood in his way: French defeatism and American reluctance to allow de Gaulle's political agenda to determine Allied troop movements.

Americans and French still saw the war from different perspectives. The United States wanted to defeat the Axis as rapidly as possible. Although the State Department favored rebuilding French strength, FDR and his generals had little patience with de Gaulle's "political" maneuvering. The Americans sought to postpone most political questions until after the war, when U.S. economic might would command maximum leverage in war-torn Europe. While condemning de Gaulle's intrigues, American and British generals shaped Allied military strategy to fit the broad political interests of their nations. Inevitably, political and military issues intertwined.

That inseparability became apparent on 19 August 1944, when the Communist-dominated Paris FFI rose up against the weakened Germans. De Gaulle welcomed this outburst of French spirit, yet feared the consequences if either the Communists or the Americans liberated the capital. Paris remained the heart of France. If the FFI controlled the city, it might take the country. Partly because of Moscow's order to preserve a united front against the Germans, the Communists accepted de Gaulle's wartime leadership. But the Communists and other FFI groups planned on radical social changes that conflicted with de Gaulle's ambition for revitalizing French grandeur. The United States shared de Gaulle's concern about the now-popular Communists. The American military had airlifted most of its supplies to the FFI in rural areas, hoping to stem the rise of the more radical urban groups. The FFI presented a challenge to de Gaulle, but also gave him leverage against the Americans.

On 19 August American troops camped only 25 miles from Paris, while French troops under General Jacques Leclerc stood 100 miles away—despite Eisenhower's promise that the French would participate in the city's liberation. De Gaulle valued the Americans' proximity to Paris as insurance against the Communists' taking Paris, even though a U.S. liberation of the French capital would shatter the prestige of his movement and the psychology of victory. The general also feared the Americans might strike a Darlan-type deal with Pétain or former premier Edouard Herriot.

For Eisenhower such political concerns were soon outweighed by military priorities. At first he decided to bypass Paris. He was driving against the Germans as hard as possible, and taking the capital would mean diverting to its civilian population at least 4,000 tons of supplies daily, enough for seven divisions. Eisenhower also did not want to risk the city's destruction in a battle with the Germans. Therefore he rejected de Gaulle's plea to have Leclerc liberate Paris at once. Defiant, de Gaulle directed Leclerc to seize the capital. In turn Eisenhower, by now aware that Paris was too important a symbol to leave untaken, ordered Leclerc and a U.S. division to move into Paris simultaneously, dressing his political decision in military clothes by describing it as a reinforcement of FFI forces.

Leclerc still disobeyed American orders by using roads assigned to U.S. troops. Meeting heavy German resistance and throngs of overjoyed citizens, he fell behind schedule. Disgusted, American commanders decided to take the city without waiting for the French to "dance their way in." When he learned of the American decision, Leclerc rushed forward a token detachment, which avoided the enemy and made it to the city shortly before midnight 24 August. De Gaulle and the Americans followed the next day.

Dramas large and small marked the capital's liberation. Hitching to Paris on an American bomber, Bullitt (now an officer in the French army thanks to an appointment by de Gaulle) unlocked the U.S. Embassy gates, closed four years before. When he gave the victory sign from the balcony, crowds cheered enthusiastically—mistaking the former ambassador for General Eisenhower. De Gaulle planned a victory parade to dramatize his nation's revival and his paternity in that rebirth. The American commander, General Leonard Gerow, forbade the march, fearing it might draw fire from either dissident Frenchmen or the few German troops still in the city. The French determined to parade anyway. Many Parisians confused *Gerow* with *Giraud*—or at least professed to do so. On 26 August de Gaulle relit the flame at the Tomb of the Unknown Soldier, then led the victory march down the Champs-Elysées. Some 2 million turned out, cheering wildly. With tears streaming, he led the crowd in an off-key rendition of "La Marseillaise." France had begun recovery from the despair of June 1940.

As de Gaulle entered Notre Dame cathedral, shots rang out. He bravely ignored them. But when Eisenhower arrived the next day, de Gaulle made two requests: that the Americans show support for the FCNL by having two U.S. divisions march through Paris on their way to the front, and that Eisenhower allow Leclerc's division to remain in the capital for a week to consolidate the FCNL's authority. Eisenhower, sharing de Gaulle's dread of civil strife with the Communists, readily agreed.[72]

Besides relying on U.S. military strength, de Gaulle also depended on American supplies. Starting in November 1941 the United States gave the Free French $2.3 billion in military equipment and supplies, most of it after D-Day. An additional $548 million of wartime aid under the Lend-Lease program went to the French civilian economy in 1944–45.[73]

After freeing Paris, Allied forces advanced rapidly eastward, stretching their lines of supply. In December 1944 the Germans counterattacked in the Ardennes, and the ensuing Battle of the Bulge threatened to roll back the

U.S. soldiers and French citizens share the joy of Liberation. *Courtesy of the National Archives*

Allies. To consolidate his exposed defenses, Eisenhower ordered the evacuation of Strasbourg, capital of Alsace. On the Franco-German border, Alsace and neighboring Lorraine had gone to victorious Germany in 1871, to France in 1919, and to Germany again in 1940. De Gaulle refused to withdraw from Strasbourg without a battle. If "the Allied forces retire," he ordered General Jean-Marie de Lattre de Tassigny, "take matters into your own hands to assure the defense of Strasbourg."[74] For de Gaulle, retention of Alsace symbolized the triumph over Germany. Hasty evacuation would subject the people to German reprisal and to suspicion that France could not defend them. If he abandoned Alsace without a serious fight, de Gaulle warned Eisenhower, an outraged French population might overthrow his government, spawning chaos in the rear of the Allied armies.

The dispute heated up. The Americans threatened to cut the French army's supply of fuel and ammunition. The French warned they would stop the transport of Allied supplies over their territory. Eisenhower's negotiator in this matter blew up at his French counterpart. "If he had been an American, I would have socked him on the jaw," the aide exclaimed to the supreme commander. Roosevelt cold-shouldered a personal appeal from de Gaulle; the defiant general showed "considerable nerve," the president huffed.[75] But Eisenhower conceded. Fearing unrest in the rear areas of France, he canceled the withdrawal order. The French stayed in Strasbourg. Once again de Gaulle secured a victory based on France's strategic location and America's dread of turmoil.

Despite such tactical success, respect as a great power still eluded France. The United States and the Soviet Union refused to invite France to the February 1945 Yalta Conference of the Big Three—Great Britain, the Soviet Union, and the United States. De Gaulle was "unrealistic" in seeking great-power status when "France had not done very much fighting in this war," Stalin commented to Roosevelt at Yalta. FDR responded that de Gaulle fancied himself a combination of Joan of Arc, Napoleon, and Georges Clemenceau. The American complained that the British had the idea of "artificially building up France into a strong power." After Yalta, FDR tried to make up for de Gaulle's exclusion by proposing a meeting in Algiers. De Gaulle angrily refused. How dare this American once again presume to invite a French president to French soil, the general fumed. De Gaulle also feared that conferring with FDR would imply endorsement of the Yalta decisions. For the next quarter century de Gaulle denounced the de facto division of Europe that emerged from that summit conference.

At Yalta the Big Three did make France one of the five leading states in the planned United Nations. And Churchill's prodding led the others to accept a German occupation zone for France—but "only out of kindness," Roosevelt and Stalin emphasized. What that zone would include, the Big Three would not specify until the war ended.[76] In response, de Gaulle, burning at his exclusion from Yalta, told his generals to secure as much territory as possible in southwestern Germany, regardless of Eisenhower's orders.

American troops raced into Germany too, but they pursued two other objectives. After losing the Battle of the Bulge in January 1945, German resistance sagged along the western front. Fearing the Nazis would make a last stand in the Austrian Alps, Eisenhower moved swiftly to block German escape to the forbidding mountains. He worried that rapidly advancing French troops, more interested in taking territory than in killing Germans, would drive enemy forces out of easy grasp and into the rugged terrain.

Americans jostled the French aside in pursuing another prize, Germany's atomic energy resources. As Germany neared collapse, General Leslie Groves, head of the Manhattan Project, created an Anglo-American strike force, code-named Alsos, to snatch up enemy atomic research facilities and scientists before the other Allies could grab them. A huge intelligence-gathering project pinpointed the location of key scientists, laboratories, and raw materials in Nazi-held Europe. When Leclerc liberated Paris, an Alsos team followed in a jeep just behind the first tanks. They searched out Frédéric Joliot-Curie, France's leading nuclear physicist. Celebrating the liberation with champagne drunk from laboratory beakers, the Americans probed the French scientist on the state of the German atomic program—and what he knew about the U.S. effort.

Groves and Roosevelt soon grew disturbed with Joliot-Curie. The scientist insisted on France's right to British nuclear information under the terms of a deal, negotiated by his agent after the June 1940 collapse, that also entrusted French atomic assets to Great Britain. Churchill had not mentioned this deal to FDR in August 1943 when each had pledged in the Tube Alloys accord not to share atomic information without the other's consent. In February 1945 Joliot-Curie threatened that if France did not win equality in the Anglo-American atomic condominium, it would turn to the Soviet Union. Groves took this warning to heart. He conducted the Alsos program with the assumption that "nothing that might be of interest to the Russians should ever be allowed to fall into French hands."[77] Such cooperation between France and the Soviet Union would never develop, however. In May 1945 de Gaulle would launch an independent atomic energy project, under Joliot-Curie's direction.

That program would get off to a slow start, partly because Alsos's stunning success left little atomic war booty for France. Ironically, many of Germany's atomic assets stood on territory that later passed to French control. The Americans captured 30 tons of uranium ore near Toulouse, France and shipped the radioactive metal to the United States without informing the French. In mid-April 1945, as French forces marched across southwest Germany from the Black Forest to Stuttgart—this time following Eisenhower's plan—they neared Hechingen, a rural area where the Germans had an atomic complex. At Stimson's request, Eisenhower ordered the French to halt. Unaware of the scientific prize, the French still drove forward. They aimed for Sigmaringen, where the Nazis had interned the survivors of the Vichy government. On 23–24 April a small Alsos unit led by Captain Boris Pash sprinted diagonally across the path of the French and took Hechingen. The Americans seized a number of top German scientists, a large quantity of heavy water, and more than a ton of uranium cubes buried in a field outside town. When the French arrived, they mounted no competition for the atomic booty. The hungry "French were much more interested in pigs and chickens than in atomic specialists," explained one American scientist. [78]

Unable to compete with Alsos's superb intelligence information, the French also had difficulty playing catch-up when Germany surrendered. Intent on receiving the field surrender of at least one German army, de Lattre continued fighting for hours against one unit whose overall commander had already capitulated to the Americans. French insecurities were not eased by the formal German surrender on 8 May 1945 in Berlin. Until de Lattre protested the fact, no French flag flew at the ceremonies, nor was a copy of the surrender document rendered into French. No one mentioned France in the victory toasts until de Lattre himself did so. France had overcome its defeat, but not its humiliation. [79]

Meanwhile, as the European war ended, a crisis brewed in northwest Italy that almost set Americans and French to fighting each other. Seeking revenge for 1940 and security against another Italian attack, de Gaulle wanted to annex some strategic Alpine districts. Although people in these areas spoke French, most preferred to remain part of Italy. On 29 April de Gaulle ordered General Paul Doyen to advance further into Italy and take the coveted districts. De Gaulle argued that since the Americans and British had excluded him from the Italian armistice negotiations of 1943, France could set its own peace terms with that neighbor. Like the Soviets in Eastern Europe, the French intimidated inhabitants into supporting the takeover. Trying to bolster the shaky Italian government against domestic radicals and Yugoslavia's demand for territory in the northeast, the Americans and British grew furious at de Gaulle's grab. Foreign Minister Georges Bidault confided to American ambassador Jefferson Caffery that the French Foreign Office opposed the seizure. This offered small comfort because de Gaulle still dominated the government. When American troops entered the disputed territory, Doyen protested this "serious and unfriendly act." [80] Backed by de Gaulle, he warned that any U.S. attempt to challenge the French government in the area would be resisted "by all necessary means without exception." [81]

The Truman administration responded to the crisis with thinking that prefigured the postwar era. When Americans looked at France, they saw a nation whose empire and strategic location between Germany and the Atlantic made it vital to U.S. interests. France's importance magnified the problem of handling defiant leaders such as de Gaulle. In disputes with the French government, American officials tended to assume they had the approval of the French people. Polls suggested otherwise. In December 1944 a survey revealed that U.S. attitudes toward France pleased only 33 percent of the French public; 53 percent expressed dissatisfaction. In contrast, 63 percent of the French approved of Britain's stance, and 53 percent favored Soviet policy toward France.[82] Top U.S. analysts ignored these data, instead often viewing troublesome French leaders as being out of touch with their own people. De Gaulle and other insolent challengers were emotional, crazy, or simply wrong, Americans concluded. Washington used aid as a lure to win over these recalcitrants and to bring forward other Paris officials more in tune with the assumed pro-American feeling of the French public.

On 6 June Stimson briefed Truman on the crisis. He and Army Chief of Staff Marshall were "very much troubled over the possibility of a clash with France," particularly since de Gaulle's troops "lay right across the line of communications for the deployment of our troops in the Asiatic war." Truman, agreeing that de Gaulle was "psychopathic," aimed to "curb" the general's power while working with "French government men who were on our side in trying to hold back de Gaulle."[83] In this case, Truman quickly brought de Gaulle to heel by cutting off all American military aid except food for his troops. Noting that it was the anniversary of D-Day, Truman scolded de Gaulle for "threat[ening] that French soldiers bearing American arms will combat American and Allied soldiers who . . . contributed to the liberation of France itself."[84] Themselves at sword's point with the French in Syria and Lebanon, the British backed the Americans. The French pulled their troops out of Italy—but later negotiated the border adjustments de Gaulle wanted. The harsh dispute hardened U.S. opposition to French participation in the Pacific war and the July 1945 Potsdam summit conference. France's exclusion sparked further resentment and quarrels.

Northwest Italy proved to be an exception among the military disputes that followed D-Day. At Paris, Strasbourg, and elsewhere, de Gaulle skillfully levered the Americans' fear of turmoil to bend Anglo-American military strategy. He paid for those victories in incurring the wrath of U.S. officials, including the new president. Even Eisenhower, among the most sympathetic of Americans, grumbled that "next to the weather . . . [the French] have caused me more trouble in this war than any other single factor."[85]

The average G.I. shared some of Eisenhower's gripes about the French. In every war allied soldiers and civilians quarrel. But in 1944–45 hostility between Americans and French grew particularly intense. Both French prefects and U.S. intelligence officers blamed much of the trouble on the soldiers' "lax discipline." The military police tried to crack down, but the violence worsened, particularly after Germany surrendered. "The French in Havre are terrified by the Americans, both black and white," wrote a prefect in November 1944; "they run after the women, the children, the men. 300 women are under treatment at the hospital. Yesterday on the radio they asked for word about 5 boys, aged 10 to 14 years, who had been kidnapped by Americans." Robbery, rape, murder, and looting were the most common crimes. Displaced persons and others dressed in American uniforms may have committed some of the offenses. Yet American army officers admitted to "extreme and undisciplined behavior . . . [by U.S.] troops in Cherbourg, November 1944, in Fountainebleau, December 1944, [and] in Reims, January 1945." In some areas there was a "reign of terror."[86] In part, such violence stemmed from the common criminals in every mass army. And the French did not suffer alone. Some American soldiers in occupied Germany also ran amuck with rape and pillage, including the $3 million theft of the crown jewels of Hesse.[87]

Much of the hostility between Americans and French arose not from such apolitical crime but from longstanding national antagonisms. Each people harbored prejudices against the other, stereotypes with a kernel of truth. After D-Day the war threw together millions of ordinary French and Americans. Old grudges and complaints—dating from tourists in the 1920s, the doughboys in World War I, and before—now resurfaced. G.I.'s caricatured the French as lazy, inefficient, profiteering braggarts. In July 1945, 32 percent of G.I.'s polled expressed a favorable opinion of the French people, while 42 percent liked the Russian people and 43 percent the British.[88] The French painted G.I.'s as crude, materialistic "gangster types." There lingered in France the smell of German propaganda and resentment of U.S. bombing.

In August 1945 a concerned Brigadier General G. Bryan Conrad distributed to top U.S. officers in Europe an extensive analysis of this hostility. The U.S. embassy also studied the epidemic of anti-American feeling. Like many Americans after World War II, Conrad interpreted French resentment of the United States as evidence of a feminine illness: "The French are hurt, sensitive, suffering from a collective inferiority complex. . . . "La Grande Malade" is flat on her back but hypersensitive to remedies suggested by U.S. doctors and unable, so far, to cure herself. . . . France today is sick, hungry, proud and hard to handle." Conrad sympathized that France chafed "under an occupation, dependent on the United States." "High-handed" behavior by many U.S. Army officers had aggravated this feeling, particularly by "treat[ing] the French merely as a nuisance."[89] Less understanding than Conrad, Ambassador Jefferson Caffery diagnosed French complaints that "Americans treat us like children" as symptomatic of "post-liberation neurosis."[90]

Conrad perceived the clash in French and American attitudes. The average G.I. believed—like presidents Wilson and Roosevelt—that "America's way of doing things is the best way, the only right way, and that her good intentions are self-evident." Expecting gratitude for the Liberation, Americans resented the fact that the kissing and flowers ended in a few days. The French were so delighted to see us, griped the soldiers, "that they wait[ed] fully 45 minutes before tripling prices." Conrad blamed the suspicion of U.S. designs on the French empire on German propaganda, not on FDR's policy.

A large gap separated the highly equipped and trained soldiers of the United States and the lightly armed, irregular troops of the Resistance. *Courtesy of the National Archives*

Popular French complaints about America's generosity toward Germany and miserliness toward France foreshadowed postwar differences between the two governments. "Americans everywhere are feeding vast quantities of oranges to German prisoners," the French groused. As after World War I, U.S. soldiers often found Germans more compatible than French. "One German POW can and does outwork three Frenchmen," they claimed. Conrad heard "increasing numbers of Americans . . . openly stating their preference for the Germans over the French." Others observed that G.I.'s liked fräulein better than mesdemoiselles. The French had fantasized about America's capability to deliver enough relief supplies and unfairly blamed their shortages on a stingy Uncle Sam, Conrad and Caffery agreed. Meanwhile, hungry, cold French civilians felt exploited when the rich Americans requisitioned French facilities. The Americans took over so many luxury hotels, many just evacuated by the Germans, that SHAEF (Supreme Headquarters, Allied Expeditionary Force) really meant "Société Hôtelière des Américains en France," the French quipped. Many went so far as to claim that "France was much better off under the Germans than under the Americans."[91]

However exaggerated, these French feelings of injury and envy grated on Americans, who expected gratitude for the Liberation and aid. This clash of attitudes reflected the reality that proud France depended on the United States. France's soldiers carried American equipment, its economy needed dollars, and its political influence suffered from the U.S.-Soviet decision to exclude France from the Yalta and Potsdam conferences.

In December 1944 de Gaulle had tried to balance this dependence by signing a pact with the Soviet Union. The treaty promised Franco-Soviet cooperation in Germany after the war. Most French applauded the pact, for it revived the tradition of an alliance with Russia against Germany, fit the domestic reality of a strong Communist party, and most important for de Gaulle, it promised leverage against the United States and Great Britain. "A dazzling sign of French grandeur reconquered," exulted a legislative leader.[92] Many French liked the idea of their nation as the natural mediator between East and West. This recalled Pétain's dream of arbitrating between the Axis and the Allies. De Gaulle's balancing act never made it to the stage because the Soviets refused to play along. Irked by the general's refusal to endorse Soviet control of Poland and contemptuous of French military power, Stalin opposed adding France to the Big Three at the Yalta and Potsdam conferences. Slapped in the face by the Soviets, de Gaulle had not gained much room to maneuver.[93]

All alliances are rent by division and resentment. Even the close bond between Roosevelt and Churchill could not overcome Anglo-American differences. Yet wartime relations between France and the United States proved particularly acrimonious. Americans felt united and jubilant over their triumph over evil. The French endured a more complex and less happy experience: struggle nearly alone against Germany; surrender; division into two zones by the Germans and into many factions by collaborators and resisters; invasion by American and British liberators who, though a relief from the Germans, shared the enemy's cavalier attitude toward its sovereignty. Having liberated and aided France, Americans understandably expected gratitude. Yet such thanks were hard to express for a nation that still smarted from defeat by the enemy and dependence on its friends. Although most French by 1944 applauded Germany's downfall, significant numbers dreaded an Allied invasion and valued the occupation as protection against social revolution and a promoter of European integration.

Stubbornly believing he knew what France needed, FDR backed a series of losers: Pétain, Darlan, Giraud. American and French troops fought side by side only in 1943–45, and even then the generals quarreled over strategy. Many ordinary French and Americans agreed they did not like each other. Conflicts over France's sovereignty during the war and its fate as an imperial power afterward divided Roosevelt and de Gaulle—and Roosevelt and Churchill. FDR angered de Gaulle with his designs on French colonies.

The two wartime leaders wrestled to a draw. De Gaulle won recognition and power in France despite FDR's dogged opposition. Yet FDR proved prescient, for less than a year after the president's death, de Gaulle would resign because the French refused to follow him. Both understood that France needed a more powerful exectuive, a reform that de Gaulle would finally win when he returned to power in 1958. After 1958 de Gaulle would implement the decolonization policy that FDR had pushed 15 years before.

Neither of these two charmers could win over the other. Yet common interests softened their quarrels. Roosevelt and Eisenhower shared de Gaulle's and Pétain's opposition to revolution in France. De Gaulle and the Americans needed each other to defeat the Germans and to contain the French Communists. France depended on U.S. aid; the Americans required French transportation and communication facilities to get to Germany. Although the two nations had taken very different paths to victory, by 1945 these requirements gave them important mutual interests. Would their common concerns produce cooperation or more acrimony?

Chapter 2

THE RELUCTANT COLD WARRIOR:
FRANCE AND THE UNITED STATES, 1945–1950

In 1947 drought cut France's wheat production to the lowest level since Napoleon's time. The United States sent large amounts of wheat and corn. Yet the French, who loved their *baguettes,* could not stomach bread made with cornmeal. The French Communist party (PCF) began a whispering campaign that a steady diet of corn meal led to male impotence and sterility. American officials feared that in a nation where love-making amounted to "a favorite indoor-outdoor sport," this propaganda could prove disastrous. The State Department counterattacked. We "flooded the country," recalled John Hickerson, the director for European Affairs, "with pictures of colored [families] in the U.S. with 8, 10, 15 children, whose *sole* bread was corn bread."[1]

This episode points to a central problem in U.S.-French relations for the years 1945–50: while Americans were trying in many ways to shape France into a loyal ally of the United States, the French were inclined to resist such molding even when they needed the United States. Washington officials such as ambassador Jefferson Caffery understood that brusque demands on the French only aggravated what he called their "well-known inferiority complex."[2] Instead of bludgeoning the French, the United States lured them with aid. Washington's assistance to France totaled nearly $1 billion a year in the period 1945–54. The preferred method for shaping French policy, American officials explained, was "finding, or creating through persuasion, influential groups in [the] French Government who want to see instituted . . . [what] we

44

have in mind and working with them towards its accomplishment."[3] By offering economic aid, technical advice, and protection against the Soviet Union, the United States cleared the path to France's becoming a capitalist-oriented ally. Although France retained considerable independence, the United States dominated the two countries' relationship. Though America became a major player in the internal life of France, France played no such role in U.S. society. Most French welcomed U.S. assistance but resented their dependence on America and their restricted sovereignty. When the French divided on whether to follow America's lead in the worsening cold war, Americans diagnosed this ambivalence as French weakness and emotionalism.

Fear that Paris might go its own way made Washington officials more anxious to shape France's policies. That war-ravaged nation could veer in one of two directions, observed Paris-based diplomat Livingston T. Merchant in February 1946. A top State Department French expert, Merchant explained that France could "gamble on a new world" by rebuilding its economy on the American model of private enterprise, modernization, and expanded trade with all nations. This path fit Washington's fervent aim for a vibrant, capitalist-oriented world economy, but it also required American loans to France "on a grand scale." Unless France received such credits, it would surely choose the other road of "economic self-containment," Merchant warned. This alternative meant extensive government subsidies and control of key industries and limited trade through bilateral deals. The self-sufficiency track enjoyed "greater popular and political appeal" in France, for it "cut . . . dependence" and "conform[ed] to 'reality' and the desire for national accomplishment and strength," Merchant reported. But this second choice "would be extremely disappointing to all our hopes for a liberalized, expanding world trade." Restrictive policies had choked off world trade and economic recovery in the 1930s and had spawned dictators and world war, Americans believed. Merchant and others stressed that the United States could head off a repeat of these catastrophes with dollar aid and deft direction of French policies. When weighing the expense of loans to France and other nations, Congress should also "calculate how many hours a billion dollars lasts in fighting an all-out war," he argued.[4]

Dread of communism helped loosen congressional purse strings and underscored France's importance. In Washington's eye the PCF, France's largest party, loomed as a double threat. Communists tended to favor the restrictive economic practices Americans abhorred. And if France—whether by peaceful elections or by Soviet conquest—adopted a Communist government, the United States could no longer "live safely," the Joint Chiefs of Staff warned in 1947.[5] Washington needed at least reluctant cooperation from France in order to build a strong non-Communist Western Europe. Such concerns gave non-Communist French leaders some leverage in Washington. France also remained a key element in plans to build a democratic Germany and integrate it into a peaceful Europe. France's empire retained its strategic importance, especially in North Africa and Indochina. Americans pressed the French—with mixed success—to grant these areas more independence, in the hope of heading off gains by Communists or dangerous nationalists.

France remained crucial to postwar strategy, yet "very difficult to deal with," complained H. Freeman Matthews, a top State Department official.[6] Even after the 1944 Liberation, Americans often viewed France as ailing, emotional, and womanish—chronically incapable of caring for itself or judging its own best interests. U.S. experts tended to belittle the foreign policy of this apparent "convalescent" nation, suffering "moral and physical shock."[7] "Since the First World War the French have been devitalized, since the Second World War they have been demoralized and exhausted, and for the last year they have been in a state of acute jitters," asserted Hickerson in 1948.[8] President Harry Truman dismissed French fears of Germany as "remote" and "exaggerated"; the State Department found these worries "archaic," "confused," and "obsess[ive]." Americans often slighted French concerns as obstacles to be jumped or bulldozed out of the way. "Nobody took little Bidault seriously," recalled Matthews, referrring to Georges Bidault, the most important architect of French foreign policy from 1944 to 1948.[9] Viewing France's history since 1940, U.S. officials found that nation's virility directed more toward "indoor-outdoor sport" than toward fighting Nazi or Communist takeover. This weakness—and America's own national security—seemed to require saving France from the French.

In France, however, existentialist philosopher Jean-Paul Sartre and President Charles de Gaulle shared an aspiration in opposition to the American goal, namely, saving France for the French and for humanity. In October 1945 Sartre asserted that precisely because the atomic bomb and the American and Soviet giants cast such an ominous shadow, France carried special responsibility for the rest of the world. Even though "our country has lost much of its power," he declared, "France is our concrete situation . . . our only chance. . . . And if we decide to take our chance on life . . . we have to take our chance on France, and commit ourselves to finding a place for France in this tough world, this humanity in danger of death."[10]

De Gaulle likewise took his chance on French independence, but he also recognized the need for cooperation with powerful America. The canny general wanted to keep Germany contained while striking a balance between the two superpowers. He saw the Soviet takeover of Eastern Europe—and the dread that sparked in the West—as a lever to boost French independence and pry aid from the United States. "I would much rather work with the USA," de Gaulle assured Caffery. But "if I cannot work with you I must work with the Soviets . . . even if in the long run they gobble us up."[11] The Soviets, however, showed little desire to work with de Gaulle. Stalin belittled the power of the French, differed with them over Germany and Eastern Europe, and hesitated to challenge the United States in Western Europe. Moscow's indifference forced the French to look more to Washington. A French Foreign Ministry analysis of 20 July 1945 noted the "marked incomprehension" between France and the United States, but emphasized that the Soviets, unlike the Americans, stood "industrially incapable of furnishing us with the equipment necessary to rebuild our industry."[12]

At the same time, Washington was preparing to do more to assist French recovery. In early 1945 Roosevelt had approved the State Department's plan to rebuild France as a major power. The United States should make allowances for the "psychological" damage resulting from 1940 and treat France "on the basis of her potential power rather than . . . her present strength," the department urged.[13] This would bolster the non-Communists. Looking for allies in the postwar containment of Germany, the State Department wanted France as the fourth occupation power. It hoped these concessions would create "a more cooperative spirit among the French." Reviving the French economy, moreover, would restore an important market. We "desire to export," Caffery explained to de Gaulle, "and we cannot export if you are not prosperous enough to buy." The issue remained aid on whose terms. The general wanted help without strings. The Americans expected loyalty in return. "Don't create difficulties for us," Caffery warned.[14]

Personal relations bettered after Roosevelt's death. Truman referred to de Gaulle as an "s.o.b.," but got along with him.[15] De Gaulle observed that like FDR, Truman believed France should simply pattern its postwar reconstruction on the U.S. model and accept the leadership of Washington. De Gaulle had clashed with FDR over this issue of independence. But now with France needing reconstruction aid and the Soviet Union occupying all of Eastern Europe, he grew more accommodating.

Despite the improvement in relations, differences persisted over France's domestic policy and stance in Germany. At a series of meetings in Washington on 22–23 August 1945, Truman and Secretary of State James F. Byrnes accused de Gaulle of trying to curtail American influence in France. The Americans protested what they saw as the pervasive anti-U.S. bias of the French press. De Gaulle had ignored Truman's earlier request that Paris launch a public relations program to boost America's image among the French people. The president objected "that certain American businessmen . . . had been badly received by members of the French Government." His complaint touched a broader issue. "It would be unfortunate if France should isolate herself behind a high wall" with tariff and currency barriers, Byrnes stressed. Foreign Minister Bidault, who accompanied de Gaulle to Washington, agreed that world trade was important, but he also argued that in its present feeble condition, France had to protect its "traditional industries," so much weaker than "the huge American industries." To encourage the French to open up their economy, Truman approved in principle a postwar loan. Finally, the president queried de Gaulle about the powerful French

Communist party. Americans worried that the PCF would block U.S. access to France. Truman stressed his eagerness to aid French recovery, as long as France remained receptive to American influence and business.[16]

While Truman focused on keeping France open, de Gaulle worried about how to close off the threat of yet another German revival. When it came to Germany, Americans and French operated on different wavelengths. After toying with the idea of keeping Germany weak, U.S. policy shifted toward rebuilding Germany (at least the three western zones) as part of a prosperous Europe. Americans tended to admire the Germans' economic and military prowess. Having experienced two German invasions of France in his lifetime, de Gaulle hoped to detach the Rhineland from Germany, set up international control of the coal-rich Ruhr, and divide the rest of the Reich into dependent states. France wanted a large and secure supply of coal as reparation from its late enemy. If allowed to reunite, the four zones of Germany might ally with Moscow and "be even more dangerous than in the past," the Frenchman warned. The Americans disagreed. They argued that Germany stood utterly devastated; the United States would not allow it to rearm. Truman and Byrnes protested that French proposals to destroy German industry would cripple European reconstruction. Nor did they accept international control of the Ruhr, which would open the gate to Soviet influence. France should stop being obsessed with Germany, curb its appetite for German coal, and focus on rebuilding its own economy, the Americans lectured. They promised that the atom bomb and the United Nations guaranteed against German aggression. Unconvinced, de Gaulle and Bidault reiterated their aim of detaching the Rhineland and the Ruhr. And so it went round and round, to the frustration of both sides.[17]

U.S.-French differences over Germany peaked in 1945–48. Discord within the Truman administration complicated the picture. Responsible for the U.S. occupation zone in Germany, the Department of the Army pushed for recovery of a unified Germany as envisioned at the 1945 Potsdam summit. France had not been invited to Potsdam and did not feel bound by its agreements. The French repeatedly used their veto in the Allied Control Authority to block coordinated administration of the four zones. This infuriated General Lucius Clay, the outspoken and powerful governor of the American zone. The French acted worse than the Soviets, Clay raged, and Washington should cut off loans to Paris. The State Department disagreed, and its reasoning prevailed with Truman. America's position in Germany would stand isolated and untenable if the Communists gained control in France, the State Department argued. Cutting off aid would only hand France to the PCF. As relations with Moscow deteriorated, the Truman administration grew more determined to insulate the three western zones from Soviet influence. Yet this concern did not mean that the United States adopted the French thesis on Germany. Washington still opposed France's ambition to detach the Rhineland and internationalize the Ruhr.[18]

France's failure to get all the Ruhr coal it wanted deepened its dependence on the United States. It got some coal from the Saar mines in the French

Despite his troubles with the U.S. government, de Gaulle remained popular
with the American public. Here the general receives from Mayor Fiorello
LaGuardia the honorary citizenship of New York City. *Courtesy of AP/Wide
World Photos*

zone. But France needed much more to repair war damage and to become, as de Gaulle hoped, a great industrial power. If France could not get enough coal in reparations from Germany, it would have to buy it with U.S. dollars. France also needed dollars to purchase food, machinery, and other vital imports. Lend-Lease, which funded those supplies during the war, coincidentally ended the day de Gaulle came to Washington in August 1945. The contrast between France's poverty and America's riches astounded the general. Impressed by America's "overpowering activity and intense optimism" he wondered how France might tap that wealth without surrendering its independence.[19]

Part of the answer came from Jean Monnet. A global salesman for his family's cognac business who was to become perhaps the foremost internationalist of the twentieth century, Monnet, in a variety of jobs in both world wars, cut through red tape to direct resources to where they were most needed. Of course this particularly helped France, generally poorer than its associates. Monnet spent much of World War II in Washington, where he became friends with many influential people in government, business, and academia. These contacts proved useful in the postwar era, when Monnet became a facilitator for Western European and transatlantic cooperation. Sharing de Gaulle's admiration for American industry, Monnet studied the organizational methods that directed this wondrous machine. Before returning to France in November 1945, he negotiated a $550 million loan from the Export-Import Bank, a U.S. government agency to promote American exports. Proposed during the de Gaulle-Bidault visit in August, this loan provided enough dollars for a few months.

For the longer run, Monnet, de Gaulle, and others hatched three ambitious, interrelated schemes to bolster their nation's power and autonomy: uniting Europe under French leadership, keeping that Europe as independent as possible of superpower rivalry, and modernizing French industry. How far a united Europe would extend to the east; whether it would include Great Britain; how it would control Germany; to what extent it would supplant national sovereignty; whether its bonds would be primarily economic, political, or military; what its relationship would be toward the superpowers—all loomed as questions in 1945 and would remain so for many years. Monnet and de Gaulle would later split over those issues. Yet there existed a consensus that French revival required expanded markets and some scheme to get Germany's coal while containing the former enemy's power.

Unity and neutrality provided the obvious remedy to Europeans dwarfed by the superpowers. The semiofficial newspaper Le Monde urged that the European bloc try to maintain an equal understanding of and an equal independence from Moscow and Washington. Otherwise Europeans would suffer as pawns of the superpowers. This fit the popular concept of France as the "wedding ring" or "hyphen" between East and West. "An alliance with the West?" "Yes," Bidault affirmed in late 1944. "But an alliance with the East as well."[20] Such ideas also suited the governing coalition of the Mouvement Républicain Populaire (MRP, or Christian Democrats), the Socialists, and the Communists. PCF officials ran several of the economic ministries. Until mid-1947 most French remained highly reluctant to enlist in the cold war. Like the yearning for European unity, French sentiment for a neutralist, independent Europe stood frustrated in the immediate postwar years, but it remained an outlook shared by many.

The modernization of France's economy proved easier to attain. De Gaulle, Monnet, and others hoped to use American dollars to help reconstruct the efficient, expanding economy necessary for French power and independence. France faced the choice, as Monnet put it, of "modernization or decadence." He and de Gaulle understood that launching the modernization plan would increase France's dependence on American aid and hence on the United States. In particular, France's need for dollars made it more difficult for Paris to oppose Washington's policy to revive western Germany. The Monnet Plan also implied a general shift toward the United States in that the market-oriented recovery scheme helps align France's economic, social, and political structures with those of America. But most French leaders figured it worthwhile to accept some loss of autonomy in order to secure what Monnet called the "promise of future independence."[21] In late 1945 Monnet and de Gaulle began preliminary negotiations for another American loan.

Meanwhile Monnet's experts analyzed the problems of a backward economy. They realized that France needed modern technology and a scale of operation larger than the family businesses that had predominated. The most efficient French steel plant dated from 1906, installed by the Germans when they owned Lorraine. In 1946 French experts drafted a modernization program, which became known as the Monnet Plan. American example inspired their work. In contrast to French tradition, the new plan rested on a faith in economic growth, productivity, statistical analysis, informal personal contact, and the active involvement of labor, industry, and consumers in the planning process. Monnet and several of his deputies had absorbed this approach to modern production in the United States, and now they wanted to apply it to France. The French tapped the skills of economist Robert Nathan, who had helped direct the U.S. Office of War Mobilization. In Paris Nathan advised Monnet's group on everything from analysis of raw data to detailed policy. Monnet's team worked from the assumption that France would remain a primarily capitalist nation. At Monnet's insistence, the technicians enjoyed considerable independence from the ministerial bureaucracies. Their autonomy insulated the planners from control by the Communists, powerful in the economic ministries until 1947. The Monnet Plan's stress on modernization also helped blunt popular pressure for redistribution of wealth. Its authors hoped that rising productivity would finance future wage hikes, but for the present they tried to keep wages low, channeling funds into investment rather than consumption.[22]

To American astonishment, the PCF endorsed such sacrifice by workers. As part of the governing coalition, the Communist party "was a loyal and even friendly partner in our work," Monnet acknowledged. The PCF opposed strikes or wage hikes that would curb investment. Facing wildcat strikers, Maurice Thorez, secretary general of the PCF and minister of state in the coalition government, told them, "To produce, to mine coal, is today the highest form of your class duty." The workers returned to the pits, but discontent grew as living standards collapsed.[23]

From pre-Liberation days to mid-1947, French Communists and non-Communists tried to work together, despite their mutual mistrust. French patriots agreed that failure to cooperate could fatally divide the nation and undermine its independence. France's ideological divisions made many French view the cold war, like World War II, as a gray struggle rather a black-and-white one. In the early postwar years, most French wanted to minimize conflict with Communists, whether in the Soviet Union or the PCF.

The French appreciated their liberation by the United States; yet they judged the Soviet Union a better partner in keeping Germany down. According to 1945 opinion polls, four-fifths of the French public found the Americans too easy on the Germans. An even higher proportion trusted the Soviets to be properly tough. Twenty percent of the public gave first priority to relations with the United States; 33 percent put the priority on ties with the Soviet Union. While 24 percent of the population in early 1945 expected postwar aid from the United States, 29 percent expected it from the Soviets. Massive U.S. assistance changed that opinion: by 1947, 64 percent awaited continued aid from the United States; 8 percent from the USSR. Knowing where their bread came from did not eliminate suspicion of those who gave it. Shortly after Washington announced a program of generous aid under the Marshall Plan, 42 percent of the French feared the United States wanted to dominate the world, while 49 percent worried about the Soviet Union's global ambition.[24]

From 1945 to 1947 the French political party structure reflected this ambivalence about the cold war. Prewar conservative and moderate parties stood discredited by the defeat of 1940 and subsequent collaboration. Their shame made room for groups that had resisted the Germans. Most important were the Christian Democrats (MRP), the Socialists, and the Communists (PCF). Many of de Gaulle's followers joined the MRP, although later conflict split him from that group. Despite deep differences, all three parties determined to reconstruct not the tired France of the 1930s but a revitalized, productive nation capable of raising the living standard of its people. All agreed on the necessity of national economic planning. The MRP and the Socialists aimed at some happy medium between what the MRP termed capitalism's "dictatorship of money" and communism's "dictatorship of the state."

Where the PCF aimed was harder to determine. While part of the Socialist-MRP-PCF coalition government from 1945 to 1947, the Communists curbed worker demands in order to promote investment and production, essential to rebuilding the economy. Although still committed to radical change, the PCF as a coalition partner acted moderately. If the PCF had remained within the government, it might have evolved into a distinctly French party independent of Moscow. But in May 1947 the Socialists expelled the PCF from the coalition. The split between the PCF and the rest of France widened in pace with the deepening cold war and American involvement. De Gaulle illustrated the pattern. From 1943 to his resignation in January 1946, the general had a competitive but working relationship with the Communists. In mid-1947 he made anticommunism his springboard for an attempted political comeback.[25]

No lovers of de Gaulle, the diplomats who ran the American Embassy in Paris remained highly suspicious of Communists, whether those enemies were in Moscow, Paris, or Washington. Ambassador Jefferson Caffery viewed the French Communists as dangerous "extremists" who would eventually try to seize the government. One gets a sense of the near paranoia about communism among embassy officials from a statement years later by the experienced diplomat Douglas MacArthur II. "We did not dare . . . report on communist activity through ordinary [State Department] channels, for fear that it would be back to Moscow within 36 hours," MacArthur recalled.[26]

MacArthur's memory of the State Department as riddled with Soviet moles was grounded not in historical fact but rather in the near-hysterical fantasy of the early cold war that good people everywhere were under assault by Communists. Many Americans of the time regarded communism as a disease and its followers as sick. In 1946 Senator Arthur Vandenberg, ranking Republican on the Senate Foreign Relations Committee, found himself seated at dinner opposite Communist leader Maurice Thorez. Vandenberg stared at Thorez's beaming face. "How can such a healthy man be a Communist?" he kept asking.[27] To help prevent the spread of such sickness, Truman approved a War Department plan to send additional American troops into France in the event of an attempted French Communist armed takeover. United States soldiers would guard "munitions of war which might be seized and used by the Communists in their revolutionary action," the secretary of war ordered.[28] Even if Communists stayed peaceful, they remained dangerous, Caffery and other Americans believed. PCF control of the economic ministries threatened "Monnet's economic liberalism." The ambassador found the Communist ideal of a "closed economy . . . extremely difficult to reconcile . . . with our broad commercial policy objectives."[29] Like other American officials, Caffery never considered working with the PCF. Instead he tried to mold French politics by encouraging and supporting political factions open to U.S. influence.[30]

Hoping to strengthen those pro-American elements, Washington gave France a large loan as part of the May 1946 Blum-Byrnes agreement. The accord meant that France would modernize on the U.S. pattern with U.S. aid and accept American rules in its foreign trade. The agreement grew out of talks launched by de Gaulle before he resigned in January 1946 over the refusal of the Socialists and Communists to grant strong executive powers to the president of the new Fourth Republic. The new government (a MRP-Socialist-PCF coalition with Socialist Félix Gouin as president) sent as negotiator its most prestigious statesman, former Socialist premier Léon Blum. Blum had emerged from German prisons a hero. Although he had led the Popular Front government before the war, Blum now favored keeping the Socialist party independent of the Communists. Aid from the United States was essential, Blum told Americans, to assure French recovery and to keep the PCF at bay. While the elder statesman handled the public relations, Monnet negotiated. Monnet impressed Americans with his careful, statistical account of French needs. That analysis aimed at increasing French industrial production to 150 percent of 1938 levels by 1950. Byrnes rejected Monnet's bid for a large increase in German coal and a multiyear commitment of aid (the latter would come a year later with the Marshall Plan).

But the Americans agreed to loan enough Export-Import Bank funds to get the Monnet Plan started. Monnet's modernization scheme required internal investment and the importation of American equipment and supplies. Since France did not earn enough from exports to pay for these U.S. goods, it needed a steady transfusion of dollars. Building French power for the long term required increased dependence on America, at least for the short term. In effect, the Blum-Byrnes deal traded access to the French economy in return for U.S. aid.

Washington won commercial and cultural links to France in addition to the financial and industrial ties offered by Monnet. The French agreed, at least in principle, to slash import restrictions and to support the United States in forthcoming international trade negotiations. Meeting with top business and political leaders at the elite Council on Foreign Relations, economist and future premier Pierre Mendès France assured banker David Rockefeller "that France planned to let her colonies buy and sell directly in foreign countries without restrictions." Rockefeller and Mendès-France agreed that a U.S. loan, "by improving economic conditions, might . . . help to prevent the growth of communism." The French government's "nationalization would not bring about nearly as great changes as many believed," Mendès France promised these conservative Americans; besides, "labor would be more willing to work hard for a company owned by the state than for a private corporation."[31]

The State Department fought for a loan hefty enough to help France's economy and influence the upcoming French election. State proposed a $1 billion aid package involving a $650 million loan from the Export-Import

Bank, a credit sale of merchant shipping and other war surplus property, and a generous settlement of Lend-Lease.

The Truman administration's debate over the aid package revealed the deepening cold-war atmosphere. When some officials questioned giving so much loan money to one country, Will Clayton, undersecretary of state for economic affairs, suggested "that the funds could come immediately from the billion dollars which had been earmarked for Russia." Knitting ties with France seemed more rewarding than repairing those with the Soviet Union. State Department cold warriors calculated that the loan would produce votes for the Socialists and other non-Communist parties in the 2 June French election. New Deal carryovers such as Secretary of Commerce Henry Wallace and Federal Reserve chairman Marriner Eccles felt pangs about "buy[ing] a foreign election." "The French people might resent the fact that we were trying to influence the election," Eccles warned. Clayton waved aside such old-fashioned objections, arguing that communism would be a disaster in France, "the key to the whole Western European situation." The State Department won out. The Truman administration approved the full $650 million loan, running the risk that other countries would receive nothing unless Congress appropriated more loan money.[32]

The Blum-Byrnes agreement was signed on 28 May 1946, five days before the election. Despite fanfare over the loan, voters blamed Blum's party for the rampant inflation. The Socialists lost heavily, the PCF gained slightly, and the MRP surged ahead to become the largest party. MRP leader Georges Bidault replaced the Socialist Félix Gouin. News of Blum-Byrnes sent the Paris stock market soaring. The business press welcomed the accord as strengthening capitalism. If the government moved too far to the left, French businessmen warned, Washington would cut off aid, as it had done to Poland.

While Blum-Byrnes strengthened promarket forces in France, it damaged a crucial industry. Washington made just one specific trade demand during the negotiations—that France ease import restriction on Hollywood movies. Both Americans and French understood that films involved far more than commerce. Films remained "one of the most effective media for the dissemination of information regarding the United States," the American embassy recognized.[33] Barney Balaban, president of Paramount Pictures, described Hollywood's "mission . . . [of] informing people in foreign lands about the things that have made America a great country. . . . we know how to put across the message of our democracy."[34] The French public responded to this glittery message; at least they flocked to American films. Hollywood's popularity threatened a major industry and, worse, the loss of "French genius," cultural independence, and world prestige. For both sides, films became an emotional symbol. "To defend the French movie industry was the same as defending France," was the cry.[35]

The issue went back to the 1920s, when American silent movies swept world markets, including France. Understanding that Hollywood films advertised other American products, Washington promoted movie exports. The French fought back with quotas and subsidies, but Hollywood retained a strong position.[36] Under German orders, Vichy stopped Hollywood imports. With this protection the number of French film producers doubled. Their monopoly ended when the U.S. Army's Psychological Warfare Division brought to France some 400 prints of the latest films and turned them over to American companies. Hollywood's products enjoyed "great demand" with the French public, reported the embassy, and yielded "tremendous profits" to exhibitors.[37]

Trying to shield French industry and culture from the Hollywood invasion, de Gaulle's government restored some of Vichy's barriers to Hollywood movies. Yet Paris allowed freer access for films from the Soviet Union, Czechoslovakia, and England. An uproar resulted, yet another round in France's long battle over Americanization. The French government's effort to curtail imports of American movies was opposed by the many French citizens who enjoyed Hollywood fantasies and the French cinema owners, who appreciated the profits. "If you wish to stab America in the back, you shall not do it in our cinemas," the president of the owners' association snapped to the minister of information.[38]

State Department officials also protested. On most matters the department treated the French government gingerly, for fear it would fall to the Communists. On films the department became insistent. Acting Secretary of State Dean Acheson confronted Monnet with the issue "in connection with talks re financial assistance."[39] Washington pried open the door for Hollywood in the Blum-Byrnes accord. In every 13-week period, only four weeks were reserved for French-produced films; in the remaining nine weeks, theater owners could show what they wanted.

Hollywood imports soared while French film production plummeted. Usually, U.S. movie companies could recoup production costs in the home market. The Americans could rent films to French theater owners for less than domestic producers had to charge. The American industry enjoyed another competitive advantage—a huge inventory of films made during the war. By early 1948 half of France's film studios had been shut down and 80 percent of its work force was unemployed, Bidault complained to Caffery. Some of the best talent left for Hollywood, further crippling the industry. Not only jobs but national identity appeared threatened. As one French actor saw it, Hollywood imports "endanger the very existence of dramatic art. The change in French taste may well be irreversible and fatal. Accustomed to the wines of Burgundy and Bordeaux, our stomachs will now have to adjust to Coca-Cola. For a Frenchman this amounts to giving up his citizenship."[40]

This economic and cultural protest climaxed in January 1948 with thousands of film artists, technicians, and their supporters marching through the streets of Paris against "les gangsters et pin-up girls" of Hollywood.[41] The stark symbolism evoked by Hollywood's intrusion into the sacred culture of France was easily exploited by Communists and others resentful of America's growing presence in French life. "The social and political implications of this crisis . . . cannot escape you," Bidault warned Caffery.[42] Bidault had pressed the right button. Washington officials grudgingly accepted an additional week of exclusive French showings, with the remaining eight of every 13 weeks open to Hollywood films.[43] The Americans also agreed to limit the number of exported films to France to 121 per year. The Blum-Byrnes deal sketched the future path of U.S.-French relations. The United States assisted France; France in return moved closer to America's orbit. The State Department's burning concern for the film issue foreshadowed later efforts to win the hearts and minds of the French.

Despite help from the Blum-Byrnes loan, France suffered economic and political crisis in 1946–47. In the short run, the Monnet Plan aggravated problems because it favored investment over consumption, profits over wages, steel over housing. Large budget deficits accelerated inflation; PCF opposition to strikes braked wages. In 1946 workers received a 25 percent pay increase while prices jumped 74 percent. In 1947 the inflation rate galloped at nearly twice the pace of wages. The Confédération Générale du Travail (CGT), the Communist-dominated labor union umbrella, struggled to restrain desperate workers, denouncing wildcat strikers as "Hitlerite-Trotskyite[s]." Seeing little incentive in exchanging produce for depreciating paper, farmers fed grain to their cattle instead of shipping it to the cities. Despite France's begging in Washington and bluster in the Allied Control Council for Germany, it did not receive all the Ruhr coal it wanted. Then in 1946–47 nature struck with the coldest winter of the century and a withering drought the following summer. The food and fuel crisis grew desperate. The French suffered a "deep psychosis of worry and disillusionment," Caffery concluded.[44]

France did not suffer alone. Great Britain's economic stability, Germany's recovery, and America's own prosperity all stood imperiled, the Truman administration feared. Economic, political, and military aspects of the crisis intertwined. If Great Britain went bankrupt, Truman fretted, it might bring down the American and the world economies. With Great Britain staggering, the United States took over the imperial burden in places such as Greece, where leftist rebels supported by Yugoslavia fought against British-backed conservatives. In his famous Truman Doctrine speech of March 1947, the president announced that the United States would combat Communist insurrection anywhere in the world. Many observers such as State Department expert George Kennan found the doctrine too broad in its geographical focus and too narrow because of its military emphasis.

The U.S. economy's shaky postwar adjustment underlined the need for another initiative—one geared more toward economic reconstruction and focused more on Western Europe, America's best customer. Truman's advisers alternated between warnings that the U.S. economy would sink into depression and worry that soaring demand would loft inflation. Since 1945 consumer spending and booming exports had supported the economy. America's trade surplus with Europe climbed to $5 billion in 1947. These sales included coal, food, and supplies, along with the machinery to modernize Europe's economies and link them to the United States. Yet this vital exchange seemed destined to end by late 1947, when Europe would run out of dollars. Some historians now believe that European recovery would have continued at a slower pace even if the massive purchases had ended. Probably too, France could have remained capitalist, perhaps with integration of the PCF into a national consensus. But American policy makers in 1947 did not have such hindsight.

They saw a crisis—and an opportunity. If Western Europe ran out of dollars to buy U.S. products, "there will be revolution," warned Undersecretary Clayton of the State Department. "The immediate effects on our domestic economy would be disastrous: markets for our surplus production gone, unemployment, depression, a heavily unbalanced budget on the background of a mountainous war debt. *These things must not happen,*" he warned department colleagues.[45] "It is idle," affirmed George C. Marshall, now Truman's secretary of state, "to think that a Europe left to its own efforts . . . would remain open to American business in the same way that we have known it in the past."[46]

From 1947 to 1950 Marshall and other Truman administration officials did not leave Europe "to its own efforts." Americans bound Western Europe with silken threads of economic and technical aid, systematic political consultation, and, by 1949, joint military planning and integration—all under U.S. leadership. Western Europeans, particularly the French, felt torn. To a degree they resisted Washington's hegemony, particularly the prodding to move quickly toward a liberal, integrated market patterned on the United States. Yet Western Europeans sorely needed U.S. help, and they hoped to use that assistance for their own purposes. In the wake of Nazi and Soviet depredations, many Europeans found America's mass democracy and capitalist prosperity highly attractive. Thus most Western Europeans, including the French, consented to the raft of initiatives—tied to aid—that emerged during an extraordinarily creative period of American foreign policy. While Washington wooed Western Europeans, Moscow scared them with its clampdown on Eastern Europe. The combined impact of Soviet repression and American aid enabled the United States to dominate most policy debates with its new allies and, more importantly, to determine the very language and issues of the debates. The governing elites and much of the population of Western Europe came to accept the legitimacy of America's worldview and leadership. Thus Washington could create the "Free World," in orbit around the United States and dedicated to containing and opposing the Soviet Union.

Enlisting Paris in this cause required getting the French to accept their ancient enemy Germany as a partner in European reconstruction. It also meant nudging the French to jettison their wartime hope of cooperation with the Soviet Union in foreign affairs and collaboration with the PCF in domestic matters.

Though divided, Germany remained Europe's powerhouse and the center of Washington's reconstruction policy. Herbert Hoover, who had faced the same problem after World War I, warned that keeping Germany impoverished would also keep the rest of Europe in rags. Hoover and the U.S. Army wanted to unleash German industry so that it could recover and contribute to European reconstruction. German coal remained crucial. The French wanted to divert this fuel from the Ruhr to the expanded steel industry planned by Monnet. They feared that unrestricted German industry would again dominate Europe. The State Department shared the army's appreciation of Germany's importance, but wanted more of a balance between France and the former enemy. Walt Whitman Rostow, a young State Department official who in the 1960s would become a presidential adviser, suggested a way out of the dilemma. In early 1946 Rostow urged tying Germany's recovery to Western Europe's integration. Linked to its neighbors with extensive economic and perhaps political bonds, Germany could grow strong without becoming a threat. Of course Monnet, de Gaulle, and others had talked about European unification under French leadership, but Americans liked to think of integration as a U.S. history lesson for Europe.

Fear of communism brought Americans and Western Europeans together and spurred the penny-pinching U.S. Congress to finance the collaboration. The Truman administration admitted that Europe's main problem was an exhausted physical plant and a spiritual malaise, but it blamed the Communists for exploiting the emergency.[47] Cold-war tensions worsened in early 1947. To get Congress to approve aid to Greece and Turkey, Truman cast the Soviet Union as the villain. The Soviets acted out this role by installing a satellite regime in Hungary, a move that made French leaders "almost hysterically frightened," Caffery reported.[48] At the Moscow Foreign Ministers Conference of March–April 1947, Secretary of State Marshall quarreled with the Soviets over Germany, yet worked closely with Bidault. After talking with the secretary, a columnist reported that he "is eager to make a policy with France as its center if a non-Communist coalition can prove its ability to govern."[49] Caffery and other Americans let Socialist Premier Paul Ramadier understand that expelling the PCF from the governing coalition would open the door to closer relations with the United States.

Such hints encouraged the non-Communist parties along a path they were already treading. Since Liberation, France's MRP-Socialist-PCF government and balanced foreign policy had tried to straddle the gulf between Communists and non-Communists in the domestic and foreign arenas. This stance grew precarious as economic conflict and the cold-war split further widened the gap. At the Moscow conference, the Americans, British, and Soviets maintained their opposition to French plans for the Rhineland and Ruhr.

Expecting this veto, Bidault focused on the more limited goal of integrating the coal-rich Saar region of Germany into the French economy. Bidding for French support, Marshall went along on the Saar and also promised more coal from the Ruhr. In contrast, the Soviets opposed French designs on the Saar unless France agreed to support their bid for a share in the Ruhr. Furious, Bidault left Moscow declaring that "Russia did everything it could to organize the western bloc and it will get it."[50]

Meanwhile, the French Communist party had little to show for its loyal cooperation with the non-Communists in the government. Aside from a voice in social welfare legislation, the PCF had gained little say in domestic and foreign policy. Militant workers began to desert the Communist-dominated CGT in disgust. The showdown came in late April 1947 when, despite the confederation's efforts to suppress it, a wildcat strike spread through the Renault auto works near Paris. The nationalized plant stood out as France's largest factory and the pacesetter in labor relations. Unable to stop or settle the strike, the CGT came out in favor of it. Now—with the nation watching—the PCF had to choose between backing the workers' pay demands or supporting the government's wage policy. MRP and Socialist ministers refused Thorez's plea to grant a wage hike. Instead, Premier Ramadier asked the National Assembly for a vote of confidence on the issue. The Communist ministers abstained on the vote, and on 7 May Ramadier dismissed them from the government.[51]

Caffery warmly welcomed the reshuffled, non-Communist Ramadier government. It appeared Socialist enough to appeal to workers and conservative enough to exclude the Communists. On 9 May 1947 the U.S.-dominated World Bank made its first loan ever, a $250 million grant to France. Caffery warned that France needed still more aid or Ramadier would fall. The ambassador feared that a Socialist defeat would divide France between two "extremist" groups, the Communists and the ultranationalistic followers of de Gaulle. De Gaulle's return to power, he predicted, would probably end democracy in France. A Communist triumph threatened something worse: "Soviet penetration of Western Europe, Africa, the Mediterranean and Middle East . . . our position in . . . Germany rendered precarious, if not untenable."[52] France appeared to be the first in a long line of dominoes.

Caffery's warning heightened the crisis atmosphere in which the State Department crafted what became the Marshall Plan. Department experts wrestled with two difficulties: whether to invite the Soviet Union to participate in the program, and how to have Europe adopt the major elements in America's plan while having the scheme appear to be Europe's initiative. Washington resolved the first problem by "playing it straight," as George Kennan put it. Kennan and others understood that many Europeans, particularly the French, opposed the division of their continent into rigid blocs. So the United States invited all of Europe, but oriented the plan toward open economies and open records. Washington also indicated that if the Soviets joined in the plan, they should help Western Europe. This put the Soviet Union, still suffering a war-ravaged economy, in a difficult position. It could participate, which meant abandoning Marxist principles and sharing its meager resources, or it could say no, which meant assuming blame for further dividing Europe. At first the Soviets showed some interest in Marshall's proposal. Then Stalin, perhaps frightened by Poland's and Czechoslovakia's eagerness for U.S. aid, pulled back. He attacked the plan as "American imperialism" and urged Western Communist parties and labor unions to combat it. In France and elsewhere, the Soviets took the blame for Europe's division. Opposition to the aid plan also hurt the Soviet Union's image as the champion of the French working class. Though suspicious of American intentions, the French could not deny the fact of U.S. assistance.

The persistent problem of getting Europe to initiate what Washington wanted proved more difficult. On the one hand the aid program had to meet broad specifications, particularly to get through Congress. These included European integration, German participation, open economies, cost controls, and assurance that the money would not simply disappear down the "rathole of Europe." Some State officials such as Clayton argued that only American control could assure these goals. Kennan and others pointed out that overt control would backfire by feeding European resentment and adding credence to charges of American imperialism. They argued that self-help would boost European morale, and that the details of reconstruction had to be worked out by the recipients themselves. In the end, Marshall resolved the issue by deciding to exercise American power from behind the scenes.[53]

In his 5 June 1947 address at Harvard, the secretary of state summed up the analysis of the previous months. Marshall described the economic ills of Europe, pointed to their effect on the American economy, and prescribed the "remedy" of "restoring the confidence of the European people in the economic future of their own countries and of Europe as a whole." The "initiative" for a program of physical and psychological recovery "must come from Europe," he declared. The United States would contribute money and "friendly aid in the drafting of a European program."[54]

In response to Marshall's invitation, the British and French hosted a 16-nation European meeting to sketch a recovery plan. Differences soon emerged between the Europeans and the Americans. The Europeans continued to focus on separate national recoveries. Washington wanted Europe to integrate its economies, as the United States had done after 1789. The French favored a European customs union, but only after achieving recovery. The Truman administration decided to be flexible. Building an economic and political alliance with Western Europe seemed more pressing than the details of the construction. In September 1947 the Europeans submitted a list of aid requirements. After some trimming this tally became the basis for the Marshall Plan, passed by Congress in March 1948.

U.S. Marshall Plan aid helped modernize France. *Courtesy of the National Archives*

From 1948 to 1951 France received $2.4 billion in Marshall Plan aid, much of it in the food, fuel, and equipment imports needed to carry out the Monnet Plan. Marshall Plan money financed 70 percent of French public investment in 1948, and 90 percent in 1949. The French modernization effort also drew on American technology. From 1949 to 1952 Paris sent out 267 "missions of productivity" to learn from foreign experts; 211 of the groups went to the United States. Despite this vital assistance, France itself paid most of the cost of its recovery. The French invested from internal funds nine times as much as they received from the United States. As historian Alan S. Milward has put it, Marshall Plan aid supplied not the fuel but the lubricant for European recovery. The bilateral Marshall Plan agreement of 28 June 1948 also contained provisions that galled the weaker nation. Washington pressured the French to buy American cigarettes, dried fruit, and chewing gum, products that the French considered not exactly vital for economic recovery. The United States insisted on the rights to oversee the exchange rate of Marshall Plan dollars and to obtain needed strategic materials from French colonies.[55]

Similarly, the United States did not drive the French economy—but it did keep a hand on the steering wheel. Washington pointed the French government down the road to reduced public spending, stable prices, fair wages, equitable taxation, minimal trade restrictions, and European integration. The Marshall Plan's success required "substantial sacrifices . . . by all French citizens," lectured David Bruce, the plan's director in France. He added pointedly that American taxpayers and the Congress expected greater French efforts.[56] Such plain talk fueled French resentment. A chorus of newspapers from left to right condemned Bruce for interfering in France's internal affairs. French sensitivity made U.S. officials cautious. They feared that heavy-handed criticism of France could backfire by feeding charges of domination and increasing the danger of Communist or right-wing takeover. Economic pressure could similarly boomerang by igniting inflation. Committed to keeping moderate, "Third Force" governments—that is, administrations of neither the extreme right or left—in power, Washington found itself with little room to maneuver.

The counterpart controversy demonstrated Washington's dilemma. Counterpart francs were the francs French importers paid when they bought U.S. products supplied through the Marshall Plan. By controlling the release of these counterpart francs to the French government, the United States theoretically held a large say in the direction and level of public spending. A similar mechanism existed in other Marshall Plan countries. "He who controls the so-called lire fund," predicted the U.S. ambassador to Italy, "will control the monetary and fiscal, and in fact the entire economic policy of Italy."[57] In fact, however, counterpart money proved a clumsy tool for shaping policy in France and in other Marshall Plan nations. Repeatedly U.S. officials insisted that they would not release counterpart funds unless the French government met specific targets to cut the budget deficit and to dampen inflation by reducing the amount of francs in circulation.

Paris almost never fulfilled these pledges. The French government chronically overspent its budget, particularly on the Monnet program of modernization and investment and on the increasingly expensive war against Communist nationalists in Indochina—two expenses the Americans agreed were necessary, though they complained about French prodigality. Americans feared that if they withheld counterpart funds, French budget deficits and inflation would mushroom, with poisonous effects on economic and political stability. The Americans' own division also weakened U.S. clout. Worried about Communist influence in the working class, State Department officials urged the French government to raise wages, while Marshall Plan officials thought it more important to check pay increases so as to rein in inflation. So time and again the French failed to meet their promises and the Americans, after agonizing over the issue, released more counterpart funds to the French government. France also failed to honor repeated promises to remove trade and foreign exchange restrictions, partly because the rest of Europe retained barriers against French goods. France did edge toward a more open economy, but it did so slowly and fitfully. Washington's commitment to French economic recovery and to a non-Communist, non-Gaullist government tied U.S. hands. Third Force leaders knew how to exploit Washington's predicament. "It helps the Communists when Americans insist on France balancing her budget," Minister Jules Moch solemnly warned journalist Walter Lippmann.[58]

Although the French could often manipulate their rich benefactor, they still felt aggrieved at U.S. meddling in French internal affairs. More than most Americans, Lippmann empathized with French pride. Pending passage of the mammoth Marshall Plan, Washington approved a measure for interim assistance to Western Europe. Discussing the aid agreement the United States submitted to the French parliament in early 1948, Lippmann wondered how Americans would feel if Congress had to ratify a document written by the French national legislature. Washington's insistence that Paris distribute the aid fairly and charitably seemed reasonable. Yet if America sat in France's position, "compulsory fairness, compulsory charity, like compulsory gratitude, would somehow stick in our throats."[59] When Paris begged for cosmetic changes to make the agreement appear less a dictate, the State Department, its eye on Congress, refused. Nor did it accept Bidault's proposal to have the agreement signed in Washington, thus minimizing embarrassing publicity in Paris. Instead, the U.S. Embassy arranged for extensive press and radio coverage to make sure the French appreciated their benefactors.

The Marshall Plan affected France in matters far beyond pride and dollars. The plan used U.S. power and prestige to draw in Western Europe as America's economic and political ally. The now-radicalized PCF fiercely fought that effort. With the aid of American labor unions, the Truman administration counterattacked with deeper intervention in French politics and labor relations. This was not a struggle of the United States against France. Rather the United States became a key actor in an internal French drama. American intervention sharpened the French conflict and helped the non-Communists win victory.

As the State Department understood, three major groups competed in French politics: the Communists, who dominated the labor unions; the largely right-wing Rassemblement du Peuple Français ("rally of the French people" [RPF]), sparked by de Gaulle; and the Third Force, consisting of the MRP, Socialists, and other moderate parties. Washington's first objective was to "isolat[e] and ostraci[ze]" the Communists, agreed Hickerson, Matthews, Charles Bohlen, and other State experts. That meant shepherding the moderate left, particularly the Socialists and the MRP, into an anti-Communist coalition. "Politically speaking the break must come to the left of or at the very least in the middle of the Socialist Party," those U.S. officials calculated. "Translated into labor terms, the healthy elements of organized labor must be kept in the non-Communist camp."[60] De Gaulle's opposition to all labor unions threatened this strategy. The State Department appreciated the general's anticommunism, but feared that his coming to power would drive workers into the arms of the Communists.

Other objections to de Gaulle's return to power recalled wartime conflicts. Hickerson criticized the general's "mystical (and illusory) idea of France as a great power." Echoing FDR's jokes about de Gaulle the reluctant bride, Hickerson jeered that "he talks about economics as a woman talks about carburetors. His advisers are ill-assorted, incompetent, self-seeking and unstable."[61] Others feared that de Gaulle would stiffen French resistance to American objectives, such as reviving Germany and loosening the bonds of the French empire. Even where the general agreed with U.S. aims, he would insist on independence. Nonetheless, Americans agreed that despite his faults the imperious Frenchman remained a safer bet than the Communists.

Best of all to Americans was the moderate Third Force, more democratic and more receptive to advice than either de Gaulle or the PCF. The United States supported the Third Force governments of Ramadier, Bidault, Robert Schuman, Henri Queuille, and René Pleven. The multitude of premiers during the short period of 1947–52 seemed evidence of the Fourth Republic's turbulence. Yet a basic stability prevailed, since many important ministers served in cabinet after cabinet. Enjoying close rapport with many of these ministers, U.S. officials gave (and were asked for) informal advice on internal French matters.

The United States also used covert means to combat Communist influence. Marshall and other American officials warned French leaders that if the Communists reentered the government, Washington would cut off aid. State Department officers dared not be so direct in public. "Open" action against the PCF would "raise the cry of direct interference in French internal affairs and turn large sections of French public opinion against the U.S.," they worried. Bohlen and other officials decided on "a substantial secret fund" to subsidize anti-Communist organizations.[62] The new Central Intelligence Agency (CIA) administered the money. Coordination of diplomatic and covert political warfare operations had become essential, Marshall directed the Paris embassy. The Americans also tried, by overt and covert means, to influence the French press. In the midst of a propaganda battle with the Soviets, Acting Secretary of State Robert Lovett instructed Caffery to "inspire in [the] French press . . . an editorial or statement . . . calculated to be as . . . newsworthy as possible in order to receive widest initial coverage in French and world press and provide sound basis for exploitation by Dept and field."[63] From 1948 on, such measures became part of the Truman administration's broad program of open and covert actions to fight the Communists in France.

The United States also influenced organized labor. State Department officials believed that labor unions held the key to French production and to the success of the Marshall Plan. Americans expected labor to endure cuts in purchasing power and harder work. Both the Marshall and Monnet plans gave first priority to investment, not consumption. Economic experts warned that cooperative labor unions were crucial to get workers to accept sacrifices in their standard of living and other difficult adjustments. Hostile unions could cripple Washington's plan for France by blocking shipments of goods and convincing Congress that help to Europe was futile. Yet collapsing living standards made workers desperate. Prices had skyrocketed 26 percent in three months, the State Department noted anxiously in late 1947. Faced with a potential labor explosion, American and French officials encouraged non-Communist union leaders to break away from the Communist-dominated CGT. With the "healthy" unions organized under a new labor umbrella, the CGT could be isolated and contained.

The American Federation of Labor (AFL) and the Congress of Industrial Organizations (CIO) had already mobilized to fight the Communist labor unions. In 1946 the AFL established a European office headed by Irving Brown. "France is the area where we must fight," he declared at a State Department briefing. Brown agreed with State officials that "France is the immediate key to the problem of Western European democracy [though] in the long run Germany will be the decisive question."[64] His first priority was to change the internal French situation by splitting the PCF-dominated labor movement. To do this, Brown helped finance and organize anti-Communist splinter groups. He cooperated closely with the State Department's labor attachés and funneled secret CIA funds to anti-Communist factions. Brown identified anti-Communist militants worthy of U.S. government subsidy.

These efforts paid off when the Force Ouvrière (F.O.), a minority group of Socialist unions, broke off from the CGT. Though Caffery exaggerated when he bragged that he personally had been responsible for breaking up the C.G.T.,

American intervention had stiffened the non-Communists. "Our job was to be the reinforcing rods in the concrete," Brown explained. The F.O. gained strength among bureaucrats and school teachers while the CGT remained preeminent among industrial workers. F.O. leaders still faced daunting organizational problems, particularly since they had left behind the union halls and equipment of the CGT. The AFL stepped into the breach. "They needed a few francs for a mimeograph machine and a full-time organizer. But most of all they needed to feel they were not alone," Brown recalled about one union he had helped.[65] The AFL sent regular payments to the F.O., and Caffery gave supplies to the organization. Once established, the F.O. and other non-Communist unions lined up behind the Marshall Plan. Their support helped counter Communist charges that the recovery plan was antilabor.

After the creation of the North Atlantic Treaty Organization (NATO) in 1949, Communist-led dock workers called strikes to block arms shipments to France. The CIA gave Brown money "to pay off his strong-arm squads in Mediterranean ports so that American supplies could be unloaded against the opposition of Communist dockworkers," a top agency official recalled.[66] U.S. aid hamstrung the Communists while helping non-Communist unions. Yet Washington's client unions had only modest success in meeting workers' needs. The subsidized groups focused more on cold-war issues than on the mundane tasks of organization and worker benefits, non-Communist labor leaders recalled. When U.S. funding dried up in the mid-1950s, so did many of these unions. Discouraged by the feuding, many workers dropped out of unions altogether. "Europeans are tired of little men who run around with little black bags," later observed a Brown critic.[67]

Brown's hiring of muscle men to keep U.S. weapons flowing into French ports demonstrated how American aid helped intensify the polarization and confrontation between Communists and non-Communists. Before mid-1947 both France and Czechoslovakia aspired to keep their national independence and to bridge the differences between the superpowers. Then France edged closer to the Americans in order to obtain Marshall Plan dollars for the Monnet Plan and other recovery efforts, while Czechoslovakia found itself deeper in the Soviet camp when Moscow vetoed Czech participation in the Marshall Plan. On 25 February 1948 Czechoslovakia adopted a Communist government under the threat of a Soviet invasion.

On 5 March General Lucius Clay in the American zone of Germany warned that the coup in Prague might be the prelude to a Soviet war of aggression. Although the war scare soon subsided, the Truman administration raced ahead with plans to increase the military budget and reinstitute the draft. Washington was also determined to build a viable West German state capable of joining the Western camp. Alarmed, Moscow in June 1948 began an 11-month blockade of all surface routes into the Western-held sectors of Berlin, deep inside the Soviet zone of Germany. The American ambition to revive West Germany also conflicted with French plans to keep Germany weak and to use German coal for French industry.

The worsening cold war left France with fewer—and harder—choices to make. The Soviet move in Prague frightened the French and discouraged the many who had, like Socialist President Vincent Auriol, viewed neutralist Czechoslovakia as a model and a partner for France. More than half of the French public now worried that Moscow would launch a war of conquest. Even some pro-PCF newspapers protested the Soviet aggression. For many French the neutralist option appeared still desirable but no longer tenable. French officials felt trapped between Soviet brutality and American overreaction. General Clay has "lost his head to anti-Communism," worried René Massigli, the French ambassador in London.[68] Most French leaders agreed with the May 1948 assessment of Maurice Couve de Murville, the Foreign Ministry political affairs director, that Washington's "creation of a West German government . . . is the most provocative act one could possibly think of against the Soviet Union."[69] The French feared that Moscow, outraged at Washington's revival of the German enemy, might launch a war that would destroy France.

Moreover, as the French well knew, the Americans did not intend to shield France from a Soviet invasion. Pentagon plans of 1947–48 envisaged a quick withdrawal to Great Britain and North Africa. From these bases the United States would attack the Soviets with atomic bombs. For the French this scenario theatened horror worse than that of 1940–45. "The Russian hordes will occupy the area, raping women and deporting the male population for slave labor in the Soviet Union. . . . France and Western Europe will be . . . devastated by the Soviet hordes and [then] atomized by the United States," worried Foreign Minister Bidault and Armed Forces Minister Pierre Teitgen.[70] Premier Queille feared that "the next time the U.S. would probably be liberating a corpse and civilization would be dead,"[71] In contrast to the Americans, who planned to fight from Europe's periphery, the French had the overwhelming priority of avoiding an invasion of their country. That meant stopping the Soviets in Germany before they reached France. American officials such as Hickerson dismissed French fears as "hysterical" while pointing to a basic contradiction in the French argument: How could the West stop the Soviets on the Rhine without rearming the West Germans?[72]

After the Communist takeover in Czechoslovakia, most non-Communist French leaders concluded that they had to swallow their differences with the Americans and accept Washington's lead on Germany and on the cold war. But this shift also opened some possibilities for renewed French independence. "In our present miserable condition," France needed dollars, Foreign Minister Bidault told the Cabinet, and "there is not the ghost of a chance of benefiting from Marshall aid while also obstructing [the rebuilding of] Germany." Moreover, Bidault noted, once revived, Germany would "be at least half compatible with our views."[73] Here the foreign minister hinted at what

In the early 1950s, many French feared that the United States might provoke a war with the Soviet Union. *Courtesy of the National Archives*

would later become the creative policy of building up West Germany as a support for France—and an independent French-led Europe. A Foreign Office memorandum suggested that France would "offer to a future German government a third solution between American economic expansionism and Soviet political expansionism."[74]

In June 1948 France dropped its long-held opposition to forming a West German state. Bidault had already begged Secretary Marshall to "tighten . . . the political and . . . military . . . collaboration between the Old and the New World."[75] In effect, Bidault offered to place France under American leadership in return for Washington's pledge to defend France at the Rhine—not just from Great Britain or North Africa. In the scary days of the early cold war, France joined the Western camp because it seemed the least horrible alternative.

In late 1947 Bidault and British foreign minister Ernest Bevin had suggested to Marshall a military pact with the United States. Marshall replied that Western Europe should show some self-help by first forming its own defense alliance. The secretary hoped this initiative would impress Congress and ease domestic resistance to an entangling alliance, the first since the United States escaped the tie with France in 1800. In March 1948 Great Britain, France, and the Benelux (comprising Belgium, Luxembourg, and the Netherlands) fulfilled Marshall's request by signing the Brussels Pact, which pledged members to come to each other's aid in the event of an attack. Responding to this initiative—and to smooth flattery from the Truman administration—key Republican senator Arthur Vandenberg sponsored a resolution calling for "association by the United States, by constitutional process" with the Brussels Pact. The Joint Chiefs of Staff began discussions with their British and Canadian counterparts. Suspicious of leaks to the Communists, the talks did not include the French. This proved ironic, since Soviet spies had already penetrated the British high command. The French resented this latest exclusion from Anglo-Saxon decision making.

Relations did not improve when Washington admitted France to the talks. "The French are in our hair," complained Robert Lovett, the chief U.S. negotiator. He fumed when Ambassador Henri Bonnet "had the effrontery" to set "conditions" for France's joining the pact. France wanted "an automatic commitment" in the event of attack, "immediate re-equipment" of its forces, and a unified allied command in which it would have a voice. These demands had "such an irritating effect on General Marshall that . . . he felt like calling off the Atlantic pact negotiations at once," Lovett reported. Yet France's geographical location made it essential to Western European defense. France exasperated Americans because it punctured their self-image as Europe's wise and selfless benefactor. The French lived a "fantas[y]," Lovett exploded; the United States, not France, was "doing the favors" in creating a military alliance.[76]

In truth, Washington and Paris both gave and received "favors" in building the alliance. Within little more than a year after the creation in April
1949 of NATO, Pentagon planning shifted toward defending Western Europe. The United States extended over France and other member nations a
defense umbrella. America's nuclear monopoly made its pledge credible,
though the umbrella soon sprang leaks—Moscow exploded its own atomic
weapon in September 1949. Still, Washington analysts did not expect a
Soviet invasion of Western Europe and did not plan to commit many U.S.
troops to NATO. "I do not know of any responsible high official, military or
civilian . . . in this government or any other government who believes that
the Soviet now plans conquest by open military aggression," testified John
Foster Dulles, adviser to the Truman administration and a ranking Republican foreign policy spokesman.[77]

While the French valued NATO because it committed the United States,
Americans appreciated the new organization as a corral for France and the
other allies. Washington worried about Western Europe backsliding to neutralism. "A general stiffening of morale in Free Europe is needed," asserted
Hickerson, who guided the treaty's development.[78] Without the military
alliance, "there would be a reorientation" in Europe leading to "a restrength-
ening of those that believe in appeasement and neutrality," warned W.
Averell Harriman, who had been ambassador to Moscow in World War II and
an architect of U.S. policy since then.[79]

Such experts believed that NATO would solidify or institutionalize the
influence that the United States had gained in Western Europe through World
War II and through the Marshall Plan and other aid programs. The military tie
offered a new, more permanent vehicle for guiding French development. Even
if French Communists or nationalists won an election, an ongoing military link
with the United States would make it more difficult to escape the American
orbit. This intent became clear during the treaty negotiations, when the
United States proposed that the members undertake to protect each other
against "internal aggression" as well as armed attack. This provision would
justify armed intervention to "rescue" an ally from Communist control even if
it came about through peaceful election. Although spirited British and French
opposition scotched this measure, it revealed how Americans looked to NATO
to keep Western Europe in line. Through NATO's Standing Group, Pentagon
officers gained the leading voice in planning Europe's defense and the deployment of European military forces.

NATO held military and economic benefits too. The alliance warned the
Soviets not to attack Western Europe. It stepped in where the Marshall Plan
was failing. The plan certainly boosted national economies (in France, indus-
trial production climbed 32 percent from 1947 to 1951), but its goals of
European integration and closing the dollar gap remained distant. Indeed,
Europe's shortage of dollars worsened. The alliance and the Military Assis-

tance Program (MAP) that Truman launched in connection with it offered another means, more amenable to Congress than "give-aways," to pursue those aims. U.S. officials hoped that military supplies and the promise to come to Western Europe's aid in a Soviet attack could overcome the continent's "fear psychosis" and secure the confidence necessary for sustained economic growth.

In sum, NATO arose as a military pact when analysts, particularly American officials, did not expect imminent war. Aside from atom bomb–carrying B-29s flying out of Omaha, Nebraska, the alliance lacked the strength to fight if war did come. In essence, NATO was an attempt to banish anxieties—about Soviet intentions, American dependability, and Western European loyalty—with the hard, tangible certainties of tanks, planes, and military commitment.

Even as the NATO treaty emerged in 1948–49, there appeared many of the issues that remained until the French left the organization in 1966: In the event of war, would the United States actually come to France's defense, especially if the Soviet Union threatened Washington with nuclear annihilation? Would the United States risk its own destruction to save France? Would Congress's role block a U.S. military response? Would France share in the alliance's decision-making process? To what extent would the United States supply military equipment? Did the alliance extend to overseas French territory?

As Vandenberg's June 1948 resolution had warned, Congress would not give up its constitutional power over the decision to go to war. This ruled out the ironclad promise desired by the French. The final treaty provided that an armed attack on one of the signatories would be regarded as an attack on all, but left each member free to respond "as it deems necessary." Originally the French wanted NATO to cover all of North Africa. Unwilling to underwrite what it regarded as bankrupt colonialism, the United States agreed to include only Algeria, and even that reluctantly. This pointed to future differences over colonial policy in North Africa.

The issue of military equipment proved easier to settle. Responding to persistent French requests, the Truman administration in late 1948 gave some equipment to French forces in Germany. A few hours after the NATO treaty went into effect, Truman submitted to Congress the $1.1 billion Military Aid Program for France and other NATO nations. With an escalating war in Indochina, France needed still more supplies. Washington helped but objected to French desires to hold on to the colony (see chapter 3).

Another long-running controversy centered on France's role in the command of NATO. Americans repeatedly advised their ally to build up the infantry and rely on U.S. naval, air, and nuclear forces. The French feared this would reduce them to dependent foot soldiers in an atomic world. From the start of NATO, de Gaulle found it unacceptable that an American would oversee the defense of France. Like the French government, the general argued unsuccessfully for a unified NATO command in which France would enjoy a significant voice. The French also sought a leadership role in NATO to keep a privileged position over the emerging West German state.[80]

NATO became a milestone in U.S.-French relations. It measured the distance France had traveled from its neutralist stance of 1945. The United States had nudged France down that road while helping to push the French Communist party off to the wayside. NATO helped keep France on America's path. The different directions from which the two nations entered NATO, however, pointed to future conflict over military and colonial matters.

The Schuman Plan of May 1950 marked a turning point in another perennial issue, Germany. Since 1945 the United States, backed by Great Britain and the Soviet Union, had blocked French efforts to detach the Rhineland and Ruhr and keep the rest of Germany divided into weak states. In June 1948 Bidault agreed to merge the French zone into a proposed West German state. This change signaled the bankruptcy of previous policy, the need to keep the Americans in a generous mood, and the hope to win influence over Western policy in Germany. France did gain some voice in the restrictions placed on the emerging West German state, yet its rearguard effort to suppress German industry and rearmament fizzled.

Monnet rued France's weakness in the Franco-German-American triangle. West Germany wanted again to increase its allowed steel production, he reported to Foreign Minister Schuman. "We shall refuse, but the Americans shall insist. Finally, we shall state our reservations, but we shall give in."[81] France feared Germany as a distressingly powerful neighbor that had smashed across the border three times in a lifespan. Dismissing French protests as irrational—"a natural pathologic Gallic reaction," Bohlen explained—the United States rushed German revival.[82] Already by 1950 steel production, the measure of modern power, was cheaper in West Germany than in France.

The Schuman Plan broke through this impasse by forging a new path for Franco-German relations, an avenue America wanted Europe to take. A product of Monnet's fertile mind, the Schuman Plan proposed a common market for European coal and steel production. An international high authority, whose decisions would be binding on governments, would guarantee equal access to steel resources, promote modernization, and develop a joint trade policy. The iron ore of Lorraine and the coal of the Ruhr formed a natural economic unit over which the two nations had repeatedly fought. Now France and West Germany would share the resources. For France this promised access to cheap Ruhr coal and some international control over the West German economy, even after the postwar restraints on the defeated enemy expired. Economic integration would make it difficult for West Germany again to attack its neighbors. The Schuman Plan presumed the division of Germany, and so it underlined France's new stake in the cold war partition of Europe. For West Germany, the plan meant a quicker end to the controls, better access to European markets, and renewed economic ties with the Saar, still under French administration. Monnet hoped that integration of this central industry would lead to further European economic and political unity. Along with other French leaders, he understood that a united Europe could be more independent of the United States and possibly take its own stand toward the Soviet Union.[83]

The Schuman Plan underscored a central American dilemma. If Western Europe did unite, it might challenge U.S. policies and cut its own deal with the Soviet Union. "The greatest safeguard we have against th[is] perversion"— that is, European neutralism—"rests in the existence of NAT[O] itself," State Department officials reassured themselves.[84] American leaders understood that the Schuman Plan meant tougher competition for the U.S. steel industry, yet they stood willing to take this risk because America's economic superiority seemed unbeatable and because they hoped the Schuman Plan would boost Europe's lagging recovery.

After the triumphant signing of the NATO treaty, American foreign policy had suffered some reverses. In the fall of 1949 the United States lost its atomic monopoly to the Soviet Union while "losing" China to the Communists. With the four-year Marshall Plan already half over, Western Europe's trade deficit with the United States had only grown worse. The Marshall Plan's goal of a united Europe, efficient enough to compete on an open-door basis, remained unachieved, largely because the British blocked such rigorous competition. Despite billions in aid, the United States had failed to banish the threat of economic stagnation. If Western Europe remained economically fragmented, America "faced . . . diminishing European trade . . . [and] a very definite adjustment in the economic and political situation in the States," Harriman warned.[85]

A strong, economically integrated Europe also appeared crucial to what John McCloy, the American representative in Germany, called the "struggle for the soul of Faust."[86] West Germany's fast rising development already was "taking a familiar and dangerous nationalist turn," feared Dean Acheson, who had become secretary of state in January 1949. Unless the United States "harnessed" West German power to an integrated Europe, the former enemy would strike a deal with the Soviets to recoup lost territories. That threatened a recurring American nightmare: the "Russo-German domination" of Europe, as a worried Acheson put it.[87]

Until the fall of 1949 Washington officials assumed that Great Britain, their closest ally, would take the lead in integrating Western Europe. But the Labour government did not want such narrow ties with the Continent. Suffering a sagging economy, Labour leaders feared that membership in a European common market would hamstring their commitment to full employment. London preferred close links with the Commonwealth and a special relationship with the United States. In September 1949 the British economic crisis necessitated a drastic devaluation of the pound. Acheson concluded that Great Britain should employ its diminished resources outside of Europe, particularly by bolstering the crumbling Western position in the Far East.

With Great Britain occupied elsewhere, France became "the key" to integration, Acheson decided.[88] Although many State Department officials doubted that Paris could do much without London's leadership, the secretary encouraged France to reach out to West Germany.

In May 1950, when Paris, for its own reasons, proposed the Schuman Plan, American and French policies on Europe swung into broad agreement. Instead of trying to suppress German power, France would try to harness it, as the Americans and Monnet had long urged. After tortuous negotiations, in which the United States intervened to support France against rising West Germany, the European Coal and Steel Community came to life in 1952. With Great Britain standing glumly aside and America cheering them on, France, Germany, Italy, and the Benelux moved toward a common market.

Like joining NATO, France's commitment to integration with West Germany dramatically showed how France had changed since the Liberation. Thoughts of bridging the gap between East and West, remaining neutral in the cold war, or siding with the Soviet Union no longer animated French foreign policy. Such cold-war heresies would recur, however, and they remained alive among some intellectuals and the PCF. The Communists had fallen from war heroes who by right participated in the government to loud, marginalized outcasts. Even their stronghold in the labor movement suffered from the rise of non-Communist unions and from worker apathy. The Monnet Plan directed modernization along efficient, capitalist lines. America's economic aid and political influence helped that development. In contrast to Soviet control in Eastern Europe or America's own actions in areas such as Central America, U.S. direction in France remained deft and sophisticated. The French "can be tactfully led but not driven," explained David Bruce, who succeeded Caffery as ambassador.[89]

However tactful, foreign direction irritated a nation that had once ranked number 1 and that still prided itself as the world's cultural center. Like the United States, France liked to think of its culture radiating out to a receptive world. In culture too, the two nations stood as rival allies.

France's cultural influence, like its national power, suffered from wartime destruction, postwar divisions, and overshadowing by the superpowers. French painting, which before the war had dominated the art world—and the lucrative U.S. market—faced new problems. Like almost everything else in France, culture polarized between the Communists and non-Communists. The united front of writers and artists formed in 1945 collapsed when the MRP-Socialist-PCF coalition broke up in 1947. French art found it difficult to regain momentum. The crisis threatened pocketbook and pride. "Foreign [art] sales . . . contribute to our balance of payments and extend our influence and renown," worried critic René-Jean.[90]

Meanwhile American avant-garde painters such as Robert Motherwell and Jackson Pollock made New York the new global center for modern art. Many

American collectors now preferred native painters. Along with industrial and political superiority, "the main premises of Western art have at last migrated to the United States," trumpeted American critic Clement Greenberg.[91] New York's triumph over Paris did not surprise State Department officials confident that cultural influence "corresponded with the rise and tide of national power."[92]

Ever bold, the Paris fashion industry successfully bucked this tide of American national power. For a century Paris had dominated the world market for couture: those fashions custom-made by the most prestigious designers, worn by the world's richest women, and eventually sold by the millions in cheaper, mass-produced versions. Although Paris designers lost ground to New York during the Occupation, they surged ahead after 1944, encouraged by their government. To French officials this industry glittered as a small gold mine, since an evening dress costing relatively little in material could fetch a fantastic export price—as much as a new car. For rich Americans, who bought most of the custom-made dresses, couture's exorbitant price only enhanced its snob appeal. Meanwhile the rest of the important French apparel and perfume industry profited from the spinoff of glamour and the foreign licensing of dress patterns.

In February 1947 designer Christian Dior consolidated Paris's postwar grip on fashion with his sensational "New Look." Dior burst on a scene still marked by the uniformlike styles (padded shoulders and moderately short skirts) born of the war and by the casual, practical "American Look." The New Look challenged this austerity with elegant, round-shouldered, hour-glass-shaped dresses with long, billowing skirts. Dior's models displayed this sumptuous clothing in the depth of the cold, hungry winter of 1947. Enraged, Parisian women cried, "40,000 francs for a dress, and our children have no milk!" as they ripped the dresses off the models' backs.[93] In prosperous, postwar America, where women were again being plugged into traditional roles, Dior's extravagantly feminine, almost Victorian styles fit a national mood and appealed to wealthy trendsetters. "One expected to be corseted," explained Evangeline Bruce, wife of the ambassador to France.[94] In the summer of 1947 polls showed that a majority of U.S. women disliked the new styles (and perhaps the forced feminization they implied) but would wear them anyway. Indeed by 1948 hemlines had dropped and padded, mannish shoulders had disappeared from women's fashion. Thus male French designers played a role in shaping the image of the postwar American woman.[95]

Though important, fashion proved an exception to the trend of 1945–50. By most measures of national power—cultural, political, economic, or military—France stood subject to the United States. In ways subtle and striking, America conditioned and shaped French development. The proud French found it hard to swallow this dependence, even if it arose from their own weakness. At times their resentment exploded.

Such an outburst happened in early 1950 when an alliance of wine growers, journalists, and politicians tried to shut out that American icon, Coca-Cola.

The controversy sparked high emotions because each nation saw at stake its values and culture as well as money. Both sides vented resentments building since the war. The Coca-Cola company's victory underscored U.S. influence, especially among those French who wanted closer cooperation with the powerful Americans.

Marketed at first in the American South as a temperance drink, Coke was originally spiked with cocaine (later replaced by caffeine). Through millions of dollars of advertising, the soft drink became an emblem of "the American Way." Coca-Cola's global expansion marched forward when the company pledged to make the drink available to G.I.'s anywhere in the world for 5¢ a bottle, no matter what the cost. Convinced that ice-cold Coke would boost G.I. morale, General Eisenhower ordered eight bottling plants soon after landing in North Africa. Coca-Cola plants followed American troops into France. In Berlin, Eisenhower gave a case of Coke to the Soviet marshall Georgy Zhukov.

The gesture was significant because both Communists and non-Communists agreed with Coca-Cola president Robert Woodruff that every bottle contained "the essence of capitalism."[96] "You can't spread the doctrines of Marx among people who drink Coca-Cola," explained one columnist. "It's just that simple."[97] Despite the hyperbole, the drink did stimulate American-style business. The Coca-Cola company sold only concentrate abroad. In each country it licensed bottlers and trained technicians (some at the Coca-Cola Production School in Atlanta) in the proper formulas for making, advertising, and distributing the drink. In lesser-developed areas, Coca-Cola sparked demand for ice and electricity; in Paris, it allied with powerful liquor and ice firms; wherever it was sold, its bright red delivery trucks signaled spreading American influence.

An odd coalition of Communists, Catholic wine growers, and moderate journalists spearheaded the defense against this "Coca-Colonization." When Coca-Cola opened its first postwar bottling plant in late 1949, the Communists responded with a law to ban the soft drink on health grounds. With the support of Premier Bidault's MRP, which represented wine growers fearful of losing markets, the measure passed the National Assembly 366 to 202.

Even non-Communists feared Coca-Cola's distinctively American, aggressive sales campaign as a threat to economic and cultural autonomy. Coca-Cola appeared as just "the advance guard of a tremendous offensive aiming at the economic colonization of France," warned the Jesuit newspaper *Témoignage chrétien*.[98] Influential *Le Monde* launched a probe into American corporate investment in France, a subject of continuing concern. The danger came less from the drink itself than from "the civilization, the style of life of which it is . . . a symbol," *Le Monde* explained. "Red delivery trucks and walls covered with signs, placards and advertisements"—the effect recalled totalitarian propaganda, by which "whole peoples have been intoxicated. The moral landscape of France is at stake," *Le Monde* concluded.[99] This imagery recalled the defeat of 1940, with France again facing soulless, efficient invaders too adept at mass persuasion.

Even as the Coca-Cola controversy crystallized French resentment, it hardened American anger at French ingratitude. The head of Coca-Cola's export division was former Democratic boss James Farley, who had managed Franklin Roosevelt's 1932 and 1936 campaigns. Farley still had many friends in high places. When hearing of the French law banning Coke, he exclaimed that "Coca-Cola wasn't injurious to the health of the American soldiers who liberated France from the Nazi. . . . This might be the straw to break the back of the camel hauling billions of American dollars to France."[100]

Despite Farley's bluster, the Truman administration would not shut down the Marshall Plan aid over this issue. But in the context of delicate negotiations over counterpart funds and military aid, Ambassador Bruce's formal protest carried weight. The American public took offense at the ban and the measure had "serious implications," Bruce warned Bidault and Schuman.[101] Meanwhile, Congress discussed retaliation against imports of French wine and perfume. Bidault and Schuman dared not resist such pressure. They killed the anti-Coke law in the upper house of the legislature.

"Good wine is sufficient. We want neither Coca-Cola nor vodka," declared *Témoignage chrétien* during the dispute. Yet "good wine," in the sense of an independent French alternative to Soviet or American domination, proved inadequate from 1945 to 1950. Fear of the Soviet Union, geography, internal division, economic need, and the appeal to many of liberal capitalism and parliamentary democracy opened France to U.S. influence. In effect Washington offered France, particularly the Third Force governments, a matrimonial deal Moscow could not match: generous aid and general autonomy in domestic affairs (within broad, open-door tenets) in return for accepting U.S. leadership in foreign and defense affairs. Still, the French chafed at their dependence. In 1950 half the French people judged their nation no longer independent in foreign affairs; a three-to-two margin picked the United States, not the Soviet Union, as the country that "meddle[d] too much in French affairs."[102] "The French did not like Americans," historian Thomas Bailey observed in 1947.[103]

Americans tended to dismiss such resentment as petty French emotionalism, the resentment of people often blind to their true best interests. Like Roosevelt in World War II, American officials in the cold-war era assumed they knew what France wanted and need. U.S. policymakers worked hard to make France an ally in the containment of the Soviet Union and Germany and in the construction of an open world economy. Driving the French with a stick would only backfire, Americans understood. Far better to lure the French with economic aid and the dazzle of American culture. As Coca-Cola's victory demonstrated, France could resist American influence, but it could not stop it. The heat of the dispute suggested that the United States could make France an ally but not a friend.

Chapter 3

THE "WEAK SISTER," 1950–1958

A "flash-fire of anti-Americanism" was sweeping through France, Ambassador C. Douglas Dillon alerted Washington in June 1953.[1] President Dwight D. Eisenhower was feeding the blaze with his refusal to stop the execution of Julius and Ethel Rosenberg, convicted on shaky evidence of conspiring to pass atomic secrets to the Soviet Union during World War II. Posters throughout France pictured the famous Eisenhower grin with every tooth an electric chair. Though sharply divided on other matters, the French Catholic church, the Communist party, a group of former premiers, and the president all called for clemency. Over 7,500 petitions flooded into the American embassy, protesting the death sentence on grounds of humanity.

The French found the Rosenbergs' June 1953 execution so "shattering," as the pro-Western *Franc-tireur* put it, because they saw it as further evidence that America, France's supposed protector, had succumbed to the virulent anticommunism of Senator Joseph McCarthy.[2] "Who governs America? Eisenhower or McCarthy?" fretted the moderate newspaper *Paris-Match*.[3] Many worried that a McCarthy-dominated, nuclear-armed America might drag France into a world war. The Catholic leftist *Esprit* saw the Rosenbergs as "the first victims of atomic warfare."[4] Some French mistook Joseph *McCarthy* for General Douglas *MacArthur*, who in the 1950–53 Korean conflict pushed for total war against the Chinese Communists. This confusion and lumping together of American militants aggravated French anxieties that the United States was slipping into fascism. "Eisenhower—Another Hindenburg," headlined a usually friendly newspaper, drawing a parallel between the American president and the elderly general who preceded German dictator Adolf Hit-

SON FAMEUX SOURIRE

"His Famous Smile." President Dwight D. Eisenhower's decision not to stop
the execution by electric chair of accused spies David and Ethel Rosenberg
provokes widespread protest in France. *Courtesy* L'Humanité

ler.[5] "How can Western Europe accept the leadership of a nation given over to a furious demagogue?" asked *Paris-Match*.[6] According to Dillon, many French found "the acts of McCarthy . . . identical in pattern with Hitler's Nazism."[7]

The Rosenberg controversy pointed up the mutual though different suspicions with which French and Americans viewed each other. Non-Communist French remained nervous about the PCF and the Soviet Union, but increasing numbers believed that Washington was "just as bad as Moscow" in threatening the peace, the American ambassador reported.[8] As the French recovered from the destruction of World War II and the shock of the Soviet takeover of Eastern Europe, they grew more restive about their dependence on the United States.

Fired up with their cold-war crusade, Americans dismissed French fears about the United States launching a world war or turning fascist. Americans diagnosed French anxieties and neutralist leanings as symptoms of illness, cowardice, or lack of manliness. Shortly before his 1952 election, Eisenhower commented that France had lost its moral nerve. Frustrated with France's parliamentary divisions and its resistance to Washington, Dillon labeled that nation "the weak sister of the Western Alliance."[9] Secretary of State John Foster Dulles agreed that "France seems to be deteriorating as a great power and losing capacity to govern itself or to deal with its problems."[10] An Air Force captain stationed in Europe said it more bluntly: The French "won't fight simply because they don't care to—freedom isn't that important to them. Besides, as a nation, they're yellow. They have some noble individuals but collectively they're useless as a fighting ally."[11]

In this cloud of mutual suspicion, the two allies quarreled over the major issues of the 1950s: Germany, France's voice in the Western alliance, and the fate of the French empire. The topics recalled old squabbles between Roosevelt and de Gaulle. As during the war years, America tried to bribe, cajole, and bully the French into swallowing some bitter medicines, remedies Washington considered essential to the health of France, to the Western world, and not least to the United States. Yet the France of the 1950s wielded more independence than had the war-torn nation of the 1940s. Such resistance challenged American officials, who responded with elaborate, only partly successful strategems to manage France, clip its sovereignty, and mold it into a staunch but malleable ally.

Both Paris and Washington succeeded in frustrating each other's policies at times, but in the end the United States usually had its way. Washington's ambitious propaganda campaign failed to stem the tide of French neutralist opinion, though France did remain in NATO. Paris blocked Washington's scheme to rearm West Germany through the European Defense Community, but the Americans achieved a German army anyway. France tried to use U.S. military aid to hold on to Vietnam, but at Geneva it lost the northern half to the nationalist Communist Ho Chi Minh and the southern portion to the Americans, tragically confident they could succeed where France had failed.

France bitterly resented the Americans' lagging support in colonial North Africa and their opposition during the Suez crisis. Washington also quarreled with London over Suez, but that relationship remained special. Washington often consulted closely with the British and aided their atomic weapons program. The United States refused France even this junior partner status.

Offstage, de Gaulle criticized much of America's policy and France's humiliation by it. He would act on that criticism when France, frustrated by colonial war, parliamentary instability, and dependence on America, would turn to him in May 1958. The wave of nationalism and resentment that would bring de Gaulle to power grew throughout the 1950s.

The frustration of many French citizens with the U.S. alliance had been there from the start, but it deepened after the onset of the Korean War in June 1950. Uncomfortably dependent on their giant ally, the French felt threatened whether America appeared to be winning or losing in Korea. This conflicting sentiment appeared in the pages of Le Monde, the most elite, influential newspaper of France. Beginning in April 1950 Le Monde published a series of articles by Etienne Gilson, a respected figure in the pro-American MRP. Gilson urged France to take a sharp turn in policy: withdraw from NATO and maintain only benevolent neutrality toward America in the cold war. After all, the United States had remained neutral in 1914–17 and 1939–40 when France had faced a mortal enemy, Gilson recalled.[12]

In June 1950 Le Monde, like most French opinion, applauded when the Americans went to South Korea's rescue. France itself sent a volunteer battalion of 1,000 soldiers. Then the spectacle of North Korea sweeping the Americans nearly into the sea shocked the French with a frightening look at their own probable fate if the Soviet Union marched westward. A Le Monde editorial feared another turn in the cycle of invasion-occupation-landing-liberation. Paris could only hope for "peaceful coexistence" between the superpowers and neutrality for France, the newspaper decided.[13] Then MacArthur's vigorous counterattack raised the obverse fear of a U.S.-provoked world war. An editorial condemned the bombing of villages and the use of napalm as American "war crimes."[14] (Ironically, at this time the French government was pressing Washington for additional aircraft for bombing Viet Minh rebels in Vietnam.) By late 1950 an influential, articulate minority of non-Communist French espoused these neutralist sentiments.

Yet many other French rejected neutralism and opted to stay in NATO. Indeed the various French governments, despite differences with the Americans, took no steps to leave the organization. Many French officials still feared the Soviets. Moreover, no weak coalition government dared risk the storm such a break with NATO would have caused. Some intellectuals such as Raymond Aron sympathized with the yearning for neutralism, but thought it impossible to stay out of a U.S.-Soviet war. Aron endorsed de Gaulle's point that "French feelings of dependence upon the United States" crippled the nation's morale.[15] In contrast to the general, however, Aron thought France could recover its pride while staying close to the United States. Like some exasperated Americans, the conservative newspaper Le Figaro diagnosed French neutralist sentiment as a failing of vital masculine powers: "Neutral France does not exist"; rather "there are neutral [French]men, in the sense that they are impotent.'[16]

Impotent or no, "widening circles of Frenchmen" had become neutralist, Ambassador Dillon reported in 1953.[17] Reasons included the Korean War, the rise of McCarthyism, the stationing of American troops in France, high U.S. tariffs, the Soviet Union's effort to woo the West with promises of peace, the ominous escalation of the arms race with the first explosion of a hydrogen bomb, and French disputes with America over Germany, Indochina, and North Africa.

Another impetus was the rebirth of a vibrant Gaullism, reminiscent of the war years. De Gaulle's Rassemblement du Peuple Français (RPF), a group supposedly above party, had in reality become a refuge for static conservatives, including former Vichyites. Hoping to bring down the weak Fourth Republic, de Gaulle ordered his deputies to abstain from parliamentary politicking. In 1952–53, however, conservatives RPF deputies abandoned the austere general to support, and later join, the center-right coalitions of premiers Antoine Pinay, René Mayer, and Joseph Laniel. Disgusted, de Gaulle dissolved the rump RPF as a political party.

Gaullism did not die, but reemerged a phoenix: a popular, less conservative movement dedicated to progressive, independent, "eternal" France. Now de Gaulle commanded a greater voice, and he amplified left-wing criticism that France suffered as an American protectorate that America did not and could not protect. The general wanted France to remain within the Atlantic alliance, but to have more power in directing Western policy. Like the Communists, neutralists, and others, the Gaullists denounced the U.S.-backed plan for a European army that would submerge the French army's separate identity. By 1954 the general urged an end to the war in Indochina. He blamed the Americans for prolonging France's agony in Vietnam after they had accepted a compromise peace in Korea. When an observer pointed to the many shared positions with the PCF, a Gaullist spokesman offered the startling explanation that the general was defending France and the Communists were defending Russia. Had not Russia and France often allied in the past? Reviving his policy of 1943–46, de Gaulle defined France's mission as bridging East and West. "Above all," he cried, "let us remain France, sovereign, independent and free!"[18]

French sentiment in France did swing toward neutrality—more than in other Western European nations. In 1952, 42 percent of the French wanted to be with the West in the cold war, 4 percent with the East, and 43 percent neutral. By 1958 only 26 percent picked the West and 4 percent the East; a majority of 57 percent opted for neutrality. By contrast, 28 percent of West

Germans, 44 percent of Italians, and 38 percent of the British chose neutrality in 1958. Polls also suggested less French confidence in the United States.
When asked in 1954 whether "America is doing all it should to prevent a new
world war," 25 percent of the French answered yes, as compared with 48
percent of the West Germans, 42 percent of the Italians, and 39 percent of
the British.

Polls showed that the French felt the weight of U.S. hegemony and disapproved of particular policies. Still they had an overall positive attitude toward
the United States. The French public welcomed American aid but not American troops. However, relations between G.I.s and French civilians were better
than they had been in 1945, perhaps because government policy kept the two
groups largely separate. By overwhelming margins, French opinion disapproved of Washington's policies in Germany, Indochina, and North Africa.
When describing American characteristics, 70 percent of the French checked
"treating the French like poor relations," 64 percent "over-hypnotized by hatred of communism," and 56 percent "meddl[ing] in affairs that don't concern
them." Yet 61 percent said they felt sympathy with the United States, 32
percent gratitude, and 19 percent admiration.

A basic question was, How much did American and French interests coincide? In 1956, 29 percent of the French perceived agreement with American
objectives and 36 percent saw disagreement. That same year only 18 percent
of West Germans, 16 percent of Italians, and 13 percent of the British
considered their interests to be in conflict with America's. In their hearts and
minds, the French people simply stood further from the United States than
did other European allies.[19]

France's ambivalence toward the cold-war alliance mounted just as Washington geared up the superpower struggle. In 1949 American anxieties deepened after the Soviet Union tested its first atomic bomb and China became
Communist. The Truman administration responded with NSC 68, written
largely by State Department policy-planning chief Paul Nitze. This April
1950 policy document urged the United States to take its allies in tow and
pursue the cold war more vigorously. When the North Koreans surged south
in June, Truman and Acheson seized the opportunity to put NSC 68 into
effect. In contrast, many French longed for a cold-war truce, particularly after
the mid-1950 war scare blew over and it became clear that the Korean War
was not part of a global Soviet offensive.

France's restiveness with the cold war pointed up a persistent problem: how
could the United States shape the policies of allies like France, nations that still
enjoyed some autonomy and whose interests often conflicted with those of
Washington? The Marshall Plan, NATO, the Military Assistance Program,
and the effort to combat indigenous Communist parties (see chapter 2) helped
keep the allies in line, but these programs also fed "mounting . . . resentment
[of] the U.S. and our policies," observed William R. Tyler, a key State Department expert on France.[20] A "majority" in France "feel outraged by what they

regard as American interference in French domestic affairs," noted Gladwyn Jebb, the British ambassador to Paris.[21] Washington's self-righteous leadership sparked a nationalist, anti-American backlash. In France the working class, much of which still voted for the PCF, and the intellectuals, most of them leftist or neutralist, deepened this resistance to intervention.

A few perceptive officials, such as Harlan Cleveland in the State Department and Richard Bissell in the Marshall Plan agency, grew concerned with Washington's "increasing degree of intervention in Western Europe and . . . increasing U.S. supervision of their [sic] policies and actions." This "partial satellization" of once-proud nations heightened the danger that Western Europe might escape U.S. influence in search of independence and neutrality. Unlike Nitze and other enthusiasts of incremental U.S. control, these experts understood that European "self-respect and morale are the necessary conditions of a long-term working partnership." Cleveland and Bissell made the essential, and usually ignored, point that Washington's hegemony made real Atlantic partnership impossible.[22]

Despite such cautioning, American officials eagerly steered Western Europe into Washington's orbit. In diagnosing the problem of French "indifference or resentment" toward American programs, Tyler recommended still deeper intervention with a concerted propaganda campaign. The United States had to "exercise our leadership and power in a direction sufficiently calculated to rally to us the loyalties and enthusiasm of the millions of [French] workers," Tyler urged in May 1950. By this he meant an intense, sophisticated public relations effort aimed at such "targets" as workers and intellectuals.[23]

Tyler's suggestion arrived in Washington at a time when the government was already gearing up for psychological warfare—"psywar." On 29 August 1950, Secretary of State Dean Acheson ordered Paris and other embassies to launch a global "informational offensive . . . to create psychological strength and resistance to Communism and Soviet imperialism."[24] As part of the NSC 68 cold war drive, Washington vastly expanded the United States Information Service (USIS), an arm of the State Department. (In 1953 the USIS would become the independent United States Information Agency [USIA].) In April 1951 President Truman created the Psychological Strategy Board, which worked closely with the USIS, to coordinate the government's effort to "influence men's minds and wills" in France and in other danger zones. In January 1952 the Board approved a "Psychological Operations Plan for the Reduction of Communist Power in France."[25] Within a few months, 289 U.S. and French employees were engaged in a comprehensive propaganda campaign headed by Tyler. This marked a further step in America's intervention in France's internal affairs—from economic, labor, political, and military matters to public opinion.

The propaganda campaign suffered fatal flaws: it offered no plausible alternative to French leftists still seeking radical change; many French had grown

disaffected with militant anticommunism; and despite its cunning and covert-
ness, the campaign lapsed into clumsiness.

Although the degree to which the public relations blitz affected French
opinion remains difficult to gauge, the campaign graphically illustrates assumptions and problems underlying U.S. policy in the 1950s. Americans
regarded France as a sick, seriously confused nation, chronically unable to
perceive its own true interests. Confident they knew what France needed,
USIS officials tried to manipulate French opinion.

Americans understood that years of Nazi, Allied, and Communist manipulation had hardened the French against overt propaganda. Thus the USIS
planted its stories in the French press and tried to disguise their American
origin. This way "the patient does not have the sensation of receiving an
injection," explained Tyler, who used this metaphor twice in an important
memorandum.[26] Operating "invisibly, through French channels" was like
"giv[ing] medicine to a sick child," another official suggested.[27] Otherwise
sensitive to French concerns, USIS operative Harold Kaplan labeled "quasi-
schizophrenic" and "irrational" the conflicting sentiments of wanting American help and lamenting France's lost independence and greatness. Le Monde's
neutralist editorials demonstrated "confusion," he believed. Americans had
to exercise "patience" and "tolerance . . . if we are to help France emerge
from her crisis and become a stronger and more steadfast ally of the U.S.,"
Kaplan explained with palpable condescension.[28] Nearly three years into the
propaganda offensive, Tyler portrayed France's "psychology," economy, and
politics as "basically unhealthy and unhopeful."[29]

By habitually using language that coded the French as sick (or, on other
occasions, as womanish and thus requiring the ministrations of a healthy,
implicitly masculine superpower), Americans legitimated and reinforced the
practice of belittling France and trivializing its perspective and concerns.
USIS officials viewed the French as objects to be manipulated.

A prime "target" for such manipulation was the influential French intelligentsia, the USIS memorandum "Cultural Affairs Policy for France" instructed staff. Officials had to "convince" French thinkers that the United
States had no desire to dominate France, and that America "has basically the
same values as Europe. Hardly anyone believes this," the USIS ruefully admitted, "but it is true."[30] The USIS calculated that university students and other
youth "are our most promising material, since being young and uninformed,
they are the most 'mouldable' material." The agency believed that French
citizens who utilized the USIS libraries just to find a how-to manual or simply
to enjoy a good read—"technological or pastime readers" in USIS jargon—
"do not serve our purpose." "The technological reader must be induced to
read [also] books that will present American civilization and American foreign policy in a favorable light," the USIS directed. Librarians should display
such books prominently, "get all favorable American books reviewed" for
French patrons, "eliminate from the library trivial and outmoded works," and

advertise a list of the " 'Ten Best Magazine Articles of the Month' . . . 'Best' means conforming most closely to [USIS] objectives."[31]

This 1953 directive appeared at roughly the same time that Roy Cohn and G. David Schine, aides to Senator Joseph McCarthy, toured USIS libraries in Europe to root out "subversive" books like *Huckleberry Finn*. Dillon warned the State Department that such "book burning" horrified the French, and some U.S. officials quaked at McCarthy's witchhunt.[32] Yet "Cultural Affairs Policy for France" did not read like a defensive response to McCarthyism. Instead the document shared McCarthy's premise that all was fair in the war against communism.

With this assumption, a one-page USIS instruction on academic exchanges repeated the word *indoctrination* five times. French students and professors who applied for USIS travel grants to the United States "should be considered targets for USIS indoctrination," the agency ordered. Although not all candidates would be accepted, "the mere possibility of going to the United States may induce many to extend, clarify and correct present impressions" of America, the USIS calculated. If professors or students returned from the United States with "faulty impressions," USIS officials should "correct" them with "suggested reading. It is imperative to find out what the returned grantee is thinking."[33] Such obtrusive manipulation fed the very anti-Americanism that the public relations effort was supposed to combat.

In addition to the inherent contradiction of intervention, there was the long-standing U.S.-French difference over revolution. In late 1950 Allen W. Dulles helped set up a Council on Foreign Relations (CFR) study group to wrestle with this problem of divergent revolutionary heritages. A master spy in World War II and the brother of Eisenhower's secretary of state John Foster Dulles, Allen Dulles would become deputy director of the Central Intelligence Agency (CIA) in 1951 and director in 1953. A club for elite government officials, businessmen, and academics, the CFR organized private lectures and study groups. At one such session CFR members worked through the idea of the United State wooing "the revolutionary forces" of France. "We should cease worrying about the fate of the ruling classes" and resuscitate democracy as a radical, burning faith, some argued. Reviving democracy as a "subversive" force would outflank the Communists and ignite French zeal for the cold war. Yet this happy scenario was disrupted by the contradictions in playing Thomas Jefferson to twentieth-century French revolutionaries. The study group found "no clear revolutionary objective for us to seize upon in France"—at least no acceptable one. Nor could Americans figure out how to encourage dissent and still build what Dean Acheson called "situations of strength" in the cold war. As a revolution, 1776 seemed ill-suited to compete with 1917 as heir to 1789.[34]

Despite such problems, the USIS enjoyed some success, particularly in the French provinces, where small, underfunded newspapers and libraries welcomed its services. Working unobtrusively, the agency tried, as Ambassador

James Dunn put it, to "plant . . . ideas in Fr[ench] minds where they can be propagated by the Fr[ench]."[35] Partially funded with Marshall Plan counterpart francs, the USIS distributed bulletins in French on American economic, scientific, artistic, and political developments. The agency gave French newspapers an indexed guide to embarrassing statements made by Soviet leaders, lent books to tiny community libraries, translated American books into French, supplied schools with subscriptions to American newspapers and maps of the United States, and offered films to the fledgling French television system. The USIS targeted sports films at youth groups, "frequently under Left-Wing leadership and otherwise difficult to penetrate," an officer reported.[36] Along with the sports movies, the agency included others on the American political system. The USIS sent to rural areas films such as the *Holtville Story,* which celebrated the independent initiatives of a New York farm community. This message was "particularly valuable" in France, "where too much reliance is placed on the Government," Tyler commented.[37]

The USIS helped keep popular magazines pro-American. When publisher Jean-Jacques Servan-Schreiber, inspired by *Time,* launched *L'Express,* an official urged that Servan-Schreiber receive "the cooperation of this Embassy" since the new magazine could "be useful in influencing opinion."[38] In response to a request from *Réalités,* another glossy publication, the American Embassy subsidized and assisted production of a special issue on the United States. The State Department arranged travel grants for *Réalités* staff, helped plan where the French journalists visited, and supplied photographs. The department also financed and helped word the questions for a *Réalités* opinion poll about the United States. After a few months in the States the journalists "returned with great enthusiasm about what they saw," USIS officials reported. Americans congratulated themselves that this special issue would "influence French opinion along the lines which USIS-France is striving to direct it." Yet the success would sour if "any disclosure of the relationship" with *Réalités* leaked.[39] Apparently such covert subsidies were routine. Ambassador Dunn observed that some USIS activities had slipped over into areas "which properly lie within the province of the CIA rather than the Department of State."[40]

The CIA was quite generous in trying to buy friends in France. A former agent claimed that the CIA bribed at least one long-term minister in the French government.[41] Through dummy foundations, the CIA funded the Congress for Cultural Freedom (CCF). In June 1950, as North Koreans crashed across the border into South Korea, more than a hundred worried European and American intellectuals met in West Berlin. They founded the CCF as an organization of liberal, antifascist, and anticommunist writers who challenged communism's grip on the European intelligentsia. Many members were apostate Communists, now eager to denounce their former faith. A powerful influence from 1950 until 1967, when its CIA funding was exposed, the Paris-based congress operated in 35 countries: sponsoring magazines, conferences, and exhibits; helping intellectuals flee the Soviet bloc; and competing with Moscow's own program to win over cultural and intellectual leaders.

At an early CCF meeting, held in the Paris home of writer Arthur Koestler, the group decided that its first priorities were France and Italy because almost all French and Italian intellectuals stood on the far left. The respected philosopher and political commentator Raymond Aron stood out as a notable exception. The most influential figure on the CCF Executive Committee, Aron operated from the assumption "that for an anti-Stalinist there is no escape from the acceptance of American leadership."[42] The congress organized the widely read intellectual review *Preuves* and also established throughout France branches of the Friends of Liberty—a "useful instrument of anti-communist activity," explained CCF general secretary Nicolas Nabokov.[43] The Friends of Liberty sponsored women's, youth, and film groups; seminars; and anti-Soviet protest demonstrations. Between November 1956 and November 1957, for example, the Friends of Liberty organized seven art and photographic shows, 14 musical events, and the publication of three brochures on the Soviet bloc. The CCF liked to emphasize the contrast between the government-dominated, politicized intellectual life of the East and the freedom, independence, and private funding of the West—even as the CIA secretly subsidized the congress through the Fairfield Foundation and other front organizations. With similar irony the congress sponsored "private" art festivals to show the American people's commitment to high culture.

In May 1952 the Congress for Cultural Freedom launched the ambitious Festival of Paris. In one month the CCF presented 100 symphonies, ballets, and operas, including Alban Berg's *Wozzeck* (performed by the Vienna Opera), Gertrude Stein and Virgil Thomson's *Four Saints in Three Acts*, and works by Russian composers banned in the Soviet Union. The whirl of events included an exhibition of some 150 modern paintings and sculptures, many of them by European artists. William Faulkner, Katherine Anne Porter, James T. Farrell, and other American writers debated with French writers. Ostensibly financed by wealthy Americans, the CIA-funded extravaganza was designed to win the respect of French intellectuals, Nabokov explained.

Instead, the oversized festival demonstrated the difficulty in American intervention. The events attracted full houses, but also hostile press reviews. An example was *Combat*, a neutralist, non-Communist newspaper that published Sartre and had the leftist intellectual readers "targeted" by the CCF. *Combat* had no inkling of the CIA's involvement, and it certainly appreciated the art. Yet the newspaper found offensive both the festival's exclusion of all Communist writers and its glittery lavishness. *Combat*'s criticism was probably sparked by a combination of envy at America's riches (particularly in European art) and intuition as to what was going on. The newspaper interpreted the sudden artistic interest as an American "offensive . . . with propagandistic purposes." Both sides in the cold war had politicized art; "totalitarianism is triumphing everywhere," *Combat* lamented.[44] Not surprisingly, the CCF had overreached itself. A final ironic twist came from the fact that *Combat* was among the newspapers secretly subsidized by the CIA. The Americans could spend their money in France, but they found it difficult to buy French public support.[45]

U.S. efforts enjoyed more success when they corrected distortions in the stereotype of aggressively modern, cold-war America. An exhibition of paintings by Grandma Moses set an attendance record at the Paris USIS office. Many visitors felt relief, as one put it, to see this "rustic, kind, peaceful and serene America without any machines, movies, chic young women, atom bombs, an almost Breughelian America." Pleased with the turnout, the cultural attaché noted that it had reached "a completely different group of individuals who are most important to influence."[46] An exhibit of Steuben glass enabled viewers, as one French woman expressed it, "to see you in a different light, less forbidding and less utilitarian."[47] This eagerness to view America's softer, human side pointed to the difficulties of enlisting France in a militant cold-war crusade.

In addition to this direct propaganda campaign, the United States worked through the French government, the leadership of which had become strongly anti-Communist. At American urging, Premier Queuille set up the Democratic Union for Peace and Liberty. An ostensibly private, mass movement of French citizens committed to "genuine" peace, the Democratic Union was dedicated to opposing the Soviet peace offensive. In reality, the organization was covertly funded by the CIA and directed by France's governing political parties and police forces.[48]

To what extent did the propaganda campaign succeed in making France a more dependable ally? A definitive answer is impossible, since there existed no counterfactual case, no "other" France without such a campaign. U.S. propaganda remained only one of many factors that influenced French opinion. Polls showed that French neutralism grew in the 1950s. After nearly four years of propaganda effort, "American prestige in France, particularly in influential non-communist intellectual circles, has dropped to the lowest point we can remember," State Department officials reported.[49] In 1956 British ambassador Jebb, worried about the "disturbing proportions" of anti-American sentiment in France, lay much of the blame on "the United States Information Services—and United States policy-makers in general—[who] are incapable of understanding or defending the interests of other countries except when they coincide with those of the United States."[50] Such evaluations suggest that American propaganda efforts failed, or succeeded only in limiting the swing toward neutralism.

Just as Americans failed to mold French public opinion, Washington proved unable to fold the independent French army into the proposed European Defense Community (EDC), a U.S.-dominated European armed force.

In both matters the basic issue was American influence over France. Although challenged by the French, U.S. hegemony still prevailed: however fitful, France remained an American ally, and however recalcitrant, France could not block the rearmament of West Germany. Nor could France retain even a marginal role in Vietnam after it suffered defeat from colonial rebels and displacement from its Washington ally.

In 1954 the issues of German rearmament and Indochinese war fused in a global crisis. "France is creating a vacuum in the world wherever she is," Dulles fretted. The United States had to "fill that vacuum . . . [or] we could lose Europe, Asia and Africa all at once," he concluded.[51] Ambassador Dillon offered an equally ominous scenario. Military defeat in Vietnam could trigger a "neutralist government in France that would recreate the wartime Franco-USSR alliance in order to prevent German rearmament." An angry Congress might then pull "our troops from Europe," destroying NATO. America would then stand alone—forced into "isolation."[52]

Several elements linked the crises over German rearmament and the colonial war in Vietnam (which along with Laos and Cambodia had constituted French Indochina). Events brought them to a head at the same time. In both, France, after years of agony and indecision, finally rejected the roles in the cold-war drama assigned to it by Washington. Significantly, the United States would not accept these parts for itself. The first role involved the French colonial war in Vietnam. Washington feared much of Asia might be lost if the nationalist and Communist Viet Minh, led by Ho Chi Minh, drove the French from their country. Yet the United States remained reluctant to commit its own troops. Instead, Washington sent money and equipment to the French and urged them to continue fighting. Both Paris and Washington saw this aid in Vietnam as partial payment for a big sacrifice: France would deposit much of its army and some of its sovereignty in the European Defense Community. Again, the United States would not make such a sacrifice itself (nor did it insist that Great Britain do so). This inequality aggravated French resentment of the United States and opposition to the EDC. The French government linked the EDC and Vietnam by warning Washington that without a military victory in Southeast Asia, the French people would never consent to submerging their army in the European force. Americans argued that their assistance to the French war effort in Vietnam meant that France should ratify the EDC. In contrast, the French believed that because they were fighting in Asia, they should not have to endure the additional sacrifice of accepting the proposed EDC. Although the EDC and Vietnam issues intertwined, their complexity requires separate analysis.

The Truman and Eisenhower administrations committed passionately to the EDC plan because it promised Washington so many benefits at so little cost. The scheme addressed the delicate problem of how to maintain American predominance in an alliance of largely independent nations. The United

States hoped the EDC would reorient its members (West Germany, France, Italy, and the Benelux) from narrow, nationalist, separatist interests to common concerns, largely defined by Washington.

Americans hoped the EDC would help with another perennial concern: binding West Germany into the Western alliance. With its Ruhr industry, strategic location, and energetic population, West Germany glittered as the chief prize of the cold war. Happily, Chancellor Konrad Adenauer stood eager to have his Bonn government accepted as a sovereign ally of the West. General Omar Bradley, chairman of the Joint Chiefs of Staff, enthused at the prospect of "cracker jack" German divisions. "Germany is a better keystone for our arch than France, and the thing that will snap the French out of their morass is to see Germany building up," said another top Pentagon official.[53] Bradley pointed out that a sizable German army would force the Soviets to concentrate their forces in any invasion of Western Europe. Then the United States could deploy its atomic bombs to destroy the massed Soviet troops. "We don't have enough atomic weapons to plaster all of Europe," he explained.[54]

Yet recent history showed that a German army could prove highly dangerous. Both Americans and French worried that only Moscow could satisfy West Germany's desire for reunion with East Germany and recovery of territory lost after World War II. Would not Germany, perhaps after Adenauer, cut a deal with the Soviet Union as it had done in 1939 or go to war as it had done in 1941? Paris and Washington drew different conclusions from this nightmare scenario. Having suffered three invasions in 70 years, France opposed any rearmament of its too-powerful neighbor. From a more protected geographical position, the Americans saw a safeguard in the EDC. A European army could contain German power by integrating the West German, French, Italian, and Benelux armies into a single force, under NATO and hence American command. Integration would bind the West Germans more tightly than could any written agreement. The EDC would draft German soldiers while guarding against German military independence. Anxious to move up from former enemy to ally, Adenauer would agree to limits on German rearmament. Yet he opposed blatant discrimination. The question was how to contain the Germans while minimizing their resentment. The prospect of French resentment seemed less important.

Washington hoped to avoid overt discrimination against West Germany by limiting the sovereignty and autonomy of all EDC members. Without its own army, a nation could not have an independent foreign policy. A supranational institution such as the EDC meant "giving up a lot of what is called sovereignty," Secretary of State Dean Acheson explained to the U.S. Senate.[55] The EDC did not discriminate against West Germany, Acheson and other Americans argued, because the proposed plan would treat all the Continental allies equally. This meant putting France in nearly the same restricted position as recently defeated Germany. Eisenhower wanted to tie the Germans to France in a "federation from which they could not break loose," he told

Foreign Minister Georges Bidault. But Bidault realized that such union meant the end of France's independent army, its pride for centuries. "There was no pleasure in integration," he answered Eisenhower.[56]

For the United States, the hobbles on France and the other allies appeared useful. Moscow could use tanks to enforce obedience in its part of Europe; Washington had to be more subtle. In 1948 and 1949 Americans had pushed the NATO treaty in large part to cement transatlantic economic and political ties and to prevent Western Europe from drifting toward neutralism. Yet the danger persisted that governments that had voted for the NATO treaty could one day vote against it. "If you lost an election . . . it may cause the collapse of the whole thing," Dulles worried.[57] The EDC would help anchor the alliance against such shifts in public opinion while allowing West Germany to rearm within the confines of an American-dominated European army.[58] The Americans hoped that the EDC members would contain each other's adventurist or neutralist tendencies. A European army would also make another Franco-German war impossible and so focus Western Europe's military efforts against the Soviet Union. Finally, the EDC would offer another channel for American influence since the integrated army would become part of NATO, led by the United States. The American NATO commander "could take any unit in the European Army and put it wherever he wants," Acheson explained.[59]

Dulles believed that in addition to helping Washington control Western Europe, the EDC would bind the United States and Europe together with close, institutional ties. If Congress saw Europe move toward unity through the EDC, it would become more willing to station U.S. troops there. "Much more was at stake here than . . . a treaty," Dulles preached. If EDC failed, we of the West would "los[e] our illusions," he feared, with "each one turn[ing] in upon himself." Dulles believed such "isolationism" terrifying because the American way of life could survive only in a world open to U.S. business and influence.[60]

Clearly the EDC offered many more benefits to the United States than to France. American officials obscured that fact—even to themselves—by emphasizing the origin of EDC in the significantly different Pleven Plan, drawn up by French economic expert Jean Monnet. Monnet's faith in American leadership and supranational institutions like the European Coal and Steel Community (see chapter 2) or the proposed European army ran against the tide of French nationalism and anti-Americanism in the early 1950s. Yet he enjoyed considerable influence in the French government because of his close ties with leaders in America and Europe and because of the success of the postwar Monnet Plan for economic recovery. Monnet played a key role in the French response to the Soviet war scare and the American NSC 68 offensive of 1950. Many French feared that North Korea's June 1950 assault on South Korea foreshadowed a Soviet lunge into Western Europe. Many French also understood that defending Western Europe required using German territory and troops, but they remained horrified at the thought of reviving German militarism. Typical was Jules Moch, the strongly anti-Communist defense minister who could not forget that Germans had strangled his son, who had been active in the French resistance.

At a NATO meeting in September 1950, Secretary of State Acheson had shocked Moch and others by pushing for the rapid creation of 10 German divisions. The Truman administration would keep the former enemy under control by putting the German divisions in an integrated command headed by a U.S. general and by stationing several American divisions in Europe. To sweeten the deal, Acheson promised more military aid. Other Western Europeans reluctantly accepted Acheson's plan, but Moch and Foreign Minister Robert Schuman vehemently opposed rebuilding German divisions. The NATO meeting ended without agreement.

Many French also objected to the idea of rearming West Germany without first assuring France a privileged position as one of the Western Big Three. Bidault, who had become premier in October 1949, pushed in 1950 for the creation of an "Atlantic High Council for Peace," that is a NATO directorate with permanent seats for the United States, Great Britain, and France.[61] The French had made a similar bid to institutionalize their great power status during the 1948 negotiations for the the NATO treaty; they would persist in making such demands until they left NATO in 1966. The Americans, unwilling to give up their near monopoly on alliance decision making and reluctant to antagonize West Germany and other allies, remained just as consistent in rejecting the French requests.

With the Americans pressing hard for rearming West Germany, Monnet advised Prime Minister René Pleven that "we must resolutely oppose America's present policy. But we . . . [must] give our opposition a positive content."[62] By this Monnet meant extending the supranational principle of the Schuman Plan from coal and steel to military forces. The Pleven Plan would preserve the French army's autonomy and add a European armed force to include German troops organized in small units. West Germany would contribute soldiers, but have no army of its own. The aim was to keep Paris's "control . . . over German rearmament," the French government affirmed.[63] The Germans would "fight under French command as helots," an American observed.[64] In the war scare atmosphere of 1950, the Pleven government desperately pushed this scheme as a means to tap German strength while blocking Acheson's plan for German divisions.

After lengthy negotiations in which the United States played an unofficial but central role, the Pleven Plan emerged—fundamentally changed—as the EDC treaty. In May 1952 the French government reluctantly signed the agreement, but then stalled on asking the National Assembly to ratify the increasingly unpopular accord. As part of the EDC deal, West Germany would regain limited sovereignty and France would secure the right, denied to Germany, to station troops overseas and to develop atomic weapons. In contrast to the Pleven Plan, however, the EDC provided for rebuilding German military units commanded by German officers. Even more disturbing to the French, the EDC would fold not only German but also French divisions into the European army. "This would mean the disappearance of the French national army. This was unthinkable," a close associate of de Gaulle protested to General Eisenhower in 1952.[65] Responding to the chorus of dismays at the EDC proposal, the Foreign Ministry drew up a list of reservations, the "French Additional Protocols," that would preserve the French army as a unit in the European army. In February–March 1953, however, the other five would-be EDC members (with U.S. officials hovering in the background) refused to amend the EDC treaty to include the additional protocols. To mollify the National Assembly, France's partners accepted the additional procotols as mere "interpretive texts" that did not affect the EDC treaty itself.[66] The EDC plan still required "the disappearance of the French Army as such," top French and British officials commented in January 1954.[67] Many French also grew concerned that military "equality" with Bonn would really mean German superiority, because of West Germany's economic power and because the flower of the French officer corps was being cut down in the jungles of Vietnam.

To counter German strength, the French tried to bring in the British. London refused, arguing that its global responsibilities precluded tying its hands with the EDC or any other supranational institution. Washington did not insist that Great Britain sacrifice its sovereignty. Nor would the United States put American troops under international command. "While urging others to surrender sovereignty, the US is unwilling to do so itself," noted David Bruce, who later became Washington's chief lobbyist for the EDC.[68] De Gaulle commented that if the United States found union such a good idea, "why does she not merge with Mexico and Canada and South American countries?"[69] The only EDC member with a claim to world rank, France was expected to meld with two recently defeated enemies and three minor powers. NATO commander Eisenhower recognized, but had little sympathy with, France's desire "to act . . . in Europe very much like we do and like the British do."[70]

Neither the Pleven Plan, the EDC, nor any other plan for German rearmament ever had deep support in France. In 1951 the French public approved the idea of a European army by a 42 percent to 26 percent margin. Many advocates of EDC feared that the alternative of an independent Germany army was far worse. By August 1954, however, public support had melted to 31 percent in favor and 36 percent opposed.[71] Increasing numbers of French preferred to ease the cold war with Moscow rather than arm the Germans. Paris officials resented the EDC as a "trap for France," Lippmann reported.[72] Support for the scheme dissipated for a variety of reasons: declining fear of the Soviet Union and rising apprehension about the United States; the June 1951 election, which strengthened anti-EDC forces; resentment of U.S. pressure; and the strain of the French Indochina War.

The Soviet Union's peace campaign, intensified after Stalin's death in March 1953, fed French opposition to EDC. If the Soviets were eager to lower tensions, why risk arming the Germans, many French asked. Dulles reacted differently to Soviet peace overtures, telling the Eisenhower Cabinet that "we ought to be *doubling* out bets, not reducing them—as all the Western parliaments want to do. This is the time to *crowd* the enemy—and maybe *finish* him, once and for all."[73] Like Acheson before him, Dulles worried that Moscow's peace offensive could destroy the allies' willingness to endure the cold war. The Soviets highlighted the danger by asking to join NATO, appropriately enough on April Fools' Day 1954. Yet despite the smiles the Soviets remained their own worst enemies. They sent in tanks to crush the East Berlin uprising of June 1953, reawakening fears of the bear's embrace.

Although French officials wanted more independence from Washington, they dared not risk a reversal of alliances. Aside from economic and cultural ties, France depended on the United States for military equipment, particularly in Vietnam. In 1950–52 France received from the United States $500 million in military hardware each year, more than did any other European ally.[74] A generation of French officials had based their careers on the American tie. The French government did not seriously challenge Washington's leadership in negotiating with the Soviets. Nor did the Soviets reach out seriously to the French. Apparently Moscow concluded that a meaningful deal could be made only with the United States. In sum, a spectrum of French leaders thought it unrealistic to break the alliance with the United States. Yet they saw little rush to rearm Germany or to sacrifice French independence in the EDC when the Soviets seemed ready more to talk than to fight.

The June 1951 elections of the National Assembly strengthened scepticism about the EDC. With inflation rising, the governing parties lost votes. The pro-EDC MRP (the party of Bidault and Monnet's ally Robert Schuman) dropped from 169 to 96 seats in the new parliament. Isolated but not dead, the Communists garnered 25 percent of the voters and 101 seats. The Gaullists shot up to 121 seats, the most of any single party. The election results meant that the Communists and Gaullists, hard-core EDC opponents, held 222 out of 627 votes. The EDC had only lukewarm support or opposition from the Socialists and Conservatives. From 1952 to 1954 government after government resisted American pressures and stalled bringing EDC ratification before the National Assembly. Tepid suport for the EDC grew cooler. French army officers were distributing to their troops leaflets denouncing the scheme. In July 1954 Premier Pierre Mendès France told Dulles that parliamentary approval of the EDC with only a slender margin could fatally split the already fractured French nation. Deaf to such pleas, Dulles replied that the "essential thing" was to pass EDC, "even if it is only [by] one vote."[75]

EDC sparked a confrontation not only over issues but over styles of government. French procrastination infuriated U.S. officials, who liked quick action. The campaign for EDC became a missionary "crusade," recalled Evangeline Bruce, wife of Washington's chief lobbyist for the plan. Earnest proselytizers, the Bruces felt "destined to assure to the Europeans a unity necessary for their happiness and their defense."[76] Dulles sermonized about climbing "the mountain top" and seeing the "vision" of EDC.[77]

The French saw not salvation but unsavory choices. They were more capable of making such decisions than the Americans thought. Though chaotic and frustrating, the Fourth Republic's parliamentary system did work, after its own fashion. The same ministers resurfaced in succeeding cabinets, lending important continuity. The labor of the bureaucracy and planning groups originated by Monnet progressed regardless of who was prime minister. After 1952 the French economy took off, sparked by innovations introduced by government planners and private industry. The National Assembly's deep divisions, however, encouraged compromise and obfuscation. American officials regarded their own executive-dominated governmental system as healthier and more "normal" than the Fourth Republic's. French drift on EDC understandably frustrated Americans. Yet there was an underlying progression. The repeated postponement and final defeat of EDC ratification was France's way of considering a complex, divisive issue and then saying no to its powerful ally. Blinded by their crusading spirit, American officials labeled as pathology France's policy differences with Washington.

In early 1954, with the EDC still stalled, top Americans considered how they might further pressure France. Dulles feared time was running out. He took seriously Adenauer's warning that the Germans, who had already ratified EDC, might soon get disgusted and turn to Moscow for a deal. "The first thing you know, Germany is going to be stolen right from under our noses," Dulles fretted at a secret Senate committee session.[78] He concluded the United States had to push France harder or risk losing West Germany. Yet this could also be dangerous. General Alfred M. Gruenther, supreme Allied commander in Europe, acknowledged Germany's importance in the defense of Western Europe. But "the real estate of France" was even more essential, the general advised lawmakers. Like many U.S. officials, Gruenther thought that France represented a "sick man status," a "psychopathic situation." The problem was how to "get tough" without having France rebel.[79] Senator J. William Fulbright of Arkansas urged Dulles to apply private threats "to the limit," but warned that public pressure would stiffen resistance to the "big bully."[80]

In 1953 Congress had passed the Richards amendment cutting off future military aid unless France (and Italy) ratified EDC. This had proven toothless since there was so much matériel already in the supply pipeline. On Gruenther's and Dulles's advice, the Senate committee scuttled the idea of stopping the flow in the pipeline, a move that would imperil America's investment in the French and Italian armies and threaten "a disintegration of NATO."[81] With Vietnam in the balance, some senators feared that too much pressure would drive France to "conclude a treaty with [Soviet foreign minister Vyacheslav] Molotov.[82] As Dulles recommended, the Senate voted to adopt the House measure providing for a slowdown rather than a cutoff of military supplies.

In this frustrating situation, several points were obvious. Rather than choose between France and Germany, Washington wanted both as allies, so that they could contain each other and help contain the Soviets. Americans respected the Germans as fit fighting partners; they disdained the French while valuing France's strategic location. Officials in Congress and in the Eisenhower administration understood that too much pressure on Paris could endanger America's stake in France and in Vietnam. Nevertheless Washington leaned on the French in a way that it dared not (and did not have to) do with the Germans. The State Department used what it called "shock treatment" on "wayward, unreflecting, illogical" France.[83]

The shocks only stimulated French opposition to EDC. At a Paris press conference on 15 December 1953 Dulles threatened an "agonizing reappraisal" of U.S. foreign policy unless France ratified EDC. This public warning reinforced private ones that the United State might pull back its defense perimeter to England or to North America, abandoning France. Michel Debré, a future prime minister, protested this "intolerable interference in internal French affairs." What President Vincent Auriol labeled Dulles's "tirade" only further reduced French support for EDC.[84]

The secretary had expected the explosion, but the bomb failed to move the French, partly because it was more fuse than powder. Talk about pullback was a bluff, Dulles admitted to Pentagon officials. "We are defending ourselves and not merely the French," Eisenhower told the National Security Council; "our front line now runs east of the Rhine."[85] De Gaulle came to the same strategic conclusion about pullback. "Go as far as you like," he said with a smile.[86] Effort to make the threat credible led to nasty exchanges. Americans would never withdraw from Europe because its industry was too important, a French expert told U.S. Embassy officials. The Americans replied that "it would of course have to be destroyed in the case of war." "But it is very much dispersed," the Frenchman rejoined. "C'est la drame," the Americans retorted.[87]

Despite all the straining to get Paris to ratify EDC, American officials never seriously considered the one concession that might have won France to the scheme. A succession of senior Paris officials begged the United States to treat France as "a partner" in the Western alliance, that is, to consult seriously on issues, to respect French viewpoints, and to enable France "to participate with the U.K. and the U.S. in all great decisions," as Prime Minister Mendès France put it.[88] With its army part of EDC, France "would be just one of many European countries," Foreign Minister Bidault worried. He feared that "EDC meant resurrection for Italy and Germany with arms in their hands."[89] Dulles replied that he desired no such diminution of France so long as Paris exercised responsible "leadership" in the world—such leadership, of course, to be defined by Washington's criteria. Dulles and other American officials refused to assuage French anxieties by accepting proposals for institutionalized tripartite discussions. While giving the usual assurance of regular consultation, Dulles vetoed any "formal machinery" for such talks.[90] American leaders refused to commit themselves to real sharing of decision making in NATO, especially with the effete and apparently declining French. When other French leaders sought closer consultation with Washington, Ambassador Dillon suggested that talks "with very little substance" would suffice.[91]

Instead of assuring the French, Washington played on their fears. Bruce argued that France's great power status "depend[ed] on our good offices," a telling contradiction.[92] What America gave it could take away. Dulles told Bidault bluntly that if EDC failed, it meant an "end to the role of France as a great power."[93] Americans warned that they might cut the French out from Western councils and knit closer ties with Great Britain and with rapidly reviving West Germany. Indeed Dulles, who enjoyed a particularly close relationship with German chancellor Konrad Adenauer, was already turning toward Bonn.

This pressure from Washington grated on French nationalists and sharpened opposition to EDC. As a few State Department officials perceived, such lobbying heightened resentment that Americans wanted to "tell the French what to do in all fields, foreign and domestic."[94] Meanwhile, Ho Chi Minh's forces battered the French in a different way, besieging and then taking the symbolic stronghold of Dien Bien Phu on 7 May 1954. The French felt drained of emotional and military strength.

In the depths of the EDC-Vietnam crisis, Pierre Mendès France became prime minister. An economist descended from Portuguese Jews who had dabbled in the sugar trade of Santo Domingo, Mendès France had joined de Gaulle in 1940 and later had helped draft the proposal for the World Bank. In June 1954 he dramatically pledged to settle the French Indochina War within a month or else resign. He also promised to end the two-year procrastination over EDC. For the first time since de Gaulle's resignation in 1946, France had a vigorous, popular leader.

Mendès France wanted to keep the alliance with America while carving out a more independent role in world affairs. This meant ending the hopeless colonial war, reforming ties with the rest of the French Union, moving toward détente with the Soviet Union, invigorating the economy, reconciling Germany while escaping its domination, and developing an atom bomb. Much of Mendès France's program foreshadowed de Gaulle's policies after 1958. Ahead of his time, Mendès France excited the suspicions of American cold warriors. David Bruce found him "a devious character."[95]

Americans feared that Mendès France had bought peace in Indochina by promising the Soviets he would kill EDC. The possibility of such a deal certainly occurred to French leaders; France and Russia had historically been allies, and both nations disliked the idea of rearming West Germany. As foreign minister in the Laniel government, Bidault had considered such a bargain, but apparently the Soviets had not been interested. On 10 July, during the Geneva Conference, when Soviet foreign minister Molotov proposed talks with the French on European and Asian problems, Mendès France declined. The French leader doubted that the Soviets would concede much for a pledge to bury the EDC because the scheme already faced intense opposition in the French National Assembly. Yet Mendès France remained interested in better East-West relations and disarmament, and he sought a Big Four summit conference that could lead to détente. Exaggerated and distorted reports of these conversations fed the American and British distrust of the French leader who talked of moving beyond cold-war orthodoxy. Gossip also had it that the premier's closest adviser, Georges Boris, was Russian (he was Alsatian).[96]

American suspicions of Mendès France deepened at the August 1954 conference in Brussels of the six would-be EDC members. With the French Indochina War over (and the United States already moving into Vietnam's southern half, saved from immediate Communist rule), Secretary of State Dulles ratcheted up the pressure. Mendès France proposed to modify the EDC so that only armed forces stationed in West Germany would be integrated. This change would preserve the French army's autonomy, a condition essential to ratification, the prime minister argued. With American prompting, the other five said no. Spurred by Adenauer's warning that delay would drive West Germany into the arms of the Soviet Union, Dulles pushed harder on France. He underscored Paris's isolation by urging that the other five would-be EDC allies get together without France to discuss German rearmament. This was the "strongest and most indiscreet pressure that I have ever seen brought to bear on a French government," a top Foreign Ministry official observed. He concluded that such bullying demonstrated how little "will remain of French independence" if Paris ratified EDC.[97]

Much of France felt humiliated and angry by the American pressure. Public support for EDC dropped.[98] In the final National Assembly debate, Mendès France took an ostensibly neutral position and cautioned that the Americans and British would rearm West Germany regardless of what France did. The final blow to EDC came from the 82-year-old former premier Edouard Herriot, near death, who dramatically denounced the scheme as "the end of France" and "a step forward for Germany."[99] On 31 August 1954 the EDC went down on a procedural vote, 319 to 264. With the tally announced, the Communists jumped up to sing "La Marseillaise." The Gaullists were the first to join them. "Are the French deliberately saying they are going to tie up with Russia?" Eisenhower worried.[100]

Dillon responded to this defeat with a cable setting out American concerns and perspective on France. Keeping West Germany tied to the West remained the first priority, the ambassador emphasized. France could help with this objective even though it had rejected EDC. French territory remained essential for access to Germany and for the defense of Western Europe. Like American officials in other crises, Dillon believed that outright hostility would only drive the French further away. He remained confident that France would eventually "pull herself together" and come around to Washington's view. Hence the distraught ally required not punishment but therapy. "France is undoubtedly ill . . . [with a] high fever," Dillon cabled Washington. "Shock treatment is indicated, merited and sound therapy. But the voltage must be carefully controlled so as not to kill off the patient." Like many other Americans, Dillon coded France as womanish, emotionally unbalanced, and susceptible to revolution. This "weak sister in the Western alliance" suffered "selfish, nationalistic, or stubborn contrariness," "delusions of grandeur," and an individualism so extreme as to be "almost fatal in organizing the disciplines and restraints" necessary for effective government.[101] Dean Acheson explained on another occasion that "France is like a member of our own family who is mentally ill."[102] As the wise doctor or husband, the U.S. had to "exercise almost superhuman patience and forbearance"—while carefully controlling the voltage.

Other Americans shared the ambassador's stereotyping. A few weeks after Dillon's telegram, Marshal D. Shulman, who had been a close adviser to Secretary of State Dean Acheson, reported to his old boss on his observations of France during the EDC debate. Like Henry Adams and other Americans, Shulman enjoyed and disdained the atmosphere of France—that "pleasant after-glow of a dying culture." He characterized as "neuralgic" and "non-rational" France's opposition to rearmament of its long-time enemy. Shulman's opinion that "neither logic, French national interest, nor calm reason were factors in the [EDC] discussion" echoed venerable American judgments of France.[103]

In the months after August 1954 Dulles administered the shock therapy. He emphasized France's isolation, snubbed Mendès France, cut aid down to a trickle, and made it plain that Washington would rearm West Germany and restore Bonn's sovereignty whether France liked it or not.[104] Dulles hoped the pressure would convince the French to participate in some other formula for German rearmament.

Meanwhile, the harrowing, four-year debate had clarified French thinking. None of the French enthused about rearming Germany. But EDC seemed "unthinkable" because it threatened "the disappearance of the French national army," as an associate of de Gaulle put it.[105] A week before the EDC vote, Mendès France had outlined a compromise: the six would-be EDC members, including rearmed West Germany, would join with Great Britain to form "a little box in the big NATO frame."[106] He urged British participation as a protection against both German dominance and the American enthusiasm for "supranational" schemes that restricted other nations' autonomy. Indeed, the Americans and British had extensively discussed such alternative plans for West German rearmament, but had kept those talks private in hope that the French would ratify the EDC. West Germany's willingness to renounce production of atomic weapons and so concede potential nuclear superiority to France opened another way out of the EDC impasse.

In the anguish over the French Indochina War and EDC, France had stepped up its small nuclear program, under way since 1945. The French were

"Vicky's International Fashion Show," a London cartoon reproduced in the *New York times*, portrays Foreign Minister Georges Bidault, who favored the EDC; Premier Pierre Mendès France, who resisted U.S. pressure for the EDC in the interests of France's "freedom of movement"; and the austere de Gaulle, who opposed the EDC as unbecoming French *grandeur*. *Courtesy London Daily Mirror*

developing the capability to produce civilian atomic power—and atomic bombs if the government should so decide. This program had moved ahead slowly, in part because the French had received no assistance from the United States, which had rejected Paris's request to share research information. In 1951 Félix Gaillard, the government minister in charge of the French Atomic Energy Commission, had ordered the drafting of a five-year development plan, which had concluded that "France depends on us today to remain a great modern nation ten years from now."[107] In July 1952, the National Assembly had endorsed this plan, rejecting by a wide margin a PCF amendment that would have forbidden the development of a French atomic bomb. Such atomic ambitions had been threatened by the EDC proposal, which would have restricted each member's plutonium production to 500 grams per year. This was "an unacceptable limit for France," declared Bertrand Goldschmidt, a top French nuclear scientist.[108] By 1954 some military officials, echoed by de Gaulle, argued that the growing Soviet nuclear arsenal undermined the credibility of America's deterrent, and that France needed its own atomic bomb. Atomic weapons might have prevented France's humiliation in Indochina, some believed. Atomic advocate General Charles Ailleret recalled that when he was attached to Eisenhower's NATO command, the Americans did not take the French seriously. Along with others, Ailleret believed an atomic arsenal would win respect from France's allies and enemies. A nuclear-armed France would also enjoy an edge over West Germany, restricted to nonnuclear weapons.

In October and December 1954 Mendès France asked for feasibility studies on production of atomic bombs and atomic submarines. Although the prime minister remained reluctant to make a final decision on building those weapons, he encouraged the technocrats and military officials who dominated the French Atomic Energy Commission to accelerate their development. After 1954 the atomic program would accelerate in response to war in Algeria, the Suez crisis, Germany's recovery, America's refusal to share information, and the Soviet Union's launching of Sputnik with a powerful rocket.[109]

France's guaranteed nuclear advantage, freedom from the fetters of EDC, and peace in Indochina made it easier to accept German rearmament, especially with the compromise Mendès France had outlined shortly before the EDC vote. After EDC's defeat, the British helped patch together a plan. Winston Churchill, once again the British prime minister, had never liked EDC. He preferred "German armies march[ing] by our side" to the "sludgy amalgam" of EDC.[110] Characterizing Dulles as "a bull who carries his china closet with him," Churchill directed Foreign Secretary Anthony Eden to mediate between the secretary of state and Mendès France.[111] London made a major concession by agreeing to station a sizable British army in rearmed West Germany.

The Western powers worked out a deal on German rearmament at conferences in London and Paris in September–October 1954. The Western European Union, created in 1948, became Mendès-France's "little box" to group the six nations, along with Great Britain, in a loose unit within NATO.[112] Although West Germany technically suffered no discrimination, the Bonn government renounced production of atomic, biological, and chemical weapons. All German troops would be under NATO command, which gained added authority. In contrast to Germany, France could keep forces under exclusive national control and station them overseas. Germany had to accept the presence of its allies' troops (which indeed it wanted), whereas France hosted NATO forces by choice. The United States and Great Britain promised to keep troops in Germany for the foreseeable future. Washington and London also pledged that West Germany would not use force to achieve reunification or recovery of its lost territories.

The agreement stitched West Germany, which Washington already favored over France, securely into the Western alliance. "Mendès France always had his eye on little things; Adenauer always on big things," Dulles concluded from the negotiations. He appreciated that the strengthened NATO command, like the EDC proposal, "made it impossible for any single member nation to use its armed forces in Europe for nationalistic adventures."[113] This integration enlisted the military forces of Western Europe (except for French troops stationed in colonies) in the containment of the Soviet Union. A final flap occurred when the National Assembly balked at ratifying the agreement. "Those damn French!" Eisenhower exploded.[114] On 30 December Mendès France got it approved, 287 to 260. West Germany began to rearm and in May 1955 entered NATO.

The Paris agreement broke the four-year impasse over German rearmament and marked an ironic change in U.S. relations with Western Europe. Between 1945 and 1954 Washington gave first priority to containing communism and maneuvering Western Europe into close orbit around the United States. With West Germany's rearmament and integration into NATO assured, most of the components of that solar system appeared in place. Even as their handiwork neared completion, however, American officials felt confined by the transatlantic ties they had fostered. Americans worried that the alliance with France, Great Britain, Belgium, and Portugal would alienate colonial peoples struggling for independence. Western Europe's tottering empires had become battlegrounds, of colonial wars and of the cold war. The Atlantic alliance "tagged [us] as colonialists," fretted Dulles, unwilling to go down with a lost cause.[115] The problem grew most explosive in strategic Indochina and North Africa, where determined nationalists waged war against French masters.

These colonial revolts presented Washington with a new twist on the old dilemma of entangling alliances. Like the U.S.-French bond of 1778–1800, ties with France and other European powers in the 1950s weighed on America's freedom to expand influence and power. Yet the United States needed allies—to help contain communism and fight wars, to do business with, and to avoid the dread of isolation. Alliances legitimated America's hegemony over the "free world," believed Eisenhower, who had commanded the Western coalition in World War II. His "concept of leadership implied associates," Eisenhower explained; "without allies . . . the leader is just an adventurer like Genghis Khan."[116]

Still, America did not want to be hemmed in by France or by other European associates. In 1954, with France facing defeat in the Indochina war and unrest in its North African possessions, Dulles complained that NATO "stifled" America's ability to outcompete the Communists for the hearts and minds of emerging colonial peoples. He yearned to mobilize the "dynamic force" of American democracy and so revive the nation's "historic role as an apostle of political liberty."[117] With this reasoning, Dulles wanted France and Great Britain to abandon their imperial heritage, prepare their colonies for responsible (i.e., not radical or Communist) self-government, and join the United States in fighting the spread of third-world communism. Dulles aimed to go beyond the work of secretaries of state George Marshall and Dean Acheson, who had helped create a consensus in Western Europe against domestic communism and against the Soviet Union. Dulles wanted to make democratic anticommunism the overriding cause in Western Europe's empires as well.

Adopting Dulles's colonial policy would have required France to abandon its imperial glory and weaken its economic and cultural ties with former colonies—while still maintaining expensive military commitments halfway around the globe. If Washington compelled the colonial European powers to endure these sacrifices, it could "tear the free world coalition to pieces," Dulles admitted to the National Security Council. "Nevertheless, we could not go on forever avoiding these great issues. The peoples of the colonial states would never agree to fight Communism unless they were assured of their freedom."[118]

Although Dulles thought colonial peoples should have their freedom, he feared that independence could lead to revolutionary governments. The United States itself was born in a revolution. Yet that upheaval had been more an anticolonial war than a revolution on the French (or Soviet or Chinese) models—and the United States had changed greatly since 1776. Dulles underscored his distrust of revolution when visiting Arab leaders from French North Africa "brought up George Washington." He reminded them that "the U.S. has two great national figures." Balancing the Revolutionary War's General Washington was Abraham Lincoln, "who led a war to preserve the Union." Dulles instructed colonials to work for autonomy within the French Union, a loose grouping dominated by France and useful for containing communism and radical nationalism. "We must find a formula," Dulles told Foreign Minister Bidault, "which will on the one hand promote political and economic unity and on the other hand meet the . . . demand for an increasing measure of self-government."[119]

This "formula" proved elusive in both Indochina and North Africa. In Indochina the French fought from 1946 to 1954 against the Viet Minh, led by Vietnamese nationalist and Communist Ho Chi Minh. For a while during World War II, Franklin Roosevelt opposed returning Japanese-occupied Indochina to France. Valuing Ho's guerrilla war against the Japanese, the United States airlifted supplies to the nationalist leader. Legend had it that American quinine and sulfa drugs saved Ho's life from jungle disease. But Washington's opposition to French rule faded even before Roosevelt died in April 1945. The United States wanted France to "be an effective outpost of Western influence" in Indochina, an American diplomat confirmed in mid-1945.[120] After the French attacked Ho's forces in 1946, the United States quietly aided Paris's war effort with transport and supplies. The State Department's Southeast Asian experts protested that Ho was able, popular, and eager to cooperate with Washington. The department's European specialists overruled them by emphasizing Ho's communism and the necessity of winning French cooperation in Europe.

After the Chinese Communists came to power in 1949 and the Korean War broke out in 1950, Washington stepped up its financial support of the French war. The Truman administration now saw the colonial conflict as a battle between communism and democracy. Despite American aid, the colonial rulers were losing the conflict. "The biggest Viet Minh appeal is . . . land, education, and a chance to shoot Frenchmen. It is difficult to match that platform," observed Edmund Gullion, a State Department expert.[121]

American officials worried that Ho Chi Minh's victory in Vietnam would trigger a series of catastrophes, starting with the fall of all of Southeast Asia to communism. This loss would cut Japan off from its traditional markets and raw materials, forcing that key nation to orient its economy toward Communist China. The United States itself faced forced isolation, since "America without Asia will have been reduced to the Western Hemisphere and a precarious foothold on the western fringe of the Eurasian continent," concluded a joint State-Defense committee. The group argued that winning Southeast Asia would "vindicate . . . the American way of life."[122] The collapse of Southeast Asia would also hurt Great Britain, which depended on dollar earnings from Malayan tin and rubber. In December 1952 Dulles told Eisenhower that "the really important spot is Indochina, because we could lose Korea . . . but if Indochina goes, and South Asia goes, it is extremely hard to insulate ourselves against the consequences of that."[123] Senator Mike Mansfield of Montana spoke for many when he declared "that the most important area in the world today is Indochina, and it is tied up very clearly with the security of the United States."[124] With all this apparently at stake in the Vietnamese jungles, the United States assumed 80 percent of the war's financial cost, airlifted in French troops, loaned the French two aircraft carriers, and sent many planes along with almost 300 technicians to keep the aircraft flying.[125]

Despite this massive transfer of aid, the Americans and French held radically different perspectives on the French Indochina War. The French fought to maintain their global status and colonial empire. The Americans regarded that empire as an anachronism, favored autonomy for Vietnam, wanted to open Southeast Asia to trade with Japan, and had little sympathy for what Eisenhower derided as France's "frantic desire" to remain a world power.[126] During the Korean War Washington officials talked about the common U.S.-French struggle against Asian communism. But after the Americans settled for a compromise peace with North Korea and the People's Republic of China in 1953, they still urged France to continue its draining fight in Vietnam. General Jean-Marie de Lattre de Tassigny, the French commander in Vietnam, told the Washington Press Club: "We have given our shirts; now we are giving our blood. What more do you expect of us?" De Lattre needed U.S. supplies, but this aid made France "look like a poor cousin in Vietnamese eyes." He complained also that by talking about Vietnamese independence, Americans fanned "the flames of extreme nationalism."[127] When French army chief of staff General Paul Ely protested the American determination "to control and operate everything of importance," Admiral Arthur W. Radford, chairman of the U.S. Joint Chiefs of Staff, answered that the United States was "growing very impatient" with "French tendencies to overemphasize their prestige and sensitivities."[128]

Americans blamed faulty French character and policy for much of Ho's success. Radford came back from Vietnam convinced that U.S. aid could not supply what the French most needed—"guts." "Two good American divisions with the normal American aggressive spirit could clean up the situation," he believed. Eisenhower traced the central problem to the French having "used weasel words in promising independence."[129] But as the French countered, the more independence they gave to Vietnam, the less reason they had to fight.

The war—and the mutual distrust between France and the United States—climaxed at the battle of Dien Bien Phu in April–May 1954. The Eisenhower administration seriously considered intervening with air and sea power and with Marines. Probably through a misunderstanding, Bidault became convinced that Dulles had offered the French two nuclear weapons. After much debate and reflection, Eisenhower scotched plans for American military intervention when a number of things became clear: the French would give neither military control to the Americans nor independence to the Vietnamese; Congress remained skeptical; the British would not go along; and the chances for military success looked poor. Responding to "a rather hysterical" French request for an air strike to save Dien Bien Phu, Dulles snapped that "it was crazy to think" that the United States would intervene under such conditions.[130] On 7 May 1954 the French at Dien Bien Phu surrendered. The irony was that France had gone to war in Indochina to hold on to the empire it considered essential to independent world power. After eight bloody years, the French left the conflict—dependent on the United States in Indochina and under assault in other colonies.

The day after the French fortress fell, a Geneva conference including the United States, Great Britain, France, the Soviet Union, Communist China, and representatives from the Viet Minh and the French-created Vietnamese government took up the Indochina issue. Haunted by the specter of the French collapse in 1940, Dulles feared that the newly elected Mendès France would "collaborate with the Soviets just as the French Government of the summer of 1940 collaborated with the Germans."[131] But Mendès France proved to be no Red Pétain. He negotiated a war settlement that won back much that France had lost on the battlefield. "This guy is terrific," Dulles exclaimed.[132] Luckily for France, the Chinese, Soviets, and the Vietnamese were suspicious of each other and worried that unless the war ended, America might intervene. Dulles fed such fears by pushing negotiations for a Far East anti-Communist pact. In September 1954 this effort led to the South East Asia Treaty Organization (SEATO), under which the United States, Great Britain, France, Pakistan, the Philippines, Australia, and New Zealand pledged to consult in the event of Communist aggression.

Meanwhile at Geneva the Soviets and Chinese pressured the victorious Viet Minh to withdraw from Laos and Cambodia and to accept a temporary, military division of Vietnam. According to the Geneva Agreements, the Viet Minh would regroup to the north and the French to the south of the seventeenth parallel. In two years, nationwide elections would be held to reunify the country. The American representative at Geneva estimated that Ho Chi Minh would win 80 percent of the vote.

For that reason, Dulles from the beginning planned to thwart the planned elections. As the Geneva Conference was winding up, the secretary confided to a closed session of the Senate Foreign Relations Committee: "We are not as urgent about elections here [Vietnam] as we would be in either Germany or Korea, because as things stand today, it is probable that Ho Chi Minh would get a very large vote. . . . the military regrouping will . . . become a live de facto political division.[133] In August 1954 Dulles affirmed that "our real objective should be to avoid having any such [all-Vietnam] elections."[134] Thus was born South Vietnam and America's disastrous commitment to that fragile country.

After the Geneva Conference, Mendès France believed that France could best protect its remaining interests in Southeast Asia by cooperating there with the increasingly powerful Americans. He also hoped that the French might restrain American impulses to violate the Geneva Agreements and thereby trigger a renewed Viet Minh assault. With the rejection of the EDC, America's pet project for Europe, Mendès France was eager to show Washington that Paris was a loyal ally in Asia. Mendès France also courted the Americans in hopes of obtaining aid to suppress the Algerian revolt, which erupted on 1 November 1954. On the American side, Dulles and other officials believed that, in the short term, the remaining French could be useful in helping stabilize South Vietnam and the now-independent states of Cambodia and Laos.

Despite French efforts at cooperation, relations quickly soured as the Americans elbowed the French out of the way. Washington strongly backed the anti-French South Vietnamese premier Ngo Dinh Diem, ostracized North Vietnam as an enemy state, and rushed military aid to South Vietnam in violation of the Geneva settlement. Unlike the cold-war crusading Americans, Mendès France hoped to woo North Vietnam away from dependence on China and the Soviet Union. In Indochina Mendès France sought "peaceful coexistence," Dillon worried. On 22 October Eisenhower told the NSC that it was time to "get rough" and "lay down the law" to the French, who opposed building up a South Vietnamese army devoted solely to Diem.[135] During a visit to Washington in November 1954 the French leader complained that the United States was "replacing France" in South Vietnam. He proposed "formal procedures" for U.S.-French consultation on Indochina. Unwilling to commit to shared decision making with France on this or any other matter, Dulles agreed only to "flexible procedures," which he could more easily evade.[136]

Washington and Paris also differed over French hopes of maintaining a cultural influence in Indochina strong enough to moderate the Vietnamese Communists. Indeed, Ho had proposed such cultural ties. "French pride in cultural penetration borders on fatuity," reported the U.S. ambassador in Cambodia. The American feared that such cooperation would prove to be a "Trojan horse" in which the Communists could gain entry into French councils.[137] While the French offered literature, Americans bid dollars. Lavish American military aid enabled Diem to hire enough soldiers to oust his rivals, favored by France. Losing out in South Vietnam, France tried to recoup in Cambodia. Here too, France could not match America's resources in either military or economic matters, the American ambassador reported.[138] Within a year of the Dien Bien Phu defeat, the United States had displaced France in South Vietnam and Cambodia. A top French official concluded that in Indochina "the Americans behave like imbeciles and we too for not being able to tell them."[139] The French gave way in Indochina in part because they became desperate for American aid in colonial conflicts in North Africa, closer to home and closer to their hearts.

In the French North African territories of Algeria, Morocco, and Tunisia, nationalism mixed with religion rather than with communism, but the combination was no less potent. Algeria presented a special case since it was legally a part of the mother country, a status France had insisted be written into the NATO treaty. In 1943 Franklin D. Roosevelt had signaled America's postwar interest in the strategic area by meeting privately with the Moroccan sultan. This infuriated the French and sparked the widespread (though false) belief that the president had promised independence. Arabs fantasized that U.S. General Omar Bradley had Arab origins. Roosevelt's visit, the spectacle of France's 1940 defeat, and contact with American and British soldiers quickened North African nationalism. On 8 May 1945, VE-day, the French deployed aircraft and artillery to quash an Algerian nationalist demonstration in which more than 100 Europeans and 6,000 Muslims died. Paris determined to hold on, convinced that North Africa, even more than Indochina, was essential to French world power.

The United States had also become vitally interested in North Africa, Secretary of State George Marshall affirmed in 1947. The Pentagon planned to occupy the strategic territory if the Communists gained control of France. The United States established key military bases in French Morocco. As the State Department observed the buildup of nationalist aspirations in the early 1950s, it pondered whether to support the French or the North Africans. Backing France would allow the Communists to exploit frustrated nationalism. The other choice endangered America's interests in Europe and its air and naval bases in Morocco. The State Department arrived at a "middle-of-the-road policy": encourage the French to make reforms and the North Africans to stay within the French Union. Yet America's middle-of-the-road position still gave France the right of way. If "open revolt" broke out in Morocco, State Department analysts concluded, "the United States would have to support France."[140]

In 1953, when senators such as William Fulbright and Theodore Francis Green of Rhode Island argued that the United States should champion the Moroccans, Secretary of State Acheson made clear his priorities: "We want these bases. . . . If we start telling the French we think they had better run the whole country differently they are likely to say, 'I guess we don't need your bases here.'"[141] U.S. diplomats assigned to North Africa or to Indochina tended to be more sympathetic to nationalism than were those who focused on relations between Paris and Washington. But almost all American officials viewed the emerging nations as pawns. "The main issue everywhere is to decide who can capture nationalism and whether nationalism can be channeled in the right direction," asserted one top diplomat touring the Near East and South Asia.[142]

Encouraged by the spectacle of French humiliation in Indochina (where many Muslim draftees died in battle), North Africans stepped up their agitation for independence. Sympathetic Arab states tried to bring the issue before the United Nations. The United States tried to keep the question off the agenda, and when that effort appeared doomed, lobbied to moderate the debate. In 1953 France angered much of the world, including the United States, by deposing the popular Moroccan sultan. Nationalist violence sparked counterterrorism by French settlers. Tunisia and Morocco quieted down only when France promised independence for those territories in 1956. In Algeria, however, the French grimly determined to hold on.

Friction between Washington and Paris over colonial issues increased when Secretary of State Dulles replaced Acheson in January 1953. Both men doubted the ability of colonial peoples to govern themselves, and both picked communism as the overriding issue. But Acheson had a more of an imperial outlook. "Big Peoples just cannot allow Little Peoples to intefere with their vital interests," Acheson believed.[143] Dulles agreed that power ruled, but he also understood that the calculations had become more complex. "We have to be spokesman for those wanting independence or we will be licked. That is the basic communist strategy," Dulles insisted.[144] And that strategy confronted the United States with the quandary of entangling alliances.

Dulles had to deal with that problem in November 1954 when Algerians revolted against French rule. Two weeks after the uprising began, an anguished Mendès France visited Washington to beg for help in stopping the flow of aid going to the rebels from Egypt and other sympathetic countries. NATO recognized Algeria as an integral part of France, the prime minister reminded the Americans, and now the Algerian part of France faced external attack. Dulles agreed that North Africa was probably "the most serious problem that we faced," but he defined the crisis differently.[145] In Algeria, France suffered not outside aggression but a colonial revolt. Both men saw the Indochina war as an ominous precedent. Mendès France wanted to avoid another colonial defeat; Dulles determined to avoid another war for French colonialism. The secretary declared that if the French wanted U.S. help, they had to give up political and military control in North Africa—which of course would have led to the independence France was fighting to prevent.

French colonialism made a last stand in the Algerian war of November 1954–April 1962. Some 1 million Algerians died, and hundreds of thousands of European settlers fled to France. The Algerian revolt also wounded French pride because it appeared to repudiate France's "civilizing mission," a crucial component of its national self-image. Americans mocked France for being so pious about its imperialism, a favor the French repaid a few years later when the United States bogged down in Vietnam.

As the Algerian war escalated, the United States tried in vain to please both sides. As a discouraged State Department expert on North Africa put it, the United States was "trying to sit on a fence which is not there." Washington wanted to "support a liberal French policy," but French policy was not liberal enough to grant what most Muslim Algerians wanted, independence.[146] Therefore the United States backed the French only part way, thereby antagonizing both the French and the Algerians. At first the war only sharpened French determination to hold on to Algeria. In February 1956 a poll showed a 2 to 1 margin in favor of keeping Algeria an integral part of France. A year and a half later only 18 percent of the French wanted complete independence for Algeria.[147] Washington could find no middle of the road in this fierce battle.

As the war dragged on, many French scapegoated the United States for encouraging colonial independence. Some saw the Americans as bumbling idealists (the "sorcerer's apprentice") or as grasping hypocrites. Other French answered U.S. critics by pointing out that Europeans had emigrated to both North Africa and North America. In North Africa, French settlers had civilized the inhabitants; in North America, the pioneers had annihilated them. Alluding to the civil rights struggle in the American South, where Eisenhower had to send in federal troops to enforce school desegregation, French commentators pointed out that Arab children in Algeria did not need soldiers to protect them from their classmates. Many French people resented America's ambivalent support at the United Nations. In a poll, French citizens picked U.S. policy on Morocco as the worst American irritant.

Such criticism helped confirm American stereotypes about the French. "There is a stronger anti-American feeling in France now than at any time in the last 5 years," observed General Alfred Gruenther, the NATO commander. Like many Americans, he dismissed French thinking as "badly disorganized."[148] Robert Murphy, a State Department expert on France since his intrigues in Vichy North Africa, blamed the "psychological phenomena" of anti-Americanism on France's "frustration and failure."[149] Ambassador Dillon's successor in Paris, Amory Houghton, recalled that rational discussion on Algeria "was something beyond [French] comprehension."[150] These American attitudes seemed to justify marginalizing France's position in NATO. Dulles commented that he valued regular talks with the British and other allies, but that "lately he had consulted France less owing to French irresponsibility."[151] The French bitterly complained that they had committed their nation to NATO, only to receive little in return. Both the war in Algeria and the Suez crisis, which grew out of that conflict, strengthened this nationalist, neutralist sentiment in France.

In October–November 1956 tensions in North Africa and the Middle East exploded in the Suez crisis. Aided by Israel, France and Britain struck at Egyptian leader Gamal Abdel Nasser, a champion of rising third-world nationalism. Meanwhile the people of Hungary rebelled against their Soviet oppressors.

France played a central role in the Suez affair. As the Algerian war deepened, the French fixated on the moral and material aid flowing to the rebels from Nasser. The French found a ready ally in Israel, beleaguered by the Arab states and anxious to take strategic border territories from Egypt. France and Israel cooperated in nuclear research, and top French leaders had worked closely with Palestinian Jews during World War II. France lied to the United States about the large amounts of military equipment it sent to Israel, supplies that violated the Anglo-American-French pledge of 1950 not to fuel an arms race in the Middle East. France became the link between Israel and Great Britain, which had distrusted each other since the days when Israel had been part of the British-controlled Palestinian mandate. When the British had second thoughts about the invasion scheme, the French urged them on. And it was France that overruled the British and Israeli suggestion to wait until after the U.S. election so as not to embarrass Eisenhower.

The French blamed the United States for setting in motion the events that led to the crisis. Angered by Nasser's overtures to the Soviets and Chinese, Dulles in July 1956 suddenly backed away from his promise to help finance the Aswan Dam. The dam would vastly increase Egypt's arable land and, Southern senators complained, competition for American cotton exports. Dulles's move was "stupid . . . uselessly provocative," recalled Maurice Couve de Murville, later de Gaulle's foreign minister.[152] Within a few weeks, Nasser recouped by nationalizing the Suez Canal. He now held a source of revenue for Aswan, the route for Europe's critical oil, and a venerable symbol of British and French imperial power. For the British, who had had a protectorate in Egypt and who saw their worldwide empire crumbling, this was going too far. "I don't want Nasser neutralized," exploded Prime Minister Anthony Eden; "I want him destroyed!"[153] Comparing Nasser to Adolf Hitler, both Eden and Socialist Premier Guy Mollet suffered from the "Munich syndrome," that is they were haunted by their nations' disastrous appeasement of Nazi Germany in the 1930s. British and French leaders also believed that unless they used military force to humiliate and depose Nasser, their nations would sink to third-rank status.

Dulles and other U.S. officials had a different perspective. They wanted to keep the third world open to Western, particularly American, influence. Especially important were the oil-soaked lands of the Middle East such as Saudi Arabia. Dulles wanted to protect the huge stakes there of American oil companies and minimize Arab resentment of Western help to Israel. The secretary tried to drag out negotiations over the nationalized canal, hoping British and French tempers would cool. If London and Paris used force, he warned Eisenhower, a series of colonial wars would follow, and Soviet influence would shut the West out of "the Middle East and most of Africa . . . for a generation, if not a century."[154]

This nightmare scenario seemed to be coming true when Great Britain, France, and Israel defied American advice and attacked Egypt. With its cities protected by French air units, Israel on 29 October 1956 lunged against Egyptian targets. Eisenhower exploded: "Damn it, the French, they're just egging the Israelis on—hoping somehow to get out of their *own* North African troubles. Damn it . . . we tried to tell them they would repeat Indochina all over again in North Africa. And they said, 'Oh no! [Algeria's] part of metropolitan France!'—and all that damn nonsense."[155] Tempers got still hotter. By prearranged plan and without prior notification to the United States, Great Britain and France issued an ultimatum ordering both Egypt and Israel to pull away from the Suez Canal area and allow Anglo-French forces to occupy it. This was a transparent ruse, since the Israelis were far away from the canal. When Nasser, in Churchillian tones, pledged that his people would fight the invaders to the end, Great Britain and France bombed Egyptian military targets. With the greatest massing of naval and air forces in the Mediterranean since World War II, the British and French on 5 November invaded Egypt and came close to seizing the canal. Chief of Naval Operations Arleigh Burke ordered the U.S. Sixth Fleet to prepare for any contingency. "Who's the enemy?" asked the fleet's commander. "Don't take any guff from anybody," Burke replied. Later he confessed, "I didn't know who the damned enemy was."[156]

Meanwhile the Hungarians rose up and deposed their pro-Soviet leader. On 31 October Soviet tanks withdrew from Budapest, and Americans hoped this marked the beginning of the end for the Soviet Union's Eastern European empire. That hope was crushed on 4 November when a Soviet force of 4,000 tanks destroyed the rebellion. The day before, Dulles underwent surgery for abdominal cancer. Two days later, Americans went to the polls.

Before entering the hospital, Dulles briefed the National Security Council on the background of the crisis. For a long time, the United States had "been walking a tightrope" between the alliance with France and Great Britain and the need to win the newly independent nations. "We could not walk this tightrope much longer," he argued, without losing the new countries to Soviet influence. Although the Suez crisis marked "the death knell for Great Britain and France," the United States would not go down with them. Dulles was furious that "at this very time, when we are on the point of winning an immense and long-hoped-for victory over Soviet colonialism in eastern Europe, we should be forced to choose between following in the footsteps of Anglo-French colonialism . . . or splitting our course away from their course."[157]

In the heat of the crisis, the Eisenhower administration did choose. The United States led the opposition to Great Britain and France in the United Nations, crippled London's finances by refusing to support the British pound, and refused help when the Arabs cut off Great Britain's and France's oil supply. They should "boil in their own oil," Eisenhower angrily remarked.[158] The president did not "see much value in an unworthy and unreliable ally."[159] The Soviet Union exerted its own form of pressure on 5 November by threatening Great Britain and France with atomic rocket attack if they did not pull out of Egypt.

The U.S.-Soviet pressure and the condemnation from most of the world, including many Britishers, proved too much for Eden, like Dulles a sick man. Shortly after midnight on 6 November he called Prime Minister Mollet to say that Great Britain was backing out. Mollet urged him to stay the course until Nasser was deposed. At 3 A.M. Mollet summoned Dillon to a meeting. The French were "scared to death," about the Soviet threat, Dillon recalled. Would the United States honor its NATO commitment? When Dillon said yes, Mollet replied, "Well, *you* say that, but what about Washington? They've been saying all these terrible things about us."[160]

The Suez crisis strained the Western alliance, but did not destroy it. Washington publicly warned that it would retaliate against a Soviet attack on Great Britain or France. Privately, the United States passed to its allies the CIA estimate that Moscow was bluffing. "The important thing to remember . . . is that 'the Bear' is still the central enemy," Eisenhower reminded Dulles in his hospital room.[161]

Although reassured against the Soviets, Eden had refused to press the attack even though Anglo-French forces had come close to retaking the Suez Canal. Israel had achieved its limited territorial objectives and stood pat. The French military and government came away bitter at the prospect of yet another defeat. Unlike the divided British, the French (aside from the Communists) united in approving the Suez intervention. Yet the French, who had agreed to integrate their fighting units with those of the British and to put the combined armed forces under London's comand, could not continue the fight once the British decided to stop. In decades following 1956, France did not forget what appeared to be this latest betrayal by Great Britain.

Yet many French put the major blame for the Suez debacle not on the British, Soviets, or Egyptians but rather on the Americans. "During this crisis they chose to ensure our defeat," concluded bitter French diplomats. Christian Pineau, French foreign minister in 1956, commented a decade later that memories of Suez still poisoned French feelings about America.[162] Such criticism of America was unfair because it ignored France's own culpability at Suez. One reason the acrimony became so intense was that after the Arab nations cut off oil supplies from the Middle East, the United States blocked oil relief from the Western Hemisphere until the British and French actually withdrew their troops in December. Washington was "trying to rub their noses in it," Dillon thought. "You had to go in your overcoat" to the Embassy and to the Foreign Ministry, he recalled, because France had no oil for heat.[163]

Great Britain and France drew different conclusions from Suez. London determined to stay close to Washington, even if the Americans called the shots. In return, Eisenhower in 1957 agreed to renew the wartime practice of sharing some atomic secrets with Great Britain. "There is an extremely close relationship" with London, Dulles informed American diplomats in 1958, but they had to keep it quiet or the French and others "would want to be in on it."[164]

Being shut out of such close cooperation strengthened French determination and self-reliance. A RAND study concluded that Suez convinced French legislators of their deep differences with the United States and "the necessity of acquiring an atomic arsenal if France was not to be compelled to align her policy with that the United States."[165] On 10 November 1956 Mollet, originally an anti-nuclear Socialist, reversed course and accelerated the program to build a French atomic bomb. Like Mendès France, Mollet and Pineau tried to improve relations with the Soviet Union. The French also focused on negotiations that in March 1957 led to the Treaties of Rome and the creation of the European Common Market, a crucial phase in Europe's unification.

Yet for France, North Africa remained the burning issue. After his victory, Nasser gave the Algerian National Liberation Front (FLN) equipment abandoned by the French and British armies. The Algerian war escalated, Paris sent more conscripts, and French inflation skyrocketed. A series of weak governments replaced Mollet.

American sympathy for France dwindled further after the Algerians launched a modest but successful public relations campaign in the United States. Intelligent, sophisticated Algerians spoke on college campuses, reached out to journalists, and cultivated influential Americans such as economist John K. Galbraith and Senator John F. Kennedy. They publicized instances of the French torturing Algerians, and they embarrassed French officials who refused public debate. American television broadcast pictures of French brutality into U.S. living rooms.

In July 1957 Senator Kennedy spoke out in favor of Algerian independence. Kennedy hoped to enhance his own foreign policy credentials while showing the Republicans as insufficiently committed to liberty. The speech won support from antiwar figures in the United States and France, but it was sharply criticized by establishment Democrats such as Dean Acheson, who worried about keeping the French in NATO and the Communists out of Algeria. Kennedy then backed down somewhat. Publicly he hedged the call for complete independence; privately he told aides he did not want to become known as "the Senator from Algeria."[166]

The Eisenhower administration clung to a policy midway between the positions of Kennedy and Acheson. The secretary leaned a little toward the third world; the president edged a little toward the French. In November 1957 the Eisenhower administration decided to ignore French objections and sell small arms to Tunisia, which was aiding the FLN. American officials feared that if they sent nothing, Tunisia might turn to the Communists. The French protested that the weapons would go to the FLN. "Your bullets are being used to kill our boys," a French official angrily told Ambassador Houghton.[167] Eisenhower worried that "if the French suddenly drop out of NATO we are out of Europe." Dulles breezily assured him they "would get over it since they needed our help."[168]

The next crisis toppled the wobbly Fourth Republic. Infuriated by the FLN's use of Tunisia as a safe haven, the French sent a squadron of American-built B-26 bombers to flatten the border village of Sakiet. "Bombing an open town on market day, slaughtering women and children, was pretty bad business," Dulles grumbled.[169] He saw another nightmare scenario: If Tunisia and Morocco got dragged into the fighting, they would turn to the Soviet Union for support. France could suffer "a military defeat such as Dien Bien Phu. . . . Afterwards, the French will say we cannot go on, and would turn over North

Africa to Communist domination. A regime which did that could turn to neutralist policies in other areas. The government which surrendered Indo-China killed the EDC. The fall this time could be on a greater scale."[170] Always about to fall or fail, France remained for Americans the weak sister of the alliance.

To head off catastrophe, Eisenhower and British prime minister Harold Macmillan offered a "good offices" mission after the bombing of Sakiet. The weak Félix Gaillard government accepted, setting off howls in France about Anglo-Saxon interference. Officially the mission was to mediate between the estranged French and Tunisians; unofficially it was to encourage negotiations between the French and FLN. Strangely, Dulles appointed Robert Murphy as the U.S. representative on the mission. Within the State Department Murphy had a reputation as anti-French; the French remembered him for intriguing with Vichy and favoring General Girard over de Gaulle. "The only solution is Algerian independence," he told an American newsman.[171] Right-wing French groups, especially those who wanted de Gaulle to overthrow the weak Fourth Republic and save Algeria, burned at the appointment. They "considered it treason to accept the mediation of an American," Pineau recalled.[172] Such resentment further undermined the Gaillard government and the even weaker one by Pierre Pflimlin that followed.

In March 1958 the Paris head of the CIA offered a sad commentary on U.S.-French relations in the previous eight years: "This place is going to blow up very, very, very soon. De Gaulle is getting stronger by the day. . . . The only thing that the extreme left and right mobs would agree upon . . . would be anti-Americanism."[173] Such scapegoating of America may have been unfair, but it reflected France's discontent with its share of the costs and benefits of the Atlantic alliance.

Feeding on that discontent, de Gaulle swept into power determined to rewrite the equation of U.S.-French relations. France's problems from 1950 to 1958 and its resistance to U.S. goals had reinforced the American stereotype of French weakness and sickness. Despite its superior power, the United States had failed to shape French public opinion, to integrate the French army in the EDC, or to bring the French to a winning position in Vietnam. The United States had responded to these disappointments by strengthening ties with Great Britain and West Germany, by letting Bonn into a more integrated NATO, and by undertaking its own commitments in Indochina. France remained in the Western alliance, but as the poor, dependent relation. De Gaulle found this status unacceptable.

Chapter 4

THE ALLIANCE IN THE DEEP FREEZE:
DE GAULLE AND THE AMERICANS, 1958–1968

In November 1960, President Dwight D. Eisenhower and Atomic Energy Commission chairman John McCone discussed one of the many problems arising from President Charles de Gaulle's persistent efforts to make France more independent of the United States. France was planning to build a costly uranium gaseous diffusion plant to secure its own supply of the uranium isotope U-235 for French atomic weapons and power plants. Eisenhower and McCone hoped to stop this plan and have the French instead become dependent on buying the much cheaper U-235 uranium available from the United States. Such French purchases would offer the United States three advantages: Washington would gain some control over French nuclear developments, the deal would help relieve the mounting American surplus of U-235, and the sales would improve the American trade balance. McCone explained to the president that "we could insist that [French atomic weapons made with] this U-235 be placed in the NATO stockpile"—that is, under the ultimate control of Washington. Eisenhower became enthusiastic about the prospect of a global export market for American uranium, particularly for overseas nuclear power plants. The president proposed that if the radioactive metal became a commonly traded commodity, "we could place some of it [in] our stockpile at Fort Knox and announce that uranium, as well as gold, will be used to back up our currency."[1]

This conversation, which took place on the day that John F. Kennedy and Lyndon B. Johnson were elected president and vice-president, highlighted many of the problems and concerns which shaped relations between France and the United States from de Gaulle's ascent to power in June 1958 to the crises of 1968, which nearly wrecked the administrations of the two nations. As McCone suggested to Eisenhower, American officials expected Western European allies such as France to build powerful military forces yet still accept Washington's strategic leadership, to become confident and prosperous nations yet still remain loyal helpmates of the United States. Like Kennedy and Johnson who succeeded him, Eisenhower believed that America's chronic balance of payments deficits and gold outflows obliged the prosperous Western Europeans to do more to help Washington. "The United States lost $4.3 billion in gold last year," Eisenhower fretted in 1959. "We are spending too many billions all around the world without the Europeans taking a commensurate load."[2] The president hoped that "selling U-235 overseas" might reduce "our outflow of gold."[3]

De Gaulle looked differently on these matters of uranium and gold, of NATO and independence. The stubborn general determined to revive France as a world power, the leader of a Western European bloc linked to the United States but independent enough to negotiate on its own with the Soviet Union and other nations. He dreamed of a Europe "from the Atlantic to the Urals," with the hated Yalta division undone, with American and Soviet troops withdrawn to their borders, with Germany perhaps united but certainly contained by its neighbors, and with France again the focus of Western European diplomacy. Such independence and greatness required that France control its own defenses, insisted de Gaulle, who still smarted from the humiliations of World War II. Accordingly, he began to separate French armed forces from NATO and accelerated development of French autonomous nuclear capability. De Gaulle built the costly uranium plant expecting that it would bolster France's nuclear independence. He also calculated that an independent French nuclear force (the *force de frappe*) would enhance Paris's position within the Western alliance and that it might, in an emergency, deter a Soviet attack. Such proud self-reliance fit de Gaulle's belief that the French people, particularly after their defeat of 1940 and their frustrating wars in Indochina and Algeria, needed a foreign policy of grandeur. He argued that a glorious foreign policy would undercut support for the left in France and inspire the French people to work together, overcoming their past debilitating divisions.

France's ability to build and finance the sophisticated uranium facility pointed to Western Europe's growing challenge to U.S. economic and technological predominance. Eisenhower's problem of too much U-235 and not enough gold—and his unusual suggestion that more uranium could somehow right the balance—foreshadowed the conundrum of the following decade, when rising military expenditures, particularly for the Vietnam War, deepened America's balance of payments crisis. Washington expected increasingly prosperous Western Europe to shoulder more of the financial burden of America's military expenditures and aid to underdeveloped nations.

From Paris, the payments deficits appeared not as America's sacrifice, but as the dollar's imperialism. French leaders feared that the outflow of dollars threatened them with inflation. Worse, many of the dollars were being used to buy up French industry. No doubt relishing the reversal in economic roles, the French scolded the Yankees as spendthrifts. The deficits would burgeon as the Vietnam War escalated. Johnson's single-minded pursuit of the Southeast Asian war, despite its financial, social, and political costs, would convince de Gaulle that the United States had become a colossus, overeager for military intervention. Eisenhower, Kennedy, and Johnson all would fail in their search for a painless solution to the payments deficits. The painful fact remained that America no longer could afford all that it wanted to do in the world. Meanwhile, France's prosperity boosted de Gaulle's confidence that he could afford the uranium plant, the *force de frappe*, and the other trappings of independent power.

Although most Fourth Republic leaders had lacked de Gaulle's nerve and verve, they had prepared the way for France's resurgence, particularly after their bitter experience in the 1956 Suez crisis. Paris officials concluded from that debacle that France could rely on neither Great Britain nor America, and that allied military integration often imperiled vital French interests. Even as the Fourth Republic collapsed in confusion, Premier Félix Gaillard, the former junior minister who had accelerated the nuclear program in 1951, scheduled France's first atomic bomb test for early 1960.[4]

The turmoil in April–May 1958 led to de Gaulle's return to power and the rise of the Fifth Republic. As during World War II, the canny general displayed his talent for dominating swirling events. A revolt by French army officers, frustrated by the indecisive colonial war in Algeria, knocked the tired Fourth Republic to its knees. Almost no one in France wanted a civil war, not even the Communist party, inhibited by its isolation and declining numbers and by Moscow's appreciation of de Gaulle's hostility to U.S.-dominated NATO. "It is a tremendously explosive situation," worried Secretary of State John Foster Dulles and his brother, CIA director Allen W. Dulles. They fretted that right-wing army officers might try to seize power, plunging France into chaos and killing chances for a negotiated settlement of the Algerian war, or that the Communists might take over. De Gaulle seemed preferable to these extremists on the French right and left, despite the general's well-known agenda for reviving France's world power and revising NATO's integrated military structure. The CIA "has a fellow who is in touch with him all the time," Allen Dulles assured his brother.[5] De Gaulle positioned himself as the indispensable savior of the torn nation through adroit maneuvers and Delphic statements crafted to appeal to conflicting sides. On 1 June 1958 he became the last premier of the Fourth Republic. He promised to end the fighting in Algeria—on what terms he purposely did not say—and to draw up a constitution for a Fifth Republic, which would provide for the strong presidential powers he had been denied in 1946.

Sharply aware of the link between domestic and foreign affairs, de Gaulle intended to unite France and solidify his own power with a glittering foreign policy, one appealing to patriots of diverse classes and political parties. Indeed, many French felt suppressed by the cold war and the Atlantic alliance. "What kind of government does Dulles think we have had during the last twelve years?" snapped a top French Foreign Ministry figure in May 1958. "Does he think we have been satellites? Does Dulles think *I* have been working for *him?* I have been working for France and for the cause of the whole western world."[6] A few days later, a leading Communist party official spat out his resentment of Moscow's authority: "We are not going to follow them forever. We represent the left. We are French. We will not be their slaves."[7] De Gaulle fanned these feelings, welding together a nation rent by the Algerian war. "At this critical moment," he told Secretary Dulles on 5 July 1958, "there is nothing more important for the French people than to be made to believe again that France is a great power."[8]

Viewing de Gaulle himself as a great—indeed, patriarchal—power, Americans generally stopped feminizing France. After mid-1958 U.S. official documents and press reports rarely referred to France and the French in terms coded as womanish or weak. The NSC described the new France as "stronger, more constructive and stable," terms that suggest masculinist control and normality.[9] Unlike the Fourth Republic, which had empowered a divided group of weak legislators—"half are commies or fellow-travellers," a disgusted Dulles had commented in 1954—the Fifth Republic had ordained a single "Providential Man," who was "towering," "lionhearted," "magnificently strong," and had "iron composure," the *New York Times* and *Time* magazine rhapsodized.[10] In 1960 France exploded its first atomic bomb, and in 1962 it ended its draining colonial war in Algeria, both moves reinforcing the sense in America and elsewhere that France under de Gaulle was again a serious power that could not be trivialized. Indeed, the six-foot-six-inches tall president seemed to American leaders not simply to be looking them in the eye but to be looking down at them. Washington officials found overbearing de Gaulle's insistence on an equal voice for France in managing NATO and his push for a more autonomous French policy. They often coded de Gaulle's stubbornly nationalistic policy as pathological self-aggrandizement and the crotchets of a too-old leader, as the product of the general's overblown sense of France's natural place and his underdeveloped appreciation for the "reality" of America's power and wisdom. As Eisenhower put it, he did not intend to treat de Gaulle as if he were "like God."[11]

This conflict over France's rank in the Western alliance dominated the first official meeting between Dulles and de Gaulle, held on 5 July in Paris. Dulles first genuflected before the French shrine—"the spirit of France is the spirit of

Western civilization," he assured the suspicious general—then moved on to explain that the power of the West would remain concentrated in the United States.[12] Dulles made this remark only two days after Eisenhower and the Congress had amended the Atomic Energy Act to provide for assistance to the nuclear-weapons program of Great Britain but not that of France. Arguing that France did not need to develop its own atomic weaponry, Dulles repeated the pledge to defend France with NATO's bombs. The secretary also proposed to station U.S. tactical nuclear warheads in France and to help train French troops in the use of the new weapons. Incensed at the preferential treatment of London, de Gaulle emphasized that France would continue to develop atomic bombs on its own. He also pointed to the strings in the American offer: Washington still retained final control over the nuclear weapons in NATO and over any deployed in France. Continuing the policy of the Fourth Republic, de Gaulle refused to allow American warheads in France unless Paris could decide when and how to use them. Meanwhile the French leader wondered whether, in the event of a Soviet attack on Western Europe, America would indeed retaliate with nuclear weapons, thus risking assault by Moscow's newly developed intercontinental ballistic missiles.

Dulles confided to de Gaulle that the Eisenhower administration planned to send troops to Lebanon to prevent the toppling of its pro-Western government by radical Arab nationalists inspired by Egypt's Gamal Nasser. The British would dispatch paratroopers to prop up the royal government in Jordan. Eisenhower had already decided that "it would be a great mistake if the French . . . participate[d]" in the military action.[13] He did not want to dirty America's Middle Eastern intervention by associating it with France, tarred as the colonial oppressor in Algeria. Yet Lebanon had been a French mandate; the Lebanese president had asked for French as well as American troops; and France had, along with the United States and Great Britain, assumed special responsibilities for the Middle East in the Tripartite Declaration of 1950. Despite all this, Dulles urged de Gaulle to stay out of Lebanon. He warned further that if France tried to establish itself as a world power, it would antagonize West Germany and Italy.

Although excluded from Lebanon, France was subjected, along with Great Britain and the United States, to Soviet leader Nikita Khrushchev's blistering threat that such intervention could lead to nuclear holocaust. A few weeks after this unsuccessful bluff, the Communist Chinese began to bombard the Chinese Nationalist–held offshore islands of Quemoy and Ma-tsu. Fearing that the Communists might next attack the Nationalist government on Formosa (Taiwan), John Foster Dulles warned of American military retaliation. Khrushchev countered that any U.S. assault on China would be considered an attack on the Soviet Union. Such a series of crises could threaten war in Europe. Thus far-off problems, in which Europeans had no say and little interest, threatened them with catastrophe. De Gaulle chafed at the thought of France's powerlessness in such crises.

De Gaulle sprang from this box with an incredibly ambitious effort to escape the American protectorate and restore France as an independent world power. The audacious general had no set plan for this diplomatic revolution. Instead, as French government officials later described it, his method amounted to "throwing a stone in the water and then wait and see how the ripples grow, and act accordingly [sic]."[14] In September 1958 he threw three stones into the water. Their impact rippled through international diplomacy for the following decade and beyond.

On 14 September, at de Gaulle's private home in Colombey-les-Deux-Églises, he met for the first time with German chancellor Konrad Adenauer. The two men shared a conservative, Catholic, early-twentieth-century background. Both came from the border region over which French and Germans had fought since Charlemagne's day. The modern Charles the Grand charmed the crusty chancellor, who afterward startled journalists with the mistaken comment that the general "is not a nationalist."[15] Adenauer warmed to de Gaulle's vision of burying the ancient quarrel in a close entente through which France would help protect German interests. Although Adenauer never shared the general's antipathy to NATO, he soon matched the Frenchman's distrust of the Americans and British. De Gaulle appreciated that Germany's economic might and political timidity (the latter stemming from its Nazi past and divided status) made it the perfect helpmate. With West German backing, France could lead a Western European bloc. That grouping would be strong enough either to command an equal voice in the Atlantic alliance or to go its own way if the Americans refused to share power.

On 25 September de Gaulle created bigger waves with memoranda addressed to Eisenhower and to British prime minister Harold Macmillan. Pointing to the crises of Lebanon and the offshore Chinese islands, the general observed that France suffered the "risks" of the Western alliance but did not enjoy a commensurate share in the decision making. In the past, America had monopolized the West's nuclear weapons and responsibility over their use, but this "no longer corresponds to the actual situation," he bluntly declared. He demanded that the responsibility be divided, "that an organization comprising the United States, Great Britain, and France should be created and function on a world-wide political and strategic level." This three-power directorate "would make joint decisions in all political [and military] questions affecting global security . . . especially as regards the use of nuclear weapons."[16] This meant "that de Gaulle actually wants a veto power over the use of our Strategic Air Command," grumbled General Lauris Norstad, the American commander in Europe.[17] The French president had foreshadowed his triumvirate proposal in statements made before he came to power, and indeed some Fourth Republic leaders had quietly voiced similar ideas. But de Gaulle made the project a top priority, and to underscore his seriousness he warned that further French "participation in NATO [was] contingent" on setting up the directorate.[18]

On 26 September the French leader threw the third stone by launching the French Community. Through this commonwealth he hoped to keep the soon-to-be-independent French colonial territories linked to the mother country. Such ties would demonstrate France's worldwide interests and sympathy for former colonial peoples. Although there developed some competition between American and French interests in Africa, Washington officials generally favored the French Community as a buttress of anti-Communist stability. Meanwhile, de Gaulle consolidated his grip on power within France. His smashing 4 to 1 victory in the 28 September referendum on the Fifth Republic's draft constitution, followed by triumphs in the legislative and presidential elections at the end of 1958, fueled his drive for peace in Algeria and power in the Atlantic alliance.

In meetings with American leaders from 1958 to early 1962, the proud general, who hated to ask for anything, repeated his request for a central role in governing the Western alliance. "The trouble with de Gaulle," complained French expert C. Douglas Dillon, "was that he always returned to his September, 1958 letter on the *directoire.*"[19] At first the French leader urged a formal directorate. When that met opposition from the other NATO allies as well as from the Americans and British, he pressed for an informal but binding tie. Regardless of the shift, de Gaulle focused on the substance of sharing real power over the West's military and political policies. He cared little for the shadow of "consultation," the pattern whereby the United States informed the allies of a decision it had already made, or polled its associates and then did what it wanted.

Shortly after John F. Kennedy's inauguration, Jacques Chaban-Delmas, president of the French National Assembly, arrived in Washington on a "personal mission" from the general. A "fundamental reconstruction" of the Atlantic alliance had become essential, he asserted to Kennedy. France wanted "intimate coordinat[ion]" through "decisions taken beforehand at the level of the conception of policies and not belatedly at . . . their implementation." In place of America's near-monopoly on decision making, Chaban-Delmas urged that the Western Big Three divide the power along geographic lines. For example, France's ties with West Germany and other neighbors made it the "natural channel for the coordination of policies on the continent." Similarly, a common policy in North Africa would reflect, above all, French concerns. In effect, de Gaulle tried to get the ripples to converge by winning Washington's support for the Franco-German entente and for French leadership in Europe and North Africa. The French leader wanted Washington to share its governance of the Western alliance. If the Americans, like Faust, clutched this power for themselves, they would be "tempted by the devil," Chaban-Delmas warned Kennedy.[20]

Eisenhower and Kennedy administration officials saw devilish ambitions displayed in Paris, not in Washington. The Americans favored de Gaulle's effort to revive France as a strong, stable nation, yet they disliked his attempt to make France independent of the United States, and they opposed de Gaulle's campaign to get Washington to share its management of the Western alliance. De Gaulle was troublesome to Washington because he refused to become a loyal helpmate.

"The key issue confronting U.S. policy is the extent to which . . . [Washington should] cooperate with General de Gaulle . . . to recreate French power and prestige," the National Security Council concluded in a major policy analysis approved by Eisenhower. In some issues, the United States would try to mollify and assist de Gaulle, particularly by helping him to extricate France from Algeria. Yet the NSC doubted "the extent to which we can actually meet De Gaulle's proposals without sacrificing *more important interests.*" For example, de Gaulle's triumvirate plan would set back NATO's military integration, antagonize anticolonial third-world nations, and, not least, "seriously impair U.S. strategic flexibility and . . . giv[e] France a virtual veto power on the use of U.S. nuclear weapons."[21] The Eisenhower and Kennedy administrations also worried that if France graduated to officer class in the alliance, other nations still in the lower ranks, particularly West Germany and Italy, would become restive. This concern recalled American thinking in the early 1950s about the European Defense Community: the United States should minimize German resentment by keeping all the continental allies on a par with each other—equally subordinate to Washington. De Gaulle's scheme also conflicted with the Kennedy administration's "Grand Design" for tying Western Europe even closer to the United States. Both Eisenhower and Kennedy tried to deflect the French by agreeing to talk about global policies, without giving up their prerogative to decide them.

Eisenhower set the pattern shortly after receiving de Gaulle's 25 September 1958 memorandum. He directed Dulles to set up a middle-level committee with the French and British for "*discussing*" but "*not . . . carrying into* effect De Gaulle's plan."[22] For some reason Dulles assigned the talks to Robert Murphy, de Gaulle's wartime nemesis, who had again offended French pride in the "good offices" mediation after the Sakiet bombing. The tripartite discussions continued in various forums through the remaining Eisenhower years, but they made little progress. The Americans preferred to talk about political issues; the French focused on military-strategic questions. The French pressed for binding agreements and shared decision making; the Americans would make no such commitments. The British tried to mediate, but usually sided with Washington. The Americans "play[ed] political games with committees," de Gaulle complained to Dulles.[23] In February 1959 a French delegation went to Washington to take up Eisenhower's offer, made in December 1957, to sell a nuclear-powered submarine to any NATO nation. The French came away disappointed, however, when the powerful atomic energy committee of Congress vetoed the sale of submarines to any ally other than Great Britain. De Gaulle underlined his dissatisfactions—and the threat in the 25 September memorandum—by withdrawing the French Mediterranean fleet from the NATO command. "Gaullist France will be a headstrong and difficult ally," the NSC concluded in November 1959.[24]

Within a year of de Gaulle's return to power, one could discern the attitudes and policies that cooled U.S.-French relations to the freezing point. De Gaulle's challenge to American hegemony in Western Europe and his brusque manner, which alternated with melting charm for maximum effect, offended Americans. U.S. officials were then not used to such cheek from anyone other than obstreperous third-world leaders or the Communists. And indeed Americans began to talk about the French leader's aspirations in terms heretofore reserved for the Soviets. "It is impossible to satisfy de Gaulle's appetite," General Norstad warned Eisenhower.[25] The French leader's "obsession" with his nation's honor also hampered compromise, the president complained, adding that de Gaulle "wants to make France the first nation of the world with himself the first Frenchman."[26] Americans found such ambitions doubly difficult—hard to square with U.S. interests and with a view of the world centered on Washington.

The French leader was unrelenting. He publicly declared that someday the United States and the Soviet Union might "agree to divide the world," "unite," or "wipe out . . . Western Europe from Moscow and Central Europe from Washington."[27] Angered at what Dulles called these "nasty cracks," Eisenhower asked de Gaulle to apologize for drawing "an equation . . . between my country and the Soviet Union."[28] Pending declassification of key documents, it is unclear whether de Gaulle did apologize, but most likely he smoothed relations with Eisenhower, while leaving in the public mind this seed of doubt about America.

Despite such squabbling, most U.S. officials who dealt with de Gaulle from 1958 to 1969 opposed a public fight, which might inflame the French people and extend the quarrel into the post–de Gaulle era. Norstad laid out the strategy. the United States should "present a calm, pleasant, orderly front" and then "do what is right."[29] It seemed easier to ignore and to outlast the general (69 years old in 1959) than to try to meet his demands.

Moreover the Atlantic alliance did endure, despite the tensions, name calling, and withdrawal of French forces from the integrated NATO command. When war threatened, as during the 1958–61 Berlin crisis or the 1962 Cuban missile crisis, de Gaulle pledged to stand by America's side. The general probably was sincere. Yet this remained an easy commitment, since he did not expect war. The Soviets would back down in the face of America's superior power, de Gaulle told Americans during the Berlin and Cuban crises. With Moscow checkmated by Washington, de Gaulle believed that France could maneuver only if it had some input into U.S. policy or some distance from the powerful Americans. The United States reacted coldly to both of these French alternatives.

Eisenhower, more than Kennedy or Johnson, tried to breathe warmth into relations with the French. He empathized with de Gaulle's resentments and nationalism and recalled Franklin Roosevelt's humiliations of France and of the proud general. The president even commented that "we would react very much as de Gaulle does if the shoe were on the other foot."[30] But by the end of his term, after meeting his wartime comrade several times and exchanging many letters, even Eisenhower had lost patience. "I must confess, my dear General, that I cannot quite understand the basic philosophy of France today," he concluded in a letter rehashing the issues of the directorate, French independence, and NATO integration.[31] The president balked at admitting the pushy French into the Anglo-American club. He sought instead a "common understanding" with London on "the problems posed by de Gaulle."[32] Kennedy, too, would find it easier to work with the more pliable British.

De Gaulle repeated the directorate proposal to the new administration—in his May 1961 meeting with Kennedy, through the Chaban-Delmas mission, and on several other occasions. By late 1962 he had dropped the issue, concluding that Kennedy administration officials were even less willing to share power than their predecessors had been. The ripples from the 25 September 1958 memorandum had broken up on the hard shore of the United States.

Denied senior rank in the Western alliance, de Gaulle dropped back to his old goal of autonomy. The general read the events of 1961–62—Cold War crises over Berlin and Cuba; U.S.-French rivalry over West Germany, nuclear arms, and the future of Europe; near civil war in France—as proof that his nation could and should move toward greater independence.

In early 1961 the Soviets reheated the Berlin crisis by repeating a 1958 threat to sign a peace treaty with their East German client. The Soviets argued that such a treaty would end the American-British-French prerogative to be in West Berlin by right of conquest in World War II. The Western powers, which had refused to recognize the East German regime out of deference to Bonn's claim to be the only legitimate German government, would then have to negotiate with East Germany about their rights in West Berlin. In the ensuing crisis Washington insisted on West Berlin's freedom, its access to the West, and the continued presence there of American, British, and French troops. Apart from these three essentials, Kennedy, worried about nuclear war, stood ready to compromise. Privately he considered accepting the East German government, the wall erected in August 1961 to divide East and West Berlin, and Germany's post–World War II loss of territory to Poland. Adenauer, whose people still yearned for reunification, opposed such concessions.

Probably calculating that the Soviets would never permit German reunification anyway, de Gaulle backed Adenauer's resistance to negotiations with the Soviets. Negotiations could lead to concessions. De Gaulle wanted to show

Adenauer that France, more than the United States or Great Britain, stood up for German rights. The general also worried that if the Western powers conceded too much, the Germans might bolt and make their own deal with the Soviets. The West should simply insist on its rights; the Soviets did not want war, the French leader argued. What infuriated the Americans was that de Gaulle, for all his solidarity with Adenauer, had already accepted the German-Polish frontier, shied away from using force to defend West Berlin, and dreamed of an eventual deal with Moscow, inevitably at Germany's expense. By late August 1961 Kennedy decided to ignore France's and Germany's objections to negotiations. They "must come along or stay behind," Kennedy told Secretary of State Dean Rusk. "We cannot accept a veto from any other power."[33] De Gaulle stayed behind and fed Adenauer's fears that the American and British talks with Moscow would barter away West Germany's interests.

The 1962 Cuban missile crisis further aggravated the general's restiveness with U.S. dominance of the Western alliance. Washington consulted none of the European allies about its decision to challenge, at the risk of nuclear war, the Soviets' deployment of missiles in Cuba. Excluded from the decision making, the allies had sunk to "protectorate nations," observed Raymond Aron, the pro-American French commentator.[34]

Advising Kennedy during the crisis, former Secretary of State Dean Acheson suggested that because the United States was not going to consult with de Gaulle, it should at least inform him "in an impressive way." Perhaps thinking that Acheson was as impressive as anyone, Kennedy asked the elder statesman to go to France. De Gaulle greeted Acheson with the central question: "In order to get our roles clear . . . have [you] come . . . to inform me of some decision taken by your President—or have you come to consult me about a decision which he should take [?]" When Acheson replied, "I have come to inform you," de Gaulle dropped the issue. Argument was useless and undignified. But the general added this incident to his list of black marks against the Americans. De Gaulle agreed with Acheson that Khrushchev probably was bluffing and would withdraw the missiles. But whatever happened, he declared, "France will support [Kennedy] in every way in this crisis."[35] Though the general did not expect to have to make good on his promise, it fit his image of France as an ally loyal in wartime but independent. And he was setting a precedent for American loyalty in a European emergency.

For de Gaulle and Adenauer, the Berlin and Cuban crises pointed up important lessons. The Americans held to their monopoly on decision making. Yet Washington's choices touched Europe's vital interests, including the basic question of national life and nuclear death. Adenauer questioned the Kennedy administration's competence and toughness in Berlin and Cuba. De Gaulle encouraged such doubts about American dependability, hoping to nudge the West Germans toward French leadership. The general interpreted Moscow's withdrawal of its missiles as an admission of Washington's superior strength and as a signal that neither superpower wanted war. De Gaulle concluded that France had less reason to huddle under the American defense umbrella and more ground to resist the Yankees' overweening power. Adenauer's growing distrust and de Gaulle's mounting dislike of U.S. leadership fed their opposition to Kennedy's Grand Design for Western Europe.

The architects of the Grand Design included Undersecretary of State George W. Ball, who as a private lawyer had helped Jean Monnet plan the European Coal and Steel Community; State Department policy planning chief Walt Rostow; David Bruce, now Kennedy's ambassador to Great Britain; and a number of other State Department officials. Dubbed the "theologians," they stayed true to the creed underlying the Marshall Plan and the aborted European Defense Community. They fervently believed that Western European integration remained essential to contain West Germany and the Soviet Union, to provide a safe outlet for German energies, to create a prosperous market for European and American products, to prevent the growth of European neutralism, and to dilute European nationalism to safe levels.

Kennedy and McGeorge Bundy, his national security adviser, never shared the zeal of the "theologians," but from early 1961 to mid-1963 they became intrigued by the prospect of bolstering America's sagging position by shaping Western Europe's unification. Europe's economic and productivity growth rates, particularly in the Common Market countries (France, West Germany, Italy, Belgium, the Netherlands, and Luxembourg), were outpacing the American economy. The Grand Designers aimed to increase exports to Europe by reducing transatlantic tariff barriers through the Trade Expansion Act and the Kennedy round of international tariff negotiations. To help keep Europe within the American orbit, the Kennedy administration pushed hard for the admission of Great Britain to the Common Market. The Grand Designers calculated that Great Britain's desire to preserve its "special relationship" with the United States meant that London would serve as Washington's ear and spokesperson within the Common Market. The Americans also hoped that Great Britain's tradition of global trading would insure that the Common Market developed not into a closed Western European bloc but into a low-tariff group open to world commerce. Finally, with Great Britain's strength added to it, the Common Market would be more able to contain West Germany and less likely to come under de Gaulle's control.

In both nuclear and trade matters the Grand Design tried to extend into the 1960s the post–World War II formula of European integration under American auspices. Ball, Rostow, and the other advocates hoped to satisfy Germany's nuclear aspirations by allowing it to participate in the proposed Multilateral Force (MLF). They conceived the MLF as a fleet of surface ships, manned by a mix of NATO nationals and armed with nuclear missiles. Each participating nation would hold a veto over the weapons' use, giving the Germans and others a finger near but not on the nuclear button. Americans valued the MLF as a device that appeared to give the allies a share in the

West's deterrent while in reality consolidating Washington's control. The MLF, of course, challenged de Gaulle's concept of national nuclear forces. Washington hoped that the MLF might absorb the *force de frappe* in the post–de Gaulle era.[36]

In nuclear, economic, and political issues, Kennedy's Grand Design conflicted with de Gaulle's own grand design to win the leadership of Western Europe. Although opposed to the Common Market before taking power, the general soon recognized its utility for wielding French influence within Western Europe. He sought a confederation of European nations, led by France, rather than an integration in which France might lose its identity. De Gaulle agreed with the Americans that Germany had to be contained, but he hoped to do so by tying that economic powerhouse to France. He wanted Paris to dominate Western Europe, not to share leadership with London. London would "always be too intimately tied up with the Americans," he bluntly told Harold Macmillan. London's acquiescence to Washington appeared perilous since "America wants to make Europe into a number of satellite states."[37] De Gaulle feared U.S. domination of the Common Market, through the British Trojan horse or through powerful American corporations. Opposed to the MLF as a dangerous extension of NATO integration, he was determined that the *force de frappe* remain an autonomous symbol and guarantor of French independence.

Americans viewed an independent French nuclear capability as dangerous because it challenged Washington's centralized control of the West's nuclear deterrent. Such control was essential to "flexible response," the Kennedy administration's military doctrine of meeting Soviet aggression with a carefully calibrated counterforce. If the Soviets seized Hamburg, for example, Kennedy did not intend to launch immediate, all-out nuclear war. He would counterattack with conventional forces or by dropping a few nuclear weapons on Soviet military facilities, thus giving Moscow a chance to negotiate and avoid a holocaust. With a small, relatively primitive nuclear force, the French could not wage limited nuclear war. They viewed the *force de frappe* as a deterrent to Soviet attack, and so targeted Soviet cities. If the French dropped a bomb on Moscow during a crisis, Washington officials feared, it would trigger a nuclear war with the Soviet Union that the United States would have to enter.

Americans also disliked the *force de frappe* because it left West Germany as the only major nonnuclear Western power. In the Paris Agreements of 1954, Bonn had pledged not to build such weapons. In talking with French foreign minister Maurice Couve de Murville, Ball drew the parallel with the disarmament provisions forced upon Germany in the Treaty of Paris after World War I, resentment of which had helped Adolf Hitler come to power. "The Germans would never be content with a permanent position of discrimination," Ball warned. As the French nuclear force developed, "the pressures within Germany for a national [nuclear] system would become increasingly difficult to deal with."[38] "The mere prospect" of German nuclear weaponry, Kennedy officials worried, "would shake NATO to its foundations" and inflame East-West tensions.[39] The French shared this concern, but thought they could contain the danger by binding West Germany tightly to France. The Americans did not want to see Paris-Bonn relations that close and doubted that France was strong enough to hold West Germany.

Unable to control the *force de frappe*, the Eisenhower, Kennedy, and Johnson administrations tried to hobble it by refusing to sell France nuclear equipment or technology. The Americans hoped that the weapons program would prove so slow and expensive that French leaders, perhaps after de Gaulle, would abandon their nuclear ambitions. Although the proud general probably wanted nuclear assistance, he never formally asked for it and remained unwilling to sacrifice his force's independence to obtain such help. McCone's suggestion that Washington sell cheap U-235 to France in return for control over French nuclear weapons never appealed to de Gaulle. One U.S. senator suggested that the French president acted like the "little kid who stands outside the pastry shop with his nose up against the window and looking at the cakes."[40] Of course, the general was making cakes of his own—not as good, perhaps, but his own. Meanwhile Washington officials, particularly in the Treasury and Defense departments, sought to ease the yawning balance-of-payments deficit by selling other goodies—conventional weapons—to Paris. French military officials came over to shop, but concluded, "You don't want to sell us what we want to buy."[41]

Like so many other U.S.-French disputes, nuclear aid centered on the issue of independence. In early 1962 President Kennedy conducted "a most searching review" of the no-aid policy and ended up reaffirming it. A top official explained that "the finally persuasive argument" was that nuclear assistance "would not bend General de Gaulle to our purpose but only strengthen him in his."[42]

Despite the differences with de Gaulle, the Kennedy administration did not seek to undermine the man who had contained the Communists in France and who allowed Algeria to become independent in 1962. In 1961–62, disgruntled French officers and settlers in Algeria launched several coup and assassination attempts against de Gaulle. The most serious plot occurred in April 1961 and involved former French Air Force chief Maurice Challe, who had served in NATO's Paris headquarters and who maintained close ties with U.S. officers. General Challe warned his American friends that an independent Algeria would fall to communism, and he promised that the French army would reintegrate into NATO after de Gaulle was eliminated. There is no available evidence that any American officers helped Challe, although some sympathized with him. Over the tapped French telephone system, NATO supreme commander General Lauris Norstad described Challe as "a good man . . . a talented leader, which is a pretty rare thing in the present crop of French generals."[43] Receiving reports of such talk, de Gaulle growled "that some officers of the US Government had encouraged Challe."[44]

Meanwhile, Kennedy offered de Gaulle assistance and ordered American military units in France to help block the rebels. "We don't want the ultras to take over France," Kennedy explained; "with all his faults the General is the only hope for a solution in Algeria."[45] Despite Kennedy's support for him, de Gaulle still worried that powerful American military officers attached to NATO headquarters in Paris could intrigue with French plotters. This vulnerability violated de Gaulle's sense of an independent France.

Similarly, Great Britain's effort to join the Common Market while deepening its special nuclear relations with the United States conflicted with de Gaulle's ambitions for a French-led, autonomous Western Europe. In 1960 Eisenhower had promised to develop and sell to the British the air-launched Skybolt missile. Although the British saw Skybolt as a cheap way to maintain a modern, independent nuclear force, the missile only increased their dependence on the Americans. In early December 1962 Skybolt's poor test performance prompted the Kennedy administration to scrap the missile and focus instead on the submarine-launched Polaris missile. "We knew of course the arrangements with Britain," a senior Kennedy official later recalled, "but they didn't influence us."[46] On 14 December Macmillan met with de Gaulle and explained British intentions of trying to buy Polaris missiles from the Americans. The prime minister also stressed Great Britain's desire to enter the Common Market. De Gaulle took offense at Macmillan's intention to put one foot in Europe while leaning closer to the United States on nuclear matters. The general apparently suggested that instead of asking for Polaris, Britain might join with France economically and militarily, through joint development of a missile to replace Skybolt.[47] Macmillan deflected this proposal, aware that Washington officials opposed what one U.S. senator termed a nuclear "unholy alliance."[48] De Gaulle may have decided at this point to block Great Britain's admission to the Common Market; in any case ensuing events confirmed his view of Great Britain as an American satellite.

A few days later Macmillan flew to Nassau to meet with Kennedy; there he pressed for the sale of Polaris missiles to Great Britain. Kennedy was torn between his desire to phase out Great Britain's nuclear independence (a potential precedent for post–de Gaulle France) and the need to support the pro-American Macmillan, who warned of a storm of anti-U.S. opinion if he returned home empty-handed. The president relented and agreed to sell the Polaris missile. Hoping to mollify de Gaulle, JFK offered to sell Polaris to France as well. Yet, as one of Kennedy's advisers warned, the offer would be read as "insulting," because France had neither the warheads nor the submarines required for the Polaris missile.[49]

According to witnesses, when the general learned of the Anglo-American deal at Nassau, he flew "into a tremendously violent temper"—directed mostly at the British, whom he denounced for "betraying Europe" and as "no longer worthy of being considered a free country."[50] On 14 January 1963 de Gaulle poked a gaping hole in Kennedy's Grand Design by vetoing Great Britain's application to the Common Market. Once admitted, Great Britain would tip the Common Market toward close cooperation with the Americans, he feared. London would probably find support among the many West Germans who also had Atlantic leanings. This would doom de Gaulle's dream of harnessing German power to France.

De Gaulle also rejected the Polaris offer. Mocking the Kennedy administration's effort to centralize the West's nuclear deterrent in Washington, he observed that "in strategy . . . as in economics, monopoly . . . appears to him who holds it as the best possible system." France would continue to develop its own nuclear force. The general argued that the Cuban missile crisis had demonstrated that America, without consulting its allies, might initiate nuclear war to protect its interests. No one could say whether the United States would risk the same for Europe. While rebuffing the British and Americans, de Gaulle snuggled closer to the West Germans. Despite pressure from Washington and from more Atlantic-minded officials such as Foreign Minister Gerhard Schroeder and Economics Minister Ludwig Erhard, Adenauer signed a friendship treaty with France a week after the general's Common Market bombshell.[51]

The explosion shook the Kennedy administration. The president grew "extremely concerned" over intelligence reports (later shown to be false) of a Franco-Soviet deal to shut the United States out of Europe.[52] Officials feared the strong-willed general might mold the Common Market into an autarkic bloc, closing out American business through discriminatory tariffs and investment policies. Kennedy worried that the nation's "world leadership" was under attack. On 31 January 1963 Kennedy drew up a list of "questions to be settled in the coming months," an enumeration that expressed his concern with de Gaulle's challenge: "What kind of a deal can deGaulle make with the Russians which would be acceptable to the Germans[?]"; "Will deGaulle top us" with the Germans?[53] To head off any Franco-German nuclear entente, Kennedy pushed hard for the MLF, hoping it would "increase our influence in Europe, provide a way to guide NATO . . . [and] weaken de Gaulle's control of the [Common Market] Six."[54]

Yet the MLF scheme suffered a fatal contradiction. De Gaulle's policy appealed to the French and to many other Europeans because it addressed the vital issue of autonomy. Americans designed the MLF to mask that issue and to keep Europe dependent. The independence question surfaced in secret Senate hearings, when Senator Frank Church of Idaho criticized the MLF proposal as "inconsistent and contradictory." "If I were in France, I would raise the same questions Mr. de Gaulle is raising," Church declared. Rusk tellingly replied, "Well, Senator . . . since I am an American, I think we have to look at this from the point of view of . . . American national interest."[55]

Despite American lobbying, the MLF won few European supporters outside West Germany. By June 1963 a variety of developments made the MLF proposal appear less attractive to the Kennedy administration. In May the German parliament bowed to American pressure and attached to the Franco-German treaty a preamble reaffirming Bonn's ties with the United States. The danger of a nuclear deal between Bonn and Paris had become more remote. Kennedy administration officials noted that the MLF proposal alienated a broad spectrum of French leaders, including some otherwise pro-American ones who, Washington hoped, might succeed de Gaulle. The intelligence rumors of a Franco-Soviet deal were false. De Gaulle apparently had no Soviet card to play. But Kennedy did have such a card, the prospect of a limited nuclear test ban treaty with the Soviets. This "is now a factor of real importance," Bundy emphasized. In an era of budding détente, the United States should not appear "as the nuclear rearmers of Germany." JFK accepted Bundy's advice to stop pushing so hard for the MLF.[56]

This decision marked another milestone in America's slow shift away from its Western Europe–oriented policy of the 1940s–50s. With the Grand Design stalled and the Berlin crisis eased, Kennedy focused less on Europe and more on the proposed nuclear test ban treaty with the Soviet Union and on the growing war in South Vietnam.

On both questions the United States and France found themselves at odds. The established nuclear powers—the United States, the Soviet Union, and Great Britain—negotiated the test ban treaty of July 1963, intending that, once signed by most of the world's nations, the accord would slow nuclear proliferation. With just a nascent force, de Gaulle refused to participate. The treaty permitted only underground tests—more expensive and more difficult to monitor than atmospheric explosions. Americans hoped that other nations would hesitate to go nuclear if they had to pay the huge costs and face negative world public opinion. "The central problem," Rusk remarked, "is France." Despite Kennedy's personal plea and offer to share technology on underground testing, France would not compromise its independence by signing the pact. This holdout made it harder to crack down on the nations whose nuclear potential was most feared—the People's Republic of China and, to a lesser extent, West Germany. Asked whether the Soviet Union would join in "coercive action against China," Rusk replied, "If we got everybody but China to sign . . . we could . . . take some action along this line."[57]

In August 1963 de Gaulle further undermined U.S. efforts to isolate China by publicly criticizing Kennedy's intervention in South Vietnam. This touched off a wave of resentment in official Washington. Gallic criticism of America's persistent payments deficits also pricked, particularly when France in 1962 ran the world's largest payments surplus.

By the end of the Kennedy administration, U.S.-French "relations . . . had really deteriorated," recalled Foreign Minister Couve de Murville. Yet, he added, JFK "was certainly very popular" in France.[58] Couve pointed to a

President John F. Kennedy and Jacqueline Kennedy charmed de Gaulle during their May 1961 visit, but U.S.-French relations deteriorated nevertheless. *Courtesty of the National Archives*

central irony. Even as Kennedy's Grand Design fell apart and U.S.-French differences festered, JFK's personal popularity with the French (and with other Europeans) soared. The president "talked over the heads of government to the hearts of people," recalled a top adviser.[59] JFK's youth, good looks, wit, intellect, and reputation as a connoisseur of the fine arts appealed to the French. Elegant, French-speaking Jacqueline Kennedy charmed both de Gaulle and the people of Paris during the Kennedys' 1961 visit. "I am the man who accompanied Jacqueline Kennedy to Paris," the president quipped.[60] Many French admired JFK's triumph over anti-Catholic prejudice and his push (though belated) for racial integration.

Kennedy's assassination stunned the French as it did people around the globe. "I felt a great choke," a French woman wrote to Mrs. Kennedy.[61] Jean Médecin, mayor of Nice since 1938, reported that not even "the Fall of France and the death of President Roosevelt . . . compared to the loss felt by the common man. . . . [T]he sight of Italian and French construction workers stopping to cry while building new apartment houses was . . . almost unbelievable."[62] Even French officials, Ambassador Charles Bohlen observed, "act almost as if they had lost their own head of state."[63] Seventy-two percent of the French people rated JFK "a United States President of exceptional ability."

The televised spectacles of JFK being gunned down in the streets of Dallas and of Jack Ruby shooting Kennedy's assassin two days later dramatized de Gaulle's thesis: France should not depend on distant, troubled America for its defense. The assassination damaged American prestige, concluded nearly two-thirds of the French people. Only 19 percent believed Lee Harvey Oswald had acted as the lone assassin; a plurality of 33 percent blamed "a racist organization."[64] De Gaulle showed his respect for the slain leader by personally attending the funeral in Washington.

While in Washington, de Gaulle met briefly with President Lyndon B. Johnson. Both were tall men with forceful personalities, masters at charming or humiliating those around them and used to getting their own way. Both ranked as geniuses at political manipulation and harbored immense ambitions. Yet their personal styles clashed. One need only imagine how out of place the formal general would have been at one of LBJ's Texas ranch barbeques. More important, their national goals conflicted.

De Gaulle saw the cold-war logjam breaking up, opening room to maneuver for French grandeur, independence, and global influence. Johnson dreamed of building a "Great Society" at home and around the world, particularly in Southeast Asia. But first he had to defeat the Communists in Vietnam. Johnson's widened war soon poisoned relations with de Gaulle and weakened America's international position. Like the general, LBJ hoped to exploit the Sino-Soviet split and develop better relations with Moscow. Johnson, however, wanted to keep the Western allies lined up behind Washington, leaving little room for French grandeur.

The two men had met before in Paris when Johnson was vice president. "What are you here to learn?" the imperious general had asked then.[65] Now, at the funeral, de Gaulle turned on his renowned charm, as he had done in meetings with American presidents since FDR.

Though cordial, their conversation revealed basic differences. Johnson and de Gaulle reaffirmed the Atlantic alliance, each pledging that his nation would aid the other in the event of an attack. Yet two days earlier the general had repeated his doubts that the United States would risk its cities to defend France. Within weeks he was criticizing the growing American involvement in Vietnam. In Washington the general spoke more candidly about his ambition to "organize Europe—continental Europe—from an economic point of view and . . . perhaps also from the political point of view." This plan meant a French-dominated Western European bloc, with Germany lashed to Paris and Great Britain excluded. After this "organization is completed," he told Johnson, "Europe will open negotiations with the United States on economic questions." Slipping comfortably into his self-appointed role as Europe's spokesman, de Gaulle assured LBJ that the bloc would keep "all windows open" to foreign business.[66] Washington, however, preferred the freer passage of open doors, negotiated with individual nations unable to match America's economic clout. As the conference ended, Johnson invited the general to return in early 1964.

Such a visit did not take place, though both presidents stayed in office for five more years and met repeatedly with other world leaders. Aside from a six-minute conversation at Adenauer's funeral in 1967, the two men never saw each other again. De Gaulle had tentatively agreed to return Kennedy's 1961 visit in early 1964. But the modern Charles the Grand decided that his social obligation had died with the young president and that Johnson should first visit him, the West's senior statesman. De Gaulle offered the compromise of a meeting on the French West Indies island of Martinique, but Johnson stubbornly insisted on U.S. soil.

The impasse over the visit symbolized the dead end in U.S.-French relations from late 1963 to mid-1968. De Gaulle understood that closer ties with the United States meant compromising French independence. Why make that sacrifice, particularly when the Americans seemed bent on entangling themselves in Vietnam? Although Johnson's advisers appreciated the stability that de Gaulle had brought to France, they viewed him as an adversary. The general's stubborn autonomy—and penchant for throwing stones—posed a "challenge to U.S. leadership and so to you," Bundy told Johnson.[67] Given his combative personality and the manner of his succession, LBJ was particularly prickly about any such defiance.

During the Johnson years the American and French governments clashed in many ways. "The main thrust of French policy . . . runs counter to many of the long-term objectives of the United States," Bohlen advised Rusk in early 1965.[68] Paris and Washington differed over Vietnam, NATO, Germany, relations with the Soviet Union and China, nuclear policy, and monetary matters. The CIA, which ran a large number of operations out of its Paris office, faced opposition from the French intelligence agency. The CIA reported on the "anti-American" campaign of government-controlled radio and television. Embassy officials bitterly remarked that the broadcasts of the French government had stolen the Communist party's anti-American thunder. Meanwhile high French officials, including Couve de Murville, complained that the U.S. government was funding de Gaulle's political opposition. The French government sent a debugging team to its Washington embassy to look for microphones hidden by the United States; American officials also feared that their quarters in Paris were bugged.[69]

The Johnson administration's strategy for handling the French recalled the tactics employed by FDR in World War II and Eisenhower in 1958–60: quietly deflecting de Gaulle's challenge while waiting for that better day when the French people's basic pro-Americanism would produce a leader more accommodating to Washington. This policy meant "paying no attention to General de Gaulle," as Acheson bluntly put it.[70] Both the American and French governments abandoned serious diplomacy with each other. The United States need not bother to compromise on major issues, Ambassador Bohlen advised, because "no concession or courtesy or personal contact will have any effect upon de Gaulle's policies or attitudes." Negotiations could not move the general; only "an actual change in the conditions under which he is operating" would shake him.[71] This conclusion recalled some of the thinking that had led Washington to shift from diplomacy to containment at the onset of the cold war with the Soviet Union.

De Gaulle appeared too difficult to deal with, and so old as to make the effort unnecessary. The general suffered "megalomania," Bohlen claimed.[72] Rusk saw the French leader as a bitter man, acting out his "tragic . . . final chapter."[73] The "messianic" general amounted to only a "temporary" ruler, soon to be followed by a government "more responsive to public opinion, hence more favorable to NATO, United Europe and the United States," argued Douglas Dillon in a memorandum endorsed by Bundy and Rusk.[74] "He is a lot older than I am," Johnson told a journalist, "and I am going to outlive him."[75] Ironically, de Gaulle's presidency outlasted Johnson's. The real test became not which man lived or stayed in power longer, but which nation could longer endure the burden of its leader's ambitious foreign policy. Like FDR, Johnson administration officials naively assumed that the basic concerns of France and the United States coincided. Washington could watch out for "French views and interests" while dismissing "de Gaulle's personal predilections [sic]," Secretary of the Treasury Dillon argued.[76]

Again like FDR, Dillon underestimated the appeal of de Gaulle's forceful nationalism. When asked in 1965 which side had the right in U.S.-French disputes, the French people picked their own government, 53 percent to 5 percent. They endorsed de Gaulle's policy toward the United States by a 46 percent to 21 percent margin.[77] Bohlen admitted that grandeur appealed to the French much more than had the "European and Atlantic policies" of the Fourth Republic. De Gaulle added "a layer of nationalism . . . to the French cake . . . which tastes better and better to many Frenchmen," he reported.[78]

Growing differences with America over the third world fed this appetite. From 1958 to 1963 U.S.-French disputes had remained confined to Germany, Europe, and military issues. Washington's complaints about French colonial policy had quieted with the Fourth Republic; Americans applauded de Gaulle's decision to let Algeria become independent. Aside from rivalry in Laos and France's disapproval of the United Nations' role in the civil war in the former Belgian colony of the Congo, Washington and Paris had no serious quarrels over the third world. This relative amity ended in 1964 when de Gaulle cast two stones into the stormy waters of the third world. By that time, two of his earlier initiatives had run aground. The Americans had rejected the directorate, and the Germans continued to cling to the Americans. Only the policy of aiding the third world, especially former French colonies, won a positive response. De Gaulle again made waves by reaching out to the People's Republic of China and to independent-minded nations around the globe.

In January 1964, after giving the United States only a few hours' notice, France recognized the government of the People's Republic of China. De Gaulle found impossible and absurd the American policy of trying to quarantine the world's most populous nation. Beijing shared Paris's distrust of both superpowers and could be useful in efforts to play off the United States against the Soviets. The French also calculated that the Asian giant was crucial to any negotiated settlement of the growing war in Vietnam. Washington, however, viewed "Red China" as an enemy state and spearheaded drives to deny the Beijing government Western technology, political recognition, and admission to the United Nations. Kennedy officials had even considered dropping a hydrogen bomb on China's nuclear weapons plant. America was getting involved in Vietnam in large part to contain Chinese "expansion." Now the French had breached the wall around China, and "the shit has hit the electric fan," a journalist reported after talking with Bohlen.[79] "De Gaulle simply believes that Mao, Ho, and Prince Sihanouk and all the others are Gaullist" nationalists, a top French diplomat told startled Americans.[80]

If the general saw natural allies in other nationalists, he found the enemy in the hegemonic superpowers, particularly the expansive United States. He concluded that nationalism had become the driving force in world affairs, not the sterile (and self-serving) struggle between Soviet communism and American capitalism. France had shed most of its own empire, and it could now shine as the "guiding light" for smaller countries jealous of their independence, Paris leaders hoped.[81] In March 1964 de Gaulle declared "France is violently opposed to the blatant American imperialism now rampant in the world. France will continue to attack and to oppose the United States in Latin America, in Asia, and in Africa."[82]

For all the general's bluster, however, France lacked the leverage to "attack" the United States in any important area of the third world—except in South Vietnam, where French cultural prestige and economic influence remained high, and where the United States was making a huge investment of blood and treasure. From 1964 to 1968 the Vietnam War became the most bitter issue dividing the United States and France.

To de Gaulle, the Vietnam War demonstrated what was fundamentally wrong with U.S. foreign policy: naive self-righteousness, a readiness to quash smaller nations' independence, a tendency toward military actions that could engulf France in a world war, and wrongheaded persistence in containing "Communist" expansion while underestimating the Sino-Soviet split and Vietnamese nationalism. Though estranged, Vietnam remained, in Paris's eye, a French offspring. Even the Communists acknowledged cultural and sentimental ties with France, and economic and personal ties continued to hold. As de Gaulle viewed it, the United States had backed the French insufficiently before 1954, had shoved them aside after the Geneva conference, and had mistakenly refused to allow the 1956 elections to reunify the country. Naturally a civil war had resulted, and now the Americans were trying to prevent the inevitable with massive military force and intervention so complete as to eliminate any vestige of South Vietnamese independence or French influence. France had learned from its mistakes in Indochina and Algeria; now the the Americans were ignorantly repeating the same errors. De Gaulle grew impatient as Washington remained deaf to his advice.

In 1961 de Gaulle had warned Kennedy that victory would prove elusive in Vietnam. Throughout the 1960s, he predicted defeat: "You cannot succeed in Indochina. The ground is rotten. It is impossible. We in France know. We failed and you will fail."[83] Kennedy and Johnson officials saw no parallel between the French war and their own. The French had been colonists, they told themselves; the United States wanted only to defeat the Communists and then get out. Americans dismissed French warnings. Belief in American failure was "a comforting conclusion for a Frenchman," Bundy assured Johnson.[84]

De Gaulle's criticism escalated along with America's deepening involvement in the war. In August 1963 he deplored foreign intervention in Vietnam and pointedly referred to "the country as a whole"—a direct challenge to Washington's view of independent South Vietnam as the victim of the North's aggression. French officials facilitated the conversations between North and South Vietnam that took place in the fall of 1963. Intent on victory, Washington saw these talks as yet another reason to allow disgruntled South Vietnamese generals to overthrow the unpopular Diem. The generals who replaced Diem looked more than ever to Washington, not to Paris.

Nevertheless, France still cast a large shadow in its former colony. In late January 1964 de Gaulle shook the morale of the Saigon generals when he publicly urged cooperation with China to neutralize Southeast Asia, including South Vietnam. His statement had a "larger than lifesize effect [in South Vietnam] because of a French social, economic and cultural presence there," LBJ fretted.[85] Johnson himself felt pressure from the ambassador in Saigon, Henry Cabot Lodge. He had sent Lodge, the Republican vice presidential candidate in 1960, to Saigon as insurance against expected Republican attacks on Vietnam policy in the forthcoming 1964 presidential election. Now Lodge insisted that Johnson make de Gaulle agree that such neutralization would not include South Vietnam. From Paris, Bohlen warned that the difficult general would reject such a declaration. Asking him would only give him more leverage with which to press for a U.S. withdrawal from Southeast Asia.[86] As Johnson administration officials discussed whether to escalate the war, they viewed the French not as experts who might help head off an American catastrophe but as wrongheaded and annoying critics.

In June 1964 LBJ warned de Gaulle that by raising "doubts of our strength" and prospects for victory, the general increased the chances that "the United States Government would have to prove its determination by military action." In other words, the French had better suppress their skepticism about America's Southeast Asian adventure or Washington might have to lash out to uphold its precarious military credibility. If war should occur, Johnson wanted de Gaulle's promise of support "as a friend and ally as . . . in the Cuba crisis of '62."[87] The general refused such a pledge, cautioned against military escalation, and urged a political settlement by reconvening the 1954 Geneva Conference. "On Southeast Asia, there is no common ground" with France, a White House staffer noted.[88] This conclusion came a year before the United States began bombing North Vietnam or sent large numbers of combat troops.

On 6 February 1965 Johnson seized the pretext of a Viet Cong attack on U.S. forces at Pleiku, South Vietnam, to begin bombing North Vietnam. Fearing that the French might warn the North, the Johnson administration apparently gave them even less notice than it offered other nations. In an ironic footnote to de Gaulle's directorate proposal, Bohlen had to ask Washington for permission "to deal with French on equal basis with [the] other allies."[89] Meanwhile de Gaulle sent Ho Chi Minh a sympathetic letter and agreed with the Soviets, Chinese, and North Vietnamese that the Geneva Conference should be reconvened. Although he denied it, de Gaulle probably would have liked to mediate a peace.

In Washington a worried French foreign minister met with top officials. The Communists "had killed a number of our boys," Johnson noted grimly. He "was not going to write them a thank-you note for this." LBJ recalled de Gaulle's support during the Cuban crisis, warned of American disenchantment with the European allies unless they helped out in Asia, and concluded that "if we were to abandon Vietnam, we . . . would be back to Hawaii and San Francisco." Couve de Murville feared that bombing North Vietnam could escalate into a general war. If war did come, France probably would "not . . . be involved," he warned. He also relayed Moscow's dismay at the bombing, aggravated by Soviet premier Aleksei Kosygin's presence in the North Vietnamese capital at the moment of the U.S. assault. "The essential problem was: how to get out," the Frenchman emphasized. He argued that China, North Vietnam, and particularly the Soviet Union wanted a negotiated settlement for America's eventual withdrawal, but not humiliation.[90] The French hoped for a Titoist solution—a Communist South Vietnam probably linked with the North, but independent of China and Russia. Couve's views aroused little interest among Johnson officials. Instead, Rusk complained again to the French government about "its public needling regarding Viet-Nam and its public posture of concerting with the Soviet Union on this problem."[91]

Bitterness increased in late April 1965 when Johnson dispatched the Marines to prevent Juan Bosch, an elected president of the Dominican Republic, from retaking power after a military coup had ousted him. Johnson feared that the Communists would dominate a new Bosch government. This latest military intervention sparked widespread dismay in France and seemed to confirm de Gaulle's suspicions of Washington's "overwhelming power."[92] The U.S. Embassy reported that usually pro-American French journalists and officials felt that the Vietnam escalation was hard enough to swallow, but that Santo Domingo "was too much."[93] Only 14 percent of the French approved of Johnson's intervention in the Dominican Republic, while 42 percent disapproved.[94]

When de Gaulle toured Mexico and South America in 1964, he proclaimed sympathy for nations dominated by the United States. A year later, the general deplored Washington's apparent view that "force would solve everything."[95] When Vice President Hubert Humphrey visited Paris, de Gaulle lectured him that in light of America's proud history as a "champion" of human rights, "its present position was particularly distressing."[96] The remark that irked Johnson and Bundy the most, despite their effort to ignore de Gaulle, was the general's comment in June 1965 that "the U.S. was the greatest danger in the world today to the peace."[97] Thus de Gaulle had come out squarely against America's war in Vietnam, a month before Johnson began sending massive numbers of troops there and before large-scale antiwar protests began in the United States or in Europe.

A wide spectrum of the French people shared the general's opposition. Future secretary of the treasury Henry H. Fowler observed that even those French who were anti–de Gaulle and pro–United States "disagreed . . . vehemently" with U.S. policy in Vietnam.[98] In July 1965 the French picked the Vietnam War as the most important world event. A consistent antiwar bias in the French broadcasting fanned public disgust. The drama of the world's most powerful nation pulverizing a backward, former French colony tugged at

Gallic hearts. The French people disapproved of American bombing near Hanoi by a margin of 81 percent to 8 percent; they disliked overall U.S. policy in Vietnam by a tally of 71 percent to 8 percent. When asked in 1965 which world leader posed the greatest danger to world peace, 32 percent named Chinese leader Mao Tse-tung; 30 percent picked Johnson.[99] Some White House staffers attributed LBJ's unpopularity to "Gaullist attacks."[100] One of Johnson's principal advisers on France blamed the antiwar sentiment on "the political castration of much of the [French] population."[101] Meanwhile, the USIS deluded itself that a "more intensified" information program could win over the French people.

Antiwar protests near the American embassy in Paris intensified from 1966 to 1968. Each week the embassy received hundreds of petitions bearing thousands of French signatures. When Vice President Humphrey visited Paris in 1967, demonstrators hounded him at almost every stop; threw eggs, paint, and stones; and attacked his American Marine guards. The U.S. Embassy protested that the Paris police had stood by without aiding the Americans; the police later apologized. Angered by reports of this hostility, the American Legion urged retaliation against the perfidious French. Representative Mendel Rivers, chairman of the House Armed Services Committee, recommended that the bodies of America's war dead be dug up from French graves and reburied in U.S. soil.[102]

Despite its vehemence, French opposition to the U.S. onslaught in Vietnam was mostly words. The French government did not try to block American war operations. Nor did Paris give significant aid to North Vietnam and the Viet Cong, aside from verbal encouragement. The general exchanged warm letters with Ho Chi Minh, but turned down an invitation to visit Hanoi. The alliance with the United States remained in the deep freeze, but it remained. De Gaulle saw no reason to sacrifice all influence with Washington by going over to the other side.

France actually had little impact on the course of the war. The general repeatedly asked the United States to declare a permanent bombing halt as a prelude to serious negotiations. Several times Johnson interrupted the bombing, but he resumed when the North Vietnamese refused to come to the bargaining table on American terms. Washington had some contact with the North Vietnamese through Paris, but it did not sufficiently trust the French to use them as a major intermediary. In September 1966 de Gaulle made his last major statement on the war before a cheering crowd of 100,000 Cambodians in Phnom Penh. Citing the example of France's withdrawal from Algeria, he called on the United States to pull out its troops and accept Vietnamese self-determination (meaning North Vietnam's control of the South) and an accord with China. Washington never willingly accepted these conditions. Even in 1973, when President Richard M. Nixon would finally agree to withdraw all U.S. troops, he would do so intending to resume bombing to forestall the North's takeover of the faltering South.

Although France had little say about the war's outcome, the conflict boosted French diplomacy. America's pursuit of victory in the Vietnam War created an atmosphere in which de Gaulle's own will-o'-the-wisp—global grandeur—appeared almost reachable. Brought by television into French living rooms, the Vietnam War offered graphic proof of de Gaulle's thesis that America had become too powerful and too careless, and that military ties with the giant could be dangerous. The conflict also seemed a lesson in the general's teaching that ideological struggles had become atavistic in the age of nationalism. Blinded by anticommunism, the United States pounded futilely at a small but determined people battling for nationhood. Many French, like some American antiwar protesters, romanticized the Viet Cong and North Vietnamese as brave defenders of human freedom. That they were Communist seemed almost irrelevant, even to anti-PCF French people. Meanwhile, France prided itself for escaping the clichés and confinement of the cold war and for reaching out to the East. Speaking on Soviet television in 1966, de Gaulle declared that "my visit to your country is a visit of eternal France to eternal Russia."[103] Like many people in the 1960s, de Gaulle believed that sweeping change was possible. Perhaps he remembered that bold words could transform events, as had his broadcasts from London in 1940.

"Vietnam . . . runs like [an] endless thread through all French thinking on world affairs," Bohlen observed.[104] The thread also ran through the rest of Western Europe, where journalist Walter Lippmann found growing "dissent and doubt and anxiety about the wisdom and competence" of American foreign policy.[105] The war was worsening the U.S. payments deficit, sharpening U.S.-French quarrels over the dollar, gold, and foreign investment.

The Johnson administration itself viewed transatlantic ties through the lens of Vietnam. At a NATO meeting in late 1965 Dean Rusk and Harlan Cleveland, the American ambassador to NATO, informed the allies that the United States would "judge its bilateral relations" according to how other nations "join[ed] us" in the "peacekeeping business." "The only way" Europeans could prevent the war "from degrading NATO is to join that effort themselves," the Americans bluntly warned. Cleveland believed that the United States had to "convert" its allies "from affluent protectorates to active participants in policing world order." That "will be uphill missionary work," he admitted.[106] Indeed, the allies never did "convert," and differences over the third world continued to plague American relations with Western Europe. As the Americans plunged deeper into the morass of Vietnam, de Gaulle, who had secured his leadership in France by winning the presidential elections of 1965, distanced his nation further from the United States.

On 7 March 1966 de Gaulle sent Johnson a letter stating that France was leaving NATO and asking the Americans to remove NATO headquarters and U.S. soldiers from France. Within a year the United States evacuated its 30 military bases, 26,000 military personnel, and 37,000 dependents from

French soil. De Gaulle's decision grew out of his fear that Washington could drag France into an unwanted war, his inability to win American approval for the triumvirate proposal, his longtime distrust of military integration, and his bitter experience with Anglo-American military domination in World War II. The general figured that a Soviet attack on Western Europe was highly unlikely and, if such an assault did occur, the Americans would have to defend France in order to save Germany. Significantly, even after Paris withdrew from NATO's integrated military command, France continued as a member of the alliance; that is, it remained pledged to fight against unprovoked aggression on a NATO member. But what constituted unprovoked aggression? France would decide whether to do battle alongside the rest of NATO only when an actual war crisis occurred. Couve de Murville suggested that in wartime the Pentagon might be allowed to use former American bases in France, but he declined to guarantee such access. Given the example of American military intervention in Santo Domingo and in South Vietnam, France refused to be sucked into any unwanted wars.[107]

De Gaulle's withdrawal from NATO stung many Americans. Discussing the order to remove American soldiers from France, Rusk asked de Gaulle, "Does that include the dead Americans in military cemeteries as well?"[108] *Le Monde* editor André Fontaine claimed that angry restaurant owners in New York "pour[ed] their bottles of French wine in the streets of the city to protest against . . . de Gaulle."[109] A key American diplomat worried that de Gaulle's independence could prove contagious, infecting other European states with assertive nationalism.[110] That development would multiply Washington's problems in directing the Western alliance.

Although alarmed by de Gaulle's 7 March message, the Johnson administration responded with calculated restraint. Administration experts wanted to build both a "golden bridge" for France's future return to NATO and some protection for themselves from "historians" who might "unfairly blame" them "for splitting Europe." Johnson's carefully worded reply—"this will be one of your most important state letters," top adviser Francis Bator told Johnson—concluded with a strangely ungrammatical sentence: "As our old friend and ally her place will await France whenever she decides to resume her leading role [in NATO]." As Bator explained to Johnson, the letter emphasized the "distinction between deGaulle (and *his* policies), and France (and our relations with *her*)." But the syntax of the letter to de Gaulle, with its dangling modifier, created a further distinction. In the context of the sentence, "our old friend and ally" referred not to France but to the *place* of France, a place currently empty because of that country's evacuation from the alliance. According to the logic of this construction, France could be a "friend and ally" only when she was in her "place." Although references to a nation as "she" and "her" was rhetorical convention, this juxtaposition of gender-coded words did more. It feminized France as a nation led astray by de Gaulle's seductive promises of grandeur. The legitimate and genuine interests of

France lay in a different "place," the letter implied, namely with the dependable man at home, who loyally waited for her to take up her "leading role" in NATO—which he dominated.[111]

In December 1967 the French moved further away from the United States when French chief of staff Charles Ailleret declared that the *force de frappe* "should not be directed . . . at one theoretical enemy, but be able to strike . . . in any direction." France had to be able to defend itself from all adversaries, including the United States, which might "want to use [French] territory or resources in the struggle."[112] Ailleret's fear of an American grab for French bases was not far-fetched. Cleveland, the U.S. ambassador to NATO, recommended that "if the French were to remain neutral or hostile in any war with Russia," the United States should "seize such installations as we require on French soil even if . . . [this meant] 'fighting a two-front war.' "[113] As Cleveland bluntly suggested, France's military independence remained limited, despite its bold words. "The *force de frappe* is deaf, dumb, and blind without our help," explained National Security Adviser Walt Rostow; "it needs radar, early warning, and intelligence."[114] France continued to depend on the NATO air alert system (NATO Air Defense Ground Environment [NADGE]), giving the United States crucial leverage in the event of a war crisis.[115]

Although France's military autonomy did not match the aspirations of Ailleret or of de Gaulle, the nation exercised considerable diplomatic freedom. In 1966–67 de Gaulle demonstrated that autonomy with a series of initiatives in the Middle East, the Common Market, Canada, the Soviet Union, and Germany. With America mired in Vietnam and West Germany immobilized by its refusal to accept formally its post–World War II territorial losses, Paris remained free to dance a minuet with Moscow. Convinced that America and its client Israel had become so powerful as to upset the Middle Eastern balance, de Gaulle leaned toward the Arabs in the 1967 Six-Day War and voted with the Soviets at the United Nations. The general exchanged visits with the Soviet president, not with the American leader. In 1965 de Gaulle hobbled the European integration movement by insisting on France's right to veto Common Market policies. Two years later he again vetoed British admission to the Common Market. In Canada he urged the independence of French Québec; in Warsaw he advocated revival of the Franco-Polish alliance.

In official documents and in press reports, Americans interpreted de Gaulle's freewheeling defiance of U.S. policy and Cold War orthodoxy as evidence of mental unbalance. "Really, the old boy is going off his rocker," exclaimed Bohlen.[116] De Gaulle incensed much of the American press when, in the wake of the Six-Day War, he described Jews as "an elite people, self-confident and domineering." A *New York Times* editorial condemned de Gaulle's "anachronistic nationalistic imperialism," reminiscent of Hitler, and concluded that his "illusions" had advanced with his years. *Time* magazine declared the general's "rationality . . . tangled." Russell Baker caught the mood when he joked after one of de Gaulle's press conferences that the general's "announcement that France would withdraw from earth was hardly unexpected."[117] Meanwhile, U.S. officials coded as lascivious the French nation's overtures to the Soviet Union. After a "rather indecent flirtation," the French had climbed "in bed with the Soviet Union," they complained.[118]

De Gaulle regarded détente or a relaxation of tensions with Moscow as a rational response to the cold-war stalemate—despite the Vietnam War, the Johnson administration was talking to the Soviets—and as the first step toward ending the postwar division of Europe. The general believed that détente between East and West would lead to a thinning out of the superpowers' troops and nuclear weapons in Europe, enable commerce and culture to flow more freely, and encourage a loosening of Moscow's grip on Eastern Europe and on the Soviet people. De Gaulle still dreamed of a Europe "from the Atlantic to the Urals," with France the preeminent power in Western Europe and Russia in the East. Together they would contain Germany and launch an economic and political dialogue between Europe and the third world. In December 1964 he declared that "externally [the Eastern bloc] is changing toward peace and détente and internally it is changing toward liberty." De Gaulle's analysis proved correct, but his timing was off by a quarter century.[119]

For all his emphasis on détente, de Gaulle did not intend to reverse alliances by linking up with Moscow against Washington. Rather, he concluded that America had become so globally powerful and so grasping that the Soviet Union was reduced to a relatively weak regional power, suitable as a limited partner of France. "We oppose any hegemony, American or Russian," he explained.[120] Despite French distaste for integration and for NATO (that "thingamagig," Couve de Murville called it), de Gaulle and his advisers valued the residual security of the 1949 North Atlantic treaty—the simple pledge to come to each other's assistance if attacked.[121] After all, the Soviet Union—or Germany—could again become a menace.

Germany remained "the great stake in the game of European policy," Bohlen recognized.[122] Wealthy West Germany loomed as the only major European power with territorial grievances. The United States and France, along with the Soviet Union and the rest of Europe, worried that in the future Germany might again upset the cart by grabbing for reunification or for lost lands. This fear had prompted the United States to push for West Germany's integration into NATO and the Common Market. The French had long favored such integration for Germany, though many rejected it for themselves. After France departed NATO, de Gaulle maintained that "because of Germany, it is normal that American [troops] should be in Europe"—even as he kicked them out of France.[123] Although Paris and Washington agreed on the containment of Germany, their rivalry there sharpened as the United States staggered under worldwide burdens and as France reached for a global role. West Germany's purchases of U.S. weapons helped Washington afford to keep troops stationed in Europe while waging war in Vietnam. America's influence in Western Europe, particularly West Germany, gave Washington clout over Moscow. "Russia recognizes that America is the real power, and would prefer to deal directly with Washington," the CIA concluded in a study of the Franco-German-Soviet triangle.[124]

Yet Washington found its authority in Europe slipping. While the United States focused on Vietnam and considered pulling soldiers out of Europe, the NATO allies viewed Soviet overtures as a chance to cut back their military spending. At an NSC meeting, Humphrey warned that peace in Europe threatened "the dissolution of the alliance" and thus "the loss of our diplomatic cards in dealing with the Russians."[125] The juncture of war in Asia and détente in Europe undermined America's international position, built on a foundation of global cold war. The Johnson administration also sought détente with Moscow in the late 1960s, but it wanted Washington, not Paris or Bonn, to shape the new relationship.

De Gaulle had tried to bind West Germany by cultivating Adenauer and by signing the 1963 treaty. In 1965 he held out the carrot of reunification. This could be won "only by Europe because it is Europe's concern," the general declared.[126] This plan would give Moscow a larger voice than Washington in any reunification talks. "Obvious nonsense," snapped Bundy.[127] De Gaulle calculated that the Soviets shared his objective of keeping a reunited Germany under tight restrictions. He feared that Washington, in contrast to Moscow and Paris, would "demand for Germany, as the Germans would like, frontiers and armaments comparable to those of others."[128] The general worried needlessly. The Johnson administration remained uninterested in reunification and saw it as only a remote possibility. Concerned instead with stability, the Americans feared that West German or French diplomacy could upset the comfortable status quo.

De Gaulle's strategy of reaching out to the Soviets for an eventual deal on Germany suffered from a fatal flaw. The Soviets already had a powerful silent partner in managing the Germans—the Americans. In edging away from Washington and toward Moscow, Paris hoped to bring Bonn along. Yet the West Germans stayed close to the more powerful Americans. Ironically, with France estranged from NATO, West Germany found itself playing more of a leader's role in the Atlantic alliance and in the Common Market. De Gaulle's policy probably accelerated West Germany's maturation as an independent European power. After late 1966 a new German government, with Social Democrat Willy Brandt as foreign minister, reached out on its own to the Soviet Union and to Eastern Europe. French mediation became unnecessary.

In transatlantic relations, too, de Gaulle's waves could only splash against other nations' superior power. When Chancellor Ludwig Erhard replaced Adenauer in late 1963, de Gaulle lost a loyal deputy. West Germany considered itself America's "most faithful ally," Erhard assured U.S. officials.[129]

When Johnson resurrected the MLF project for a while in 1964, the chancellor endorsed it as "the best way to neutralize the 'force de frappe.' "[130] Bonn disapproved of France's recognition of China and its refusal to cooperate with NATO or to sign the nuclear test ban treaty. Franco-German consultation continued as prescribed in the 1963 treaty, but the talks became, Washington noted with some relief, "a dialogue of the deaf."[131] Under pressure to choose between France and the United States, Germans leaned westward while trying to maintain ties with Paris. Paris sat by as Bonn and Washington stepped up consultation, especially on military matters. "De Gaulle appears to be now thoroughly disgusted" with West Germany and with Erhard, Bohlen concluded in early 1965.[132] Rebuffed by West Germany, the general bounced back by building closer ties with the Soviet Union and with the third world.

The disputes over political and military issues spilled over into economic relations. In 1967 U.S. sales to France, America's fifth largest export market, rose to a record $1.1 billion. But American purchases of French goods, particularly wine, perfume, and other luxury products, stayed flat at $600 million. The U.S. Department of Commerce observed that demand for French products was hurt by scattered boycotts of French goods. Although the United States enjoyed a favorable trade balance with France, it faced sharper competition from the rest of Western Europe and from Japan. America's annual trade surplus—traditionally the fund out of which the United States paid for other overseas expenditures—shrank from $5.9 billion in 1960 to $1.4 billion in 1968. This decline, coupled with heavy military and foreign-aid spending and investment abroad, lofted the U.S. balance-of-payments deficit to $3.5 billion in 1967. The dramatic shift in gold reserves reflected America's weakening monetary strength. From 1958 to 1966 U.S. gold reserves shrank 39 percent to $14.9 billion while those of the Common Market climbed 97 percent to $24.1 billion.[133] The outflow of dollars, a result of Americans' huge overseas purchases, weakened the U.S. currency.

Yet at the same time, the payments deficits served American interests by enabling the U.S. government and its citizens to buy—with paper dollars—supplies for the Vietnam War, factories in France and elsewhere, visits to the Louvre, and other tangible benefits. Other countries had to cut back when they overspent abroad, but the United States could continue to run deficits, thanks to the Bretton Woods monetary system established after World War II. Under this arrangement, Washington had promised to exchange gold for dollars at $35 per ounce. This made the dollar as good as gold (at least until Washington's gold reserves ran out), and many countries kept greenbacks as a reserve backing for their currency. The willingness of other nations to hold dollars allowed the United States to spend more than it earned. This system began to fall apart in the 1960s. Mounting American payments deficits and doubts about the dollar led foreigners to turn in greenbacks for gold, melting U.S. reserves of the precious metal. Washington began to wriggle out of its gold pledge by pressuring Allied governments to hold on to dollars rather than convert them into gold. Canada, Germany, and Japan agreed, but France refused.

De Gaulle intended not to destroy the dollar but to dethrone it. The proud general chafed at a system that bloated U.S. power and helped to finance the Vietnam War and the "expropriation" of French firms by Yankee investors. In February 1965 he urged the replacement of Bretton Woods with a gold standard. He criticized the existing arrangement for allowing the United States "to contract interest-free debts abroad." Americans could "pay—at least in part—with dollars which they can create at will and not with gold, which has a real value, whose possession one has to work for."[134] To pressure America to curb its deficits, he began cashing in dollars for gold, $600 million in the first six months of 1965 alone.[135] The general dramatized his defiance by not allowing the United States to move the newly purchased gold to the vaults of the Federal Reserve Bank of New York, which held the gold of other nations. Instead, he sent special Air France planes to pick up the precious cargo and fly it to Paris. France was trying to "undercut the dollar as a world currency," Bohlen fumed.[136] Recalling the James Bond movie *Goldfinger*, columnist Russell Baker joked about "de Gaullefinger." The quarrel over monetary matters continued as de Gaulle opposed American efforts to shore up the weak British pound and to create a new international borrowing facility for countries in deficit, the Special Drawing Right (SDR). Yet France lacked the economic clout to block the SDR system, which went into effect in 1970.

Similarly, France's economic weakness relative to the United States forced de Gaulle to abandon his campaign against massive American direct investment in French industries. In the early 1960s large U.S. corporations gobbled up companies throughout booming Western Europe, although fewer in France than in Great Britain or in West Germany. Yet in 1963–66 it was the independent-minded French who decided to limit such purchases. In mid-January 1963, as de Gaulle denounced both Great Britain's application to the Common Market and America's Nassau nuclear offer as schemes to curtail French power, the Chrysler Corporation angered the French leader with its sudden purchase of Simca, one of France's largest automobile makers. Other American behemoths, such as food processor Libby McNeill and electronics giant General Electric, bought up French companies or established branch plants. Many French felt like lilliputians as the press reported that France's entire electronics industry did 5.5 billion francs of annual business while General Electric had sales of 27 billion francs. While only number three among U.S. automakers, Chrysler had an output larger than the entire French automotive industry. Aside from bigness, there was the matter of French independence. "It is not possible for us to leave certain sectors of our economy . . . in the hands of companies whose head offices are in Chicago or Detroit," argued Hervé Alphand, the French ambassador.[137] In 1962 the French subsidiaries of General Motors and Remington-Rand suddenly laid off hundreds of workers

Beginning in 1962, Telstar satellite helped broadcast into French homes images of the United States. Shown here is France's 1886 gift to the United
States, now fully Americanized. *Courtesy of the National Archives*

without any provision for relocation, provoking widespread outcries of "brutal" behavior by unfeeling American giants. French executives gulped at stories of incoming American bosses purging old managerial staffs. The French business press reported that Libby's giant new cannery in the Languedoc region regimented farmers into producing "à l'américaine."[138] Tire manufacturers found shocking the deep discounts given by the subsidiaries of Goodyear and Firestone. Widely published accounts of aggressive behavior by American corporations built public support for de Gaulle's effort to limit such investments. Such reports probably also fed popular French resentment of all mammoth institutions of power and so helped prepare the ground for the rebellion of May 1968.

Meanwhile, French officials in 1963 sharply tightened existing regulations for approving foreign takeovers after having failed to interest other Common Market countries in controlling American capital. Annual direct U.S. investment in France fell off from $210 million in 1963 to $149 million in 1966, while such annual investment in West Germany rose from $304 million to $646 million.[139]

This drop meant a success for de Gaulle's policy, but it also posed a problem for French industry, which needed to modernize and stay competitive. Bypassing France, many American corporations bought or built factories in France's Common Market competitors. West Germany, Belgium, and Italy benefited from the increased jobs and enhanced technology often brought in with American investment—while France imported the products made by those U.S. subsidiaries. Although the French yearned for independence, they lacked the financial, industrial, and technological clout necessary for their firms to compete with the Americans. For example, when General Electric sought to buy a controlling share of Compagnie des Machines Bull, the most important French computer manufacturer, de Gaulle blocked the deal. A short while later, Bull was taken over by three other companies, which turned out to be half-owned by Americans. "The U.S. is producing a form of economic imperialism," complained Georges Pompidou, de Gaulle's prime minister. "Already the only [powerful] calculating machines . . . are made by IBM and General Electric. Now the French electronics industry is entirely in U.S. hands."[140] Worried that France was falling behind in the technological race, French business and political leaders urged elimination of the restrictive policy on investment. In early 1966 de Gaulle, ever the realistic nationalist (at least by his own standard), again held out the welcome sign to American companies, particularly those that would bring in new technology.

In 1967 the issue of American investment grew hotter with the publication of Jean-Jacques Servan-Schreiber's *The American Challenge*, which became France's best-selling book in the 1960s. A glamorous publisher and gadfly, Servan-Schreiber struck a sensitive chord by depicting how the huge American companies with highly advanced technology and managerial skills were taking over France. But he also prescribed a solution—Americanization. Rather than try to shut out the Americans, the French should try to copy their success by building their own giant, well-managed, research-oriented corporations.[141] The Communists and Socialists such as future president François Mitterrand criticized such unabashed capitalism. Yet the Communist party lost importance in the following decades, and many Socialists, particularly Mitterrand, came to embrace the solution of Servan-Schreiber. Meanwhile, many French firms did modernize, particularly by combining with other European companies.

By 1967–68 the problems of America's gold drain and the Vietnam War were building to a crisis that rocked domestic affairs in both France and the United States as well as the relations between the two countries. The two issues intertwined in various ways, aside from the drain of dollars the United States spent overseas to wage the war. Saigon's black-market merchants generally banked their huge dollar profits in France. France cashed in the dollars for gold.[142] Worried about the gold loss and resenting Europe's refusal to help out in Vietnam and de Gaulle's slaps, many in Congress supported the Mansfield Amendment to reduce the number of U.S. troops in Europe. That measure would undercut U.S. leverage in Europe and with the Soviets. With its back to the wall, the Johnson administration pressured Europe to contribute more for NATO and third-world aid. European leaders resented the pressure and felt under duress from their own people to distance themselves from Washington's Asian obsession.

A May 1967 National Security Council meeting on Europe revealed how sour transatlantic relations had become:

> Treasury Secretary Fowler: France is trying either to expel us completely from Europe or at least to diminish our power there. . . . The French effort in Europe affects our ability to be effective in other parts of the world.
> Vice President Humphrey: Europeans . . . resent U.S. power. Détente is what they want. Their young people are causing many problems. . . . The Europeans are selfish.
> USIA Director [L.H.] Marks: USIA has a serious problem communicating with Europe. The European press is hostile, especially the Agence France press.
> U.N. Ambassador [Arthur] Goldberg: The Europeans are causing problems for us in the United Nations. We no longer have a solid bloc of western allies behind us. The view of the European delegations . . . is that the U.S. is neglecting Europe for Asia. They complain of only being informed rather than consulted.

Perhaps the most telling comment came from the president himself. After listening to this litany of problems, Johnson framed the "solution" as getting the Europeans "to make a larger contribution to the cost of NATO defense."[143]

In a followup memorandum to the president, Fowler addressed a major quandary of American policy. Since World War II Washington had encouraged

Western European integration, expecting that a united continent would assist the United States. While working to strengthen the allies, some American officials had also worried that a more powerful Western Europe might pose problems as well. Now Western Europe offered American producers stiff competition. Partly owing to de Gaulle's insidious influence, the continent balked at helping the United States finance its payments deficit and fight the war in Vietnam. Shifting emphasis from traditional U.S. policy, the treasury secretary doubted that it was in America's interest to strengthen "the Common Market, either by widening its membership or by seeking to improve its technology." "While the Europeans may be interested in closing the 'technology gap,'" Fowler argued, "this could adversely affect the United States by reducing our receipts . . . and adding to . . . [the] gold drain."[144] As Fowler feared, the gold outflow did accelerate, especially after February 1968, when Washington released the figures on the huge 1967 payments deficit.

By March 1968 the gold losses had undermined the Bretton Woods system and Johnson's hopes for victory—in both South Vietnam and in the November presidential election. Johnson collapsed under the combined weight of the spectacular January Tet offensive against American forces, the speculation against the dollar, rising antiwar protest, humiliation in the New Hampshire Democratic primary, and advice from top political and business leaders that the country no longer could afford the economic and social costs of the war. He dropped out of the presidential race, pushed for higher taxes, put a ceiling on U.S. troop levels in Vietnam, and sought negotiations to end the conflict. Johnson promised that the United States would continue to sell gold to foreign governments, but he announced that it would no longer do so to private individuals. However, since Washington had already won a pledge from other major governments—with the exception of France—not to buy any more American gold, the promise remained an empty one. In effect, the United States backed away from the Bretton Woods system because it could no longer afford to abide by the rules, which it had written in 1944.

Like Johnson, de Gaulle could play in the world arena only so long as he enjoyed political backing and financial stability at home. In the spring of 1968 both leaders found their homefronts under siege by street rebels, currency speculators, and ordinary citizens. The squeeze in France and America reflected a shared crisis. Despite the frigidity between official Paris and Washington, North America and Western Europe were becoming an economic, cultural, and intellectual community.

On both continents the Vietnam War ignited explosive emotions, radicalizing students and some workers. Young Europeans fixated on the war with fascinated horror. They had grown up with images of America as the paragon democracy, the model for new fads and factories, the liberator from the Nazis, the defender from the Red Army—in short, as the engine of Western liberal capitalism. Now they saw television images of well-built, heavily armed G.I.'s destroying villages of helpless Asian peasants. Many Europeans, particularly the young, felt prodded to question the made-in-America Western alliance and the very legitimacy of their postwar societies, which also bore the imprint of American hegemony.

Two of the world's most respected moral philosophers, Jean-Paul Sartre of France and Bertrand Russell of Great Britain, challenged America's claim to moral righteousness by organizing the International War Crimes Tribunal. Composed of citizens from non-Communist countries and from Cuba, the tribunal convened in May 1967 in Stockholm to judge America's war in Vietnam. The Johnson administration refused an invitation to submit its own witnesses and evidence. Before a global television audience Sartre compared the Americans to the Nazis who "killed the Jews because they were Jews. The armed forces of the United States torture and kill men, women and children in Vietnam *because they are Vietnamese.*"[145] As Sartre's vehemence suggested, public revulsion against the war was escalating in pace with the killing in Southeast Asia. Perhaps sensing that such emotions could get out of hand in France or interfere with his diplomacy, de Gaulle, who had been one of the first to oppose America's conflict in Vietnam, had refused to allow the planned war crimes tribunal to meet in Paris.

In March 1968, when the French government tried to clamp down on antiwar protest, it set off the biggest explosion of student and worker rebellion since the Paris Commune of 1871. In response to the government's arrest of protesters who had attacked the American Express office in Paris, students at the Nanterre campus of the University of Paris seized the administration building and launched the "March 22 Movement." Although opposition to the Vietnam War had sparked the action, students at Nanterre and at other French universities had many other grievances: crammed lecture halls, remote professors, an antiquated curriculum, and prohibitions keeping men from visiting women students in their dormitory rooms. Partly because of the overcrowding, the universities regularly failed one-third to one-half of all students before graduation. In his pursuit of grandeur, de Gaulle had lavished resources on France's nuclear force, foreign policy, and economic growth while shortchanging the universities. Growing tensions between students and Paris university officials exploded on 3 May 1968 when the administrators appealed to the minister of the interior, who called in riot squad police. Students confronted the police, the administration closed the school, and the students then occupied the Sorbonne, heart of the 700-year-old university. For the next four weeks the Left Bank of Paris became a battleground, with mass marches and police assaults, young rebels barricading the streets, and angry police rampaging through student apartments beating and teargassing indiscriminately. The uprising was largely uncoordinated and in some respects contradictory. Some students protested that the university had prostituted itself by becoming a training school for giant corporations; others objected that the antiquated curriculum did not prepare them for good jobs.

Despite the contradictions, the revolt would have a long-term impact on French thought and life, in part because radical student leaders such as Daniel Cohn-Bendit succeeded in linking petty grievances over antiwar protest and dormitory regulations with such larger issues as the hidden authoritarianism in democratic society and the alienating coldness of modern life. Sartre assured the occupying students that the Vietnam War had enlarged the "field of possibilities" for militants in Europe and America.[146] In the supercharged atmosphere of waiting for a police beating or debating how to structure society afresh, young thinkers tried to break free of traditional strictures. Wall posters proclaimed "Everything Is Possible," "Take Your Desires for Realities," and "It Is Forbidden to Forbid."[147]

Some ironies developed out of this heady sense of unlimited prospect. Many French protesters grew attracted to trends in America's youth rebellion, just as in the 1970s and 1980s—after the 1960s' antimaterialism had worn off—many French would become entranced by the cornucopia of America's consumerist society (see chapter 6). French dissenters borrowed from America techniques (sit-ins, teach-ins), issues, rock music, slogans ("Burn, baby, burn!"), and blue jeans. American antiwar leader Tom Hayden met with student protesters in Europe and returned home believing that an informal international of radical students had arisen. Touring France, the U.S.-based Bread and Puppet Theater impressed French leftists with the power of street theater. Disillusioned with the Communist party, some French radicals found an appealing alternative in the American New Left, with its decentralized organization and its fresh agenda of racial, feminist, gay, and environmental issues. "In Amerikka, our brothers and sisters are on the front line," argued *L'Idiot international,* not only in opposing the Vietnam War but also in "changing their lives, in transforming their relationships with people, in getting rid of the cop in their psyche."[148]

The conflicting theories of American sociologists were sometimes the battle ground on which French university authorities and students waged their heated debate. Shortly before the 22 March occupation at Nanterre, sociology students boycotted their examinations, explaining that their subject matter was an "import from across the Atlantic," designed for manipulating people so that they would fit into a repressive, technocratic society.[149] Other French dissidents criticized the dehumanized managerial practices brought in by U.S. companies or by French firms trying to copy Yankee success. Meanwhile, social theorist Herbert Marcuse, a refugee from Nazi Europe who had stayed in America after the war, inspired much of the new criticism of modern, technocratic society. Of course, such French thinkers as Claude Lévi-Strauss, Michel Foucault, and Jacques Lacan became enormously important contributors to the new ideas and ideologies swirling about in 1968 (see chapter 6).

A final irony of the 1968 revolt was that the French Communist party and Marxist ideology came out heavy losers in the competition for the hearts and minds of French youth. The PCF proclaimed itself the vanguard of Communist revolution, but the uprising revealed its advanced ossification. At first, the Communists denounced the student rebels as "pseudo-revolutionaries . . . [with] the impertinence to think that they can give lessons to the working class."[150] Reversing course, the Communists on 8 May tried to take control of the Sorbonne occupation, only to be met by students ridiculing them as "Stalinist creeps."[151] The PCF tried to keep such brash militants away from factory workers, fearing that the students' New Left ideas of direct action and decentralized worker control would undermine the party's grip on blue-collar labor.

Yet neither the PCF nor de Gaulle's government could prevent the revolt from spreading to French workers, burdened with a 48-hour week and some of the highest taxes and lowest wages in Western Europe. Beginning on 14 May more than 9 million French workers walked off their jobs or sat in at their workplaces without any person or organization calling for a general strike. Not only auto, ship, and chemical workers but also white-collar postal employees, air traffic controllers, and teachers refused to work. Steamers on the English Channel stopped running. Civil servants at the Ministry of Finance and other government agencies picketed outside their offices. Employees at the state-run television network demanded better wages and, more importantly, an end to heavy government censorship of programming. The strikes involved more than money issues. After a decade of the general's paternalism, many French had grown restive living in a society that remained sharply hierarchical and authoritarian, even as it became more technocratic. On 27 May, after long negotiations with employers and union officials, Prime Minister Georges Pompidou announced a program of wage hikes and reduction of the workweek. Beaming union bosses, including the head of the Communist CGT, proudly brought these concessions back to members for approval, only to meet instead catcalls and boos from workers who wanted some control on the job as well as money.

By late May the French economy ground to a halt. The CIA estimated that the strikes cost France about $800 million per week in lost production. Gold stocks melted away as the wealthy took their money out of the country. Traffic built up on the roads leading to Switzerland, where some French had secret bank accounts. The American Express office in Paris converted its open-top sightseeing buses to evacuation vehicles to transport stranded tourists to Belgium or Italy.

On 29–30 May de Gaulle, who had tried to ignore the May crisis by proceeding with a trip to Romania in the middle of it, reasserted his control. He paid a secret visit to French military authorities to make sure that the army would be with him in case of civil war. Then de Gaulle televised to the nation a dramatic address, which blamed the revolt on communism, appealed to French patriotism, repeated the 27 May wage offer, dissolved the National Assembly, called for new elections, and threatened a crackdown if the rebellion did not cease. The general gave a powerful push, and the pendulum of

French opinion began swinging back toward order. Almost immediately a huge demonstration of de Gaulle supporters surged up the fashionable Champs-Elysées. Well-dressed people shouted "France back to work! Clean out the Sorbonne! We are the majority!"[152] The many who had grown tired of the strikes, barricades, and uncollected garbage rallied behind the government as it crushed, often brutally, the remaining strikes. In the short election campaign for the new parliament, both the Gaullists and the PCF posed as the champions of patriotism, order, and social stability. Not surprisingly, the Gaullists won that competition. The Gaullists racked up a resounding victory while leftist parties, including the PCF, suffered defeats.

Despite the dramatic turnaround, France and the de Gaulle government could not afford a simple return to the period before May 1968. The French economy had suffered a severe loss in output, gold reserves had fallen, and the government had committed employers to paying higher wages. The universities and the social network obviously needed more resources. Though still a powerful leader, de Gaulle no longer had the money or the mandate for a policy based on grandeur.

Since 1958 the general had pursued a grand foreign policy in part because he believed that overseas glory would divert the French people from their fatally divisive tendencies. For most of his presidency de Gaulle was supported by the wide spectrum of citizens who appreciated his domestic and foreign successes. With adroit maneuvering, he let Algeria go free while heading off insurrection by disappointed colonists and military officers. He replaced the political turmoil of the Fourth Republic with the stability of the president-dominated Fifth Republic. Most French applauded de Gaulle's drive for independence from the United States and his high-profile effort to reestablish France as a world power, negotiate with the Soviets and Chinese, and claim a voice in Southeast Asia, Latin America, Québec, and elsewhere.

But by May 1968 the allure of foreign glory had faded, particularly because it had become apparent that de Gaulle's dazzling style could not disguise France's place as a middle-rank power. Despite its fading predominance, the United States still outclassed France when it came to holding West Germany's loyalty or to striking up new ties with the Soviet Union. A French defense truly independent from the United States proved horrendously expensive and technologically difficult. Emphasizing international prestige, de Gaulle had piled up huge gold reserves while starving the domestic economy with low wages and neglect of social services. A few months after May 1968 the Soviet invasion of Czechoslovakia and a run on the franc further restricted French foreign policy options. Although de Gaulle's ambitions were stymied in 1968, his vision of an end to the cold war and the achievement of Western European unity would come true two decades later—although not with the glory for France for which he had hoped.

Both de Gaulle and Johnson had launched ambitious overseas projects—the general's quest for French grandeur, the Texan's aim for a Great Society in Vietnam. Each had been confident that his nation would accept the cost of these aspirations, and that foreign success would reinforce his political strength and his nation's unity. Both these master politicians fatally overestimated their power abroad and the patience at home. The crises of 1968 wrecked the grandiose plans of de Gaulle and Johnson, and so prepared the way for their less audacious successors to warm up U.S.-French relations.

Chapter 5

THE SLOW THAW, 1969–1980

On 22 June 1973 President Richard M. Nixon signed with Soviet leader Leonid Brezhnev an agreement to improve consultation between Washington and Moscow to reduce the risk of nuclear war. The French feared that such superpower deals shunted Western Europe to the margins of international diplomacy. Shortly after Brezhnev left the Western White House at San Clemente, California, French foreign minister Michel Jobert arrived for two days of talks. When Jobert complained about the superpower duopoly, National Security Adviser Henry A. Kissinger startled the French official by offering help with another thorny problem—how to stabilize the spin of the submarine-launched nuclear missiles France was developing. Jobert eagerly accepted the overture, adding that France would also welcome American technical assistance in other nuclear problems. Kissinger answered that he and Nixon wanted to initiate a covert program to provide that information to France.

In September 1973 French president Georges Pompidou sent Minister of Defense Robert Galley to Washington to work out the details of the program with U.S. Department of Defense officials. Yet Galley returned to France bitterly disappointed because American officers at the Pentagon denied knowing anything about Kissinger's offer and refused to help. Kissinger had not lied to Jobert about the nuclear assistance. "We want to get better relations [with the French]," Kissinger told a senior Nixon administration official, "and this is one way to do it."[1] But the secrecy of the illegal endeavor made it complicated to establish and coordinate. The information finally began flowing to France soon after Galley's abortive Pentagon visit. The covert program con-

160

tinued through the 1980s, escaping detection in 1974 when the revelation of the Nixon administration's other secret, illegal activities forced President Nixon to resign. In return for the nuclear help, the French secretly agreed to plans that would facilitate wartime coordination between the *force de frappe* and NATO's military command. In the Ottawa NATO communiqué of June 1974, the United States publicly acknowledged that the French nuclear force had an important role in the West's deterrent.

As this episode suggests, the relations of France and the United States from 1968 to 1980 had emerged from the deep freeze, yet the attempts of the two nations to work together were limited and sometimes misfired. After mid-1968 France traded some of the independence that de Gaulle had wrested from the United States for a measure of cooperation from Washington, cooperation that helped Paris maintain its global status. Many developments contributed to the Nixon administration's acceptance of the *force de frappe*. France's explosion of its first hydrogen bomb in 1968 underscored the fact that the United States had not been able to starve out the *force de frappe* by withholding technical aid. The danger of West Germany's copying France and developing its own nuclear force seemed less threatening in the 1970s, particularly with Bonn busily building ties with Eastern Europe. Washington had, moreover, cut back its ambition, enunciated by Defense Secretary Robert S. McNamara in 1962, to monopolize the West's deterrent.

In neither military nor economic might could the United States command the preeminence in the 1970s that it had wielded in the first postwar decades. Worsening economic problems made the United States more interested in protecting its own narrow interests and less concerned (and less able) to shape developments in Western Europe. That generation of U.S. officials who had forged the Marshall Plan and who had passionately tried to implement the European Defense Community and the Grand Design had largely passed from the scene by the 1970s. Of course, the United States still remained the preeminent Atlantic power, and it still dominated France and the other Western European nations, especially when they were unable to unite on an issue. But as the United States distanced itself a little from Europe, Paris found it somewhat easier to move closer to Washington while maintaining a measure of French independence. In the postcolonial, post–Vietnam War era, the French and Americans sometimes intervened together to uphold their interests in the third world.

The thaw in U.S.-French relations began at the end of two imperial presidencies, during which those relations had frozen solid. In the spring of 1968 domestic turmoil forced Charles de Gaulle to curtail visions of grandeur and Lyndon B. Johnson to begin negotiations with North Vietnam. By that time, France had exited from NATO, the United States was moving toward détente with the Soviet Union, and de Gaulle consequently found "no reason for major differences" with Washington.[2] The French leader's sharp disappointment in Czechoslovakia added another reason for rapprochement with the Americans. De Gaulle had tried to reduce American influence in Western Europe in the hope that the Soviet Union would loosen its grip on Eastern Europe. But in August 1968 the Soviets smashed his dream of "Europe from the Atlantic to the Urals" by invading Czechoslovakia and destroying the reformist Prague Spring. Frustrated, de Gaulle blamed the 1945 deal at Yalta, which had allegedly given Eastern Europe to the Soviets. The French further diluted Moscow's guilt by faulting West German "provocation," meaning Bonn's new links with the Soviet satellites.[3] The invasion amounted to only "an accident along the route" to a reunited Europe, French officials staunchly maintained.[4] But the debris blocked de Gaulle's progress, at least for a few years—which was all the 78-year-old leader could hope to have.

Meanwhile, economic trouble and renewed fear of Germany added pressure for de Gaulle to improve relations with the United States. After May 1968 the general tried to buy off domestic discontent with generous, but inflationary, wage increases. That, along with the effect of capital flight and lost output during the upheaval, led to an attack on the franc. Speculators sold massive amounts of the French currency for stronger currencies, particularly the German mark. They expected that the French government would have to devalue the franc—that is, reduce its value in terms of other currencies and gold. Then the speculators could buy back francs at the cheaper rate, reaping a handsome profit. For reasons of prestige, de Gaulle resisted devaluation. Fearing that a successful assault on the franc would encourage speculators to attack the dollar and other weak currencies, the U.S. Federal Reserve and European central banks gave credit infusions to the ailing French.

A more lasting solution than the credits, and for the French an answer more palatable than a franc devaluation, would have been West Germany's revaluing of the mark—that is, raising its value in terms of other currencies and gold. More efficient than America, France, and other competitors, West Germany was ringing up huge trade surpluses. This trend put upward pressure on the German currency, a force intensified by the wholesale purchase of marks by speculators hoping to profit from revaluation. At central bank meetings in November 1968 the French, Americans, and British—West Germany's former occupiers—urged the heretofore compliant Bonn government to revalue the mark. Such a move would buy off the speculators, who could then walk away with their profits. Revaluation would also give Germany's competitors a break by making goods valued in marks more expensive. Unwilling to suffer the economic and political costs of revaluation, the German government refused, the first time since the war that it so blatantly defied the former victor powers. An economic giant, Bonn had grown tired of being a political lilliputian.

"Bonn has become giddy with power," Foreign Minister Michel Debré grumbled.[5] "Now that Germany reemerges," the Soviet Union became more important to France, de Gaulle observed.[6] Yet with Bonn piloting its own

Ostpolitik, Paris had little to offer Moscow. Closer by lay Great Britain, which for centuries had thrown its weight against those of its continental neighbors it considered too powerful—a tack Washington had endorsed. A top State Department official suggested to the French that "to us the natural and prudent way to organize Europe was on the foundation of the Entente Cordiale"—a reference to the Anglo-French alliance directed against Germany before World War I.[7] De Gaulle did edge closer to the British, and his protégé and successor Georges Pompidou removed the French veto on British admission to the Common Market (also known as the European Economic Community [EEC]). This shift pleased American policy makers, at least when they thought in terms of the traditional goals of anchoring West Germany and of creating a strong Europe. Yet many Nixon administration officials, particularly those in the Treasury, Agriculture, and Commerce departments, saw Great Britain's admission as adding to the EEC's threat to American trade interests.[8]

Taking office with no grand design for Europe, President Nixon and his national security adviser, Henry Kissinger, did not press France to fit back into NATO or join any other American-dominated structure. Relations between Paris and Washington improved because "American leadership has at last recognized that friendship doesn't necessarily mean alignment," Debré asserted soon after Nixon took office.[9] Nixon's and Kissinger's admiration for de Gaulle also warmed U.S.-French relations. Soon after his January 1969 inauguration, Nixon broke the five-year impasse over who owed a visit to whom by going to Europe and calling on the French president. "The high point of this trip personally and substantively was my series of meetings with de Gaulle," Nixon recalled.[10] Nixon idolized the confident, charismatic general. During his Paris visit the American president effusively praised the seasoned French leader. The imperious de Gaulle responded with kind words and even attended a dinner at the American Embassy.

Nixon and de Gaulle agreed on the need to negotiate with the People's Republic of China and to pursue détente with the Soviets. Yet Washington should avoid any "Yalta idea," that is, a renewed deal to divide Europe, the general cautioned.[11] De Gaulle proposed coordination of the two nations' foreign policies, an idea the American president promptly endorsed and quickly forgot. Nixon understood that American policy would remain crippled until he settled the Vietnam War. France could help, because Paris maintained diplomatic relations with Hanoi and Beijing, and the French capital "would be the best place to open secret channels of communication between us and them," Nixon calculated.[12]

Even the cynical Kissinger felt awe at "the Colossus of de Gaulle"—who towered a foot above the academic-turned-diplomat. When the general outlined his view of a Europe independent of the superpowers, the national security adviser asked how France could keep Germany from dominating such a Europe. "Through war," de Gaulle answered simply.[13] While Kissinger and

Nixon pondered that startling option, the general promised to visit the United States in early 1970.

Nixon returned to Washington aglow over de Gaulle, calling him "the giant" of Europe's leaders. The new president even declared that the world would be "a much healthier place . . . if there were a strong European community to be a balance . . . between the United States and the Soviet Union."[14] Here Nixon endorsed a Gaullist vision American policymakers had usually regarded as a nightmare: America would lie stripped of its European support, and united Europe would stand as a third force between the superpowers. The president soon cooled this hyperbole. A few months later, after the glow had worn off, Nixon explained why he was putting the Continent on the back burner. There was no chance of Europe's unifying, "and we all know that. Of course, I'll go on making the proper noises—but it isn't going to happen."[15] Meanwhile, de Gaulle resigned in April 1969 after losing a national referendum on a domestic issue. With his political and physical powers failing (his death would come in November 1970), the general had determined to retire with his faculties and pride intact.

His successor, the portly Georges Pompidou, had risen from the peasantry of the hardy Auvergne region to become director general of the Rothschild Bank, then premier under de Gaulle, and now president. An intelligent man with eclectic interests, he enjoyed the company of Parisian novelists and artists. During the uprising of May 1968 Premier Pompidou had suggested that de Gaulle resign; after the crisis the general made his premier a scapegoat and fired him. Afterward, when foreign leaders mentioned de Gaulle's name, Pompidou would stare back with daggers in his eyes. Yet his political views remained essentially Gaullist. Within the more modest parameters dictated by the events of 1968, the new French president carried forward de Gaulle's policies, including the improvement in relations with the United States.

Carrying out de Gaulle's pledge, President Pompidou visited the United States. The February 1970 trip offered a snapshot of U.S.-French relations in the early Nixon years. Nixon and Kissinger continued to woo the French with warm personal gestures. The ever-insecure president liked Pompidou, relieved to find him not a "sophisticated . . . Parisian" but a man from the French "heartland."[16] On the Common Market issue, Pompidou found the Americans both "pleased" that a uniting Europe might assume more "burdens and responsibilities" and "disturbed" at the prospect of more serious competition.[17] Nixon assured his guest that he accepted French independence, and the two leaders agreed on the need for moving cautiously on détente with the Soviets. Pompidou made no objection to Nixon's policy of gradually pulling U.S. troops out of Vietnam and turning over the war to the South Vietnamese. While avoiding the sensitive subject of NATO integration, Nixon reminded Pompidou of the Atlantic alliance's original purpose—to contain both the Soviet Union and Germany. "Many people

'Now, Georges—what's first on the agenda?'

Georges Pompidou's 1970 visit to the United States, the first by a French president in a decade, marked the thawing of U.S.-French relations. Yet he and President Richard Nixon disagreed over the Israeli-Palestinian question, an issue that sparked vehement anti-Pompidou demonstrations by American street protesters. *Courtesy of* Washington Post thought Russia was now less threatening—although we weren't sure of this," Nixon ruminated. But "in any case it was obvious we still had to have an arrangement . . . into which Germany could be fitted."[18] The French president agreed with Nixon. Like de Gaulle in his last months in office, Pompidou tried to balance aspirations for French independence with the need to keep the Americans in Europe to help control West Germany.

Despite the broad accord and effort at creating a friendly public atmosphere, the Pompidou visit became stormy. The French had recently agreed to sell 108 Mirage jet fighters to Libya and remained a weapons supplier to Algeria and Iraq, all enemies of Israel. Still objecting to Israel's 1967 seizure of Arab territory, moreover, France maintained its embargo on arms sales to Israel, America's ally. The United States flatly opposed the sale to Libya. Pompidou thought the Soviets could help stabilize the Middle East, and he wanted to mediate Washington's and Moscow's rivalry in the area. Nixon and Kissinger vetoed both ideas. Yet this U.S.-French disagreement was neither new nor pressing. In public announcements, both Nixon and Pompidou tried to smooth over their variance on the Middle East.

Still, those differences blew up in Pompidou's face. As the explosion demonstrated the Vietnam War and other turmoil had undermined the American president's imperial authority to shape foreign relations on his own. Even before Pompidou left for America, Michel Jobert, not yet French foreign minister, had fretted over the threatening letters France had received from the United States. Enraged at the sale of jets to Libya and the embargo on Israel, American Jewish groups protested vehemently at every stop of Pompidou's tour.[19] Many representatives and senators boycotted the French leader's speech before Congress. Congressional aides and pages filled some of the empty seats to minimize Pompidou's embarrassment. Loath to alienate Jewish voters and perhaps genuinely upset by French policy, Governor Nelson Rockefeller and Mayor John Lindsay refused to attend the New York City dinner planned for Pompidou. Chicago mayor Richard Daley begged off with the excuse that he had promised Mrs. Daley to eat with the family the night scheduled for the Pompidou affair in his city. In San Francisco, however, Pompidou found sympathy from Governor Ronald Reagan, who came directly from Santa Barbara, where he had called out the National Guard to combat student demonstrations. His nerves rubbed raw by these fresh reminders of the May 1968 ordeal, Pompidou condemned youthful rebellion, which "only leads to nothingness . . . suicide or senseless murder or even drug-induced dreams."[20]

The protest in Chicago seemed to confirm Pompidou's fears. After intense pressure from the White House, Daley agreed to break his family dinner date and attend the banquet for the French leader. A large crowd of demonstrators shouted at the French guests as they arrived at the dinner hall. In sharp contrast to the hostility between demonstrators and Chicago police during the 1968 Democratic convention only 18 months before, the police now appeared "relaxed and friendly" toward the protesters, a reporter observed. Indeed, the police did not even clear a path in front of the banquet hall doorway, and the first members of Pompidou's party had to walk among the jeering protesters. "The French people were able to see on television their President and his wife getting out of the car in the midst of a screaming crowd, while the police looked on," recalled Jobert.[21] Some demonstrators actually spat on Pompidou and his wife. The Chicago police "not only permitted but . . . led [the] demonstrators," an outraged Pompidou charged. This amounted to "a stain on the forehead of America."[22] Unruffled, Daley found no fault with his police and added that "compliments are due to those who turned out to demonstrate and for the orderly manner in which they exercised their rights as American citizens."[23] From New York, concerned Jews such as former Supreme Court justice Arthur Goldberg warned the State Department that extremists might subject Pompidou to violence if he went on to New York City, the last stop of the tour. Pompidou decided to cancel the rest of his trip and return immediately to France.

At this point Nixon, who knew what it was like to face hecklers, called the shaken French leader, apologized for the insults, urged him to continue the visit, and promised to change his own schedule in order to attend the dinner in New York City. Pompidou relented. Toasting the French president at the banquet, Nixon jested that he had wanted Pompidou to see the country just the way an American president saw it, but things had been overdone. Pompidou joined in the hearty laughter. "Feathers Smoothed, Pompi Wings Home," read a headline in The New York Daily News, but from a longer perspective Kissinger later observed that "the incident reinforced Pompidou's inherent ambivalence toward the United States."[24] The French leader had subsequent meetings with American officials, but he refused to set foot on U.S. soil again.

Nixon's graciousness helped compensate for the protests which Pompidou had suffered. Yet the president himself soon began bashing foreigners. While the anti-Pompidou demonstrators objected to French policy in the Middle East, Nixon faulted other nations for America's economic troubles. Nixon's problems stemmed in part from the Vietnam War. Though no longer a festering problem in Paris-Washington relations, the conflict continued to poison America's society and economy. The protests mounted and the dollar staggered. The New York Times defied the Nixon administration by publishing the Pentagon Papers, the Defense Department's secret history of the war. The Democrats would offer a tough challenge to the president in the 1972 election, polls suggested. Nixon interpreted these problems to mean that "the United States is now reaching that period of . . . decadence" which had destroyed ancient Greece and Rome. To head off such a calamity, the nation had to revive its spirit and its economy, Nixon told a meeting of news media executives in July 1971. "Moral . . . health . . . will only come as people are reassured" by a more upbeat reporting of events, the hard-pressed president appealed to the news chiefs.[25] Meanwhile, Nixon reached out for the votes of jingoist patriots. He fanned their resentment of antiwar protesters and of jobs lost to foreign competition.

Despite Nixon's politicking, he faced a real crisis—the United States could no longer easily afford its self-appointed role as world policeman. "Economic power" remained "the key to other kinds of power," Nixon understood. Since World War II America's strength, prosperity, and way of life had flourished in large part because the United States had been able to dominate global markets. Much of the reason the United States had spent astronomic amounts of money on troops, weapons, and foreign aid was the intention of maintaining a global environment friendly to American business. Yet this military spending had overburdened the American economy and had aggravated a deterioration in the nation's ability to compete in world markets. "We face a situation," Nixon declared, where foreigners "have the capacity . . . [to] challenge us on every front."[26]

In August 1971 that challenge became immediate as the dollar tottered. The outflow of dollars had pushed the American balance-of-payments deficit to a record $9.8 billion in 1970, and it continued climbing in 1971. Even though the United States had stopped selling gold on the private market in 1968, gold reserves melted to $10 billion, the lowest level since 1936. In March 1971 France bought $282 million of the remaining gold to repay its borrowing from the International Monetary Fund (IMF). U.S. trade figures for April showed imports surging ahead of exports, producing the first American trade deficit since 1894. This commercial imbalance aggravated the payments deficits and gold losses. Nervous yet profit-seeking speculators increased the pressure by selling dollars for stronger currencies such as the mark, franc, and yen. In May the West Germans gave in to the speculators' pressure and raised the value of the mark. This made other currencies (including the dollar) and foreign goods (including American products) cheaper for Germans to buy. American authorities welcomed the German move, hoping it would boost U.S. exports.

The French were less accommodating to the speculators and to the American government. In July speculators shifted their focus to the franc. They sold dollars for francs, betting on revaluation of the franc. Unwilling to give up the trade advantage offered by the rise of the mark, French officials refused to allow the franc to follow the German currency upward. In early August France increased market jitters by purchasing another $191 million of America's dwindling gold. France was not assaulting American reserves—if Paris had wanted to do that, it had the dollars to buy billions worth of the precious metal. Still, of all the gold sold to foreigners in the first nine months of 1971, the French took half.[27]

Irritated by the dollars flooding into his country, French finance minister Valéry Giscard d'Estaing threw down a challenge. He argued that the United States should stop pressuring other nations to hold unwanted greenbacks.

Instead America should cut back its overseas spending and end its deficits—or else finance them by borrowing from the International Monetary Fund, as other nations had to do. After World War II the United States had led in establishing the IMF and the rest of the Bretton Woods system to stabilize international monetary relations and to discipline slacker deficit nations. Giscard wanted the spendthrift United States to tighten its belt. As de Gaulle had, he chafed at the idea of France's bearing the burden of America's imperial profligacy. In sum, France would neither revalue the franc nor stop buying gold, it complained about holding dollars, and it urged the Yankees to curb their appetite to fit their pocketbook, as other nations had to do. The final blow to the greenback came in mid-August, when the British government asked for a guarantee in gold for all $3 billion of its official dollar holdings.

Nixon called a top-secret meeting at Camp David to meet the crisis. Although the decisions reached would vitally affect U.S. foreign policy, he invited neither Kissinger nor any State Department official. Instead the president relied on Treasury Secretary John Connally, the wheeler-dealer rancher, banker, lawyer, and oil man; former Democratic governor of Texas wounded in the Kennedy assassination; veteran politician who, most observers including Nixon agreed, looked like a president. "The Boss is in love," old Nixon hands had concluded after Connally's appointment in December 1970.[28] Tormented by insecurity himself, Nixon became fascinated with Connally's swaggering self-assurance and readiness to reach for the jugular. "Only three men in America understand the use of power," Nixon asserted. "I do. John Connally does."[29] (New York governor Nelson Rockefeller ranked third.) "My philosophy," Connally explained, "is that all foreigners are out to screw us, and it's our job to screw them first."[30]

At Camp David, Connally urged Nixon to get tough with the foreigners. "We are meeting here because we are in trouble overseas," the treasury secretary emphasized. "Anybody can topple us—anytime they want—we have left ourselves completely exposed." He urged that the United States slam shut the gold window—that is, simply refuse to sell foreign central banks any more gold and stop defending the dollar's value at the fixed exchange rates of Bretton Woods. This presented other nations with a dilemma: they could either hold on to their billions of paper dollars, thereby enabling the United States to continue running its payments deficits, or they could sell those dollars on the free market, where the huge supply of unwanted dollars would guarantee a fall in the value of the dollar in relation to other currencies, effectively revaluing the franc, mark, yen, and others. This would make American products cheaper and render the products of France and other nations less competitive. Federal Reserve chairman Arthur Burns pointed out that this unilateral rewriting of the economic rules would cost the "good will" of other nations. "We'll go broke getting their good will," Connally shot back.[31]

Nixon accepted Connally's recommendation to gut the Bretton Woods system. In the monetary realm, this meant the end of the post–World War II era. In effect, Bretton Woods had operated like a monetary railroad link that enabled businesspeople to range for markets and supplies throughout the non-Communist world. The American engine pulled the global economy along by linking gold to the dollar at $35 per ounce and by tying other currencies to the dollar at fixed exchange rates. After the late 1950s the Europeans and Japanese also moved out on that rail line. They often traveled faster and more efficiently than the Americans, who were dragged down by outmoded equipment and heavy military expenditures. By 1971 the U.S. locomotive no longer had the strength to honor the gold/dollar pledge. At Connally's urging, the United States uncoupled gold and the dollar and broke the close ties between the dollar and other currencies created by fixed exchange rates. The United States engine remained on the same rail line with its trade partners—that is, one could still exchange dollars for francs, marks, or yen at fluctuating exchange rates—but the engine was no longer directly attached to the other cars. The world economy lost stability as the United States regained much of its freedom of action. Unencumbered by its Bretton Woods responsibilities, the American engine remained the biggest and most powerful car on the rail line. In a collision with the locomotive, the smaller cars would suffer more.

When Nixon announced his New Economic Policy (NEP) on 15 August 1971, he pitched it as a defense of the American "workingman" and "investor" against "international money speculators" who "have been waging an all-out war on the American dollar." He made no mention of the dollar's chronic weakness, America's deficits, or the solemn U.S. pledge to the Bretton Woods system. Instead he returned to the theme of malaise. His NEP would "help us snap out of the self-doubt, the self-disparagement that saps our energy and erodes our confidence in ourselves."[32] Specifically, the NEP (ironically Nixon's wordsmiths had recycled Lenin's label for his partial retreat to capitalism in 1921) provided for a 90-day freeze on wages and prices, an investment tax credit for U.S.-made capital goods, and an end to the excise tax on automobiles. To deal with the foreign troubles, Nixon slapped an emergency 10 percent tax on the value of all imports, and he refused to sell any more gold to foreign central banks. Nixon allowed the dollar to float on the international exchange markets, knowing it would decline in value and make American products more competitive in world markets.

Nixon's NEP amounted to a declaration of economic war on the other industrial democracies, Kissinger admitted later. Connally grinned, "We had a problem and we're sharing it with the world—just like we shared our prosperity. That's what friends are for."[33] He and Nixon relished shocking the foreigners and wielding America's new clout as the rogue giant. They demanded that Europe and Japan allow their currencies to float upward—which would hurt their exports while boosting America's—before Washington would even consider ending the import surcharge. Nixon and Connally also refused to devalue the dollar in terms of gold. In other words, they wanted to keep the $35-per-ounce price, even though the dollar was declining in value against other currencies and even though the United States would no longer sell any gold. Instead of increasing the price of gold as measured in dollars, Connally and Nixon wanted nations such as France to reduce the price of gold as measured in, say, francs. The American plan would make poorer millions of frugal French citizens who had squirreled away an estimated $7 billion in gold, a quarter of all the privately owned gold in the world. The French refused to accept that loss.

Supported by a broad consensus that included the PCF, Pompidou defied Nixon's and Connally's efforts to shift America's adjustment burdens onto other nations. Within a few weeks of the 15 August bombshell, France remained the only major nation that refused to float its currency upward against the dollar. Paris erected a two-tiered currency system. In the capital market the franc did move according to market forces, thereby heading off any speculative pressure. But in the larger commercial market, where francs were traded by those importing and exporting goods, the franc remained fixed at its old rate against the dollar and gold. This meant that France denied the United States the competitive trade advantage of a floating franc. In contrast, West Germany and Japan, dependent on the United States for much of their trade and military security, allowed their currencies to float upward as Washington wanted. France, however, sent only 5 percent of its exports across the Atlantic, and it had left NATO. Paris, therefore, stood better-equipped to resist the Americans. Pompidou resented Nixon's and Connally's attempt to use the 10 percent import tax surcharge as "a big stick that might possibly be transformed into a carrot" after others revalued. America's strategy assumed that France "is disposed to play the role of the donkey, which is not our intention," Pompidou declared.[34] He urged other Europeans to insist that the Americans also make some concessions, particularly by devaluing the dollar in terms of gold.

By late 1971 the Nixon-Connally war of nerves had deepened the fissures in the alliance. The EEC moved closer to forming an anti-American monetary bloc. Europeans quipped that if they ever achieved tight unity they should erect statues to the two men who had done the most to bring it about—Joseph Stalin and John Connally. American officials prepared to sue the EEC for billions of dollars in damages suffered in lost trade since the customs union was established in 1958. Kissinger and Federal Reserve officials worried that the unraveling could go too far. Indeed, while Connally and Nixon had been acting the tough guy, informal talks among central bank officials, a Franco-German summit, and the movements of the currency markets had chalked the outline of a new set of fixed exchange rates.

Agreement came on 14 December 1971 in the Azores, where Nixon, Connally, and Kissinger met with Pompidou. The Americans gave in to French demands by devaluing the dollar in terms of gold by 8.57 percent. In return, the French eliminated the two-tiered franc market and revalued their currency against the dollar by 8.57 percent. This kept constant the franc price of gold, pleasing the millions of French gold hoarders. Then Kissinger (negotiating for Nixon and Connally) and Pompidou "work[ed] out the exchange rates for every one of the world's important currencies," the national security adviser recalled.[35] The total package of American devaluation and European revaluation amounted to about 9 percent. This cheapened American products enough to yield a brief improvement in the U.S. trade and payments balances, before they worsened again in 1973. The United States dropped the import tax surcharge but never again made the dollar convertible into gold. Though tarnished, abused, and devalued, the dollar remained the currency of world trade, for no other money had the global circulation to replace it. As a European central banker put it, "When the [British] pound went, we could go to the dollar. If the dollar went, where could we go? To the moon?"[36]

On 17–18 December the major Western nations met at the Smithsonian Institution in Washington to ratify the Azores accord. The Smithsonian settlement ranked as "the most significant monetary agreement in the history of the world," Nixon crowed.[37] But the president never even referred to it in his memoirs, for in 14 months he broke the accord to allow the weak dollar to float further downward. Nixon's and Connally's rough assault on America's economic problems led to devaluation not only of the dollar but also of the Western alliance.

The "Connally approach . . . had no notion of . . . the international system," moaned Robert Schaetzel, U.S. ambassador to the EEC from 1966 to 1972.[38] After joining the State Department in 1945, Schaetzel had helped build that "system" of open trade and informal empire, in which Western Europe shone as the brightest jewel. He had assisted Secretary of State Dean Acheson in shaping the Marshall Plan, NATO, and the pattern of close personal ties that had enabled American officials "to influence quietly the course of European events."[39] When Acheson retired from the State Department in 1953, he left behind disciples such as Schaetzel who pushed for the EDC, the Common Market, the MLF, and the Grand Design. Common to all these measures were the Achesonian principles of keeping Western Europe, especially West Germany, in close orbit around Washington and safely away from Moscow. From his years of experience, Schaetzel concluded that "if we . . . allow the Europeans to have it all their own way without the subtle insinuation of our ideas," Europeans might move away from America.[40] He looked on anxiously as the Nixon administration gave Western Europe a low priority.

Still focused on Vietnam and intrigued by the possibilities of improved relations with the Soviet Union and China, Nixon and Kissinger virtually ignored Western Europe. Even the 1971 American-British-French-Soviet agreement, which defused the Berlin tinderbox, was above all a U.S.-Soviet accord. "No one in or out of authority is thinking much about Europe," Schaetzel concluded after speaking with officials in Washington and New York. "If they do think about it at all it is in a mood of irritation or outright anger."[41] Nixon's and Kissinger's determination to monopolize foreign policy making in the White House made it difficult for the State Department's diplomats to work their "quiet influence" on Europe. "We are almost cut off completely from Washington," Schaetzel observed. Reduced to reading the newspapers to figure out White House policy, State Department officials "have no real basis for even a conversation with the Europeans."[42] "I used to see [Ambassador] Chip Bohlen once a week," a top French official confirmed. "I don't think I have seen [Nixon's ambassador Arthur] Watson in three months."[43] After speaking with Pompidou at de Gaulle's funeral in November 1970, Nixon ordered interpreter Vernon Walters not even to inform Ambassador Watson of the conversation. While shutting out the diplomats, Nixon and Kissinger relied on their private contacts with Pompidou and other foreign leaders.[44]

The president also determined to keep intact the American troop presence in Europe. Those soldiers, it was assumed, gave the United States leverage in Western Europe and with the Soviets. If the United States pulled its forces out of Western Europe, "there will be a tendency to make separate deals" with Moscow, worried Undersecretary of State William J. Casey.[45] Yet the NATO organization seemed less important; Nixon in fact let the position of ambassador to NATO stand vacant for almost a year. The postwar passion for NATO had long since faded, concluded Lawrence Eagleburger, a veteran diplomat. "Like sex, NATO is a good thing to be knowledgeable about, and to experience on occasion. But it can become a bit wearing," he decided after eight months in the U.S. mission to NATO.[46] As Eagleburger's comment suggested, Achesonian activism toward Europe had nearly vanished from the U.S. government by the early 1970s.

Paris found some value in Nixon's benign neglect of Europe. With Washington busy elsewhere, the French focused on building up an independent position in uniting Europe. Paris and Washington agreed that American troops should stay in Germany, and that Chancellor Willy Brandt's *Ostpolitik* might prove dangerous. The French also welcomed Nixon's deemphasis of the NATO organization. Yet Paris also worried that the United States might pull a new Yalta, that is, sacrifice European interests in a fresh deal with the Soviets.

By 1973 this limited improvement in U.S.-French political relations was overwhelmed by the increasingly poisonous atmosphere generated by U.S.-European economic tensions. In March 1973 Washington broke the Smithsonian accord and let the dollar float downward. The EEC choked off U.S. agricultural exports with its Common Agricultural Policy (CAP), a system of subsidies for Western European farm production. When the United States protested, Europeans countered that Washington also subsidized its farmers, and that the Americans had become undependable suppliers. French cattle producers depended on high-protein soybean feed from the United States. In the summer of 1973, bad crops and high domestic demand made soybeans scarce. Without any advance notice—and literally hours before Europeans were scheduled to review the EEC's basic trade policy—the Nixon administration slapped a temporary embargo on soybean exports. The "meanest trade disputes . . . have come to dominate the Atlantic relationship," Schaetzel observed.[47] The "drift" toward a world of competing trade blocs spelled danger, warned Peter G. Peterson, Nixon's trade representative. "Wars are rarely planned," he added ominously.[48]

Kissinger worried about the serious economic rivalry with Europe—and even more about the Europeans' "race to Moscow." With the cold war thawing, the United States found it tougher to keep the Allies lined up behind Washington on East-West matters and on other issues. Brandt's Ostpolitik revived the old nightmare of a broad German-Soviet deal. U.S. influence was also diminished by the passing of the postwar generation of Europeans grateful for America's past help and habituated to accepting its advice. The State Department's shriveled contacts in both Washington and Europe did not help the problem. Finally, cold war–weary citizens in both the United States and in Europe wanted to bring troops home and reduce military spending. Were not the Russians talking peace? In early 1973 Nixon sent Peterson to Europe and Japan to assess the mounting economic challenge. Peterson came back urging that Washington seize leverage for its economic problems by linking them to security issues, where the United States still enjoyed predominance. In short, if the Europeans and Japanese wanted America's military protection, they had better make concessions on trade and monetary matters.

Nixon and Kissinger dealt with this mix of economic and political tensions by declaring 1973 the "Year of Europe." On 23 April 1973 in a speech in New York, Kissinger urged the Western Europeans (and the Japanese) to draw up "a new Atlantic charter" in time for Nixon's planned European trip that fall.[49] Europeans reacted coolly. Pompidou remarked that for France every year was the "Year of Europe"; another leader compared the American declaration to a neglectful husband announcing the year of the wife. Given its 1941 namesake, this new Atlantic Charter sparked in the French unhappy memories of the snubbing of de Gaulle. Announcing the "Year of Europe" from New York suggested that once again Europe would be the object of intrusive American diplomacy. Paris also disliked Washington's renewed effort to limit Western Europe's independence and French leadership there.

"The political, military, and economic issues in Atlantic relations are linked," Kissinger declared. This meant that the Europeans should pay for U.S. military protection in the coin of economic concessions and seal the agreement with a political Atlantic Charter. This would give the Americans a near veto over the EEC's economic decisions. Kissinger insisted that there was a clear division between America's "global interests and responsibilities" and Europe's merely "regional interests." This distinction fit the Nixonian concept of five great powers (the United States, the Soviet Union, Western Europe, China, and Japan), of which only the United States ranked as truly global. The national security adviser would subordinate "European unity" to "a larger Atlantic partnership."[50] And he made it clear that Washington intended to keep on speaking for the West in negotiations with Moscow and in setting the Western agenda in other parts of the world.

Kissinger's blunt reassertion of American hegemony and his condescension rankled Europeans, particularly the French, who had their own outlook and agenda even if they had pulled back from de Gaulle's globalism. Western Europeans also worried about the untested, cumbersome machinery of the nine-member EEC. How could the EEC deal in a unified way with the complicated issues inherent in the American call for a new Atlantic Charter, and do so in the few months before Nixon's planned fall visit? Cynical Europeans suggested a ruse. Perhaps Kissinger—"Bismarck's love child," Schaetzel dubbed him—had purposely sought to trip up or divide uniting Europe with this impossible agenda and schedule.[51]

The battle of the Atlantic Charter ended in compromise and stalemate. The EEC backed French demands for two Atlantic declarations, separating economic and political issues from military questions. In June 1974 at Ottawa, the NATO foreign ministers (including the French, who had retained their membership in the alliance while withdrawing from the integrated command) approved a military security declaration based partly on a French draft. This statement formally recognized the (at least nominally) independent French and British nuclear forces as contributing to the West's deterrent, signifying Washington's retreat from Robert McNamara's 1962 goal of tightly controlling the West's nuclear forces. Yet at the insistence of the Americans, the Ottawa document also linked military questions with political and economic matters, a connection the French had tried to avoid. The French went along, in part because Pompidou's sudden death in April 1974 led to the replacement of the combative Jobert and the ascendancy of the more conciliatory President Giscard d'Estaing. The EEC meanwhile worked on its own Atlantic charter on economic and political matters, which affirmed Europe's unity and independence. Despite American prompting, this EEC declaration left out such Atlantic buzzwords as "interdependence" and "partnership." This omission so rankled Kissinger that he mentioned it several times in his memoir of these years. By March 1974 the Nixon administration had lost interest in a political and economic accord with the EEC. The United States still wanted agreement with "the right kind of united Western Europe," a White House official explained, but such a Europe did not in fact exist.[52]

Although Western Europe, instigated by France, no longer meekly accepted U.S. hegemony, superpower agreements and the 1973 Middle East war underscored Europe's continued dependence on the Americans. At a summit meeting in June 1973 Nixon and Brezhnev signed the Agreement on Prevention of Nuclear War. The two superpowers pledged "urgent consultation with each other" if nuclear war threatened.[53] The agreement explicitly denied any diminution of either side's obligations to its allies. The French and other Western Europeans, nevertheless, worried that Washington might consult Moscow before moving to defend Western Europe from Soviet attack. Such doubts were not soothed by Washington's ruthless exclusion of its allies from the negotiations leading to the agreement. Nixon personally informed Pompidou, Brandt, and British prime minister Edward Heath two and a half days before the signing of the accord, but pledged them not to inform their defense and foreign policy advisers. These experts learned of the pact only six hours before the final ceremony—too late to have any input into the negotiations or even to develop an informed opinion about them—although Washington and Moscow had been discussing the agreement for more than a year. Humiliated, the Europeans were relegated to "ushers at the U.S.-Soviet marriage" Pompidou grumbled.[54] When Foreign Minister Jobert met with Brezhnev, he baited the Soviet leader by repeatedly using the phrase "you and your American partner." The Frenchman wanted to see how long it would take Brezhnev to interrupt and deny that the United States was a "partner." Brezhnev never once protested, convincing Jobert that a superpower entente indeed existed.[55]

After this shaking of the old, postwar order, came the earthquake of late 1973. To Western Europeans the only thing more shattering than U.S.-Soviet cooperation over their heads was a superpower confrontation on their soil. In the early morning of 25 October 1973, without any consultation with France or other allies, a small group of American officials issued a military alert that brought the world closer to nuclear war than at any time since 1962.

This startling event grew out of the Yom Kippur War in the Middle East. On the Jewish holy day of 6 October 1973 Soviet-supplied Egypt and Syria attacked Israel, allied with the United States in all but name. The Israelis soon rolled back the Arab thrust. Meanwhile the Americans and Soviets engaged in massive airlifts of weapons and supplies to their clients. Both superpowers wanted to contain and limit the conflict, however, and arranged a ceasefire. Yet Israel continued its attack, surrounding Egypt's best troops. Desperate, the Egyptian leader Anwar el-Sadat asked both superpowers to intervene to stop the fighting. Nixon said no. He did not want American soldiers in the Middle Eastern crossfire, and he certainly opposed allowing Soviet troops in there. "I will say it straight," Brezhnev phoned the White House on the night of 24 October, "that if you find it impossible to act together with us . . . we should . . . urgently consider the question of taking appropriate steps unilaterally."[56] The threat was serious, yet Brezhnev had hedged it with careful wording.

Nixon's personal crisis arising out of the Watergate scandal encouraged the White House to act tough. Vice President Spiro Agnew had just resigned under a cloud of corruption charges. On Saturday, 20 October, a desperate

Nixon had fired both Archibald Cox, the respected Harvard Law School professor he had appointed to investigate Watergate, and other top officials who put integrity before their loyalty to the president. This "Saturday Night Massacre" spawned a firestorm of public protest. The French and other Europeans wondered about America's stability. The White House saw the domestic and foreign crises as linked. "Brezhnev wouldn't understand if I didn't fire Cox," the president insisted.[57] He had to show strength, he told aides. When Kissinger, on the night of 24 October, suggested that a military response to the Soviets might be necessary, the president empowered him to act and then retired to his private quarters.

Working with Secretary of Defense James Schlesinger and some aides, Kissinger, who now wore the hats of both secretary of state and national security adviser, decided to send Brezhnev an unmistakable warning. At 11:41 P.M. on the 24th, they ordered (in clear code so the Soviets could intercept the message) American conventional and nuclear forces around the globe to go to Defense Condition (DefCon) 3, halfway up the ladder to launching a nuclear attack. In the Mediterranean, the Sixth Fleet was put on DefCon 2, the closest to actual war. The aircraft carriers *Franklin Delano Roosevelt* and *John F. Kennedy* sped toward the eastern Mediterranean; in West Germany antiaircraft missiles rose to firing position.

Only at 1:07 A.M. on the 25th—after U.S. forces in Europe and elsewhere were already gearing up for nuclear war—did Kissinger get around to informing the British Ambassador. He notified France and the other allies even later, through the NATO headquarters in Brussels, where a communications foul-up delayed word for several additional hours. Trying to justify the lack of consultation, Kissinger later explained that "we could not have accepted a judgment different from our own. It fell to us to act as custodians of Western security."[58]

The lightning crisis—early on the 25th it vanished when Brezhnev dismissed any intention of sending in Soviet troops—left France and the rest of Western Europe aghast. Within hours the two nuclear giants had moved from smiles to bared teeth and back to smiles, and the allies could say and do nothing. The clumsy superpowers mismanaged the world with "pressures and threats" aimed at the Allies and at each other, Jobert fumed.[59] The Americans and Soviets had reinforced the dependence of their Middle Eastern clients while undermining the influence of France, which had important ties with the region but could not compete with the superpowers in the polarized environment. Remembering Kissinger's Atlantic Charter speech, bitter Europeans observed that the nuclear war that could have arisen out of the U.S.-Soviet confrontation would have incinerated their continent. Yet the Americans classified such crises as "global" issues beyond Western Europe's "regional" ken. During the Cuban missile crisis Washington had not asked its allies' opinions, but it had at least informed them before acting. In 1973 Washington gave the allies no such warning. "And to be perfectly honest, there was no advance notice within the U.S. Government either," testified a top State Department official.[60] The State Department had abundant facilities for reaching allied heads of government in time of crisis, but Kissinger had shut out his own department. He also excluded Europeans from the postwar diplomacy. "Israel would not accept them as impartial, and . . . the Europeans seemed close to the Soviet position," Kissinger later explained.[61] The crisis underscored the shabbiness of Atlantic relations.

Differences on oil policy also divided Americans from Europeans during the Middle East war, when the Arabs cut oil production, quadrupled the price, and embargoed the pro-Israeli Americans and Dutch. Before the crisis began, 77 percent of France's total energy consumption came in the form of imported oil, nearly all from the Middle East. In the rest of the EEC, dependence on imported oil ranged from 42 percent in coal-rich Germany to 93 percent in Italy. In sharp contrast to Western Europe's dependence on Arab oil, imported oil made up only 17 percent of America's total energy consumption, and only one-fourth of that foreign oil came from the Middle East.[62] With relatively secure energy supplies, Washington could afford to wrestle with broader problems: to restore peace and balance to the Middle East, shut the Soviets out, woo the Egyptians and other moderate Arabs, hold on to its leverage with the Israelis, keep American Jews satisfied, and isolate the "radical" Arab regimes in Iraq, Libya, and Syria. As it turned out, the big oil companies eased the effects of the Arab embargo. Although world prices skyrocketed and some shortages appeared, the "crisis" never became critical. It seemed, nevertheless, that France and the rest of Europe had to secure enough imported oil or their economies would seize up. Even in the United States, much less vulnerable to the Arab embargo, there appeared long lines at gas stations and anxiety that the glory days of cheap energy were gone.

Determined to salvage relations with their Arab oil suppliers, the Western Europeans refused to follow Washington's lead during the Middle East war. France and most of the Western European allies did not allow U.S. planes supplying Israel to fly over their territory. Indeed the Soviets used NATO airspace more than did the Americans. Much of the Soviet airlift to Egypt flew over Greece and Turkey without serious protest. At the United Nations, Great Britain and France cold-shouldered American efforts to block Soviet proposals for a great-power peace force. France continued military deliveries to Libya and Saudi Arabia. Pompidou urged a coordinated EEC approach to the Middle East so that EEC members could prove "their capacity to contribute to the settlement of world problems."[63] The EEC responded with a document that called for greater Israeli concessions than even Egypt was seeking.

The Europeans were "craven, contemptible, pernicious, and jackal-like," Kissinger raged.[64] "I don't care what happens to NATO," he reportedly commented; "I'm so disgusted."[65] Jobert countered that Europe had been "treated like a nonperson, humiliated all along the line." Even worse, the Frenchman observed, Europe "in its energy dependence is the object of the second struggle in this Mideast war"—the fight for oil.[66] Jobert tried to lead the EEC toward a relationship with the Arabs, independent of Washington, that would secure the oil flow. Such an entente would restore France as major actor in the Middle East, whence it had been displaced by Americans, Soviets, and Arab nationalists. In January 1974 Jobert traveled through the Middle East, including visits to Iraq and Libya, on Washington's blacklist, and Saudi Arabia, long a U.S. fiefdom. On Syrian radio and television he declared that France stood ready to swap weapons for oil. He assured Arabs that "the positions of France and of the United States are diametrically opposed."[67] Kissinger and Nixon certainly opposed France's policy of bilateral deals with the Arabs. They sought instead a coalition of consumer nations directed by Washington. Kissinger and Jobert fought out these differences at the 13-nation Washington energy conference of February 1974. By this time, their personal relations had become venomous. Kissinger devoted pages of his memoir to detailing the Frenchman's outrageous behavior; Jobert did the same in his account. But more was at stake than personal pride.

Never solid, European unity began crumbling because of internal differences and American pressures. France and Italy depended more on Arab oil than did coal-rich Great Britain and Germany. Paris and Bonn conflicted on how to deal with the Americans and the Arabs. Although the French championed European unity, they too could not forget old animosities. When the Netherlands stood isolated by the Arab embargo, Pompidou reportedly told a friend, "The Dutch can't stand the French: that is the only constant in their history. They give us lectures on Europe but all they want is to chain it to America."[68]

At the energy conference the United States cracked open the already-fractured EEC. The Middle East crisis had dealt new cards to oil-rich America and left France with a losing hand. In the event of another oil crisis, Nixon and Kissinger promised, the United States would pool its oil supplies with the proposed group of consumer nations. This would give Western Europe and Japan access to the huge oil reserves of North and South America. While holding out this carrot, the Americans lifted a big stick. The object was to coerce West Germany, once again the key prize in U.S.-French rivalry. According to a French official who favored the American energy proposal, the Germans abandoned Jobert when Kissinger threatened to withdraw American troops from the Federal Republic. Many French bitterly concluded that Washington had engineered the energy crisis to jack up its sagging hegemony.[69]

After the victory at the energy conference, the Nixon administration pressed its assault on European independence. "The right kind of united Western Europe"—one open to Washington's direction, as the Achesonians had worked for—"was not achievable," a top official told reporter Leslie Gelb. Nixon and Kissinger feared that a unified Europe would be a Gaullist one, "under French leadership in opposition to the United States." Relations with Western Europe figured as "the biggest problem" for American policy, Kissinger declared in April 1974.[70] Top White House and State Department officials explained to Gelb their campaign to "shock" Western Europe back into line behind Washington. Europeans now had to "choose between Washington and Paris." U.S. officials played on European disunity by insisting on dealing with each of the allies individually. Kissinger derided the Europeans for having problems in governing themselves; how, then, could they pretend to get along without the United States? As evidence, he pointed to the reluctance of governments in Western Europe to override public objections and support Washington's military policies in Vietnam or elsewhere. Perhaps drawing on his expertise as a former political scientist, Kissinger asserted that since World War I, Europe had not had many "fully legitimate governments."[71]

Four days after his secretary of state questioned Europe's political legitimacy, Nixon underscored its military dependency. The Europeans "cannot have the United States' participation and cooperation on the security front and then proceed to have confrontation and even hostility on the economic and political fronts. . . . we are not going to be faced with a situation where the nine countries of Europe [i.e., the nine Common Market members] gang up against the United States—the United States which is their guarantee for their security. That we cannot have," Nixon warned.[72] Such tough talk probably spawned more resentment than reconsideration of policy. European unity and independence nevertheless had suffered a severe setback. The oil crisis, soaring inflation, and wrenching unemployment of the mid-1970s pulled the economies of the nine EEC nations in different directions. They found it difficult to agree on common EEC policies.

In 1974 changes in leadership improved Atlantic relations. In the British elections in February, Harold Wilson, the U.S.–oriented Labour leader, displaced the Europe-oriented Conservative Edward Heath. Forced to resign because of a spy scandal, Willy Brandt was replaced by Helmut Schmidt, who was less committed to *Ostpolitik*. In August Nixon gave up his office to escape impeachment for crimes related to Watergate. Pompidou had already died of cancer in April 1974.

A month later, Valéry Giscard d'Estaing won a paper-thin victory over Socialist François Mitterrand. Although he had been elected with Gaullist support, Giscard was a member not of the Gaullist party but of the moderate-conservative Independent Republicans. Giscard—the brilliant, elegant "French Kennedy"—acknowledged his victory in both English and French. Groused a Mitterrand supporter: "Yes. I can see it now. France will become the 51st state before Puerto Rico."[73] Giscard improved ties with Washington, as de Gaulle had done in his last months as president and as Pompidou had done before the Year of Europe controversy and the Middle East war poisoned relations. Giscard understood the fatal flaw in French efforts to build a Paris-led Europe independent of the United States. Whenever France forced Bonn to choose between Paris and Washington, the Germans picked the Americans, with their larger nuclear umbrella.

While building a special relationship with West Germany, Giscard moderated French independence in order to improve links with Washington. Unlike other French leaders, Giscard rarely "exercis[ed] his royal independence for just the hell of it," recalled U.S. ambassador Arthur Hartman.[74] Particularly in the post–Vietnam War era, when the United States had become unsure of its global role, Giscard believed it essential that American troops and weapons remain in Europe in order to help contain the Germans and the Soviets.

Giscard also appreciated the growing benefits of the secret program, begun by the Nixon administration, for exchanging nuclear information. Subverting the spirit and, at times, the letter of the MacMahon Act of 1958, which in effect prohibited the transfer of nuclear technology to any nation other than Great Britain, American experts played with their French counterparts what they called "Twenty Questions."[75] The French would tell their American counterparts their plans or hypotheses for solving a particular nuclear weapon design problem, and the Americans would indicate whether the French were on the right track, without mouthing the actual information. Of course, this verbal game broke down as the small groups of French and American experts got to know each other personally. As one senior American official acknowledged, "I found that the technicians just loved to share their triumphs; they had no inhibitions."[76] Continued and expanded in the 1970s and 1980s, this program remained a highly secret, closely held operation of the American and French presidents, who coordinated it through their personal staffs. "There was a very, very tiny list" of participants, one American recalled.[77] Although the Americans gained some technical knowledge in the conversations, the United States benefited primarily through the increased willingness of France to link its conventional and nuclear military planning with NATO and to make French territory and logistical facilities available to American forces in the event of war.

Helping Giscard to cultivate relations with the Americans and the West Germans was the new foreign minister, Jean Sauvagnargues, a career German expert, who had replaced the more rigidly Gaullist Jobert. Both Giscard and Helmut Schmidt had served as finance ministers when France and West Germany were struggling through the economic upheavals of the early 1970s. Now national leaders, the two men breathed life into the 1963 Franco-German treaty with frequent, wide-ranging consultation. Giscard and Schmidt addressed each other by their first names and spoke a common language, English. The bilateral trade between the two nations became the third largest in the world, ranking behind the United States and Canada and the United States and Japan. Based on this Paris-Bonn axis, a European policy toward the United States began to emerge. Paris stimulated a more independent tone in Bonn; the

Germans applauded France's closer working relationship with NATO. Publicly, Washington officials now appeared reconciled to France's 1966 departure from the NATO organization. Secretary of Defense James Schlesinger found "no need for France to be involved in the integrated [NATO] command structure in order to participate fully in cooperation within the Alliance."[78]

Covert nuclear aid to France remained an ongoing program even after the Watergate scandal blew up, forcing Nixon to resign. Kissinger remained secretary of state until January 1977 under President Gerald Ford, whom Nixon had appointed vice president when Agnew resigned. Kissinger continued the policy, begun under Nixon, of seeking détente with Moscow as the means to manage growing Soviet military power and to compensate for America's relative decline in strength. Although the threat of an independent, united Europe had receded by mid-1974, the danger of a Communist Western Europe appeared on the rise.

"All of Europe will be Marxist within a decade," Kissinger despaired in 1976.[79] No one expected the Soviets to march west. But the end of right-wing dictatorships in Portugal and Spain in 1974–75 allowed the resurgence of the long-suppressed Communist parties of those countries. In France and Italy, the Communists rose in popularity as they dropped old revolutionary slogans and pledged themselves to "Eurocommunism"—democracy and independence from Moscow. As in the 1940s and 1950s, Europe appeared as a row of dominoes. "The impact of an Italian Communist Party that seemed to be governing effectively would be devastating—on France, and on NATO, too," Kissinger fretted.[80]

He decided that "the dominance of Communist parties in the West is unacceptable." It did not matter if the Communists were "reasonable," independent from Moscow, or had come to power through elections. Communist governments in Western Europe would give priority to "social and economic problems" rather than to "security issues," Kissinger argued. That shift would kill support for NATO in both Europe and America. He insisted that even if French or Italian Communists came into power pledged to uphold freedoms, once in office they would strangle democracy and free enterprise. With Western Europe Communist, "the United States would be alone and isolated in a world in which we had no relations by values to other countries."[81] Here Kissinger invoked the nightmare that had driven the United States into both world wars and into the cold war—the horror that America's prosperity and way of life would suffocate if Europe adopted a very different creed. How could the United States head off this catastrophe? Kissinger at least considered the idea of naked intervention to stop an elected Communist government from taking office. In his memoirs, the secretary of state recalled his anguish at the prospect of red governments in Western Europe. "There are changes in the international balance that can threaten our nation's security and have to be resisted however they come about," he asserted.[82] He worried, furthermore, that the American people might not support such intervention.

Yet Kissinger also believed that Washington's capability to contain Western European communism was assisted by a powerful, though limited, partner— the Soviet Union. A Communist Western Europe "would be a headache for the Soviets," Kissinger told American ambassadors at a meeting in London in December 1975. Moscow would "probably prefer not to see Communist powers taking over in Western Europe."[83] At that same assembly, Kissinger and his chief assistant, Helmut Sonnenfeldt, stressed the mutual interest of the super-powers in containing the restlessness in both halves of Europe and in maintaining the boundary between East and West. The Kissinger-Sonnenfeldt doctrine prescribed that Western Europe should remain in America's orbit while Eastern Europe stayed in the Soviet sphere.

Sonnenfeldt blamed Moscow's "inept" and "unskilled" control for the dissatisfaction in the Soviet empire. "The Soviets' inability to acquire loyalty in Eastern Europe is an unfortunate historical failure," Sonnenfeldt told the U.S. ambassadors. Rising tensions in Eastern Europe could "explode, causing World War III. This inorganic, unnatural relationship is a far greater danger to world peace than the conflict between East and West," Sonnenfeldt claimed. In the interests of stability, the United States would encourage the Soviet Union to become a smarter, more sophisticated hegemon by granting more local autonomy. Washington also had to caution the satellites against any "romantic political inclinations." Making Moscow's power base in Eastern Europe more "natural and organic" would help in "managing or domesticating" the Soviets' rising global might, Sonnenfeldt explained.[84] If the Russian bear had a friendlier neighborhood, he might stay there. Le Monde saw this "Brezhfeldt Doctrine" differently. Washington and Moscow kept Europe divided whether they cooperated or competed, the French complained.

Kissinger's ambition to manage Western and Eastern Europe was undercut by sharp divisions at home. In April 1976 the London statements were leaked to the press by conservative Republican Senator James Buckley of New York. Outraged Americans, particularly supporters of conservative presidential hopefuls Democrat Henry Jackson and Republican Ronald Reagan, decried Kissinger's abandonment of Eastern Europe to godless communism. Critics smelled blood when the hapless Gerald Ford publicly maintained that Poland was not under Soviet domination. Beating a retreat, Ford and Kissinger banished the word détente from the administration's vocabulary. But the appointed president lost anyway to Democrat Jimmy Carter, who promised honesty and a fresh start after Watergate.

After his inauguration in January 1977 Carter proved naive in world affairs and worse in coordinating his foreign policy team, which pulled in conflicting directions. In 1979 another oil crisis ignited double-digit inflation. Unemployment climbed, and the dollar's value nosedived. In November 1979 Iranian militants took Americans hostage. A month later Soviet troops marched into Afghanistan to prop up a tottering Marxist government. Carter staked his prestige on resolving both crises, a fatal move since he could do little about either of them. He enraged Europeans, particularly West Germans, by first pressuring them to deploy the neutron bomb and then dropping the project. Many Americans and Europeans concluded that the former governor of Georgia lacked the capability to manage either domestic or foreign affairs. At first, Carter could not choose between Secretary of State Cyrus Vance, who favored negotiated settlements, and National Security Adviser Zbigniew Brzezinski, who leaned toward confrontation of the Soviet Union and revolutionary Iran. After late 1979 Carter swerved to the right, calling for a military buildup and a tougher stance toward Moscow.

As U.S.-Soviet relations soured, Giscard tried to salvage French trade and dialogue with Moscow. The French president operated on the following three essentially Gaullist assumptions. 1) Paris had to keep open its lines to Moscow in order to preserve both the relative independence of France in the East-West quarrel and French influence with West Germany. 2) France had to maintain a special relationship with West Germany in order to add weight to French diplomacy and to safeguard against Bonn's becoming neutralist or moving too close to either Moscow or Washington. 3) Because the Soviets and the Americans were often dangerously clumsy in their dealings with each other and with other nations, France had a vital moderating role to perform. Unlike de Gaulle, who had exited the NATO organization while remaining a member of the Atlantic alliance, Giscard cooperated more with Washington. The United States appeared weaker and less menacing than it had when Johnson was sending troops into Vietnam and the Dominican Republic. Besides, the Americans were now aiding the French nuclear effort, a favor they had refused to do for de Gaulle.

Two months after the December 1979 Soviet drive into Afghanistan, Giscard and Chancellor Schmidt held a three-day meeting in Paris to plan strategy. They focused not so much on the Soviet invasion but on how to respond to Washington's demand for punishment of Moscow. Calling the invasion the worst threat to peace since World War II, Carter cut off the sale of American grain to the Soviets and urged a Western boycott of the Olympic games to be held in Moscow. He also pledged to resist with military force further Soviet moves toward the oil-rich Persian Gulf. Schmidt boiled over with contempt for Carter, arguing that the president's "deadly game" would only antagonize the Soviets, not change their behavior.[85] Washington's policy made little military sense, since the Persian Gulf lay in the Soviet Union's front yard, not America's. Schmidt and Giscard suspected that Carter's worry about his 1980 reelection prospects had sparked the sudden tough stance. The two Europeans agreed that the Soviet move was probably defensive, to shore up the weak pro-Soviet Afghan government, rather than the first step in a drive for the Persian Gulf's oil. Giscard shared Schmidt's doubts about Carter's judgment and competence, but the Frenchman tried to moderate the German's irritation.

Giscard did not knuckle under to Washington. He allowed French athletes to decide for themselves whether to go to the Moscow Olympic games (they elected to attend). He refused to follow the American lead in slapping an economic embargo on Iran during the American hostage crisis. In May 1980 Giscard ignored U.S. objections to his summit with Brezhnev in the wake of the Soviet invasion of Afghanistan. France did not need "anyone's prior approval," the foreign minister snapped when Washington complained of no consultation.[86] Yet the fundamental interests of France remained with the West; at his Warsaw meeting with Brezhnev, Giscard warned the Soviet leader not to use Afghanistan as a launching pad into the Persian Gulf.[87]

In other tacit or secret ways, France and the United States worked together to preserve stability and Western interests during the Carter years. The secret nuclear collaboration program became more intense. "We had the best relationship with France in my memory," recalled a member of the Carter administration.[88] Giscard's government prized the nuclear cooperation not only for the information it yielded but also as "a mark of confidence between allies."[89] David Aaron, Carter's deputy national security adviser, "would go regularly to Paris, sit down with [Jacques] Wahl [a top adviser to Giscard], and go over all the things we needed to do together," recalled a Washington insider. "I'm certain we would not have been able to do that had we not had this other [nuclear] relationship."[90]

Carter needed to do things together with the French in part because of the electoral campaign he had run. Responding to the widespread public disgust with the imperial presidency and diplomatic machinations of Nixon and Kissinger, candidate Carter had run for president in 1976 promising that the United States would no longer engage in immoral interventions in other nations. Having made this pledge, President Carter found the French connection useful for carrying out the less moral side of his diplomacy. "There were a lot of cooperative things we did with the French around the world," recalled Ambassador Hartman, "real involvement in some of these countries . . . helping opposition movements or helping governments to stay in power."[91] The French were particularly powerful in sub-Saharan Africa, where they had retained effective control in many former colonies through monetary ties, financial help, cultural links, technical assistance—and through frequent military interventions to prop up or overthrow governments. As a former French foreign minister explained, Africa was "the only continent which is still the right size for France, still within the limits of its means. The only one where it can still, with 500 men, change the course of History."[92] By 1979, 26 African nations, including many former British colonies, were receiving French aid. Agreements with compliant African rulers gave France guaranteed and privileged access to strategic raw materials such as uranium and titanium. Washington often cooperated with France to keep the impoverished states of sub-Saharan Africa relatively stable and free of Communist or radical nationalist influence. In 1978, for example, the United States flew

700 French Foreign Legionnaires into Zaire to defeat a rebel force based in neighboring Angola.

Such little victories did not stem the growing sense among many Americans that Carter could manage neither foreign nor domestic policy. In November 1980 Carter lost the election to the charismatic, conservative Republican Ronald Reagan, who pledged to get tough with the Soviets, increase military spending, and cut taxes and waste in government. A former actor and governor of California, Reagan appealed to frustrated Americans who believed in his promise of simple solutions to puzzling problems. Carter's presidency proved to be a transition to the military-oriented policies of the Reagan era. In U.S.-French relations, too, Carter, like Nixon and Ford, presided over a gradual warming trend that became more pronounced in the 1980s.

In the 1970s a series of developments in America—economic trouble, political turmoil, a less-Europe-oriented leadership, and a greater appreciation of the limits of U.S. power—all had caused Washington to focus more on narrow national interests and less on shaping Western European developments. The Year of Europe and the 1974 drive against a Gaullist Europe had demonstrated that although the United States could no longer implement grand designs for Western Europe, it could still divide the Europeans against themselves. In general, the United States had backed away from the self-assured, predominant role it had played in Western Europe in the first postwar decades. More confident about its own power and bolstered by its partnership with West Germany, France found this less hegemonic America easier to deal with. In the early 1980s France would move much closer to the United States because of the renewed cold war, the surge of anticommunism in France, and the rise of West German sentiment for disarmament and ties with the East.

Chapter 6

THE ODD COUPLE, 1981–1989

Among its many humiliating losses in the 1980s, the French Communist party suffered the defection of actor and singer Yves Montand. Star of many French and Hollywood movies, former lover of singer Edith Piaf and actress Marilyn Monroe, Montand's long, highly publicized career won him the attention and affection of the people of France. A Paris critic described him as "the heart and hands of our time."[1] Montand had become the French equivalent of a Frank Sinatra or a John Wayne. But unlike those two American idols, Montand, like most French entertainers and intellectuals in the two decades after World War II, stood on the left. He signed PCF petitions, supported Communist positions, and entertained in the Soviet Union, where he met Premier Nikita Khrushchev. Montand stopped singing "C'est si bon" because a political friend decreed it too "American." Yet Montand grew disillusioned with communism, beginning in 1956 with the Soviets' brutal suppression of the Hungarian revolt.

When he spoke out against communism in the early 1980s, the French people listened to him. In one poll, 55 percent believed the entertainer's views on politics were more important than the utterances of statesmen. Montand won lavish praise from non-Communist leftist writers for "saying out loud what we've all been thinking under our breath."[2] Supporters saw a parallel with Ronald Reagan and urged him to run for the French presidency. Half in jest, Montand replied that he would not follow in Reagan's footsteps because his own acting career had not failed.

Montand in the 1980s pointed a shaming finger at the Soviet Union for repressing its own people and for being aggressive toward the outside world.

Although President Ronald Reagan was a conservative Republican and President François Mitterrand was a socialist, they brought their governments closer together in military affairs. *Courtesy of French Embassy Press & Information Division*

The French Communists had long tried to whitewash conditions in the Communist motherland, but the brutal truth remained, he argued. Furthermore, while denouncing the Communist god that failed, Montand joined other French in taking a fresh, appreciative look at the United States. Despite its faults, "America is the last rampart of democracy," he declared in 1983.[3] He told television viewers, "We have to defend democracy; that's all we've got left, kids."[4] Even Americanization, long a French bugbear, appeared more benign. "If America has succeeded in invading us culturally, it is because we like it," Montand maintained. "T-shirts, jeans, hamburgers—nobody imposes these things on us. We like them."[5]

Montand's shift from Moscow to McDonald's symbolized and helped legitimate the 1980s reconciliation between France and the United States. Political rivalry between the two nations and sharp disputes over trade and monetary questions remained. Yet the governments of France and the United States grew closer on issues of military security, particularly the question of nuclear missiles in Europe. During the renewed cold war of 1979–86, Paris and Washington sharpened their antipathy to Moscow, built up their nuclear arsenals, and worried about the *Ostpolitik* of the Federal Republic of Germany. In contrast to America and France, West Germany remained committed to détente with the Soviet Union and to closer ties with East Germany and to the rest of Eastern Europe. The mounting stockpile of nuclear weapons deployed on or aimed at the Federal Republic's territory fed German pacifism, neutralism, and nationalism. All three *isms* worried Paris and Washington. With relatively little rivalry between them, the Americans and the French tried to reassure—and restrain—the West Germans with additional military ties. Paris also edged much closer to NATO. French society became more like American society: divided by income into a small elite, a prosperous but anxious middle class, a shrinking force of industrial laborers, and a growing underclass populated especially by people of color, yet united by powerful nationalist and consumerist impulses. These drives were manipulated by patriotic appeals and powerful advertising and subject to explosive frustrations. This convergence helps explain why many French found so appealing the buoyant consumerism and capitalism that dominated American life in the 1980s. At the same time, many American intellectuals borrowed from French thinkers new theoretical approaches that exposed the subtle, often hidden assumptions and hierarchies that sustained that consumerism and capitalism.

The French and American governments got along better in part because Washington's hegemony in Western Europe and Paris's dependence on America both declined in the 1980s. With more modest ambitions in Western Europe, the United States found it easier to accept some French leadership on the Continent. More comfortable than de Gaulle had been with France's rank in the world, the French often found the Americans a useful partner in Europe, in Africa, and in nuclear issues.

Thus France and the United States drew closer together even as America became more distant from the rest of Western Europe. From the 1940s to mid-1960 officials from both shores of the Atlantic had worked together, at times with acrimony, to create the Western alliance. In the 1970s and 1980s the intimacy between them ebbed away as the founding generation left the scene. Younger Europeans saw less reason to accept Washington's leadership, particularly as America's economic and military preeminence faded. Meanwhile political power in America shifted away from the Northeast, traditionally oriented toward Europe. The nation's deteriorating trade and payments deficit and its yawning budget gap made the military commitment to Europe and NATO appear burdensome to many Americans. Europe's carping against U.S. military actions—such as invading Grenada in 1983 or bombing Libya in 1986—made the Continent seem bothersome. U.S. trade with France and Europe stagnated while commerce with Japan and other Pacific Rim nations soared. As Japanese capital poured in to finance U.S. deficits and as Asian and Latin American immigrants streamed in to alter America's ethnic balance, Europe seemed less relevant to the nation's future. Washington's old strategic nightmare, a Soviet lunge into Western Europe, appeared more remote than ever, particularly after tremendous changes within the Soviet Union and Soviet president Mikhail Gorbachev's launching of a peace offensive in the mid-1980s. In this new time of détente and diminished cold war, the U.S. commitment to NATO remained, but the alliance became more of a hollow, ad hoc arrangement. Americans, both in and out of government, stepped up their complaints that the rich Western Europeans were not doing enough to share America's heavy defense burdens. Increasingly, U.S. analysts viewed France, with its ambitious, semiautonomous defense effort, as a help to Washington rather than a competitor.

In addition to this strategic convergence, there occurred in the 1980s a rapprochement of ideas between France and the United States. To understand this critical development, we must backtrack a bit and examine the evolution of French intellectual life after 1968. In France, people who deal with ideas matter far more than they do in the United States. French intellectuals compose a predominant subculture, which plays an important role in defining the national culture of France. In contrast, American intellectuals remain on the margin as one subculture among many.

For many years after World War II, most French intellectuals used their influence in support of the left, particularly the PCF. During the war, many French thinkers forged an identity with communism. The national collapse in 1940 brought down with it the reputation of liberal democracy, ideology of the defeated Third Republic. Eagerness to collaborate with Nazis then discredited the right. "We had no choice about becoming Communists," noted respected thinker Annie Kriegel. "For a couple of years the only army advancing toward us was the Red Army. It's true that it was the Americans who liberated us—but the turning point in the war was the battle of Stalingrad in 1942. It was the Red Army that gave us hope."[6] Through the early cold war many intellectuals and artists kept their hope in the PCF and in the Soviet Union. For many, as for Montand, gradual disillusionment began in 1956 with the Soviets' brutal suppression of Hungary and with Khrushchev's revelation of Joseph Stalin's crimes. Still, leftist, often Communist, sentiment among intellectuals, artists, and the young remained strong and indeed was fanned by the 1960s struggles of Fidel Castro and Ho Chi Minh.

The prevailing French skepticism about the United States—from the media, from de Gaulle, from intellectuals, and from the PCF—ensured that postwar youth grew up with few illusions about that country. "The De Gaulle experience in the 1960's inoculated many of the French in terms of the United States," an American official noted years later.[7] Conversely, until the late 1960s many young Germans idealized America as a substitute Fatherland, as novelist Günter Grass observed, but in the 1970s and 1980s West German sentiment swung in the opposite direction.[8]

Ironically, French opinion warmed toward the United States and chilled toward communism during the Vietnam War. In May 1968 young French rebels moved beyond opposition to the war—the patriarchal general was already blowing that trumpet—to look positively at stirrings in American society. Not only French peace activists but feminists, ecologists, and gay rights activists drew inspiration from across the Atlantic. Meanwhile, the PCF's musty ideology and clumsy attempts to control protest alienated free-wheeling street rebels.

After Washington gave up and withdrew from Vietnam in 1973, America appeared less of an ogre. Indeed the harsh treatment of dissidents in postwar Vietnam and the flight of the boat people from that unhappy country made many French question their idealization of third-world revolutions. The genocidal slaughter of Cambodian people by the Communist Khmer Rouge after they took power in 1975 doubly embarrassed French Communists, since Pol Pot and other Khmer Rouge leaders were former members of the PCF. Arguments in the United States by journalist William Shawcross and others, that Washington's cynical manipulation of events in Cambodia before 1975 had set the stage for the Khmer Rouge's excesses, found little echo in the French media. Meanwhile the French jeered both Nixon's Watergate crimes and the American people's puritanical concern with such peccadillos. Yet many French, particularly on the left, found themselves admiring the American system for forcing Nixon to resign. In France such offenses would probably have been swept under the rug.

During the 1970s and 1980s French disillusionment with communism and with Marxism accelerated with the "Gulag effect." In 1974 Aleksandr Solzhenitsyn's historical novel *The Gulag Archipelago* shocked French intellectuals with its horrifying portrait of Soviet slave labor camps. "The image of the Soviet Union became totally degraded during the 70s," Kriegel observed. "France is probably the country where anti-Sovietism and anticommunism have taken root most strongly."[9] Even philosopher and novelist Jean-Paul Sartre, the epitome of the committed, Marxist intellectual, no longer spoke of himself as a Marxist, though he still advocated social revolution. In January 1980 PCF leader Georges Marchais dealt his reeling party another blow by broadcasting on French television, direct from Moscow, a justification for the December 1979 Soviet invasion of Afghanistan. In December 1981, when the Communist government in Poland imposed martial law in an effort to squelch the Solidarity labor movement, most French observers blamed Soviet pressures. The plight of Poland gripped the interest and the sympathy of the French far more than it did the Americans or West Germans. Through the centuries France had taken in Polish émigrés and had seen itself as Poland's guardian angel. When the PCF then endorsed the Polish government's crackdown, many on the French left recoiled from the party, convinced that the Communists were the enemy of real socialism and human advancement.

The near free-fall decline in the prestige of Marxism and communism after 1968 facilitated the rise of other intellectual movements in France, some of which drew sustenance from the example of American society, and some of which had a profound effect on intellectual life in the United States. Some former radicals, grouped around Serge July of the newspaper *Libération*, advocated a more pluralistic, less state-oriented society, somewhat on the American model. Among the flashiest of the groups was the "New Philosophers," most prominent in the late 1970s. Literary critic Philippe Sollers, a key theorist during the 1968 Paris uprising and later a close associate of the New Philosophers, came back from the United States enthusing about American freedom and diversity. New Philosophers Bernard-Henri Lévy and André Glucksmann, former admirers of Communist Chinese leader Mao Tse-tung, wrote best-selling books that championed individualism and denounced Marxism. Such commercial success stemmed partly from the heavy advertising effort by the publishing house Grasset, which employed Lévy as a series director, and partly from the appeal of the New Philosophers' strident message. "The Soviet prison camp is Marxist [just] as Auschwitz was Nazi," argued Lévy, adding that Solzhenitsyn is "the Shakespeare of our time, the only one who knows how to point out the monsters." Glucksmann and many others of the group favored nuclear deterrence to safeguard against these "monsters.[10]

While the individualistic and right-leaning New Philosophers won brief attention from the American media, the structuralists and poststructuralists—a group of thinkers, most of them French, including cultural theorist Roland Barthes, philosopher Jacques Derrida, historian Michel Foucault, psychoanalyst Jacques Lacan, anthropologist Claude Lévi-Strauss, feminist philosopher Luce Irigaray, and psychoanalyst Julia Kristeva—captured the sustained interest of many American scholars and sparked battles in the humanities departments of American colleges and universities. Despite the diversity among these thinkers, as a group they contributed to American intellectual discourse sophisticated probing tools, designed to poke through traditional assumptions about language, power, and society.[11] In the 1980s and 1990s both defenders and detractors of these theoretical constructs referred to them as, simply, "theory," a formulation that pointed to the authority of this intellectual influence from France.

"Theory" attained such visibility in the United States for several reasons. The high prestige in America of older French thinkers, such as Lévi-Strauss, helped create a receptive audience for other French interpretive theories. At a pioneering 1966 conference at Johns Hopkins University, leading European proponents of structuralism met with American scholars. There, Derrida, who became the leading poststructuralist, attacked the structuralists, setting the stage for further intellectual controversy and a certain competitiveness among trendy scholars as to what was le hip du hip.[12] In the 1970s and after, poststructuralism gained a hold in humanities departments at influential universities such as Yale and Cornell and in the editorial offices of certain prestigious scholarly journals. Anthropologists, literary critics, historians, and other humanists who sought to harden their "soft" disciplines with more rigorous analysis used ideas borrowed from Lévi-Strauss, Foucault, and others—that is, ideas that carried the prestige of their French progenitors. By challenging the objectivity of science and emphasizing the relational nature of all human knowledge, Foucault, Derrida, and the German social theorist Jürgen Habermas offered American humanists a weapon with which to respond to scientists' criticisms of subjectivity in history or literature.

In part, the struggle over "theory" became a generational one. In both France and the United States, the New Left movements of the late 1960s had aroused among many students and intellectuals high hopes for sweeping societal change—aspirations dashed by the reaction of the more conservative populaces and governments. By the 1970s and 1980s veterans of these frustrated social movements, many now professors or, particularly in France, part of the sophisticated reading public, found poststructuralist arguments appealing. If language and other cultural expressions powerfully buttressed the existing social order, no wonder the wide-eyed social movements of the late 1960s had been disowned by the populace and easily put down by the authorities. If language was the locus of a key power struggle within society, then intellectuals advocating social change were justified in focusing on the battle of words and symbols within the academy, instead of getting involved in parliamentary politics or labor issues. Moreover, Solzhenitsyn's Gulag Archipelago had underscored the political power of the dominant mode of discourse: unable to escape the language of Stalinism, victims of the 1930s Soviet purges had often endorsed their own liquidation. Meanwhile left-leaning intellectuals in America and France had shifted their attention away from issues of economic exploitation, becoming discouraged with the conservatism of the working class, the sluggish economy of the 1970s, and the resurgence of popular faith in the marketplace during the 1980s.[13]

Even some formerly leftist French thinkers attained a new appreciation for capitalism, especially when they observed the dynamism of America's economy and society under Ronald Reagan. At first, the French poked fun at this Hollywood cowboy president. But then many began taking him seriously, particularly when the American economy after 1982 created millions of new jobs while France continued to suffer high unemployment. Reaganism became the subject of numerous serious studies including the best-selling *The Conservative American Revolution* by Guy Sorman. A group of French intellectuals formed a French "Committee to reelect President Reagan."[14] *Le Nouvel Observateur* and *L'Express,* glossy, "smart" magazines that catered to ambitious professionals, managers, and intellectuals, lavished coverage on the latest economic, technological, and fashion trends in America. In March 1984 President Mitterrand made a pilgrimage to California's Silicon Valley and decided that France, too, should have such a center for high-technology innovators. *Entrepreneur* was originally a French word, he happily noted. Yet Mitterrand struck a balance by censuring Reagan's conservative policies for creating "all sorts of casualties."[15] Former guerrilla fighter and Mitterrand adviser Régis Debray observed that "by a unique blend of dependency and conceit, intellectual France has become infatuated with America."[16]

The venerable French critique of American "cultural imperialism" had lost much of its bite. "Sure, we love to consume the American cultural products," noted social commentator Jean-François Revel, "and after, we love even more to reject them."[17] Yet the French appeared to love the consumption more than the rejection. In 1986 *Le Nouvel Observateur* asked opinion trendsetters, Did the pervasive American cultural influence threaten France? Its effects posed no serious dangers, the magazine concluded from its responses, and anti-Americanism afflicted only "imbeciles."[18] Taking on a stale, musty odor, anti-Americanism remained strong among the remaining Communists and among the followers of the right-wing, nativist political leader Jean-Marie Le Pen. Even Le Pen, however, declared in 1984: "My model is Reagan."[19] In that year polls showed that the French gave the United States a higher approval rating than did the British or the West Germans.[20] In ways small and large, the French acted on their judgment that much in America was worth adopting.

Fast food is "a morsel of the American way of life"—suited to urban living and especially appealing to youth—explained *Le Monde* in a surprisingly positive analysis.[21] In the early 1980s Quick and Freetime, two French hamburger companies whose names sported an American ring, soared to success by copying U.S. fast-food techniques. The French firms gained the jump on global leader McDonald's because of the latter's incompetent franchisee. By 1988 McDonald's had corrected that problem and risen to number two, close behind front-runner Quick. "International is one of the key growth areas of the future," explained an executive from McDonald's, which, like many U.S. companies, faced a flat market at home.[22] With fewer fast-food restaurants than West Germany or Great Britain, France beckoned as a frontier. To penetrate this territory, McDonald's tried to adapt to French customs and tastes (less sugar and more mustard in its salad dressings, for example) just as Quick and Freetime shaped themselves to the American pattern. Through its investments and its influence, McDonald's advanced the homogenization of the globe and the internationalization of business. *Le Nouvel Observateur* observed that the French are "mixing Coca-Cola with their wine"—quite a shift from the Coca-Cola battle of 1949–50.[23]

Another hot issue of the late 1940s had been the importation of Hollywood movies. Despite the French government's persistent efforts to promote domestic films, those from America remained popular. Of the 60 top films in Paris in 1984–85, 31 were American, 27 were French, and 2 were British. Hollywood's appeal made France America's third largest film export market, behind only Canada and Japan. In the United States French movies were the most popular foreign films shown, but in 1984 revenues from the top three foreign-language movies (two French and one Spanish) accounted for less than one-quarter of one percent of total film receipts in America. Hollywood action films like *Rambo*, *Apocalypse Now*, *Indiana Jones and the Temple of Doom*, and *Star Wars* were all smash hits in France. Perhaps because they had their own problems with former colonies and evil empires, the French relished films that featured the triumph of anti-Communist white heroes and virtuous republicans. Comedian Jerry Lewis was a longtime French favorite. Although popular at home, Woody Allen became a bigger star among the French, who took seriously his intellectual humor—and who hired him as a television commentator on the 1980 U.S. presidential election. Young French directors continued to look to Hollywood for inspiration. U.S. movies did dominate, *Le Monde* concluded, but "the imperialism of American cinema is one of quality."[24] American television also became popular in France. "President Mitterrand is a *Dallas* fan he knows the story line and knows every character," reported culture minister Jack Lang in 1985.[25] René Bonnell, who bought films for the French pay television service, explained that "no one else can make films with the production values of American movies."[26] With a $3 billion surplus balance of trade in 1989, the U.S. film industry shone as one of the few bright spots in America's dismal trade picture. Sales to France and elsewhere kept the top Hollywood studios afloat, with exports accounting for 43 percent of all film revenues in 1989, up from 33 percent in 1984.[27]

Although Americans and French enjoyed seeing each other's films, they remained rivals for profit and prestige. In 1985 competing scientists Luc Montagnier of the Pasteur Institute and Robert Gallo of the U.S. National Institutes of Health (NIH) each claimed to have first identified the HIV virus that causes the deadly Acquired Immune Deficiency Syndrome. (The dispute extended to the name. Proud of their scientific tradition and their language, the French refused to accept the nearly universal English acronym—AIDS— using instead the French acronym SIDA.) At stake was more than fame. The discoverer of the virus stood to gain the lion's share of patent profits from the huge AIDS test business. On 31 March 1987 Reagan and Prime Minister Jacques Chirac agreed to what the French called a "research Yalta" to divide the royalties. However Gallo and Montagnier still argued, in the popular press and in scientific journals, about which of them had first identified and cultured the HIV virus. In 1991 other French and American researchers concluded that in 1983 a particularly virulent strain of the virus had contaminated the laboratory cultures of both Gallo and Montagnier, thereby misleading the two scientists. Each of the rivals continued to maintain that he had been right, displaying a stubbornness common in U.S.-French disputes.[28]

A week before the AIDS Yalta, Chirac signed with Michael Eisner, chairman of Walt Disney Company, a contract to build a $4.4 billion theme park, called Euro Disneyland, on former sugar beet fields 20 miles east of Paris. Building Euro Disneyland became Europe's second largest construction project, ranking behind only the tunnel being burrowed under the English Channel. When completed in 1992, "Euro Disney is going to create at least 30,000 jobs," enthused Christian Cardon, the French government official in charge of relations with the American company. "And tourists from abroad will spend almost $1 billion a year here."[29]

Lured by this bonanza, the French made repeated concessions during the two years of hard negotiations for the project. Of the $4.4 billion total, the American Disney company put up $160 million in cash. The French government provided a low interest loan of nearly $1 billion, and banks and other private investors pumped in the remainder of the construction costs. The Disney company would receive 49 percent of the profits from Euro Disneyland plus a share of the gross in admission fees, food sales, and so on. An industry analyst calculated that by 1994, Disney's share of the park's profits would reach $199 million annually, a huge return on its $160 million investment.[30] "Europe is going to be as important as the United States to the Disney company," predicted Robert Fitzpatrick, the French-speaking American chairman of Euro Disneyland.[31] In addition to its financial contribution, the French government agreed to halve the usual sales tax levied on entrance tickets and to extend the Paris subway and the high-speed train systems to the site. The French government exercised the right of eminent domain to enable the Euro Disney company to acquire 4700 acres. Because the park itself took up only a small portion of this fiefdom, Euro Disney had a huge amount of prime real estate for hotels, campgrounds, office buildings, high technology factories, and retail stores. Even before Euro Disneyland opened, the company was planning a $3 billion second phase to enlarge the theme park and develop the real estate. Both English and French would be the official languages of this empire while wine and other alcoholic beverages would be prohibited. Euro Disneyland would even enjoy a kind of extraterritoriality: a panel of three judges chosen by mutual agreement, rather than the French courts, would settle disputes arising between the park and the French authorities.

In the 1980s the French eagerly embraced American popular culture. The Euro Disneyland construction project became the second largest building effort in Europe. *Courtesy* Le Nouvel Observateur

The French made such unusual concessions because they feared that the Walt Disney Company would carry out its threat to build elsewhere. The French needed the jobs from Disneyland, and they hoped that the universal appeal of Mickey Mouse would help make Paris the leisure and high-technology capital of Western Europe. "Paris is going to be the center of Europe," French television told viewers when announcing the Disneyland project—while the whole midday news team wore Mickey Mouse ears.[32]

In previous decades, building this most American of theme parks on the outskirts of the French city of light would have ignited an explosion of controversy. In the late 1980s protest remained confined to the extreme left and right. Communist-controlled unions booed Disney's plan to introduce U.S.-style, less protective labor contracts. Le Pen's right-wing group agitated against the employment of Algerian immigrants. Neither protest had much impact. Most intellectuals polled by *Le Nouvel Observateur* focused on the project's economic benefits. Disney conducted an aggressive publicity campaign to win the hearts of local residents and the francs of potential visitors. The company invited local politicians to Disney World in Florida and hosted area children at a birthday party for Mickey Mouse. It set up a satellite-based European Disney channel and aired a Disney television special throughout Europe. The Americans agreed to devote part of the park to themes from French history and from the writings of Jules Verne. "Walt Disney borrowed a lot from European stories—for Sleeping Beauty for example—and we're trying to give some of that back," Eisner said disarmingly.[33] Another company official claimed that Walt "D'Isgny" was of French descent. The goodwill blitz seemed effective. "They're experts at seduction," a French businessman noted with awe. "The French aren't used to this kind of public relations—it [is] unbelievable."[34]

The seduction was mutual, with the French government anxious to boost the French economy and the U.S. company eager to cash in on the global appeal of American mass culture. Both sides stood to profit from the partnership, but the Americans came out ahead in terms of economic gain and cultural penetration. The multifaceted rapprochement between the two nations in the 1980s probably made the French more accepting of this added bit of Americanization and of this latest example of inequality in the U.S.-French relationship.

Perhaps the most impressive product of the 1980s U.S.-French liaison was the pyramid of the remodeled Louvre museum. In 1983 Mitterrand personally selected the Chinese-born American architect I. M. Pei to design a new public entry and underground expansion for the venerable Louvre, crammed with some of France's most prized art treasures. Critics quickly charged that Pei's design would wreck the heart of Paris, for the American was planning to build a huge, modernistic glass and metal pyramid as the entrance to the classical museum. Yet when the 71-foot-high edifice opened to the public on 29 March 1989, it charmed most critics and citizens. Like the engineer Gus-

At the July 1989 economic summit in Paris the assembled leaders pose in front of the Louvre's new Pyramid, designed by American architect I. M. Pei. President George Bush stands in the place of honor on Mitterand's right side. *Courtesy of French Embassy Press & Information Division*

tave Eiffel a century earlier, Pei played on the French love of structures both colossal and technological. The sky-lit pyramid extended deep underground. Built of crystal clear glass panels held fast by thin metal cables, the elegant building seemed to float in the Louvre courtyard. Pei achieved this enchanting effect by using advanced technology distinctly American: the concepts of domes, pioneered by R. Buckminster Fuller, and the cabling systems of the America's Cup yachts. Yet he also employed the famed French glassmakers St. Gobains to produce the unusually transparent glass.

The pyramid's marriage of American design and French craftsmanship bore economic importance—as did the Disneyland and the AIDS deals. The $1 billion expansion project created more than 650,000 square feet of new space beneath the pyramid and the Louvre's central courtyard. With French approval, the American architect focused on the marketing and delivery of art. He allocated much of the Louvre's new area to bookstores, cafeterias, computerized systems for ticket sales, and data banks for quick location of specific artworks. Pei transformed the "stodgy but glorious" Louvre "into a museum that can rank with any American one in terms of merchandising and crowd management," noted a reporter.[35] This commercialization had become an essential adjunct to art, Le Monde explained.[36]

In recasting the Louvre as an institution geared toward efficient consumption of art, Pei and the French illustrated an observation of Debray. "At the moment when the Eastern Empire [of the Soviet Union and Communism] is losing its internal relay points (parties, unions, intellectuals), the Western Empire sees its own growing (data banks, audiovisual programs, news magazines)."[37] In the late twentieth century, accelerating technological change and triumphant consumerism gave the flexible market structures of capitalism an advantage over the more rigid institutions of a planned economy. France became more like the United States and other advanced capitalist nations as a majority of the French focused on their creature comforts and personal anxieties.

In the 1970s and 1980s Mitterrand rode this erratic swing toward conservatism as he revamped and revitalized the Socialist party (P.S.) Mitterrand promised voters a vigorous foreign policy with only a limited socialism, sparking complaints from left-wing P.S. leaders such as Jean-Pierre Chevènement that their party was becoming like the American Democratic party. From 1972 to 1977 and again from 1981 to 1984, the rising P.S. joined in a coalition with the sinking Communist party. The PCF's best electoral showing in the Fifth Republic (22.5 percent in 1967) was worse than its worst performance under the Fourth Republic (25.6 percent in 1956). By 1986 the PCF had dropped to under 10 percent of the French vote. "Our fundamental objective," Mitterrand explained after signing the 1972 accord with the Communists, "is to demonstrate that, of the 5 million PCF voters, 3 million might vote for the Socialist Party."[38] Mitterrand's strategy proved sound as the

Socialist-Communist coalition coopted the hapless Communists and helped push the French left rightward. Hoping desperately to demonstrate its French nationalism and independence from Moscow, the PCF in May 1977 reversed its long-held opposition to the nuclear *force de frappe*.

The left wing of the Socialist party, composing about one-quarter of the party in the early 1970s, grouped around the Center for Socialist Study, Research, and Education, known by the French acronym CERES. CERES agreed with the PCF that French independence required an autonomous nuclear deterrent. This about-face added another layer to the Gaullist nuclear consensus. The difference lay in the dream of the CERES Socialists and the Communists that leftist France would use its independence to socialize the economy and champion revolution for the world's oppressed. Mitterrand and other moderate Socialists lacked such vaulting ambitions, despite their occasional radical rhetoric. Yet in 1978 they too abandoned opposition to the *force de frappe*. Smelling victory in the upcoming elections, mainstream Socialist leaders such as Mitterrand realized they had to appear realistic to swing voters. Traditionally, Socialists had advocated universal nuclear disarmament—an unlikely prospect. With no defense plan of their own, they bought the Gaullist nuclear thesis. Thus by the late 1970s French opinion from the Gaullist right to the Communist left agreed that the *force de frappe* helped guarantee the nation's independence and defense.[39]

The left's mainstream position on nuclear weapons probably helped Mitterrand, the Socialist-Communist candidate, win the presidency in the election of May 1981, only six months after the American people elected the conservative Ronald Reagan. A political virtuoso, Mitterrand had served in 11 Fourth Republic cabinets, ran against de Gaulle for president in 1965, nearly beat Giscard in 1974, and outmaneuvered both his Gaullist opposition and Communist allies in the May 1981 election. The Socialists consolidated their win by sweeping the subsequent parliamentary elections. Mitterrand's party rewarded its Communist partners with four cabinet seats—all of them minor offices. The PCF shared the responsibility for governing France, but the Communists enjoyed little real power. Still, Mitterrand's government at first appeared to Reaganites as dangerously to the left. Attending Mitterrand's inauguration ceremony, Vice President George Bush annoyed the French president by complaining about the Communist ministers in the Cabinet. A Reagan official reportedly asked a Mitterrand aide, who must have marveled at American ignorance, what, after all, was "the real difference between your economic policy and that of the Soviet Union?"[40]

Some Americans remained suspicious of French socialism, even after Mitterrand undertook wholesale cooperation with the United States. Back in the early cold-war years, Irving Brown, the American labor federation's agent in Western Europe, had used U.S. government and union money to help split the French labor movement and create the anti-communist Force Ouvrière (F.O.) In 1985, still operating in Europe on behalf of American labor, Brown tapped funds from the National Endowment for Democracy, a Reagan-inspired governmental foundation established to shore up fragile democracies, whose bylaws required openness in its disbursal of taxpayers' money. Brown secretly gave $830,000 in endowment funds to the center-right F.O. and $575,000 to UNI, an anti-Mitterrand student confederation reportedly linked to a far right-wing group. This farcical replay of the 1940s and 1950s sparked a flurry of resentment in France, but Mitterrand did not let the episode derail his rapprochement with Washington.[41]

Despite their ostensible ideological differences, Mitterrand and Reagan soon cooperated closely, particularly on military and strategic matters. At first Mitterrand challenged Reagan's campaign against radical revolution in Central America. Speaking in Mexico in 1982, Jack Lang, the French minister of culture, denounced what he called America's worldwide cultural imperialism. France sold arms to the Sandinista Nicaraguan government and recognized the leftist Salvadoran rebels. Yet by 1982 Mitterrand had retreated from such independent forays in the third world. Paris and Washington cooperated in Lebanon, where Syrian-backed Muslims fought the pro-Western Christian minority; in Chad, where Libyan leader Mu'ammar al-Qaddafi threatened a takeover; and in Iraq, where the French, Americans, Soviets, and others sold Saddam Hussein weapons and supplies for his war against Iran. Meanwhile the world recession and a flight of French capital compelled the Socialist president to pull back from his electoral pledge to socialize the French economy. In 1984 Lang publicly retracted his accusation of two years before. In that same year the PCF left the governing coalition while Laurent Fabius, a 38-year-old with an American mother and an upper-class family, became prime minister under President Mitterrand.

Mitterrand, who had supported NATO since its birth and who had opposed de Gaulle's 1966 withdrawal, continued the French policy, begun under Pompidou, of edging back toward the alliance. Powerful forces drove that policy. While the political and economic influence of the United States in Western Europe declined, the might of West Germany steadily grew. The Germans had become reluctant cold warriors, too concerned, the French feared, with building ties to the East. Despite their economic difficulties, the Soviets increased their nuclear arsenal, particularly those weapons aimed at Western Europe. Because of those developments, Mitterrand felt that France needed the United States and NATO to stay in Europe and help balance Soviet and German power. "The Mitterrand Government has been extraordinarily cooperative in NATO matters, more so than Giscard, more so than Pompidou," observed Senator Charles Mathias in 1985.[42]

Mitterrand became a particularly valuable ally of Washington on the explosive issue of nuclear weapons in Europe. Both the Carter and Reagan administrations worked on contingency plans for waging, and winning, a nuclear war. When Reagan talked about fighting such a conflict in Europe, it horrified Europeans. Similarly, Carter and Reagan administration officials calculated that deploying the highly accurate Pershing II and cruise missiles in West Germany and in other NATO countries would bolster the alliance's morale and checkmate the Soviets, who were installing powerful SS-20 rockets aimed at Western Europe. But instead of assuring the Europeans, the new American missiles angered and frightened them, and so generated a huge wave of antinuclear sentiment.

This tide swept across most of Western Europe and the United States, leaving France relatively untouched. (Even in France, however, the emphasis remained on deterring nuclear war, not on the American fantasy of fighting and winning such a conflict. In 1983 a poll showed that more than half of the French public favored negotiation—not resistance—in the event of a Soviet military invasion. Only 6 percent advocated retaliation with nuclear weapons.)[43] French authorities worked to buttress their national consensus on nuclear power and nuclear weapons. In 1983, when Catholic bishops in the United States and elsewhere condemned nuclear weapons, French bishops extolled the benefits of nuclear deterrence. "Saint Bomb, protect us," jeered the handful of French protesters.[44] France stood almost alone among Western European nations in not broadcasting the American television film *The Day After*, which depicted the horror of nuclear war. A Paris movie theater showed the film and drew huge crowds. In response to popular clamor, French public radio staged a call-in show with one expert to answer questions— General Pierre Gallois, a father of the *force de frappe*.[45] During the celebrations marking the 200th anniversary of the French Revolution, the government paraded nuclear weapons down the Champs-Elysées.

Amid the widespread clamor against nuclear weapons in the 1980s, France became—precisely because it was *not* in NATO militarily and had no American weapons on its soil—Washington's most dependable nuclear ally. As a French defense analyst put it, "the United States needs France—even a Socialist one—so long as it remains the only European country that is still committed to a strong defense effort, that still has ambitions for itself, and that is spared from the rising wave of European neutralism and pacifism."[46] This nuclear bond provided a strong basis for U.S.-French rapprochement during the 1980s, especially before 1986, when Reagan began to consider a drastic cutback of such weapons.

After 1982 this military alignment helped soothe the resentment left by the Siberian gas pipeline controversy. The gas pipeline battle amounted to an escalation of the U.S.-European economic cold war, declared *Le Matin*, a Socialist newspaper close to Mitterrand. Sharply diverging economic interests spawned the conflict. While the Carter embargo slashed American exports to the Soviet Union 54 percent from 1979 to 1980, French sales to the Soviets climbed 35 percent. German and British exports to the Soviet Union also rose. Even though Reagan dropped the grain embargo, by 1982 American trade with the Soviet Union reached just $2.5 billion, a tiny fraction of

Western Europe's $41 billion business with Moscow. Western Europe traded heavy machinery and precision equipment for Soviet raw materials, particularly oil. With Western European unemployment at the highest levels since the Great Depression, France and the others viewed sales to the Soviet Union as essential to keep major firms from bankruptcy. Europeans valued Soviet energy supplies because they offered a measure of energy independence from the volatile Middle East. They remembered that during the 1973 Arab oil embargo, the Soviets had not joined the Arabs, but had rushed in to increase sales to Western Europe. The Soviets depended on hard-currency earnings from oil exports to pay for needed imports, yet their petroleum reserves were running out. In 1985 the shortfall in oil production forced Moscow to cut sales to the non-Communist world by one-fourth. Exports of natural gas, of which the Soviet Union held 40 percent of known world reserves, promised to fill Moscow's hard-currency gap. After 1973 Western Europeans increased their use of natural gas, particularly in homes and businesses, as part of the effort to reduce dependence on imported oil.

In 1980 the French, Germans, and Soviets began negotiations for what some Europeans called "the deal of the century"—a 3,000-mile natural-gas pipeline across tundra, rivers, and mountains from eastern Siberia to western Europe. The Europeans agreed to finance the mammoth project; supply most of the pipe, compressors, and other equipment; and buy the gas transported through the line. The Soviets obtained $5–6 billion of credits for the undertaking, of which French banks supplied $2 billion. The deal specified that the Europeans could pay for the gas in their own currencies, thereby bypassing the unstable dollar. This exclusion was one of the many objections Washington had to the deal. The United States urged the Western Europeans to buy American coal and nuclear-energy technology instead of Soviet natural gas. The Europeans rejected this offer since the gas better suited their energy needs, and the American deal promised little help for their unemployment.[47]

The Europeans began this mammoth venture with the Soviet Union just as the Reagan administration escalated Carter's arms buildup and cold-war rhetoric. The new president horrified the allies with talk of nuclear battle. Hardliners such as Secretary of Defense Caspar Weinberger and his assistant Richard Perle openly urged a "full-court press" and economic war against the Soviet Union. In contrast to the French and other Europeans, Reagan officials sought to cut the flow of goods, technology, and credits to the Communists. They wanted to wield trade as a weapon to win political concessions and internal changes from a beleaguered Soviet Union. The administration was aghast that Western Europe would become dependent on Soviet energy. "If I were a Soviet leader, I would have rubbed my hands with delight when the Europeans signed the pipeline contracts," said a senior Defense Department official. "That's the kind of leverage strategists usually only dream about."[48]

The French and others countered that by the time the pipeline reached full capacity in the 1990s, the Soviet Union would be supplying 30 percent of the total gas consumption of France and Germany, or only 6 percent of their total energy needs. If the Soviets did cut off the supply (which would hurt their future sales prospects), Western Europe's integrated gas grid made it easy to fill an emergency gap with gas produced in the Netherlands, Austria, or elsewhere. Most of the gas went to homes and stores, and in the event of a serious military crisis a shortage of cooking gas would be among the least of Western Europe's problems. The Reagan administration also worried that the Soviets would use the $5 billion worth of francs and marks earned from gas sales for purchases that would enhance their military capacity. Here critics answered that nearly all Soviet military products were made at home and that if Moscow really wanted to buy some item, it would find the gold or hard currency to do so. Energy exports, moreover, brought in two-thirds of Moscow's foreign-currency earnings, money needed to pay past debts and buy needed imports such as grain and machinery. Which side, then, would grow more dependent because of the pipeline—the Europeans who got 6 percent of their energy from the gas or the Soviets who earned two-thirds of their hard currency from gas and oil exports?[49]

Such counterarguments convinced Reagan hard-liners that the Europeans had become spineless, greedy, almost useless allies. In December 1981 General Wojciech Jaruzelski imposed martial law in Poland in response to the rising popularity and demands of the Solidarity union movement. The Reagan administration fingered Moscow for instigating the crackdown and slapped an embargo on high-technology exports to the Soviet Union, including equipment for the gas pipeline. The United States nonetheless continued to sell grain to Moscow, in keeping with the president's politically popular pledge to American farmers in the 1980 campaign. Relieved that at least the Soviets had not invaded Poland, the French and others wondered whether the Americans intended the embargo to apply to equipment produced in Europe under license from American companies. Along with other European companies, Alsthom-Atlantique, a French nationalized firm, manufactured the giant turbines for the pipeline compressors with technology licensed from General Electric.[50]

At the June 1982 Versailles economic summit, Secretary of State Alexander Haig worked out a deal whereby the United States would help support the shaky franc in the currency markets in return for the Europeans tightening up future credits to the Soviet Union. "It was implicitly understood that the United States would not apply retroactive, extraterritorial sanctions" affecting the pipeline, Haig recalled.[51] The French, who had invested considerable prestige and effort in hosting the lavish summit, were pleased. But the deal lasted only a day. When Reagan returned to Washington, Secretary of the Treasury Donald Regan, a free-market purist, balked at the idea of supporting the franc. An angry Mitterrand pulled away from the promise to restrict future credits to the Soviets. Then, at an 18 June meeting scheduled so Haig could not attend, National Security Adviser William Clark and Weinberger convinced

Reagan to expand the December 1981 embargo. Now the United States would try to stop European companies, manufacturing in Europe, from selling to the Soviets pipeline equipment that used licensed American technology. This ban assaulted the sovereignty of France and other allies. Undaunted, the president decided, "It's time we laid the wood to the Russians."[52] Reagan based his decision on narrow evidence. Clark and Weinberger "put one over on him," a State Department official recalled." Reagan wasn't fully informed of what the options were."[53] As the meeting concluded, Haig's deputy, Lawrence Eagleburger, begged the administration at least to inform the European governments of the expanded embargo before the press splashed the news. Clark thought this courtesy unnecessary. Mitterrand and the others learned through the newspapers, an added slap in the face.

"This day, June 18, 1982 could well go down as the beginning of the end of the Atlantic Alliance," declared French foreign minister Claude Cheysson. "The United States has just declared what amounts to war on her allies in Western Europe."[54] France became the first of the allies to defy the Reagan embargo. As "an act of sovereignty," explained a high French official, Paris ordered Alsthom-Atlantique to continue manufacturing the pipeline turbines.[55] It was also a matter of economic survival. Mitterrand's efforts to stimulate domestic prosperity had faltered, and France needed all the industrial jobs it could get. U.S. ambassador Evan Galbraith warned of possible criminal penalties for the directors of European companies that ignored the ban. If such companies tried to do business in the United States, they would face "a nightmare," he told Le Monde.[56] "These sanctions, are they being applied to the Soviet Union and Poland or to the European allies?" Mitterrand asked angrily.[57]

The pipeline crisis tightened other economic tensions. Reagan's massive budget deficits jacked up U.S. interest rates. Capital from Europe and elsewhere poured into America, forcing France and other nations to raise their interest levels, worsening their recessions. "How can we defend our alliance with the United States when critics say American policy is making us bankrupt?" wondered the French finance minister.[58] Washington turned a deaf ear to Mitterrand's repeated argument that assisting third-world development would help the wealthy nations get out of recession. After the conclusion of painstaking negotiations to limit European shipments of steel to the United States, American steel companies rejected the deal. Reagan sided with the companies and levied punitive duties on European steel imports. The long-running agricultural trade dispute irritated both sides. Senator Roger Jepsen of Iowa complained that the EEC's "bad behavior" with farm subsidies "denies us a share of the foreign market."[59] "We are going to do battle with the EEC wherever and whenever it is necessary," warned Secretary of Agriculture John Block.[60] While pressing Europe not to sell the Soviet Union equipment for the pipeline, Reagan on 30 July announced a new grain deal with Moscow. "The Soviet market is the biggest in the world, and we want to recapture

Frustrated with his inability at times to communicate with Reagan, Mitterrand at one point took a commercial flight to Washington for the day. At the White House, Mitterrand was met with "smiling incomprehension," French officials told a reporter. *Courtesy of French Embassy Press & Information Division*

it. . . . Our national economy needs it," he blithely explained, infuriating Europeans further.[61]

"The United States seems totally indifferent to our problems," wailed Cheysson. "It is the major ally and we don't even talk anymore." He warned of a "progressive divorce" between Western Europe and America.[62] Reagan, who often seemed to confuse reality with what he had seen on the screen, minimized the dispute as being "all in the family."[63] Perhaps the quarrel reminded the president of the popular television series of that name—with his playing Archie Bunker to Europe's Edith. Desperate to make Reagan understand Europe's problems, Mitterrand at one point simply got on a commercial airline and went to Washington for the day. At the White House he was met with "smiling incomprehension," French officials told a reporter.[64] Observing that it had once more come to warfare with the Europeans, humorist Russell Baker offered the battle song "No More Brie for Me":

> OK, Mitterrand, by me
> No more runny Brie
> I'm through with Frenchy cheese
> Till we bring you to your knees.
> Forget it, okay France?
> If you prefer the red pipeline
> I'll switch to Liederkranz.[65]

German Liederkranz actually proved to be no alternative because Bonn and the other allies followed France's defiance of the U.S. ban. Construction of the Soviet pipeline was progressing, the CIA reported to the White House.

Reagan's embargo disrupted American business as well as the Western alliance. The U.S. Chamber of Commerce and the National Association of Manufacturers lobbied against the ban. "We now have a situation," observed Senator Jepsen, "where the Soviet market is closed to us; the Japanese have the business; the unemployment lines in Peoria have grown longer; and it appears that the Soviet gas pipeline . . . will be built anyway."[66] Reagan's and Carter's sanctions against the Soviet Union made American companies unreliable business partners and suppliers. A U.S. official in France reported that European firms "are now willing to pay a premium to be independent of American suppliers."[67]

Eventually the policy's bankruptcy became clear even to the White House. Haig, whose imperious blustering clashed with Clark, Weinberger, and other Reagan insiders, had resigned in June. The new secretary of state was George Shultz, a pragmatist who persuaded Reagan to drop the failed ban. In November 1982 the president took the occasion of Brezhnev's death to lift the pipeline sanctions. The White House tried to save face by saying that the Europeans in return had agreed to new curbs on trade with the Soviets. Mitterrand sharply denied making any such concession.

The pipeline controversy demonstrated the growing distance between the United States and Western Europe. The French and others observed that once again America had pursued its narrow self-interest without much concern for Europe. Unlike some previous quarrels such as the 1973–74 energy dispute, the Europeans hung together in defying the United States. The pipeline argument illustrated the increasingly ad hoc nature of an alliance with fewer common concerns and sharper conflicts. It underscored the decline of America's influence in Western Europe. Yet the controversy also demonstrated French dismay at Washington's disinterest in leading a community of more equal states. "*Good* alliances," said one exasperated French official, require that nations "respect themselves and make others respect them."[68]

The U.S. air attack on Libyan leader Mu'ammar al-Qaddafi was another affair in which Washington did not respect France enough to try for a common policy. During the night of 15 April 1986, 13 U.S. F-111 fighters bombed Libyan shore facilities and Qaddafi's living quarters. Qaddafi escaped, but his daughter and at least 37 other Libyans and two U.S. flyers died in the raid. Reagan was retaliating against Libya's alleged involvement in the bombing of a West Berlin nightclub in which an American soldier was killed. (Later evidence indicated that Syria, not Libya, had fomented the bombing.)

The F-111s, which took off from Great Britain, had to travel twice as far to reach Libya because Mitterrand refused to allow them to fly over French airspace. Furious, Weinberger publicly vented his "considerable disappointment" with the French.[69] *New York Times* columnist William Safire called for a boycott of French goods; on his television show Johnny Carson threw a pie at an actor portraying a Frenchman; and U.S. diplomat Vernon Walters went on French television to complain of "ingratitude" and to remind viewers of food packages sent to France after World War II.[70] Carson's pie throwing became a major news story in France as the French took offense at the hostile American reaction. *Rambo* film star Sylvester Stallone canceled plans to attend the Cannes film festival, reportedly because he feared terrorism. Stallone is "just like your foreign policy: celluloid tough," a former French defense official told Americans.[71]

Almost ignored in the swirl of emotion was Mitterrand's suggestion, before the bombing raid, "that the two of us [France and the United States] talk seriously about getting rid of Qaddafi."[72] Qaddafi worried Western Europeans, vulnerable to terrorism from nearby Libya. In August 1980 the French intelligence agency had reportedly worked with the Egyptians to try to overthrow Qaddafi. With U.S. support, France had intervened to protect its former colony Chad from a Libyan invasion. The day before the raid—after it had made its final plans—the Reagan administration sent Walters to inform the European allies. The French thought the bombing plan was too limited. "Don't do a pinprick," they reportedly urged. A meaningful discussion of options was impossible; Walters had authority only to inform. If the United States had agreed to a serious attack on Qaddafi, "France would have been at your side," a Paris official later asserted.[73] Instead Mitterrand—who had only a few hours' notice of the raid and no input into its scope—denied the United States the use of French airspace. About 70 percent of the French public supported Mitterrand's decision. Yet an equal proportion favored the U.S. action.[74] France stood out as the only major European ally in which a majority of the public approved of the bombing and in which there were no large protests against the raid.

This public support, however, won France little gratitude in the United States. Outraged Americans focused on Mitterrand's refusal, remained oblivious to the consultation issue, and lumped together the "Eurowimps."[75] In mid-1986 NATO commander General Bernard Rogers observed that anti-European feeling in the United States and anti-American sentiment in Europe stood at the highest levels he had ever seen. After nearly 40 years of marriage, the Atlantic allies felt generally irritated with each other.

Trade disputes, particularly in agriculture, heightened tensions. In 1985 a U.S. Agriculture Department expert testified that the European Community's (E.C.) highly efficient, highly subsidized farmers had edged out the United States to become the world's largest exporter of poultry, eggs, beef, refined sugar, and dairy products—all commodities the E.C. had formerly bought from the United States. Europe had elbowed itself into this position by "forcing U.S. farmers to produce less and earn less in the world marketplace," he explained.[76] A year later, when America ran a deficit in farm products for the first time since the *Mayflower* landing, Representative Lee Hamilton of Indiana exploded: "In agriculture today, we can't sell anything abroad." Why should the United States support the E.C., he asked, "when it keeps causing us more and more problems?"[77]

In this shaky condition, the Western alliance was hit by a series of political, economic, and military earthquakes that changed the landscape of Europe. The cold war—that bulwark of the post–World War II order, barrier to the integration of Eastern and Western Europe, and buttress of American and Soviet predominance in Europe—began to crumble after Mikhail Gorbachev came to power in March 1985 and pushed for arms limitation, tolerance of change in Eastern Europe, and, to revive the moribund Soviet economy, *glasnost* (openness) and *perestroika* (restructuring). Gorbachev's eagerness for détente made it harder for Washington to get the West Germans to accept additional nuclear weapons on their soil. Sharing the American worry about West Germany's rising neutralism and nuclear allergy, the French knit closer economic, military, and political ties with their powerful neighbor.

The French also became interested in reinvigorating the E.C. so as to fashion a stronger anchor for West Germany in the West. Meanwhile, the directors of the E.C. (many of whom were French) declared in 1985 that rising trade competition from the Japanese and the Americans created an imperative. Unless the E.C. quickly completed the economic integration it had begun in 1957, it would suffer stagnation and "Eurosclerosis." By 1987 the E.C. governments, with much pushing from France, agreed to remove all internal trade obstacles by 1993 and so create true economic unity. The E.C. also began discussion on political and military integration.

Meanwhile, America's burgeoning trade deficit forced increased borrowing from overseas, and in 1985 the United States became a net debtor nation for the first time since World War I. With pressing trade troubles, Americans worried that the E.C. might become "Fortress Europe," blocking other nations's exports. Despite this potential danger, a strengthened E.C. appeared useful to both the Americans and the French as a harness for West Germany. Both Paris and Washington wanted to contain and channel Bonn's rising influence in Eastern Europe, yet France's leverage was restricted by the moderate size of its economy, and the United States' leverage was limited by its yawning budget and trade deficits.

In the late 1980s, as the cost of defending NATO reached $171 billion (almost 60 percent of the U.S. military budget), many Americans wondered whether the military commitment to Western Europe remained affordable, credible, or worthwhile.[78] The centerpiece of that commitment, repeated by every president since NATO's birth, was to avenge a massive Soviet assault on Western Europe with a nuclear attack on the Soviet Union. Of course this would trigger Moscow's nuclear destruction of the United States. De Gaulle had doubted that America would honor the promise. No nation would ever die for another, he thought, and so he pushed the *force de frappe*. Skepticism about Washington's nuclear commitment had become the majority view in Europe by the late 1970s, observed *Le Monde* editor André Fontaine.

Still, former secretary of state Kissinger shocked Europeans in 1979 when he declared in public that the emperor had no clothes—and never would have any. "It is absurd to base the strategy of the West on the credibility of mutual suicide," he told NATO officials in Brussels. "Don't you Europeans keep asking us to multiply assurances we cannot possibly mean and that if we do mean, we should not want to execute, and which if we execute, would destroy our civilization," he lectured.[79] Europe was left "naked," concluded French defense analyst Pierre Lellouche. "The American [nuclear] umbrella is entirely closed."[80] It was not so much what Kissinger said that upset Europeans, but the fact that he said it. "Some things are better left unexpressed," a top American analyst commented tersely.[81]

A decade later, alliance niceties—and pretenses—had worn further away. In 1988 a blue-ribbon Pentagon commission cochaired by Deputy Defense Secretary Fred Iklé and including Kissinger, Brzezinski, and others, found it "incredible" that Europeans still believed in deterrence through mutual assured nuclear destruction.[82] The commission urged a shift in American military resources away from the defense of Western Europe to the more pressing problem of armed challenge in the third world. Both Kissinger in 1979 and the Pentagon commission in 1988 tried to shock the Continent into doing more for its own defense.

Indeed increasing numbers of Americans suspected that Europe, especially West Germany, suffered from military dependency—a malady akin to welfare dependency in the inner cities. Too secure under Washington's defense umbrella, Western Europe in the mid-1980s had apparently lost the will to defend itself. Some conservative Americans scorned the allies as "Euroisolationists"—quick to criticize Washington, slow to condemn Moscow, too lazy to provide for their own defense, too craven to help the United States police the third world, and addicted to expensive social welfare programs. "You know, [Europeans] worry a lot," commented former ambassador to the United Nations Jeane Kirkpatrick, a conservative favorite.[83] Europeans "demand the right to be protected by American troops and America's nuclear umbrella while reserving the right to undermine American security everywhere else," complained columnist William Safire.[84]

The more public opinion in West Germany, Great Britain, and elsewhere swung toward neutralism and pacifism, the more Washington valued its tacit nuclear alliance with Paris. In the early 1980s the ruling German Social Democratic party responded to mammoth public protests by backing away from its pledge to deploy the American Pershing II and cruise missiles. Helmut Kohl's Christian Democrats still favored installing these so-called intermediate range nuclear forces (INF missiles). In the middle of the German election campaign of early 1983, Mitterrand addressed the Bonn parliament. It was the twentieth anniversary of the Franco-German friendship treaty, designed by de Gaulle to keep the Germans leashed to France. Intervening in German politics, the French Socialist criticized Bonn's Socialists for edging away from the missile commitment. (Of course France would not even consider putting American missiles on *its* soil.) Mitterrand's speech won warm applause from the Christian Democrats, who went on to victory in part because of Mitterrand's tacit endorsement. This marked the first major occasion since the Cuban missile crisis that Paris had come out strongly in favor of an American policy.

Despite vehement opposition, the INF missiles were deployed in West Germany, Italy, Belgium, the Netherlands, and Great Britain, beginning in November 1983. Yet the protesters, whose reasoning and emotion penetrated even those governments that accepted the new missiles, had more success than they perhaps realized. The highly accurate, mobile-launched Pershing II and cruise missiles were potential first-strike weapons; yet they also stood vulnerable to a preemptive Soviet strike. In time of emergency, they had to be split up or suffer the fate of sitting ducks. Yet this scattering required the approval of Bonn or the other host governments. Richard Perle, a leading Pentagon hard-liner, worried that the Europeans, fearful of war, would balk at dispersing the missiles. This problem devalued the missiles as a deterrent or as first-strike weapons, and probably made the Reagan administration more willing to give them up in the INF treaty of December 1987. The West Germans' growing skittishness about nuclear weapons and the very thought of war threatened NATO's credibility while underscoring the importance of France. "By the time all the orders are channeled through NATO and agreement is achieved, there might be paralysis," feared Senator Larry Pressler of South Dakota.[85] With NATO hamstrung, the independent nuclear force of "the French might be able to do something, and that might be more of a deterrent," Pressler and Jeane Kirkpatrick agreed.[86]

Back in 1974 Kissinger and Nixon had come to the same conclusion about France and deterrence, and thus had begun covert nuclear cooperation with Paris. In the years since then, the United States secretly helped the French to miniaturize their warheads (essential for development of multiple-warhead launchers), perfect methods for shielding the bombs from electromagnetic radiation from nearby nuclear explosions, and set up underground testing facilities. In addition the United States in 1985 amended an earlier law to make it legal to transfer to France restricted data concerning the safety and security of nuclear weapons. The United States benefited itself from this cooperation. For one thing, the French had leapfrogged ahead of America in certain areas of weapons technology. The French "had stuff they showed us that was the best in the world. Better than we had," commented one American scientist involved in the exchange.[87] Further, the Mitterrand and Giscard governments promised that in the event of a major war American forces could use designated French hospitals, seaports, airports, railways, and highways. This pledge abandoned de Gaulle's effort to maintain France's freedom of action until war had actually started. Finally, the French added to their independent, anti-cities nuclear targeting strategy an alternative, NATO-oriented target plan, which envisioned close coordination with the American supreme allied commander in Europe. Thus by the late 1980s France arguably had become America's staunchest cold-war ally. Then, ironically, the international order underwent fundamental change.

The cold war began to melt under what the French, at first disparagingly, called the "charm offensive" of Soviet president Mikhail Gorbachev. In striking contrast to previous Soviet leaders, Gorbachev appealed to Westerners with his personal warmth and with his policies of openness and reform at home, peace and disarmament abroad. "We will deprive you of the Soviet threat," a Moscow official reportedly declared.[88] The easing of cold-war tensions endangered America's influence in Western Europe and NATO's already fractured nuclear consensus. "It is much easier to hold the alliance together when the Soviets are vaguely menacing than when they appear friendly," explained former defense secretary James Schlesinger in 1988.[89] As peace threatened, hard-liners looked wistfully, as Perle put it, for "some external shock . . . another invasion by Soviet military forces or some activity that [would] sober people."[90] Exasperated, former national security adviser Zbigniew Brzezinski criticized Westerners for "going bananas over Gorbachev simply because he happens to wear a tie and a clean shirt and a well cut suit and his wife does not look like a beast."[91] Unlike the Germans who "think they have some sort of special line to the Kremlin," the French government and people remained cool to Gorbachev's advances, American diplomats reported.[92]

As "Gorbymania" swept through most of Europe, a top American defense analyst saw "one bright spot on the horizon—the growing cooperation between the Federal Republic and France in military matters."[93] Washington encouraged such bonds, hoping they would stiffen Bonn's resistance to Moscow's lures. In February 1986 Mitterrand assured Bonn that, time and circumstances permitting, France would consult with the Germans before it exploded French nuclear weapons on West German territory. This was a pledge with a hedge— and implications that horrified the Germans. The French also set up a joint defense council with the West Germans and an experimental brigade with soldiers of the two nations. These ventures recalled the failed European Defense Community of the early 1950s, but this time the Europeans were uniting not as America's junior assistants but as potential senior associates. Washington favored the new military ties because they drew the French "back into the alliance," helped reassure (and contain) Germany, and eased America's burdensome role in Europe, explained Richard Burt, ambassador to Bonn.[94]

Mitterrand's growing military commitment to Germany and his approach to NATO marked some important shifts away from de Gaulle's doctrines. With American influence in Western Europe weaker than it had been in the 1960s, Mitterrand, far more than de Gaulle, wanted Washington to help contain the Germans. Mitterrand also blurred the Gaullist principle of defending only the sacred soil of France. Paris boosted NATO's capabilities with its plan for a 47,000-member Rapid Action Force, designed to fight, in cooperation with the other allies, on West Germany's eastern flank. France also planned to deploy the Hades tactical nuclear missile, able to fly over West German soil to attack in Eastern Europe. Washington applauded these projects, which fit the new NATO strategy of shifting the fight to the enemy's territory. "In operational terms the difference between [France's] being and not being a member of the integrated [NATO] Command is dwindling," observed a top French analyst in 1988.[95] These changes produced a contradiction. As France sought to play a defense role beyond its borders, it risked undermining the pronuclear consensus developed in the 1960s and 1970s. "Why should France commit national suicide to defend West Germany?" asked some Gaullists.[96]

Despite such criticism Mitterrand held together the consensus on building up the French nuclear arsenal. Mitterrand expanded to seven the fleet of nuclear submarines, now equipped with multiple-warhead missiles. Compared to the British, who had only a submarine nuclear capability, the French devoted a larger share of their military budget (20 percent) to weapons of mass destruction and in 1989 maintained 18 nuclear bombers and 18 land-based missiles. France planned to have by 1994 more than 500 strategic nuclear weapons capable of reaching the Soviet Union, a deadly force but still a small fraction of the American or the Soviet arsenals. Mitterrand calculated that cautious cooperation with NATO enhanced the *force de frappe*'s credibility even if it sacrificed some independence. He lobbied to get the INF missiles installed in Germany and elsewhere. Mitterrand figured that these additional American nuclear weapons would offset those of the Soviets, again adding to the relative weight of the French force. Perhaps more than any other nuclear-armed nation, France rested comfortably behind its deterrent—a modern day Maginot line, critics charged.[97]

The nuclear consensus among the French public withstood the 10 July 1985 killing of an innocent photographer on board the *Rainbow Warrior*, docked in New Zealand. Agents of the French CIA (General Direction of External Security [DGSE]) blew up the *Rainbow Warrior*, owned by the activist environmental group Greenpeace, most probably because the ship was leading an international protest campaign against French nuclear-weapons tests in the South Pacific. Most French regarded the affair as a bit of entertainment rather than a scandal. Only the now-small Communist party (with under 10 percent of the vote in the 1986 elections) challenged Mitterrand's attempted cover-up. Washington, which had its own complaints against New Zealand's stance against nuclear weapons, stood silent. The *Wall Street Journal* applauded "Mitterrand's finest hour" and his defense of the French nuclear program against "a flotilla of hippies."[98]

Ironically, it was Reagan, with his three antinuclear shocks, who challenged France's coziness with the bomb. In 1983 the president urged development of the Strategic Defense Initiative (SDI), a space-based shield to destroy Soviet missiles before they reached the United States. Dubbed "Star Wars," SDI would throw up an "Astrodome" over the United States while leaving Europe (vulnerable to shorter-range, lower-trajectory missiles harder to destroy from space) unprotected. Critics charged that the project would cost a huge amount and remained technologically unfeasible. Reagan tried to soothe fears that the United States would unsheath its nuclear sword once it had this shield by promising to share the technology with Moscow. Although Yves Montand went on French television to praise SDI as necessary to defend the West, Mitterrand saw the project as threatening. If the scheme worked, it might render the *force de frappe* less effective and decouple Europe's defense from that of America. America and the Soviet Union could protect their home territories while fighting a nuclear war in Europe. Even if Star Wars proved to be just a black hole for defense dollars, it would make the arms race more expensive. Alone among the major allies, France refused Washington's offer to cooperate in developing SDI. Mitterrand did, however, allow French firms to compete for SDI contracts.[99]

Ironically, Reagan's devotion to Star Wars helped save the *force de frappe*. At the October 1986 summit in Reykjavík, Iceland, Reagan and Gorbachev tentatively agreed to eliminate within 10 years all offensive ballistic missiles, including those of France and Great Britain. The accord collapsed over the American president's insistence on going ahead with SDI. Europeans suffered a "heart attack" on learning how Reagan had almost bargained away their security arrangements, a defense analyst noted.[100] Once again the United States proved ready to make deals affecting the allies' vital interests without adequate prior consultation. In response to anguished protests, State Department European analyst Rozanne Ridgway insisted that "what they [the Europeans] cannot do is make a place for Europe at that table between the United States and the Soviet Union."[101] Aside from the consultation issue, the French found it "terrible" and "frivolous" that America would consider eliminating its missiles—not to mention those of France.[102] As Reagan toyed with the heresy of getting rid of these awe-inspiring weapons, the French regarded themselves as "keepers of the [nuclear] faith."[103]

To France the 1987 INF treaty appeared as a serious threat to nuclear orthodoxy. The U.S.-Soviet agreement eliminated two whole classes of weapons in Europe, intermediate- and short-range missiles. The accord's history reached back to 1979, when Washington proposed that the NATO allies install American Pershing II and cruise (INF) missiles. The Americans wanted to discomfort the Soviets with these highly accurate weapons, soothe Chancellor Schmidt's worry about the Soviet SS-20 missiles aimed at Western Europe, and pull the alliance together after the neutron bomb fiasco. Hoping to defuse the already potent European peace movement, NATO accepted the missiles as part of a "double-track" process. While Europe was deploying the new rockets, the Americans would negotiate with the Soviets to eliminate or reduce the numbers of INF and SS-20 missiles. In 1981–82, Perle led the cold warriors, who sought some way to stall arms control while they piled up weapons. At his urging, the United States proposed the "double-zero option": Moscow would pull out all of its already deployed SS-20s in return for Washington's canceling its planned installation of the INF missiles (not ready for deployment until late 1983). Perle figured the Soviets would never accept this lopsided deal. As a bonus, the double-zero offer would show the European antimissile protesters that Moscow, not Washington, had the blame for proliferating weaponry. The European peace movement was not impressed by Perle's reasoning. Massive demonstrations erupted, particularly in West Germany and Great Britain.

In 1987 Gorbachev called the Reagan administration's bluff by accepting the zero-zero option and the intrusive measures necessary to verify the missile cutback. In return for giving up the SS-20s, the Soviet leader won points with West European opinion, excised the threat of the Pershing II and cruise missiles, and made progress toward shifting resources from the military to the ailing Soviet economy. Having achieved his arms buildup (or at least increased the defense budget), Reagan became intrigued with the idea of leaving office as a peacemaker. Hard-liners such as Perle left the administration, disappointed by the president's dealings with what Reagan had earlier denounced as an "evil empire." In December 1987 Reagan and Gorbachev signed the INF treaty. Despite the great fanfare, the accord removed relatively few American nuclear weapons from Europe, some 400 out of the more than 4,000 deployed there. Even then only the missiles were destroyed; the United States could use the warheads elsewhere.

Even though the INF treaty did not destroy any French weapons, many French feared the accord as a threat to the regime of nuclear deterrence. The INF treaty "fits very well with the consistent Soviet objective of denuclearizing Western Europe," warned a respected French expert.[104] When the treaty went before the Senate for ratification in 1988, conservative opponents pointed to French concerns. Republican Senator J. Danforth Quayle of Indiana observed that the "French are quite anxious that the INF treaty" could lead to the eventual "demilitarization of NATO."[105] "The French are totally and absolutely opposed [to the INF treaty], and if you had them come down and testify . . . they would give you 95 reasons why they think INF is a bad idea," David Anderson, former ambassador to Yugoslavia, told Congress.[106] Anderson exaggerated, but even treaty supporters such as Senator Alan Cranston of California reported "greater doubts in France than in the rest of Europe."[107] Many French, particularly military leaders and Gaullists, viewed INF as a step onto the slippery path of West German denuclearization and neutralization. But Mitterrand had to endorse it or lose his influence in Bonn and the rest of Europe.

Like Mitterrand, the Reagan administration had to press forward with the treaty or forfeit a huge portion of European public opinion. "The whole INF process was a battle for the soul of Europe," explained Richard Burt.[108] In 1983 Washington's political friends in Europe, notably Germany's Christian Democrats, had withstood a storm of popular protest and installed the INF weapons. The deployment had demonstrated that, with French help and a cold-war atmosphere, the United States could still manage European affairs. But it had been a narrow, shaky victory, dependent on the promised double-track of negotiations. By 1988, with the cold war thawing and with Gorbachev playing his disarmament card, Washington had to remove the missiles or risk losing West Germany and NATO. As a senior American diplomat put it, "the Germans are just so central to everything and so distrusted."[109] If the INF treaty died in the Senate (as had happened with the last major arms accord with the Soviets, SALT II), Germans would feel "that they had lost a reliable partner in the United States," warned Burt. He feared that Germans "on the left side of the political spectrum and on the conservative side . . . [might] seek some kind of alternative security arrangement with a superior military power to the East."[110] The treaty "discredited the so-called peace movement," argued American ambassador to NATO Alton Keel; abandoning the accord would "revive the disarmament" groups.[111]

The Americans and French each tried to bind the West Germans through close bilateral ties, through institutional links such as NATO and the European Community, and with timely concessions. But with West Germany's economic preeminence and discontent with the cold war on the rise, Washington and Paris increasingly had to follow the Germans in order to stay close with them. For example, after the INF eliminated the intermediate-range nuclear missiles in Europe, Washington planned to replace or "modernize" its short-range Lance missile, already deployed in West Germany, with a new weapon able to travel 280 miles—just under the 300-mile INF treaty limit, but far enough to hit East Germany and Poland. "The shorter-ranged the missiles, the deader the Germans," large numbers in the Federal Republic immediately protested.[112] This newest American rocket would incinerate "the other part of our Fatherland," complained West German foreign minister Hans-Dietrich Genscher, who scotched the missile deployment.[113] Genscher, who had emigrated from East Germany as a young man, shared the hopes of many in the Federal Republic that Gorbachev's fresh outlook might permit the two Germanys to edge closer together.

Complete German reunification, however, seemed like a remote prospect to the leaders of the seven richest industrial democracies assembling on 14 July 1989 in Paris for their annual meeting. The first session of the summit met in Pei's pyramid in the Louvre. As host, Mitterrand timed the meeting to coincide with France's lavish, $72 million celebration of the bicentennial of the French Revolution. Much as de Gaulle might have done, Mitterrand staged a number of simultaneous dramas: a meeting of France's powerful allies, a birthday party for France that emphasized the moderating of France's revolutionary tradition, and a celebration of the president's own longevity and majesty (French pundits regularly referred to the aloof Mitterrand as "the king" and "God").[114] To demonstrate that France had not become too rich and conservative, Mitterrand invited to the festivities 24 leaders from third-world nations, announced that he wanted the rich countries to grant substantial debt relief to poor nations, and called for a conference between the wealthy northern half of the globe and the largely impoverished south. By reaching out to the third world in this conspicuous way, Mitterrand showed that France still had an independent policy and a claim as mediator between North and South.

As cultural events, the meetings and the celebration symbolized the reconciliation of France and the United States, and the coming together of the two nations' views on revolution. At summit meetings precisely choreographed for protocol, Mitterrand conspicuously honored President George Bush above other leaders such as Kohl of West Germany or Prime Minister Margaret Thatcher of Great Britain. (Thatcher retaliated by presenting Mitterrand with a copy of Charles Dickens's novel *A Tale of Two Cities,* which contrasted the revolutionary horrors of Paris after 1789 with the happy stability of

Mitterrand leads his guests to dinner in the Pyramid. The July 1989 summit marked the lull before the revolutionary storm that swept Europe later that year. *Courtesy of French Embassy Press & Information Division*

London.) On the first evening of the conference Mitterrand invited his guests to the inaugural performance of the new Bastille Opera, where an American, Robert Wilson, staged the production. Mitterrand's championing of the third world at the conclave of rich nations cut a dramatic Gaullist gesture, but his independent initiative remained a limited one. Mitterrand did not protest strongly when Bush and other leaders of the rich seven rejected French proposals for the third world in favor of less ambitious plans. With a touch of sarcasm, U.S. treasury secretary Nicholas F. Brady remarked that "you don't get solutions to problems by bunching up areas and calling them North and South."[115] France still went ahead, however, with some debt relief to its impoverished former African colonies.

Nevertheless, France's primary interests remained with the other wealthy nations, and its conservative moderation in both foreign and domestic matters was reflected in the way France remembered its revolution. Mitterrand and most others emphasized the 1789 phase of the upheaval—that is, the early, restrained period distinguished by the establishment of a moderate republic and the Declaration of the Rights of Man—developments that Americans at the time had applauded as similar to their own revolution. In keeping with the decline in numbers and prestige of the PCF and the left, most of the French public disowned the heritage of the later, more radical years of the French Revolution. Socialist Prime Minister Michel Rocard, a revolutionary in May 1968, argued for the virtues of evolution in June 1989. Nearly 200 years after Louis XVI and Marie-Antoinette were guillotined in 1793, they lived on in the sympathy of the French people. In 1989 only 18 percent of the French public approved the execution of Louis XVI and a mere 11 percent favored the death sentence of the queen. Sixty-four percent believed that the radical Terror had been "a stain on the Revolution."[116] When dignitaries elected 1989's Marianne, the mythic feminine symbol of the French republic, they chose Inès de la Frassange, a fashion model with an aristocratic pedigree.

Frassange symbolized how France and the United States had grown together as two sophisticated, materialistic nations, both of which, though rich, suffered extremes of poverty and wealth, a growing underclass, and rising racial tensions. It was probably not just politeness that led a spokesman for the blue-blooded American president to say that Bush saw no grounds at all for complaints about Mitterrand's monarchical tendencies and lavish celebrations. In July 1989 Bush and Mitterrand felt confident about the stability of their nations and the direction of future events, at least in the short run. When Gorbachev proposed to the group of seven that the Soviet Union "integrate [itself] . . . fully into the world economy," Bush pooh-poohed the suggestion as "very premature." "We're talking about free market economies here," the president reminded the Communist leader.[117] A few months later would come the revolution of 1989–90, which would break down such easy compartmentalization between East and West and shake up the security basis for the U.S.-French rapprochement of the 1980s.

Chapter 7

PLUS ÇA CHANGE, 1989–1991

Shortly before becoming the prime minister of France on 15 May 1991, Edith Cresson recounted that only twice in her 57 years had she feared for the very existence of her country—during the dark days of German occupation in World War II and during the night when the Berlin Wall fell. She warned that if you "don't force [the Germans] to their knees, they'll be at your throat."[1] Although Cresson often met criticism for what the French called her "raw tongue," she vocalized the apprehension felt by many French leaders about the reunification of Germany. U.S. officials were more confident about handling a united Germany, but Americans shared with the French some worries about the revolution of 1989–90, which swept away the barrier dividing East and West Germany, the Communist governments in the former Soviet satellite nations, and Moscow's military occupation of that region.

Despite these tumultuous changes in Europe, the foreign policies of the United States and of France remained unaltered in important ways. Both nations still sought to contain and channel German power through NATO and the European Community, with the Americans focusing on NATO as the key institution and the French favoring the E.C. Although both Washington and Paris wanted to preserve a strong U.S. military presence in Western Europe, the French sought, as they had for decades, to minimize Washington's political say in European affairs while maximizing the leadership and independence of France. The remarkably close strategic entente between the United States and France in the 1980s, which had declined with the winding down of the cold war after 1986, unraveled further as differences developed over the reunification of Germany, the alliance structure of post–cold war

221

Europe, the crisis in the Persian Gulf, and the collapse of the Uruguay round of trade talks.

Despite their initial apprehensions about German reunification, Bush administration officials by February 1990 had decided to build a closer, special relationship with uniting Germany and to house that nation in a modernized NATO, with the United States reaffirming its traditional leadership position in the alliance. Americans believed that in order to sustain NATO's preeminence in the Atlantic arena, they had to limit the military role of potentially competing institutions such as the European Community, the Western European Union (WEU), and the Conference on Security and Cooperation in Europe (CSCE). Yet Washington still appreciated the E.C. as a stabilizing force in Europe and as a vital economic and political anchor for Germany. As the European Community moved toward closer economic and political integration, Washington sought to gain an institutionalized voice in E.C. decision making. As a senior American official explained the problem, the Europeans in the E.C. "only want to talk to us when they feel like it. We want to commit them to come to the table."[2] In response, the French questioned why the Americans should have a seat at the European table at all.

The Americans and French also differed over the orientation of the Western European Union, an institution long moribund, which many Western Europeans now wanted to revive as a European organization for military and security issues. The French wanted the Western European Union, to which the United States did not belong, to be largely independent of Washington; the Americans sought to keep it under the wing of NATO. With the support of the British, Bush administration officials stifled the development of the CSCE, a loose association of 35 nations including Europe, the United States, and the Soviet Union. American leaders feared that the CSCE might take on, as some French, Germans, Soviets, and others hoped, an important military and security role that could render NATO obsolete. On 12 December 1989, Secretary of State James A. Baker III sketched the American plan for post–cold war Europe in a speech delivered in West Berlin and entitled, "A New Europe, a New Atlanticism: Architecture for a New Era."[3] The Secretary invoked Washington's traditional policy, going back to the Marshall Plan, of encouraging the European allies to build a united Western Europe within an Atlantic framework, thereby sustaining American leadership.

Washington's effort to keep NATO preeminent in Western Europe was part of its global strategy to "manage" developments around the world. President George Bush believed that the destiny of the United States was to lead and organize what he called the "new world order" for the "next American century."[4] Baker agreed with this formulation. At his Senate confirmation hearing, he announced that his first principle as secretary of state would be "the necessity for American leadership" around the globe. Like many Americans since the early Puritans, Baker endorsed the doctrine that the United States enjoyed a special providence: "We are the largest nation. We have the biggest economy. We believe in the finest principles and have the finest traditions." With these blessings, the United States remained "the last, best hope of earth," he affirmed, quoting Abraham Lincoln.

Despite Baker's glowing confidence that the United States was the "biggest" and the "finest," his pragmatism forced him, like other officials, to grapple with the gloomy reality that deep trade and budget deficits made America's global leadership precariously dependent on contributions from "increasingly influential allies," particularly wealthy West Germany and Japan.[5] This financial limitation pinched hard. A top State Department official, frustrated by the lack of funds for new U.S. programs in post-Wall Europe, observed that "we reach into our pockets and all we have is loose change. You have to put your money where your mouth is, and we're broke."[6] The shortage of money also figured in the calculations of Lawrence S. Eagleburger, the number-two man in the State Department, who since 1957 had served at the Pentagon, NATO headquarters, the White House, and the National Security Council. From this long perspective, Eagleburger noted that "we dominate [the world] less than we used to." Yet, he believed, the United States could still lead the globe. The trick was for Washington to "manage" deftly its relations with Western Europe and Japan, that is, to tap their burgeoning wealth and power. "We dominate clearly," Eagleburger explained, "if the West can collectively act together." Eagleburger presumed that "it rests in the hands of the United States to take the country and the West . . . into the 21st century."[7]

Appropriately, Bush coined the slogan "a new world order" in the context of "a real selling campaign," as his aides put it, to raise from other nations the men, money, and matériel for Operation Desert Shield, the U.S.-led response to the occupation of Kuwait by Iraq's leader, Saddam Hussein, in August 1990. "As I look at the countries that are chipping in here now, I think we do have a chance at a new world order," Bush declared on 30 August. "We [are] tak[ing] the lead," he explained, because some nation had to organize and manage the new coalition sending armed forces to the Persian Gulf.[8] In this global division of labor, the United States would make most of the decisions, while Washington's richest allies would pay most of the bills. As congressional aides put it half-jokingly, "The Germans, Japanese and Saudis ought to meet *our* responsibilities."[9]

Although Paris shared some of Washington's general strategic goals, such as containing a united Germany and challenging Iraq's aggression in the Persian Gulf, the French saw their specific national interests as different from those of the Americans. No French leader wanted to play the junior assistant in George Bush's new world order. Yet France often lacked the national resources and the backing from other nations to counter the designs of the United States.

The French design for post-Wall Europe differed from the American blueprint. Although squeamish about further clipping their national sovereignty, the French had tried, since 1983–84, to build the European Community into a near-state with coherent economic, political, and military policies. They realized that France alone could keep up with neither the superpowers nor the Germans. French president François Mitterrand believed that only a tight Western Europe could compete with America and Japan and anchor uniting Germany. Along with E.C. commission president Jacques Delors and others, Mitterrand hoped that the European Community would become what France had aspired to be, and that the E.C. would carry out France's mission. In their more optimistic moments, the French envisioned a European Community powered by German money and guided by French shrewdness.

Possessive about French influence within the European Community, Paris reacted coldly to Baker's idea of increasing Washington's say in the community's affairs. As for NATO, the French appreciated that the alliance kept U.S. military forces in Europe and helped keep Germany tethered to the West and incapable of any military adventurism. While staying formally aloof from the NATO integrated command, French military forces worked closely with their NATO counterparts, and France cooperated with the Americans on the development of nuclear weapons. Yet French officials objected to Baker's plan to give NATO new authority in the post–cold war era. Policy makers in Paris asserted that "the E.C. is naturally better placed than NATO to cope with the new challenges, notably in Eastern Europe."[10] In contrast, then, to the U.S. geographical system centered over the North Atlantic, the French hoped to make Western Europe the core area, with ties extending westward to North America and eastward to the Soviet Union.

In both the American and the French conceptions, Germany remained the key element. Hampered by lagging growth and debt problems, the United States and France each hoped to lift its national power by tying rising Germany to NATO and the European Community respectively, that is, to supranational institutions in which either Washington or Paris had a considerable voice. In pursuing these policies, however, the Americans and the French also faced the paradox that in the future Germany might come to dominate NATO and the E.C.

In France the uncertainties arising from the collapse of the cold-war order provoked nervousness even before the Berlin Wall fell. In February 1989, as Poland and Hungary edged cautiously toward more pluralistic governments, Hubert Védrine, Mitterrand's spokesman, fretted that if such democratization continued, within a decade "Eastern Europe will leave the framework of Yalta." Ever since de Gaulle had been excluded from the Yalta conference in 1945, Yalta had stood in French eyes as a hated symbol of the superpowers' division and dominance of Europe. Yet now Védrine saw the breakup of the Yalta system as threatening "instability and risk" in Eastern Europe. "I think they are all launched on a toboggan and they do not know where they are going to end up," he feared.[11] Paris officials worried about events in Eastern Europe sliding out of control in part because they had failed to construct economic and political links with the East as strong as the ties assiduously built by West Germany. In the 1960s de Gaulle had tried to outflank Bonn by becoming the spokesman for Western Europe in Moscow and in other Eastern and Central European capitals, but neither he nor subsequent French leaders could marshal the requisite economic might and political focus. By early 1989 West German exports to Eastern Europe amounted to nearly five times French sales there, and Bonn had established a dense network of economic, political, and cultural ties with the governments and people of the region.[12] Many French concluded that they had misplayed their eastern policy in the 1980s by emphasizing human rights issues. During the decade, "the Germans were making money and conquering markets," observed Dominique Moïsi, a leading French analyst. "And now we are left with no policy and no markets."[13]

During the cold-war era France, like the United States and West Germany's other allies, had made pious statements urging German unification while assuming this development would probably never occur. De Gaulle and other French leaders sometimes talked vaguely about unification as part of a grand reconciliation of East and West, an almost millennial order in which France's special leadership role would somehow be preserved. In the summer of 1989, however, the rapid thaw in Eastern Europe reopened serious discussion of German unification, but without the privileged position for France envisioned by Paris leaders. François Mitterrand was not pleased. In July when a German reporter asked for Mitterrand's thoughts about German unity, a visibly irritated French president replied that the four World War II victor powers (that is, the United States, the Soviet Union, Great Britain, and France) still held important legal rights and the deciding voice in the matter. Mitterrand asserted that the East and West German governments had to unify before the two countries could join together—this precondition coming at a time when East German leader Erich Honecker was declaring that the unification of East and West Germany would be like the unification of fire and water.[14]

Mitterrand's stern conditions meant little, however, after the opening of the Berlin Wall on 9 November 1989. By chance the French president was holding the European Community's rotating presidency; he called an emergency E.C. summit meeting for 18 November at the Élysée Palace. Frédéric Bozo, a French analyst, observed that there was "a slightly panicky side" to those proceedings.[15] On 28 November West German chancellor Helmut Kohl, hoping to stem the flood of East German migration into the Federal Republic, announced a ten-point plan leading to an eventual federation between West and East Germany. Kohl's failure to consult with the allies before launching this scheme heightened apprehensions in Paris and elsewhere. The French responded by trying to accelerate the European Community's economic and political integration so that the grouping would acquire sufficient weight to anchor West Germany.

The French also attempted to slow down reunification. On the same day that Kohl led a dramatic ceremony to open the Brandenburg Gate of the Berlin Wall, Mitterrand was also busy in Berlin—trying to prop up the East German government. Assuming the role of spokesman for the European Community, Mitterrand on 6 December met with Soviet leader Mikhail Gorbachev in Kiev, where they issued a joint statement warning Bonn not to push too fast for reunification. Months later Gorbachev confided to the Germans that Mitterrand had asked him to prevent unification. The French president related to the press Gorbachev's dire prediction that "on the day Germany unites, a marshall will be sitting in my chair."[16] The French leader kept up the attack, telling British prime minister Margaret Thatcher "that this was the worst crisis in fifty years." Mitterrand "thinks the Germans are a people who don't know where their frontiers are," a British official related.[17] Mitterrand's efforts did not stop the German steamroller, but they did generate resentment in Bonn. "We're seeing a tremendous outbreak of hypocrisy," a West German diplomat complained as France and other Western nations contradicted their pious statements of the past urging German reunification.[18]

Hypocrisy continued, since no nation was happy to see Germany reunified, yet none wanted to risk resentment from the soon-to-be-super-Germany by overtly spoiling its reunion. Although outclassed by West Germany's greater economy and ties with the East, France had its own, more subtle assets. Much of the E.C. permanent and elected staff was French or Francophile. At least in the short run, the Germans needed close collaboration with Paris, since French approval made their expanding power appear more "European" and so less threatening to other nations. Unable to brake German reunification, Mitterrand settled for committing the Germans to a stronger European Community. At E.C. meetings in 1989 and 1990, Chancellor Kohl solemnly pledged German support for accelerated economic and political integration of the community. He promised, "We don't want to be the Fourth Reich. We want to be European Germans and German Europeans."[19] Close German-French amity appeared restored, but the question for the future was how long France could maintain political preeminence in the European Community in the face of united Germany's superior power. After all, much of Mitterrand's authority in November and December 1989 stemmed from the happenstance that he was E.C. president at the time.

At first, the Americans joined the French, Soviets, and British in trying to slow down and possibly head off German unification. In early December 1989 Baker, in an effort to bolster East Germany, became the first American secretary of state to visit that rump country. But as the East German people streamed westward and their regime lost the will to remain separate, it became apparent that, for all practical purposes, no government—neither the victor powers nor West Germany—could shore up East Germany. In effect this meant a diplomatic victory for Bonn and a diminution of authority for the former victor nations, for how could the four powers—all of which recoiled from the specter of East German instability—veto the collapse of a country? Thus, reunification ceased to be policy that could be opposed and became instead a process that appeared unstoppable.

Bowing to the inevitable, the Bush administration in early February 1990 tried to manage what it could not prevent. The administration's "top priority," testified Raymond Seitz, assistant secretary of state for European and Canadian affairs, had become "managing the transition that is going on in Europe" so that the changes "do not impair the continued American presence in Europe."[20] Washington's tactic was to assume the role of Bonn's guiding older brother, a role that America could play more convincingly than could France. A Bush administration official explained that the United States had assured the West Germans of its "total confidence" in Bonn's handling of reunification. At the same time, the official continued, America was keeping its "arm around the shoulder" of the West Germans to ensure sure that they continued to consult with the West and to bind themselves to NATO and to the European Community.[21] Relations between Washington and Bonn became particularly warm when the United States pushed to establish the 2-plus-4 talks on German unification. A plan designed primarily by Seitz, the 2-plus-4 schema empowered East and West Germany to negotiate with the four major World War II allies. Baker graphically demonstrated his diplomatic priorities by first clearing the 2-plus-4 plan with the West Germans, then brushing aside objections from the French, the Soviets, and the British. France appeared less important to Washington than it had in the early 1980s. Baker and the small coterie of State Department officials who guided Washington's policy toward Europe gambled that, in the long run, a united Germany would protect and strengthen American interests in Europe.

U.S. officials figured that such help from Germany would be crucial, particularly since the easing of East-West tensions threatened to undermine American authority in Europe. The cold war was over, Gorbachev announced to admiring throngs at his December 1989 summit meeting with Bush on Malta. Gorbachev's cheery pronouncement provoked a testy reply from the American president, worried about maintaining U.S. leadership in Western Europe. Sure, tensions had eased, Bush admitted to a reporter, "but if I signal to you there's no Cold War, then you'll say, 'Well, what are you doing with troops in Europe?' I mean, come on!" When a persistent reporter asked the president, "What role do we really have to play here? We don't live on this continent," Bush struggled, "Well, I'm not sure—I'm—," then went on simply to declare that "the United States must stay involved."[22] In the next few months, the Bush administration offered a more articulate response, which predicated America's global position on its political and military leadership of NATO.

Testifying before Congress on 3 April 1990, James F. Dobbins, Seitz's deputy, made a telling statement when he declared: "We need NATO now for the same reasons NATO was created" in 1949.[23] First, there remained the risk—now admittedly remote—of a renewed Soviet military threat. But the more immediate danger was that, without the "glue" of the integrated command and American leadership in NATO, Western Europeans would revert to their bad habits, that is, renationalizing their armed forces, playing the "old geopolitical game," and "shifting alliances."[24] Dobbins's key assumption here was that, acting alone, the Western Europeans—particularly with Germany united—could not preserve order among themselves. Without the U.S. acting as the stabilizer, European squabbling would "undermine political and economic structures like the EC" and even lead to a resumption of "historic conflicts" like the two world wars.[25] In the eyes of U.S. officials, NATO served not only to contain the Soviets and to check the Germans and other Western Europeans, but the alliance structure was also needed to limit isolationist impulses arising from Congress and the American people. NATO institutionalized and solidified America's military involvement in Europe and made that involvement more popular in the United States because an American general commanded the whole structure. "Without NATO," Dobbins feared, "U.S. public and Congressional support for this engagement [in Europe] would be difficult to maintain."[26] Finally, and of key importance in the minds of Washington decision makers, NATO guaranteed the U.S. an important voice in the affairs of Western Europe.

The Bush administration's determination to retain the leading position in NATO apparently doomed the tentative negotiations of April and May 1990, when the Americans, French, and British talked about restructuring the alliance, including perhaps appointing a French general as SACEUR (Supreme Allied Commander), so that France might then resume a full commitment to the NATO organization. Since the late 1970s a number of foreign policy experts, including Henry Kissinger, had talked about the idea of making a French general the SACEUR of NATO. In effect, these discussions tried to bridge the gap between, on the one hand, America's design for Western Europe as part of a North Atlantic community, with the United States in a leading role through its command of NATO; and on the other hand, France's plan for Western Europe, as linked to NATO, but led by French guidance of an increasingly independent and powerful European Community. By 1990, with the cold war apparently over and with Western Europe asserting itself, the idea of transforming NATO into a more European-run organization had broader appeal. But would Washington accept such a reduction in authority? Citing "the importance of the United States leading the alliance," Baker in January 1989 objected to the appointment of a European general as SACEUR.[27] On 18 April 1990 Bush publicly rejected the idea of a French SACEUR, explaining that the American people had to feel wanted in Europe, and having an American in charge of NATO helped with that.[28] As some Washington officials put it sourly, the Europeans "want us to stay," but "with no say."[29] The president also had to worry about the budget-conscious Congress, where many legislators felt that if the United States could not run the NATO show, it should pack up and go home.

Although understandable, Bush's insistence on American leadership probably hurt his case on 20 April 1990 when he met with the French president at Key Largo, Florida. Bush apparently wanted Mitterrand to bring France back into the integrated NATO command, accept the stationing on French soil of American warplanes armed with nuclear missiles, and agree to a public statement endorsing NATO as the dominant military institution in Europe. One reason the Bush administration sought a more formal French commitment to NATO was its fear that a reunified Germany might leave NATO, as the result of either a deal with Moscow or an electoral victory by the more independent-minded Social Democrats. With France back in the integrated command and with American nuclear weapons on its soil, France would help to anchor Germany in NATO. (Typically, Washington wanted to deploy nuclear weapons on Allied soil as much for the political effect on the ally as for the potential destructive impact on the enemy.)[30] And if the Germans did leave NATO, America would at least have French territory as a redoubt on the Continent. With all this riding on winning over Paris, it was significant that Bush apparently did not offer Mitterrand the concession of making a French general the SACEUR. Before the meeting, French officials had been hinting that with "great flexibility . . . all kinds of new departures, including some in NATO, might become possible."[31]

Although the possibility of a deal remained, Mitterrand on 20 April apparently turned down all of Bush's proposals on NATO. "Absurd" was the way two top French officials described the American ideas for giving NATO additional political functions.[32] The gap between the American and French structures for Europe proved greater than the will to compromise. Personal relations between the two presidents also cooled, a significant matter for Bush, who liked to get friendly with foreign leaders and who had developed a particularly warm rapport with Kohl. The frequent telephone calls between Bush and Mitterrand slacked off. After an earlier meeting with Mitterrand, "Bush thought he had him," a senior American official explained, but then "Bush began to understand that the relationship ain't there. Mitterrand listens, but then he goes off and does what he wants."[33] Americans had long had trouble with French leaders who did what they wanted. Bush still persisted, addressing the austere French leader in a letter as "Old Chap."[34]

In terms of military security in Europe, this stubborn old chap arranged to have the planning conference for a strengthened CSCE meet in Paris in November 1990. Although committed to strengthening the European Community, Mitterrand also appreciated the CSCE as an institution to balance NATO, to help integrate and contain Germany and the Soviet Union, and to provide a forum in which skillful French diplomacy might muster a sympathetic coalition. Many nations in Western and Eastern Europe, including the Soviet Union, agreed that the CSCE should help guarantee the peace, though they disagreed on the extent of the CSCE's role and the degree to which it should supplant NATO. Gorbachev hoped that the CSCE might help create a "common European home" in which the Soviet Union would have an important and secure place. Washington found this talk about the CSCE threatening, particularly when Europeans stuck together against North American outsiders. A Washington official complained: "We've always operated in the CSCE with a NATO caucus; now we are confronted with a fait accompli from our European allies."[35]

The United States also felt like an outsider in disputes with the French and other Europeans over the mission of the European Bank for Reconstruction and Development (EBRD), probably the most important multilateral financial institution created since the end of World War II. In October 1989 Mitterrand proposed a new international bank to help the transition to market economies in Eastern Europe, stabilize conditions there, and balance West Germany's preeminence in the region. The French president kept tight control over the project by making Jacques Attali, his close adviser, chairman of the 42-nation committee that drew up the bank's charter. Mitterrand then lobbied to get Attali, who had no previous banking experience, chosen the first president of the $12 billion EBRD. Unlike the International Monetary Fund and the World Bank, both of which the United States easily dominated, the EBRD would be controlled by the E.C. nations, which held 51 percent of the ownership and voting rights. The United States held 10 percent of the new bank, the largest portion of any single nation. But Washington could easily be outvoted by a coalition of other nations, including the Soviet Union, which had a 6 percent shareholding. Washington's minority position became painfully clear in the organizing committee, where the United States failed to prevent the Soviet Union from being admitted to the EBRD and being allowed to borrow money from it. Washington did succeed in restricting the amount the Soviets could borrow, but after three years the bank could vote to rescind the limit. "We are being put in a position of declaring ourselves 'non-Europeans' if we don't agree," an American official commented.[36]

No longer undisputed leader in international economic issues, the United States focused more than ever on NATO as the vehicle for asserting America's will in Europe. At the 5–6 July 1990 NATO meeting in London, the Americans lobbied hard and successfully to subordinate the CSCE to NATO by having the final communiqué of the NATO meeting specify how CSCE agencies would function and where they would be located. Yet the French, the Germans, and other Western Europeans kept that NATO communiqué vague enough so that options for the CSCE might still remain open for the planned November conference. Even as the Americans tried to preserve NATO's preeminence, however, they also had to modify the alliance in order to keep the support of the Germans and to meet some of the needs of

Gorbachev, who faced increasing unrest at home. At the London NATO meeting the United States pushed through a shift in NATO's posture and strategy. Recognizing that the Soviet "threat" had indeed receded and hoping to induce Gorbachev to accept a united Germany remaining in NATO, Bush suggested sweeping changes. The American president now formally acknowledged the end of the cold war, urged abandonment of the forward defense posture so as to make the alliance less threatening to the Soviet Union, accepted withdrawal of nuclear artillery shells, suggested a nonaggression pact with the Warsaw Pact nations, and promised a new, more defensive nuclear doctrine.

This last measure meant giving up the flexible response nuclear strategy, dating from the 1960s, by which NATO stood ready (at least in theory) to respond with nuclear weapons in the event of a Soviet conventional-weapon attack. Now Bush pledged that NATO nuclear weapons would become "truly weapons of last resort."[37] This historic change, foreshadowed by the gradual deterioration in Washington's nuclear credibility, pleased the nuclear-allergic West Germans and the Soviets but angered French and British leaders, who had had almost no input into Washington's decision making. Paris's nuclear dispute with Washington harked back to France's long-held trust in nuclear deterrence rather than in nuclear or conventional fighting. Mitterrand asserted that Bush's apparent conception that war in Europe "would be a long process that can be regulated like a music score is totally contrary to reality." France would not be bound by the NATO decision, Mitterrand declared, for "we do not share the concept of last resort."[38]

While still clinging to the concept of nuclear deterrence against the Soviet Union, Mitterrand supported Kohl's effort to support the seriously sagging Soviet economy. At the 9–11 July 1990 economic summit in Houston, Texas, Kohl argued that the leading industrial democracies had to undertake a multibillion-dollar aid program for the Soviets. Kohl was particularly anxious to sweeten the Soviet attitude toward German reunification and to secure the evacuation of the 380,000 Soviet troops in East Germany. France had relatively little money to contribute, but it dreaded the prospect of the Germans doing massive amounts of business in the Soviet Union without the French at their side. Mitterrand also wanted to cultivate French ties with Moscow, and he liked the idea of Western Europe acting together in Eastern Europe. Bush opposed such a massive program to aid the Soviets, having neither the money for Moscow nor the stomach for the congressional fight such an aid bill could spark. And yet, a senior administration official warned, "the United States cannot be . . . isolated on this issue" or it would lose its leadership position in the alliance.[39] With insufficient financial and political capital to exercise leadership, Washington could do little to "manage" the allies on this crucial matter. The allies each went their own way, with the French and other Western Europeans (except the British) trailing behind the Germans. Also at Houston, Mitterrand and Kohl spearheaded successful European resistance to

Bush's drive to commit the group to eliminating agricultural subsidies. This farm subsidy dispute would lead to a breakdown in trade talks in December 1990.

On 15–16 July 1990 Kohl met with Gorbachev at Stavropol, in the Caucasus Mountains of the Soviet leader's native southern Russia. This was only a few days after Bush at the London conference and Mitterrand at the Houston conference each had gone out of his way to help Kohl by pushing for measures designed to win Moscow's accquiescence to German unity and full sovereignty. Bush believed he was investing in strengthened U.S.-German bonds while Mitterrand aimed to tighten Franco-German ties. Both were surprised by Kohl's sudden deal with Gorbachev. *The Economist's* headline, "Encounter at Stavrapallo," exaggerated the parallel with the 1922 German-Soviet pact, but the accord did suggest that Bonn and Moscow could come together in ways that excluded the Western allies.[40] Gorbachev dropped his last objections to Germany's reunification, regaining full sovereignty, and remaining in NATO. In return Kohl pledged to negotiate in the near future a comprehensive treaty with the Soviet Union that would secure Moscow's economic and political collaboration with Germany.

The Gorbachev-Kohl accord reflected Germany's new freedom to shift between East and West. Washington, Paris, and other Western capitals had long assured Moscow that they favored limits on the size of the united German army; at Stavropol, Kohl on his own agreed to a limit of 370,000 troops. Similarly, the Americans, French, and British had expected eventually to relinquish their rights, stemming from World War II agreements, to garrison troops in West Berlin; in the Caucasus, Kohl announced that the Western allies would leave Berlin when the Soviets withdrew from East Germany. Kohl and Gorbachev promised that neither of their nations would initiate a military attack on the other, a pledge that ran counter to the Federal Republic's obligation to come to the defense of a NATO ally if assaulted by the Soviet Union. Kohl also unilaterally announced that former East German territory would remain denuclearized and outside of NATO. The 2-plus-4 talks had become almost irrelevant. "Not even a fig leaf is left" to conceal that West Germany had essentially negotiated on its own for reunification, a European diplomat complained.[41] American and French officials felt affronted and a little betrayed, but could not complain too loudly lest they accent the tie between Moscow and Bonn.[42] Despite the initial confidence of Baker, Eagleburger, Seitz, and other Americans that the United States could adroitly "manage" the changes in Europe, Germany proved to be—at least in the key matter of unification—the nation that had best "managed" the others.

Almost exactly a year after the opening of the Berlin Wall on 9 November 1989, a conference met in Paris on 17–19 November 1990 to give international blessing to the unification of Germany, which had taken place on 3 October; to sign a treaty under which the NATO and Warsaw Pact nations would scrap thousands of tanks, fighter aircraft, and other conventional weapons; and to start building the new security structures of the CSCE. The conference had originated a year earlier when Gorbachev suggested a meeting to give substance to his common European home scheme, and Mitterrand seized the opportunity to organize the conclave and to host it in Paris. This should have been a grand celebration, marking the formal end of World War II, the rebirth of self-determination in Central and Eastern Europe, and the conclusion of the cold war.

But the conclave proved disappointing, particularly for the new democracies in Central and Eastern Europe. Although the cold-war order of Europe had collapsed, there appeared no new, creative structures to fill the void. The Soviets, many Eastern and Central Europeans, and some Westerners, notably German foreign minister Hans-Dietrich Genscher and to a lesser extent Mitterrand, had all looked forward to building up the CSCE as an innovative alternative to the cold-war system. But the CSCE emerged from the summit an unimpressive edifice, with only a small secretariat in Prague, a Conflict Prevention Center in Vienna, a free-elections commission in Warsaw, and a pledge by member foreign ministers to meet once a year, with summits every two years. Despite Gorbachev's enormous concessions in the former Soviet empire and his obvious troubles at home, his plea to be included in a common house of Europe went mostly unheeded. In large part, the unbuilding of the CSCE marked a victory for American and British policies. Washington and London had steadfastly opposed the construction of an institution that might compete with NATO. When some of the new democracies inquired about joining NATO, they were told no. Meanwhile, the French blocked Baker's bid for a strong, institutionalized tie between Washington and the European Community. The E.C. announced that it would not admit new members at least until the mid-1990s. President Vaclav Havel of Czechoslovakia complained that the new democracies were left "in a political and security vacuum."[43] While successful in staving off any competition to NATO, the Americans were, at the same time, packing off to the Persian Gulf much of the equipment and troops that had made up the U.S. commitment to NATO. That movement pointed up another reason why the November 1990 summit was anticlimactic. After an astounding year of peace breaking out in Europe, war was breaking out in the Persian Gulf.

The 1991 war against Iraq offered a case study of U.S.-French cooperation and rivalry in the third world. Although the two nations often had compatible strategic interests, they also had different ideas, policies, and methods for achieving their goals. The United States continued to seek loyal followers, while France insisted on taking an independent tack—if it could muster the national power and international backing to maintain such autonomy. France had long stationed thousands of soldiers (including Foreign Legionnaires) in former French African colonies to uphold stability and Western interests. In 1990 alone French troops intervened to prop up governments in Gabon and in Rwanda. France's policing actions "made a tremendous difference," a pleased U.S. spokesman commented.[44] France also gained influence, or at least a claim to influence, by selling huge amounts of military armaments to third-world nations. Some countries, notably Iraq, later aimed those weapons at the French and Americans.

Since the 1970s France had prided itself on being the best Western friend of the radical nationalist government in Iraq. France helped Iraq obtain nuclear technology, ostensibly for a power plant, which Baghdad used to try to build atomic weapons. In 1981 Israel bombed and destroyed those Iraqi nuclear installations. Under President Saddam Hussein, Iraq renewed its effort to develop atomic, biological and chemical weapons, buying parts and technology in the netherworld of illicit arms merchants. Even though many such purchases were monitored by the CIA or other intelligence agencies, the American, French, and other Western governments let most of the deals go through, largely because Iraq was fighting against the fundamentalist Islamic government of Iran led by the Ayatollah Ruhollah Khomeini. "This is a Frankenstein monster that the West created," noted a Middle East expert, referring to Saddam Hussein's arsenal of sophisticated weaponry. "We closed our eyes because some businesses wanted to make money and because Saddam was a useful tool against Iran."[45]

From 1981 to 1989 France sold Iraq more than 100 Mirage fighter planes, 600 Exocet antiship missiles (one of which hit the U.S. frigate *Stark* in May 1987, killing 37 American sailors), 1,000 Roland surface-to-air missiles, and 6,000 antitank missiles. Paris stopped deliveries in 1989 because of a payment dispute on Iraq's $5 billion arms debt to France. The United States did not directly sell arms to Iraq, but it did give Baghdad aid to buy food and other supplies.[46] In 1987, in Operation Earnest Will, the United States and France nearly went to war with Iraq's enemy Iran when they sent a sizable naval force to the Persian Gulf to protect ships of Kuwait and other gulf nations from Iranian attack. France's naval and financial contribution to Earnest Will ranked second to America's. Yet congressional and private critics often overlooked France's effort when they complained about Western Europe's lack of support for Washington's self-appointed job as world policeman. West Germany, for example, contributed neither ships nor money to Earnest Will although much of its oil came from the gulf area.

While trying to maintain a measure of independence, France supported America's military response when Iraq seized its oil-rich neighbor Kuwait on 2 August 1990. By January 1991 the United States had assembled in Saudi Arabia and the neighboring Persian Gulf a military force of 540,000 American men and women; had, with U.N backing, organized an international military coalition including Western and Arab troops; and had spearheaded an economic blockade against Iraq. Although most of the world's nations, including the Soviet Union, insisted that Saddam Hussein evacuate Kuwait, they divided on whether and when to use military force to compel that withdrawal.

The ongoing efforts of the European Community to achieve political and military unity by the mid-1990s suffered a setback when its members split over the question of employing force in the gulf. Despite the intimacy between American and German leaders in the first half of 1990, Kohl sent no troops to the gulf. Mindful of strong antiwar feelings at home and preoccupied with the enormous problems of modernizing and integrating the former East Germany, the chancellor cited ambiguous clauses in the Federal Republic's constitution that, some claimed, forbade military intervention outside the NATO area. The Germans donated money to the gulf effort, but did so reluctantly. "Whatever you get out of them, you really have to squeeze it out," a diplomat noted.[47] Some observers suggested that perhaps united Germany's influence would not extend beyond Europe. Shunted to the sidelines during the negotiations on German reunification, Paris and London now seemed anxious to demonstrate that, unlike Germany, they remained global powers. Great Britain sent to the gulf a force of 35,000 troops. "Now I hope you know who your friends really are," a member of the British Parliament admonished Americans.[48] France ranked third among the Western nations, with 10,000 troops, 54 warplanes, and 12 ships, including the aircraft carrier *Clemençeau*. "Our key interlocutors now are the British and the French," an American diplomat observed. "This crisis is restoring some balance in our relations in Europe."[49]

Weighing against closer U.S.-French ties, however, was Paris's effort to strike its own balance between getting tough with Saddam Hussein on the one hand, and maintaining French influence in the Middle East and calm among the 4 million Arab immigrants inside France on the other. And of course France insisted on at least some independence from the Americans. During the first stages of the military buildup, Mitterrand and defense minister Jean-Pierre Chevènement insisted that French forces would operate under Paris's orders. Washington objected, fearing the nightmare of uncoordinated warfare against Iraq and confused allied troops firing on each other. That danger would be particularly serious for French soldiers since much of Iraq's weaponry was French-made. Yet some French, notably Serge July, the influential editor of *Libération* protested the pressure on France to "fit into the American plan, and say farewell to 24 years of strategic independence and tactical sovereignty."[50] Of course presidents Mitterrand, Giscard, and Pompidou had already given up much of that "sovereignty" and "independence" in return for military cooperation with and assistance from the United States. Shortly before the multinational force launched an air assault against Iraq on 17 January 1991, France agreed to U.S. military command in the war.

U.S.-French differences over diplomacy proved more serious. The Bush administration, which had secretly decided on 31 October 1990 to go to war if Iraq did not withdraw, took a hard diplomatic line by insisting that Iraq evacuate all of Kuwait including disputed border areas, by upholding the legitimacy of the autocratic sheiks who had run Kuwait, by denying any connection between Kuwait and other Middle Eastern issues, and by threatening war crimes trials for Iraqis involved in looting the occupied sheikdom.[51]

Although Mitterrand sternly condemned the Iraqis, particularly after they broke into the French diplomatic compound in Kuwait on 13 September 1990 and took several hostages, he, in contrast to the Americans, held out a compromise, face-saving plan for Baghdad's withdrawal from Kuwait. Unable to match America's military might, the French pushed for a brokered settlement that could enhance their diplomatic leverage in the Middle East. For several years Mitterrand had been urging an international conference to deal with the explosive issue of Israel and the Palestinians. On 24 September, in a speech before the United Nations, Mitterrand suggested that if Iraq pulled out of Kuwait and freed the hostages it had seized after the invasion, then "everything might be possible"—including a plebiscite in Kuwait, a settlement in strife-torn Lebanon, justice for the Palestinians who wanted their own state, and arms limitation for all Middle Eastern nations, including Israel. By setting this reconciliation process in motion, Mitterrand implied, Saddam Hussein could emerge an Arab hero.[52] The French proposal embodied Baghdad's idea of a broader Middle East settlement while conflicting with Washington's policy, more favorable to Israel, of trying to keep separate the Israeli-Palestinian question and the issue of Iraq's aggression. When Bush at the November 1990 Paris summit tried to rally support for a militant stance against Iraq, France used its protocol leverage as host nation to minimize the martial overtones of the meeting.[53]

Right up to 15 January 1991, the deadline imposed by the United Nations for Iraq to begin pulling out of Kuwait, France sought a negotiated Iraqi withdrawal that would be followed by an international conference on Israel and the Palestinians. On 14 January Mitterrand made another such proposal to the U.N. Security Council, adding that foreign minister Roland Dumas stood ready to fly to Baghdad. Germany, the Soviet Union, Italy, Spain, Egypt, Morocco, and a host of smaller nations, many with armed forces in the gulf, supported France. In the NATO council, France and Germany rejected America's request for an alliance resolution giving even verbal support for a war outside of Europe.[54]

France's reaction to Iraq's aggression amounted to an alternative Western response; that is, it was a coherent policy that tried to uphold stability, even though it did not suit the United States. Yet irritated U.S. officials trivialized French moves not just as the wrong policy but as no policy at all. The peace proposal was "typically French," American officials commented, "a typical exercise in which European leaders publicly oppose steps for the sake of their public opinion that they secretly support."[55] Mitterrand was certainly concerned about French public opinion, but he also pursued a consistent policy that sought to head off war and narrow the gap between Iraq and its opponents. Despite the French peace effort, Saddam Hussein, even more intransigent than George Bush, rejected the compromise, and the American-led air attack on Iraqi forces began on 17 January, followed by a 100-hour ground assault on 24 February 1991.

Although French land and air forces fought in the short war, code-named Operation Desert Storm, France at first tried to limit its involvement. Backed by Mitterrand, defense minister Chevènement, a leader of the leftist CERES faction of the Socialist party in the 1970s and a proponent of close ties with the Arabs, announced that French forces would bomb those Iraqi troops occupying Kuwait, but spare those defending Iraq's home territory. A howl of protest and derision rose up from foreign and domestic critics, such as former president Valéry Giscard d'Estaing, who said that this policy was as if the allies in World War II had announced that they would bomb only France and not Germany.

Sensitive to this criticism, Mitterrand turned against his dovish defense minister. The French president probably also calculated that now that the war was underway and going well for the multinational force, France had to be part of the victors' circle. On the same day that Chevènement resigned, two squadrons of French Jaguar bombers attacked Iraq.[56] But Mitterrand still hoped that the confrontation with Iraq could end with a lasting Middle Eastern settlement agreeable to Arabs as well as Israelis. Bush, Baker, and other U.S. officials also wanted to defuse the Middle Eastern tinderbox, but only after they had smashed Saddam Hussein and demonstrated America's military might.

U.S.-led forces won a smashing victory, with Iraq surrendering on 27 February 1991 and withdrawing from Kuwait. Operation Desert Storm proved to be a spectacular success on the media front as well as on the battlefield, as television broadcast to people around the globe carefully censored images of America's impressive weaponry. The war boosted U.S. prestige and leverage, particularly in the Middle East. Meanwhile, France emerged as an important player in the fighting and in the diplomacy, but also as a nation still partly in America's shadow.

Although relations between Mitterrand and Bush warmed by the end of the war and the two presidents tried to cooperate on postwar negotiations, their differences on the Israeli-Palestinian question remained. At a 14 March meeting on Martinique, Mitterrand urged that the West deal with the Palestine Liberation Organization (PLO) as the de facto representative of the Palestinians, while Bush opposed the idea, pointing to the PLO's past involvement with terrorists and its support of Saddam Hussein in the recent war. Mindful of Israel's opposition, the Bush administration decided to bury "with ceremonious procrastination," as one official put it, Mitterrand's proposal for a U.N. Security Council conference on the Middle East.[57] On the crucial question of creating a separate nation for the Palestinians, in part from Arab territory occupied by Israel since 1967, Bush declared, "the position of the United

States is that a Palestinian state is not the answer," to which Mitterrand replied, "I have used the world 'state' and if you like, I can repeat it."[58]

This exchange demonstrated the constancy of U.S.-French differences over Israel and the Palestinians since the 1967 Middle East war. Yet this gap between the American and French positions also opened space for the nuanced diplomacy and compromises necessary in any lasting Middle East settlement. In late 1991, as Baker coaxed the Arab states and Israel to meet together in an international conference on the Middle East, the French, with an approving nod from Washington, acted as the West's interlocutor with the PLO.[59] Whether this conference or any other could settle the festering Israeli-Palestinian issue was a major question for the future of the world and for the future course of U.S.-French relations.

As the events in the Middle East in 1990–91 illustrated, France remained a key American ally but no client; Washington could neither count on Paris's unquestioning support nor ignore France's semiautonomous diplomacy. Paris's military and diplomatic efforts earned France an important but not independent global role; the French usually lacked the national power and the international backing to challenge the Americans effectively.

In 1989–91 the trade dispute over agricultural subsidies became another multinational controversy that pitted the United States against France. However, in contrast to the Middle East issue, in which the Americans could outmuscle the French, on the trade question France commanded leverage from the European Community. As the largest agricultural producer in the E.C., France had a huge stake and the key voice in the group's Common Agricultural Policy (CAP), through which farmers received generous sums in export and other subsidies. The 10 million E.C. farmers exerted enormous political pressure to maintain these payments, which enabled them to produce and export mountains of grain, butter, meat, and other food products, thereby outcompeting more efficient producers in the United States, Australia, and many other countries. Although the U.S. government had also erected an elaborate system of payments and import quotas that subsidized American dairy, tobacco, peanut, and other farmers, the Bush administration set as its goal in the Uruguay round of the General Agreement on Tariffs and Trade (GATT) talks the worldwide dismantling of all such farm subsidies, particularly those of CAP.

Launched in 1986 in Uruguay, the 107-nation GATT negotiations became critical as the world economy teetered between development into a single, more open, and unified global system and division into several antagonistic, more or less closed blocs separating the Western Hemisphere, Europe, and East Asia. With the approach of E.C. integration, coming in 1993 or shortly thereafter, the question of trade relations with Western Europe loomed larger. Would the unified European Community open itself to exports from the United States and other countries or would it wall itself off to become a

"Fortress Europe?" While some Western Europeans promised substantial cuts in CAP subsidies, French prime minister Michel Rocard told American congressmen that the program was "so fundamental in the EC that it cannot be reversed."[60] The State Department's Lawrence Eagleburger countered that "if Europe builds a closed, protected enclave we and the rest of the world will surely respond in kind."[61] Such statements set off alarms for those who remembered the disastrous trade wars between competing blocs in the 1930s.

By late 1990 GATT negotiations over a pending comprehensive deal reached an acute point. The four-year effort to extend GATT's free-trade regulations from manufacturing to rapidly expanding sectors of global commerce such as investment, intellectual property, services, telecommunications, and aviation—international business amounting to $1.5 trillion annually—hinged on settlement of the emotional and politicized issue of E.C. farm subsidies. "The American proposals are unrealistic," protested Daniel Gremillet, a French dairy producer. "They would crush us."[62] As 25,000 farmers demonstrated at E.C. offices against cuts in subsidies, the French government mobilized the European Community to resist the pressure from the United States and other nations for sharp reductions. Despite repeated entreaties from Bush, Kohl backed Mitterrand in opposing the cuts, and the overall GATT negotiations collapsed on 7 December 1990. "The main onus is on Mitterrand," declared a top Bush administration official.[63] Investment banker Robert Hormats observed that with the cold war over, the Western Europeans "don't need us as much as they once did; they need one another more than they need us."[64]

As the Atlantic figuratively grew wider and harder to cross, the Bush administration was already preparing to move in other directions. "Let's face it," an American trade negotiator argued, "there are other avenues that we can take—bilateral arrangements not only with Latin America but countries of the Pacific basin."[65] Washington negotiated free-trade agreements with Canada and Mexico and looked to expanding this trade group to the entire Western Hemisphere.

The accelerating economic integration within the European Community and within the forming American group intensified tensions with Japan. When E.C. Commission president Delors met with Japanese trade experts, many asked him, "There are blocs forming everywhere; what should we do?"[66] Some Japanese officials warned that they might counter with an East Asian trade zone. In the early 1990s Japan's highly successful drive to multiply exports to the European Community triggered European resentment and anxiety. Many E.C. computer, electronics, and automobile manufacturers fell helplessly behind their Japanese competitors. "This is the big battle of our time, but there is no sign that we are getting our act together," worried a top German official. "By the year 2000, the nine Japanese sisters will have a virtual monopoly on the entire range of information services, including telecommunications, semiconductors and computers. The only question is whether I[nternational B[usiness]

M[achines] will be number 10."[67] While urging France to adopt a Japanese-style plan for concerted industrial development, prime minister Edith Cresson, in her inimitable style, gibed that the Japanese were like workaholic "ants." "They sit up all night thinking of ways to screw the Americans and the Europeans," she argued shortly before taking office. "They are our common enemy."[68] But when Cresson called for united U.S.-E.C. resistance to Japanese exports, the Bush administration reportedly turned her down.[69]

In whatever pattern the emerging trade blocs and powerful trading nations lined up with or against one another, the fact of their sharpened rivalry created dangers for the whole world, particularly the poor nations. Although government leaders of the major nations ritually denied that their respective trade zones would develop into closed, protective "fortresses," they all remained under domestic pressures to limit painful foreign competition and to retaliate against real or imagined trade injuries. Tactical reprisals could escalate easily into strategic trade wars. If not reversed, the December 1990 collapse of the GATT talks could throttle the expansion of world trade and income. Already in 1991 global economic growth fell to zero while population climbed, meaning that most of the world's 5.3 billion people, particularly in the impoverished areas, suffered a decline in living standards.[70] For third-world countries trying to export their way out of poverty, the restricted trade zones of the rich nations often created higher barriers. For the United States, whose manufacturers found it more difficult to vie with Japanese and Western European rivals, the creation of a Western Hemisphere free-trade area promised more secure markets in Mexico, Bolivia, and Honduras—but little stimulating competitive pressure. Trade wars between American and European blocs threatened to terminate the transatlantic partnership, already attenuated by the end of the cold war. "Europe in the '90s could turn out to be the Japan of the '80s—the reputed enemy," warned U.S. economist C. Fred Bergsten.[71] At the July 1991 annual summit of the seven richest industrial democracies, the leaders who assembled in London proved unable to break the deadlocked GATT dispute over farm subsidies. But they promised to end the impasse by the end of 1991, thereby clearing the way for freer international commerce in services, information, and other modern businesses. The future health of both the world economy and U.S.-French relations depended on such a breakthrough.

Yet even if the European Community were to reduce its farm subsidies and become an open market rather than a fortress, the trade zone still could deal America a rude shock. Once intergration was attained in 1993 or shortly thereafter, the European Community, that "600-pound canary" as Gary Horlick of the U.S. Chamber of Commerce described it, would displace the United States as the largest market in the world.[72] Then Americans no longer could count on the automatic—and comfortable—advantage of having global trade policies and standards follow U.S. wishes. "I'm not sure we are ready for the shock when people start doing things to please the EC rather than us," warned Horlick.[73] For some Americans; accustomed to the United States' being the globe's richest, most powerful, and influential nation, the rise of the European Community produced anxiety about of loss of control. Senator Max Baucus of Montana reported that he was "overwhelmed" when he visited the E.C. offices in Brussels. "There is this gigantic black building and . . . there are so many people there it is like an anthill. And . . . they are so bureaucratic." Fearing that U.S. diplomats in Brussels were outclassed and "outgunned," Baucus urged the State Department to send "more fire-power where the action is."[74]

Worried about being "outgunned" by the European Community or squeezed out of the E.C.'s economic development, Washington relied more than ever on its military command of NATO for the authority, as a U.S. diplomat explained, to "tell the Europeans what we want on a whole lot of issues—trade, agriculture, the gulf, you name it."[75] This explanation did not mean that the Bush administration sought to decree what the Western Europeans did on every issue or that it tried to assume responsibility in every matter. For example, in 1991 Washington encouraged the European Community's efforts to mediate the civil strife in Yugoslavia. But the United States wanted to be able, at times of its choosing, to intervene decisively in European matters, and NATO remained the only vehicle for such influence. Yet after 1989 NATO appeared to many Western Europeans, particularly the French, as merely a useful relic. NATO remained useful as an insurance policy against the remote threat of Moscow's aggression, against the more immediate dangers arising from splintering of the Soviet Union into nuclear-armed, fractious republics, and against the perennial problem of German power. But it was also a relic, because U.S. hegemony in Europe was no longer needed or justified.

Although the Persian Gulf War boosted America's military prestige, the conflict accelerated the marginalization of NATO. Authorized to operate only in Europe and North America, NATO had "no role" in the Middle East, observed a U.S. Senate aide. "It couldn't play a part as a unified command structure, and there wasn't much it could do. This in fact may be a real turning point."[76] The United States sent off to the gulf much of the equipment and many of the soldiers that had made up Washington's material commitment to NATO; after the war many of the men and women went home to the United States, while much of their weaponry remained in the Middle East. Mindful of America's budget deficits and Congress's growing reluctance to pay for the stationing of U.S. troops on the territory of wealthy allies, Europeans expected that the number of G.I.'s in Europe would shrink further. The war against Iraq also highlighted the European Community's inability to come up with a common European defense or diplomacy: France, Great Britain, Germany, and the others went their own way. Yet the war also breathed life into the long-moribund Western European Union (WEU), which facilitated some military coordination among European belligerents.

On 6 December 1990 Mitterrand and Kohl pledged to create a "genuinely common security policy and common defense" for the European Community through development of the WEU and the European Political Union (EPU), the latter a new institution that would become the political arm of the European Community.[77] On 4 February 1991 foreign ministers Dumas and Genscher fleshed out these pledges with detailed blueprints for building the WEU and EPU into powerful and effective E.C. institutions. The French and Germans wanted the WEU to remain closely associated with NATO, but also to maintain its independence from the U.S.-dominated alliance.[78] This project touched off old arguments. De Gaulle and other French leaders had also tried to create a Western European security system while preserving the bare essentials of the Atlantic defense alliance and reducing American hegemony in Western Europe. Washington, which had fought off such attempts before, now moved decisively to squelch the challenge from the WEU.

Responding harshly to the Dumas-Genscher plan for the Western European Union, Baker in February 1991 sent to the French and German governments letters so hostile in tone that Mitterrand at first refused to accept his. If the Europeans dared to diminish NATO's authority by developing the WEU, Baker warned, the United States would pull its troops out of Europe. Once again Germany, pressed to choose between the United States and France, leaned toward the more powerful Americans. In March Baker met with Genscher in Washington and extracted from the German foreign minister a specific commitment to NATO's continued preeminence in Western European security matters. In return the Americans gave a vague assent to an undefined "European security identity." As one Bush administration official candidly remarked, "the Germans acquiesced in what had to happen, and we gave promises which the Europeans still have to decide how to collect on."[79]

Washington made it more difficult for the Europeans to "decide" by aggravating the differences among them. At the NATO foreign ministers' meeting in June 1991 the Americans pushed through a proposal to modernize NATO with the creation of a 60,000-soldier Rapid Reaction Corps. The Dutch, suspicious of French ambitions, and the British, promised the command of the new corps, enthusiastically supported the Americans. Abandoned by the Germans on this issue, an angry Dumas predicted that the scheme would fail and chided Washington for trying to "dictate to Europeans what they should do" for their own security.[80] If Europe did need such a force, the French minister argued, it should be part of the WEU. Once again the United States got its way by threatening to pull out its troops and by exacerbating European divisions. With the afterglow of victory over Iraq still visible, Washington won this round easily.

But the remainder of the 1990s could turn out differently. Western Europe, in fits and starts, was moving toward unity; the United States, despite or perhaps because of its military prowess, was losing much of its economic clout; and the Soviet Union had already ceased to be the frightening aggressor that cowed Western Europeans into obeying Washington. Whether the U.S. government and people would ever agree to remain in NATO while accepting a less predominant role in the alliance remained a key question for the future and an issue that touched deeply on U.S.-French relations. NATO's problems "all begin and end with France," a journalist reported after interviewing U.S. officials.[81]

CONCLUSION

In the half century after 1940 many of America's problems in the world "began with" or at least touched on France. Although U.S. influence on France far exceeded French influence on the United States, France held a special place in the American imagination as a nation well known and often desired, yet also different, difficult, flawed, "foreign," and other. Particularly in the 1940s and 1950s Americans often represented France as an ill, defeated nation, dragged down by its effete and effeminate political leadership and its impractical, rationalistic intellectual class. One recalls *Life* magazine's 1953 contrast between the stable, commonsense, "strictly unintellectual" American citizen and the emotional, unrealistic French citizen.[82] Such stereotyped representations appeared less often after 1958, when the patriarchal de Gaulle endowed France with a firm, executive-led government, but they did not disappear. When Edith Cresson became prime minister in May 1991, *Newsweek* magazine chose to include in its brief article on the event rumors, which the magazine acknowledged were old and unproven, of Cresson's "romance with Mitterrand."[83] Almost reflexively the *Newsweek* editors were literalizing *Life's* 1953 conception of the French government as "a bedroom farce."

Old stereotypes also surfaced in a front-page essay published in the *New York Times Book Review*, probably America's most influential arbiter of intellectual taste. Written by humanities professor Camille Paglia, the caustic piece, entitled "Ninnies, Pedants, Tyrants and Other Academics," condemned linguist Jacques Derrida, psychoanalyst Jacques Lacan, and historian Michel Foucault as "minor French theorists" who were nevertheless dangerous.[84] The author claimed that these French theorists had inspired an influential group of American professors—"French-infatuated ideologues" in Paglia's parlance—who "have made a travesty of the best American higher education." Paglia's widely discussed article was representative of a broad reaction, originating within academic departments and spreading into mainstream American life, against theoretical innovations criticized as either too intellectual and obscure or as giving too much weight to elements of the population and the curriculum perceived as marginal and minority. This reaction fit a mood widespread in America of assertive yet defensive nationalism. The United States was taking pride in having won a smashing military victory in the Middle East, while the political consequences of that success remained unsettling and the nation's underlying economic problems grew worse. The

United States was retreating to a protected North American trade bloc even as the more competitive, global GATT system languished. Finally, Washington seemed unable to accept any independent security arrangement of the European Community that challenged NATO's dominion.

There is no evidence that Paglia gave thought to America's difficulties with France in NATO, the European Community, and GATT, but in attempting to defend American thought and education from what she perceived as insidious French cultural influence, she revived stereotypes long used by Americans to trivialize French viewpoints, in political and security disputes as well as in cultural issues. The first stereotype was that France remained a defeated nation regardless of how many years had elapsed since 1940. When Paglia discussed why some French thinkers in the late 1960s and 1970s conceived the self as "decentered," that is, as constructed by a number of conflicting social tendencies, she explained, "of course the French felt decentered: they had just been crushed by Germany." The second conventional image was France as feminine and weak: "spinsterish" and "lying flat on her face under the Nazi boot." France at its best offered the world images of "woman's archetypal mystery and glamour." Paglia asserted that "the big French D is not Derrida but [Catherine] Deneuve," referring to the French actress famous for playing the role of feminine victim in films such as *Repulsion*. Third was the stereotype of French intellectuals as "obscurantists" given to "false abstraction," "pompous bombast," and "cheap cynicism"—pedants who had no understanding of democracy. "Lacan is a tyrant who must be driven from our shores," Paglia declared.[85] This tirade was important not so much for what the author wrote but rather for the verbal images of France that she employed. Part of the American imagination, these stereotypes have long made it easy for Americans, without really thinking about it, to trivialize France and to disparage French points of view contrary to those of the United States.

Moreover, such points of view frequently led to policies contrary to those of the United States, as a range of American policy makers from Franklin D. Roosevelt and Cordell Hull to George Bush and James A. Baker discovered to their exasperation. In mid-1991, a time of relatively good relations between the two nations, White House officials characterized the French as "difficult to keep on track."[86] Much of the problem with the American understanding of "on track" came from France's persistence in trying to manage its own train system. French foreign policy often ran along the same general lines as that of Washington, but officials in Paris, more than their counterparts in London or Bonn, held to an itinerary independent of that of the United States.

In World War II both the United States and France fought against Germany, but the Americans started fighting after most of the French had stopped. Differences in U.S.-French perspectives on the fate of the French empire, the bombing of France, dealing with the Germans, and the goals of the war compounded both the conflicts among the French and the difficulty in the personal relations between de Gaulle and American leaders. French and American officials joined together in the victory celebrations of 1945, but they had traveled along quite different roads to get there.

Similarly, the United States and France cemented their cold-war alliance by signing the NATO treaty in April 1949 after several years of differences over how to deal with the Soviet Union. Until 1947 most French, although divided on many other issues, agreed that their nation should try to straddle the East-West rift. Even after the French government decided it had to align with the United States, Paris officials still believed that the Americans were provoking the Soviets unnecessarily, particularly by building up West Germany. Motivated in part by the need to counter and contain German strength, the French launched the Monnet Plan and the Schuman Plan. Despite their differences, both these economic development schemes drew on models and help from the United States, and both expressed Paris's intention to reinvigorate the French and Western European economies and make them more independent of the Americans.

In the 1950s France determined to hold on to its empire in Indochina and Algeria and its sovereignty in terms of the French army; meanwhile many French citizens longed for neutrality in the cold war. These aspirations put the French at odds with Americans preparing for an intensified cold war and convinced that orderly decolonization could head off communism in the decrepit European empires. Washington's program of psychological warfare in France failed to bridge this gap and in fact may have exacerbated the irritation Americans and French felt for each other.

After de Gaulle came to power in 1958 he instituted a sweeping rehabilitation program that strengthened the French government and made France an independent nation with which the Americans had to reckon, even if they rejected the general's request for a privileged voice in the alliance's decision making. De Gaulle's tensions with Washington stemmed not only from his objections to U.S. intervention in Vietnam and the Dominican Republic and the rivalry over Germany and Western Europe, but also from fundamental differences over the probable course of future events. For all their talk about the future, John F. Kennedy and Lyndon B. Johnson could not see beyond their ideological cold-war blinders, although Kennedy began to do so in his American University speech shortly before his assassination. Coming of age in the era before the 1917 Bolshevik Revolution, de Gaulle believed that nationalism and national characteristics would outlast communist ideology. As de Gaulle prepared, two decades too early, for the withering away of communism and the emergence of Russia and other independent nations in Central and Eastern Europe, American policy makers dismissed his vision as impractical and even pathological.

In the 1970s the United States and France drew closer together as the two nations pruned their ambitions, respectively, for dominion and for independence. Washington and Paris also cooperated more, particularly in nuclear weaponry and in sub-Saharan Africa. Meanwhile the ending of the Vietnam

War and the disillusionment of French intellectuals with the Soviet Union improved the climate for U.S.-French relations. Yet sparks still flew, such as when Henry Kissinger and Michel Jobert clashed over the former's Year of Europe project and the latter's objections to America's Middle East and oil policies in 1973–74.

In the following decade the odd couple of Reagan and Mitterrand brought the United States and France closer together because of mutual distrust of West Germany, fear of the Soviet Union, and commitment to the doctrine of peace through strengthened nuclear capability. Mitterrand sacrificed some of France's military autonomy for the perceived benefit of closer ties with U.S. and NATO forces. French "Reaganomania" in the mid-1980s coincided with the peak of the U.S.-French entente. Thereafter, the two governments slowly drifted apart as Reagan shifted focus from building more nuclear bombs to making those weapons obsolete with the "Star Wars" project and to cutting their numbers through agreements with Gorbachev. Although the number of nuclear weapons Reagan actually eliminated was small and "Star Wars" remained largely a dream (albeit a costly one), the change in tone was important. Once again France was jilted by larger powers making deals among themselves.

Faced with a reunified Germany and a world of coalescing trade blocs, France in the early 1990s tried to build the European Community and the WEU into institutions that would contain Germany, reach out to Eastern Europe, and mobilize European power behind an agenda set, at least partially, by Paris. For a middle-sized power this scheme was highly ambitious, as audacious in fact as France's partially successful effort since World War II to maintain significant independence from its American ally. In the future the extent of French independence from America in Europe will depend on the structure of NATO, the scope of America's influence on Germany, and the degree to which a transformed or disintegrated Soviet Union threatens the West. Probably the U.S.-French alliance, like transatlantic ties in general, will become a more distant, ad hoc arrangement.

From the American perspective, France's historic contrariety appeared annoying and disruptive but not dangerous. So much more powerful than France, the United States usually shunted aside French protests as it went about its business managing the alliance. Thus Americans closed themselves off to the often acute insights of French leaders, particularly those of de Gaulle. U.S.-French policy differences involved more than just each country pursuing its own national interest. Both peoples had long manifested a sense of universalist mission; the French felt chosen to spread "civilization," while the Americans went on crusades for "democracy." As a consequence both nations at times suffered self-delusion. But there remained a difference. While America's superiority in strength forced the French to take seriously U.S. visions, France's relative weakness empowered Americans to disparage and dismiss French aspirations.

After a half century of cold alliance, the United States and France stood as opponents or as distant associates on major multinational issues such as the Middle East, trade negotiations, and the security structure of Europe. While France agreed with Germany and Italy on the urgency of a massive Western aid program to help Gorbachev and to rebuild the disintegrating economy of what had been the Soviet Union, the United States and Japan advocated going slowly. Despite these differences, the United States and France remained allies with a myriad of connecting ties and with compatible economic, political, and social systems. From their often diverging global perspectives, the two nations had mutual concerns about the power of Germany and of Russia, and about the importance of stability in Eastern Europe, the third world, and elsewhere. In response to the revolutionary changes of 1989–91, both nations applied policies that were grounded in the past and threatened problems for the future. If the European Community does coalesce into the integrated unit France has sought, this European state may well be controlled more by Germany than by France. If the United States does uphold NATO's preeminence in Europe and a renewed Pax Americana around the globe, the resulting economic strains may well worsen the standard of living and quality of life of the American people.

CHRONOLOGY

1940
    May:
    Germany attacks France.

    June:
    Charles de Gaulle escapes to London.
    France signs armistice with Germany.

1941
    December:
    Japan attacks Pearl Harbor.
    In defiance of the United States, the Free French forces of Charles de Gaulle capture from Vichy officials the North Atlantic islands of St. Pierre and Miquelon.

1942
    November:
    In Operation Torch, aimed at German forces, U.S troops invade French North Africa and encounter armed resistance from Vichy French troops. In a move that antagonizes de Gaulle and public opinion in America and Great Britain, the Roosevelt administration strikes a deal with a Vichy official, Admiral François Darlan, recognizing Darlan's civil authority in North Africa in return for his ordering French troops to cease fire and cooperate with the Americans.

1943

January:

At Casablanca Roosevelt meets de Gaulle for the first time and tries to bring him together with America's client, the politically inept General Giraud.

1944

June:

The Allied D-Day invasion of Normandy begins to free France from German occupation, while de Gaulle quarrels with the Americans over who shall govern the liberated territory.

August:

Paris liberated.

October:

Roosevelt reluctantly recognizes de Gaulle's French Committee of National Liberation as the legitimate government of France.

December:

When Germans attack Allied forces in the Battle of the Bulge, de Gaulle defies General Dwight D. Eisenhower by refusing to evacuate Strasbourg.

1945

February:

At the Yalta summit the French are not invited, but France is allotted an occupation zone in Germany and a permanent seat on the Security Council of the United Nations.

May:

Germany surrenders.

June:

French soldiers threaten to fire on U.S. troops in disputed Val d'Aosta region of northwest Italy.

July–August:

The leaders of the United States, Great Britain, and the Soviet Union meet at Potsdam to decide the fate of defeated Germany, but they do not invite France to attend.

August:

President Harry S Truman and Secretary of State James F. Byrnes meet in Washington with de Gaulle and Foreign Minister Georges Bidault. Jean Monnet begins negotiations for a $550 million loan, granted in December by the U.S. government's Export-Import Bank.

1946
January:
Charles de Gaulle resigns the presidency of France.

May:
French and American officials sign the Blum-Byrnes agreement, providing for a further loan of $650 million from the United States, a French promise to move toward freer trade regulations, and a French pledge to ease restrictions on the importation of Hollywood films.

1947
March–April:
At the Moscow foreign ministers' conference, Bidault shifts from a neutralist stance to a position closer to that of the Americans and further from that of the Soviets.

May:
Premier Paul Ramadier dismisses the Communist ministers from the French government.

June:
Secretary of State George C. Marshall invites Europeans to help draw up plans for a U.S.-financed economic reconstruction program. From 1948 to 1951 France receives $2.4 billion in Marshall Plan aid.

1948
February:
Moscow pressures Czechoslovakia to adopt a Communist government, thereby frightening many in France and in other Western European countries.

June:
France drops its opposition to building a West German state.
The Western powers institute a new currency in the three western zones of Germany, the Soviets retaliate by blocking land routes into Berlin, and the West responds with the Berlin Airlift.

1949
April:
The United States, France, Belgium, Canada, Denmark, Iceland, Italy, Luxembourg, the Nether-

lands, Norway, Portugal, and the United Kingdom sign the North Atlantic Treaty.

1950

May:

Foreign Minister Robert Schuman proposes what becomes the Schuman Plan to pool the iron and
coal resources of France, West Germany, Belgium,
the Netherlands, and Luxembourg.

August:

Secretary of State Dean Acheson directs American
embassies in France and in other nations to intensify efforts to influence public opinion.

October:

Disturbed by Acheson's proposal to rearm West Germany, the French put forth the Pleven Plan for a
European army to which West Germany would contribute soldiers. West Germany would not, however, have an army of its own.

1952

May:

Much transformed in negotiations, the Pleven Plan
emerges as the European Defense Community, a
scheme many French oppose because it would
sharply restrict the independence of the French
army.

1954

May:

French forces surrender at Dien Bien Phu after an
eight-year colonial war, financed toward the end
largely by Washington, against Vietnamese nationalists and Communists led by Ho Chi Minh. In
the Geneva Conference, which follows, Vietnam
is temporarily partitioned. The elections scheduled
for 1956 to reunify the country are never held.

August:

Despite intense U.S. pressure, the French National
Assembly rejects ratification of the European Defense Community.

October:

France accepts a plan for German rearmament that
provides for strengthening the Western European
Union, West Germany joining NATO, stationing

British as well as American troops in West Germany, and German renunciation of atomic, biological, and chemical weapons. France accelerates its atomic weapons program.

November:
Revolt in French Algeria begins.

1956

October–November:
In the crisis that follows Egypt's nationalization of the Suez Canal, France, Great Britain, and Israel ignore U.S. objections and launch an attack on Egypt to retake the canal. France feels betrayed when Great Britain succumbs to U.S. pressures to halt the military assault.

1958

June:
As France's Fourth Republic collapses, de Gaulle takes power and becomes the powerful president of the Fifth Republic.

September:
In letters to President Eisenhower and British prime minister Harold Macmillan, de Gaulle proposes a U.S.-Soviet-British-French directorate to run the Western alliance and to make collective decisions about global strategy. In a series of discussions extending into 1962, this request is rebuffed by the Americans and British.

1960

February:
France explodes its first atomic bomb.

May:
When the U.S.-British-French summit breaks up after Soviet downing of an American spy plane, de Gaulle pledges his support to Eisenhower.

1961

During the Berlin crisis, when President John F. Kennedy undertakes negotiations with the Soviets, de Gaulle, supported by West German chancellor Konrad Adenauer, criticizes such willingness to talk as a lack of resolve.

1962

October:
During the Cuban missile crisis de Gaulle promises his support to Kennedy while also noting that

once again he has been informed after Washington
has made its decisions rather than consulted in the
decision making.

1963

January:
De Gaulle vetoes British admission to the Common
Market, thereby frustrating the Kennedy adminis-
tration's plans for a Grand Design to draw uniting
Western Europe closer to the United States.

July:
De Gaulle refuses to sign the partial nuclear test ban
treaty negotiated by the United States, the Soviet
Union, and Great Britain.

August:
De Gaulle criticizes U.S intervention in South Vietnam.

November:
Kennedy's assassination provokes mass mourning in
France and elsewhere. The meeting after the Washington funeral between de Gaulle and President
Lyndon B. Johnson reveals some of the differences
that would put U.S.-French relations in the deep
freeze until mid-1968.

1964

January:
France grants formal recognition to the People's Republic of China, thereby challenging U.S. efforts
to isolate the Communist government.
De Gaulle publicly urges the neutralization of Southeast Asia, including the American supported government of South Vietnam.

1965–1967

The United States escalates its involvement in the
Vietnam War, to the vocal disapproval of de
Gaulle and much of the French population.

1966

March:
De Gaulle informs Johnson that France will pull out
of the NATO integrated military command and
asks the Americans to remove their troops and
military headquarters from French territory.

1967

Publication of Jean-Jacques Servan-Schreiber's best-
selling *The American Challenge* underscores French

unease with large-scale U.S. corporate investment in France and Europe.

June:

In the Six-Day War in the Middle East, de Gaulle criticizes the United States and Israel and leans toward the Arabs.

December:

French chief of staff Charles Ailleret declares that French nuclear forces should be able to strike against any enemy, not just the Soviet Union.

1968

March:

Strains on the U.S. economy resulting from the Vietnam War and Johnson's reluctance to raise taxes accelerate gold outflows, creating a financial crisis. Overwhelmed by domestic and foreign problems, Johnson announces a partial bombing halt in Vietnam and his withdrawal from the presidential campaign.

March–May:

Unrest among Paris students and workers explodes into a multifaceted rebellion, the economic repercussions of which undercut de Gaulle's foreign policy of grandeur.

August:

Soviet invasion of Czechoslovakia to crush the "Prague Spring" postpones de Gaulle's dream of a non-Communist Europe extending from "the Atlantic to the Urals."

1969

January:

Soon after his inauguration as president, Richard M. Nixon pays a cordial visit to de Gaulle in Paris. The modesty of Nixon's ambitions in Europe helps improve U.S.-French relations.

April:

De Gaulle resigns.

1970

February:

On his visit to the United States, President Georges Pompidou meets vehement public protest against France's pro-Arab Middle East policy.

1971   August–December:

Faced with record balance-of-payments deficits and gold outflows, Nixon abandons the Bretton Woods monetary system, severs the dollar's link with gold, and pressures France and other allies to bear most of the resulting economic adjustment burdens. Pompidou leads European resistance to this effort, and in December he and the Americans strike a compromise on foreign exchange rates.

1973   April:

Declaring 1973 the "Year of Europe," Nixon and National Security Adviser Henry A. Kissinger try to rein in Western Europe by linking military matters, in which the United States still holds predominance, with economic and political issues, on which the Europeans are showing some independence. After a year of sometimes acrimonious debate, the Americans and Europeans reach a compromise.

October:

During the Yom Kippur War in the Middle East, U.S. officials warn the Soviet Union not to intervene by issuing a military alert. As the world faces the possibility of nuclear war, France and other European allies realize that once again they have no voice in U.S. decision making.

Nixon and Kissinger begin the covert program of nuclear aid to and cooperation with France.

1973–1974   The United States and France differ over how to respond to the Arab oil embargo.

1975   December:

Meeting with U.S. diplomats in London, Kissinger spells out his vision for keeping Europe stable by maintaining American predominance in Western Europe and Soviet predominance in Eastern Europe.

1979   December:

NATO decides to deploy U.S. Pershing II and cruise missiles in West Germany, Great Britain, and

other allied countries while simultaneously pursuing negotiations with the Soviets to reduce the
number of such intermediate range weapons.
France supports this decision although it will not
permit U.S missiles on its territory.

1979–1980   As U.S-Soviet relations deteriorate in the aftermath
of the December 1979 Soviet invasion of Afghani-
stan, French president Valéry Giscard d'Estaing
joins with West German chancellor Helmut
Schmidt to try to mediate between Washington
and Moscow in the renewed cold war.
The United States and France intensify their cooperation in nuclear weaponry and in sub-Saharan Africa.

1981   January:
Republican Ronald Reagan becomes president of the
United States.

May:
Socialist François Mitterrand becomes president of
France.

1982   The Siberian gas line controversy exacerbates economic and political tensions between the United
States and France even as the two nations move
closer together on strategic military issues.

March:
The French government signs a contract with Michael Eisner of Walt Disney Company to build a
$4.4 billion theme park to be called Euro Disney-
land.

1983   January:
Mitterrand addresses the West German parliament
and criticizes German Socialists for backing away
from their commitment to deploy the U.S.
Pershing II and cruise missiles.

March:
Reagan calls for development of a Strategic Defense
Initiative or "Star Wars" project to create a space-
based shield against nuclear weapons. Mitterrand
fears that such technology could become terribly

expensive while reducing the deterrent value of French nuclear forces and decoupling the link between European and American defenses.

1984   Peak of "Reaganomania," the popular French enthusiasm for Ronald Reagan as a symbol for dynamic economic growth and neoconservative values.

1985   March:
Mikhail S. Gorbachev comes to power in the Soviet Union. Within a few years his efforts to restructure the Soviet economic and political system and his lifting of Moscow's grip on Eastern and Central Europe will change the European order. Yet many of the themes and problems in U.S-French relations will persist.

1986   April:
Intent on attacking Mu'ammar al-Qaddafi's Libya because of Libyan involvement in terrorist assaults, Reagan sends an emissary to Europe to inform the allies. Mitterrand is eager to cooperate in the planning, but the Americans have already made their decisions. Mitterrand refuses to allow the American bombers, based in Great Britain, to fly over French airspace, forcing them to travel twice as far to reach their targets. Official and popular resentment of France erupts in America.

October:
At the U.S.-Soviet summit in Reykjavik, Iceland, Reagan tentatively agrees to a sweeping elimination of ballistic missiles, including some of those belonging to France and Great Britain. Although the deal falls through, the French and other allies are incensed at Reagan's cavalier treatment of their interests.

1987   December:
Reagan and Gorbachev sign the INF treaty eliminating all Soviet and U.S. intermediate-range missiles in Europe. Although no French weapons are involved, many French defense experts worry about the progressive denuclearization of Europe. The

U.S.-French strategic entente, based in part on a shared commitment to a nuclear buildup, becomes frayed.

1989

July:

Mitterrand hosts the annual meeting of the richest industrial democracies, timed to coincide with the lavish celebration of the two-hundredth anniversary of the French Revolution. The event dramatizes the moderation of France's revolutionary tradition and Mitterrand's effort to stand close to the United States while still maintaining France's distance and independence.

November:

The breakup of the Soviet bloc accelerates when the East German government opens the Berlin Wall on 9 November. Worried that German unification could undercut French leadership in Western Europe and undermine the European Community, Mitterrand tries to slow down or halt the move toward German unity while accelerating the E.C.'s integration.

December:

When Mitterrand meets with Gorbachev in Kiev, both leaders warn West Germany not to push too fast for reunification.

1990

February:

In close collaboration with the West Germans and despite the initial objections of the Soviets, British, and French, the Bush administration initiates the 2-plus-4 talks on German unification. U.S. ties with France now appear less important to Washington than they did in the 1980s.

April:

Bush and Mitterrand meet in Florida. Despite suggestions floated by U.S. and French officials before the meeting, the two presidents are unable to arrive at a compromise leading to a more formal French involvement in NATO.

July:

Acknowledging the end of the cold war, Bush at the NATO summit in London proposes the new nuclear doctrine of "last resort," upsetting the French, who still cling to nuclear deterrence.

In Houston, at the annual economic summit, Mitterrand and Kohl side together against Bush by pushing for increased aid to the sagging Soviet economy and for retaining the E.C.'s high subsidies to agriculture.

Meeting in southern Russia, Gorbachev and Kohl make a comprehensive deal that eliminates Soviet objections to Germany's uniting and remaining in NATO and provides for large-scale German payments to the Soviet Union. The 2-plus-4 talks are now largely superseded.

August:

Saddam Hussein of Iraq invades neighboring Kuwait. The United States organizes an international military response, code-named Operation Desert Shield, in which France participates.

October:

Germany officially reunifies.

November:

At a summit in Paris, the European and North Atlantic powers give international blessing to German unification, sign a treaty providing for huge cuts in conventional arms in Europe, and establish some institutional structure for the Conference on Security and Cooperation in Europe (CSCE).

December:

International trade talks in Brussels collapse, principally because of a dispute that pits France against the United States. France leads the E.C.'s effort to preserve generous subsidies to Western European farmers and to farm exports, while the United States heads a group of highly efficient agricultural nations opposed to these payments.

1991

January–February:

In Operation Desert Storm, lasting from 17 January to 28 February, an American-led international coalition drives Iraq out of Kuwait. After failing to broker a negotiated settlement of the Kuwaiti crisis, France joins the war as a U.S. ally.

February–March:

Secretary of State James A. Baker opposes French and German efforts to build up the Western European Union into a European defense organization that could challenge NATO's role.

July:

Meeting in London at the annual economic summit, the assembled Western leaders fail to resolve the agricultural subsidies dispute or to arrive at a comprehensive plan for bailing out the sinking Soviet economy.

August:

The failed coup against Gorbachev by hard-liners in the Soviet military and secret police intensifies the issue of Western financial assistance to save the Soviet economy. Once again France sides with Germany and Italy in pushing for larger amounts of immediate help, while the United States, at least initially, remains more cautious. The aid question is complicated by the rapid disintegration of the Soviet Union as a unified country.

NOTES AND REFERENCES

PREFACE

1. U.S. Department of State, *Foreign Relations of the United States, 1952–54* (Washington, D.C.: Government Printing Office, 1983), 5:1520 (hereafter cited as *FRUS 1952–54*).

INTRODUCTION

1. Albert Boime, *Hollow Icons: The Politics of Sculpture in Nineteenth-Century France* (Kent, Ohio: Kent State University Press, 1987), 119.

2. E. B. Washburne, *Recollections of a Minister to France, 1869–1877* (New York: Scribner, 1887), 2:58, 92.

3. *Providence Journal,* 4 March 1871.

4. *California Daily Alta* quoted in Elizabeth Brett White, *American Opinion of France* (New York: Knopf, 1927), 208.

5. Arthur S. Link, ed., *The Papers of Woodrow Wilson* (Princeton, N.J.: Princeton University Press, 1969), 6:228.

6. Boime, *Hollow Icons*, 121; see also George L. Mosse, *Nationalism and Sexuality: Middle-Class Morality and Sexual Norms in Modern Europe* (Madison: University of Wisconsin Press, 1985).

7. *Life,* 26 January 1953, 34.

8. Boime, *Hollow Icons*, 131.

9. Henry Adams, *The Education of Henry Adams: An Autobiography* (Boston: Houghton Mifflin, 1961), 96.

10. Boime, *Hollow Icons,* 128.

11. U.S. Bureau of the Census, *Historical Statistics of the United States, Colonial Times to 1957* (Washington, D.C.: GPO, 1960), 550, 552, 56; U.S. Bureau of the Census, *Statistical Abstract of the United States, 1988* (Washington: GPO, 1987), 771.

12. Boime, *Hollow Icons,* 134.

13. *New York Times,* 29 October 1886.

14. See Marvin Trachtenberg, *The Statue of Liberty* (New York: Viking, 1976).

CHAPTER 1

1. Charles de Gaulle, *The War Memoirs of Charles de Gaulle: Unity, 1942–1944* (New York: Simon and Schuster, 1959), 271.

2. Ibid., 88.

3. François Kersaudy, *Churchill and de Gaulle* (New York: Atheneum), 1983), 169.

4. Will Brownell and Richard N. Billings, *So Close to Greatness: A Biography of William C. Bullitt* (New York: Macmillan, 1987), 192.

5. Ibid., 202–3.

6. Harold Ickes, *The Secret Diary of Harold L. Ickes* (New York: Simon and Schuster, 1953–54), 3:216. See also Gordon Wright, "Ambassador Bullitt and the Fall of France," *World Politics* 10 (October 1957): 63–75, and Orville H. Bullitt, ed., *For the President: Personal and Secret* (Boston: Houghton Mifflin, 1972), 355–96.

7. John McVickar Haight, Jr., *American Aid to France, 1938–1940* (New York: Atheneum, 1940).

8. *FRUS 1940* 1:250.

9. Brownell and Billings, *So Close to Greatness,* 253.

10. Ibid.

11. Charles de Gaulle, *The War Memoirs of Charles de Gaulle: The Call to Honor, 1940–1942* (New York: Viking, 1955), 61.

12. Wright, "Ambassador Bullitt," 85–86; Bullitt, *For the President,* 397–477; *FRUS 1940* 2:437–39, 452–54, 461–64.

13. *FRUS 1940* 2:464.

14. Ibid., 2:462.

15. Ibid., 2:462–63. See also Robert O. Paxton, *Vichy France: Old Guard and New Order* (New York: Norton, 1973), 3–63; Bullitt, *For the President,* 478–93; Julian G. Hurstfield, *America and the French Nation* (Chapel Hill: University of North Carolina Press, 1986), 3–30.

16. *FRUS 1940* 2:519.

17. Henry L. Stimson Diary, 27 August, 30 October, 12 November 1940, Henry L. Stimson Papers, Yale University Library; Kersaudy, *Churchill and de Gaulle,* 92–103.

18. *FRUS 1941* 2:89–206; William D. Leahy, *I Was There* (New York: McGraw Hill, 1950), 456, 71; Linda McClain, "The Role of W. D. Leahy in U.S. Foreign Policy," (Ph.D. diss., University of Virginia, 1984), 37–62; Hurstfield, *America and the French Nation,* 67–82; James J. Dougherty, *The Politics of Wartime Aid: American Economic Assistance to France and French Northwest Africa, 1940–1946* (Westport, Conn.: Greenwood Press, 1978), 36.

19. Paxton, *Vichy France,* 123; see also ibid., 117–124.

20. *FRUS 1941* 2:431. See also Richard Griffiths, *Pétain* (Garden City, N.Y.: Doubleday, 1972), 345–48.

21. Leahy, *I Was There,* 462.

22. *FRUS 1941* 2:205.

23. See Hurstfield, *America and the French Nation,* 120–38; Kersaudy, *Churchill and de Gaulle,* 170–82; Andre Kaspi, *Franklin D. Roosevelt* (Paris: Fayard, 1988), 514–18; Douglas S. Anglin, *The St. Pierre and Miquelon Affair of 1941* (Toronto: University of Toronto Press, 1966); Émile Henri Muselier, *De Gaulle contre le gaullisme* (Paris: Editions du Chene, 1946).

24. *Public Opinion Quarterly* 5 (Winter 1941): 676, 680.

25. *FRUS 1941* 2:566–67.

26. Kersaudy, *Churchill and de Gaulle,* 177.

27. *FRUS 1941* 2:556.

28. Hurstfield, *America and the French Nation,* 120–38.

29. Leahy, *I Was There,* 478, 471, 469.

30. See *FRUS 1942* 2:546–50; Stimson Diary, 10 November 1942; Robert Murphy, *Diplomat among Warriors* (Garden City, N.Y.: Doubleday, 1964), 99–143; Leahy, *I Was There,* 469–78; de Gaulle, *War Memoirs: Unity,* 45–58; Arthur L. Funk, "Negotiating the 'Deal with Darlan,' " *Journal of Contemporary History* 8 (April 1973): 81–117; Kersaudy, *Churchill and de Gaulle,* 213–32; Hurstfield, *America and the French Nation,* 162–83; Paul Victor Joliet II, "French-American Relations and the Political Role of the French Army, 1943–1945," (Ph.D. diss., State University of New York at Binghamton, 1978), 90–106.

31. Robert E. Sherwood, *Rooosevelt and Hopkins* (New York: Grosset & Dunlap, 1950), 646.

32. *FRUS 1941* 2:189.

33. H. W. Brands, Jr., *Cold Warriors: Eisenhower's Generation and American Foreign Policy* (New York: Columbia University Press, 1988), 96.

34. Kersaudy, *Churchill and de Gaulle,* 217.

35. Peter Tompkins, *The Murder of Admiral Darlan* (New York: Simon and Schuster, 1965), 139.

36. Joliet, "French-American Relations," 98–102.

37. Stimson Diary, 24 December 1942.

38. Ibid.

39. *FRUS 1942* 2:546–50.

40. Kersaudy, *Churchill and de Gaulle,* 219.

41. Ibid., 238–41.

42. Ibid., 251.

43. Ibid, 250. See also Kaspi, *Roosevelt,* 519–28.

44. Stimson Diary, 1 October 1943.

45. Kersaudy, *Churchill and de Gaulle,* 239.

46. Ibid., 288.

47. Stimson Diary, 17 June 1943.

48. Ibid., 21 December 1943.

49. Ibid., 2, 4 January 1944.

50. Memorandum by J. C. H. Bonbright, "Reasons Underlying This Government's Lack of Confidence in General de Gaulle," 20 January 1944, H. F. Matthews Files, General Records of the Department of State, record group 59, National Archives, Washington, D.C. (hereafter cited as NARG 59).

51. Joliet, "French-American Relations," 298–90; Kersaudy, *Churchill and de Gaulle,* 319.

52. Stimson Diary, 14 June, 14 September 1944.

53. Edwin C. Wilson, Memorandum of Conversation with the President, 24 March 1944, 851.00/3185 1/2, NARG 59. See also Kaspi, *Roosevelt,* 538–41.

54. George Messersmith to Secretary of State, 12 January 1945, 812.79600/1-1245, NARG 59.

55. Ibid.

56. *FRUS 1945* 4:789.

57. Edward Stettinius to Messersmith, 16 March 1945, 812.79600/3-1645, NARG

58. Kersaudy, *Churchill and de Gaulle,* 333.

59. Postwar advances in flight distance reduced Clipperton's importance.

59. Ibid., 334.

60. Paxton, *Vichy France,* 308.

61. David Eisenhower, *Eisenhower at War, 1943–1945* (New York: Vintage), 1986, 255.

62. Ronald Schaffer, *Wings of Judgment: American Bombing in World War II* (New York: Oxford University Press, 1985), 41–42.

63. Paxton, *Vichy France,* 286–329; Churchill and Roosevelt: *The Complete Correspondence,* ed. Warren F. Kimball, 3 vols. (Princeton, N.J.: Princeton University Press, 1984), 3:122–24, 127; Ronald Tiersky, *French Communism, 1920–1972* (New York: Columbia University Press, 1974), 112–37.

64. Stimson Diary, 1 May 1944.

65. Kersaudy, *Churchill and de Gaulle,* 350.

66. Ibid., 361.

67. Stimson Diary, 12, 13 June 1944.

68. Ibid., 13 June 1944.

69. Ibid., 14, 15 June 1944.

70. De Gaulle, *War Memoirs: Unity*, 269–71; Alfred Grosser, *Affaires extérieures: La politique de la France, 1944–1984* (Paris: Flammarion, 1984), 21–23.

71. De Gaulle, *War Memoirs: Unity*, 270.

72. Martin Blumenson, *Breakout and Pursuit* (Washington, D.C.: Office of the Chief of Military History, 1961), 590–628; Stephen E. Ambrose, *The Supreme Commander: The War Years of General Dwight D. Eisenhower* (Garden City, N.Y.: Doubleday, 1970), 479–89; De Gaulle, *War Memoirs: Unity*, 324–62; Joliet, "French-American Relations," 377–94; Henri Michel, *Paris résistant* (Paris: Albin Michel, 1982), 285–329.

73. At war's end, France agreed to repay $420 million at 2 percent interest. Monro MacCloskey, *Rearming the French in World War II* (New York: Richard Rosen, 1972), 182–83.

74. Joliet, "French-American Relations," 421.

75. Ambrose, *Supreme Commander*, 578; Joliet, "French-American Relations," 395–426.

76. *FRUS: The Conferences at Malta and Yalta 1945* (Washington: GPO, 1955), 572–73.

77. Leslie R. Groves, *Now It Can Be Told* (New York: Harper & Row, 1962), 234.

78. Boris T. Pash, *The Alsos Mission* (New York: Award House, 1969), 200–212; Michel Bar-Zohar, *The Hunt for German Scientists* (London: Barker, 1967), 56–64; Joliet, "French-American Relations," 442–74.

79. Stimson Diary, 30 April, 1 May 1945; Joliet, "French-American Relations," 475–525.

80. Joliet, "French-American Relations," 553.

81. *FRUS 1945* 4:735.

82. *The Public Opinion Quarterly* 9 (Spring 1945): 99.

83. Stimson Diary, 6 June 1945.

84. *FRUS 1945* 4:734–35.

85. Joliet, "French-American Relations," 581.

86. Memorandum by H. G. Sheen, "Lax Discipline as a Source for Enemy Propaganda," 17 February 1945, and enclosures, 092 France, Records of Allied Operational and Occupation Headquarters, World War II, NARG 331.

87. Paul W. Gulgowski, *The American Military Government of United States Occupied Zones of Post–World War II Germany in Relation to Policies Expressed by Its Civilian Governmental Authorities at Home, During the Course of 1944/45 through 1949* (Frankfurt: Haag + Herchen Verlag, 1983), 217–68.

88. *What the Soldier Thinks* 15 (25 July 1945): 12.

89. G. Bryan Conrad, "Franco-American Relations," 14 August 1945, 092 France 1944–45, Secretary General Staff Classified General Correspondence 1944–45, NARG 332.

90. *FRUS 1945* 4:661–65.

91. G. Bryan Conrad, "Franco-American Relations." See also Dana Adams Schmidt, "Americans Leave Dislike in France," *New York Times*, 12 November 1945; Harold Zink, *American Military Government in Germany* (New York: Macmillan, 1947), 239.

92. A. W. DePorte, *De Gaulle's Foreign Policy, 1944–1946* (Cambridge: Harvard University Press, 1968), 80.

93. Ibid., 64–83, 92–95, 162–71.

CHAPTER 2

1. John Hickerson Oral History Interview, 38–40, Harry S Truman Presidential Library, Independence, Mo. (emphasis in original).

2. *FRUS 1945* 4:674.

3. *FRUS 1949* 4:652–53.

4. Merchant to Henry R. Labouisse, Jr., 16 February 1946, Livingston T. Merchant Papers, box 1, Mudd Library, Princeton University.

5. *FRUS 1947* 1:740.

6. Steven Sapp, interview with H. Freeman Matthews, 1 August 1977.

7. For example, see Department of State, "France: Policy and Information Statement," 15 September 1946, 711.51/9-1546, NARG 59.

8. *FRUS 1948* 3:666.

9. Sapp, interview with Matthews.

10. *In These Times*, 30 April–6 May 1980.

11. *FRUS 1945* 4:686.

12. John W. Young, *France, the Cold War and the Western Alliance, 1944–49: French Foreign Policy and Post-War Europe* (London: Leicester University Press, 1990), 64.

13. Department of State, "France: Policy and Information Statement," 15 September 1946, 711.51/9-1546, NARG 59.

14. *FRUS 1945* 4:687.

15. Eban Ayers Diary, 4 May 1945, Eban Ayers Papers, box 25, Harry S Truman Presidential Library.

16. *FRUS 1945* 4:707–11. See also Young, *France, the Cold War and the Western Alliance*, 58–67.

17. Ibid.

18. See John Gimbel, *The Origins of the Marshall Plan* (Stanford, Calif.: Stanford University Press, 1976), 35–49; Grosser, *Affaires extérieures* 33–38; Reinhard Schreiner, *Bidault, die MRP und die französische Deutschlandpolitik, 1944–1948* (Frankfurt: Lang, 1985), 37–65; DePorte, *De Gaulle's Foreign Policy*, 251–70; F. Roy Willis, *The French in Germany, 1945–1949* (Stanford, Calif.: Stanford University Press, 1962), 33, 22–41.

19. Charles de Gaulle, *The War Memoirs of Charles de Gaulle: 1944–46* (New York: Simon and Schuster, 1960), 239.

20. Young, *France, the Cold War and the Western Alliance,* 17.

21. Robert Frank, "The French Dilemma: Modernization with Dependence or Independence and Decline," in *Power in Europe? Great Britain, France, Italy, and Germany in a Postwar World, 1945–1950,* ed. Josef Becker and Franz Knipping (New York: Walter de Gruyter, 1986), 266, 275.

22. Andrew Shennan, *Rethinking France: Plans for Renewal, 1940–1946* (Oxford: Clarendon Press, 1989), 224–86; Young, *France, the Cold War and the Western Alliance,* 97–99.

23. Jean Monnet, *Memoirs* (Garden City, N.Y.: Doubleday, 1978), 256; George Ross, *Workers and Communists in France* (Berkeley and Los Angeles: University of California Press, 1982) 32.

24. Klaus Hänsch, *Frankreich zwischen Ost und West* (Berlin: de Gruyter, 1972), 43, 93, 130, 175; see also A. M. Rose, "Anti-Americanism in France," *Antioch Review* 13 (1952): 471.

25. Irwin M. Wall, *French Communism in the Era of Stalin: The Quest for Unity and Integration, 1945–1962* (Westport, Conn.: Greenwood Press, 1983), 29–57; Lilly Marcou, *Le Kominform: Le communisme de guerre froid* (Paris: Presses de la Fondation Nationale des Sciences Politiques, 1977), 47–61; Ross, *Workers and Communists in France,* 25–48.

26. Douglas MacArthur II Oral History Interview, 73, Georgetown University Library, Washington, D.C.

27. Alfred Grosser, *The Western Alliance: European-American Relations since 1945* (New York: Vintage, 1982), 56.

28. *FRUS 1946* 4:435–38.

29. *FRUS 1945* 4:773–74.

30. See Monnet, *Memoirs,* 53–263; DePorte, *De Gaulle's Foreign Policy,* 192–201; Richard F. Kuisel, *Capitalism and the State in Modern France* (New York: Cambridge University Press, 1981), 219–30; Georgette Elgey, *La république des illusions, 1945–1951* (Paris: Fayard, 1965), 413–435; *L'Humanité,* 17 January 1946; Alan S. Milward, *The Reconstruction of Western Europe, 1945–1951* (Berkeley and Los Angeles: University of California Press, 1984), 128–32; Frances M. B. Lynch, "Resolving the Paradox of the Monnet Plan: National and International Planning in French Reconstruction," *Economic History Review,* 2d. ser., 37 (May 1984): 229–43.

31. Study Group on Western European Affairs, 23 April 1946 Meeting, records of groups, vol. 20, Council on Foreign Relations Archives, New York City. See also Grosser, *Affaires extérieures,* 32–33; Hänsch, *Frankreich zwischen Ost und West,* 132–33; *FRUS 1946* 5:399–403, 409–22, 425–46, 453–64; Annie Lacroix-Riz, *Le choix de Marianne* (Paris: Messidor, 1985), 45–77; Michel Margairaz, "Autour des accords Blum-Byrnes: Jean Monnet entre le consensus national et le consensus atlantique," *Histoire, économie, société* 3 (1982): 440–70; Young, *France, the Cold War and the Western Alliance,* 100–104.

32. *FRUS 1946* 5:433–34, 441–43.

33. Henry R. Labouisse, Jr., to Dept. of State, 10 February 1945, 851.4061MP/2-1045, NARG 59.

34. *New York Times*, 24 March 1946.

35. Caffery to Secretary of State, 9 April 1948, 851.4061MP/4-948, Caffery to Secretary of State, 18 June 1946, 851.4061MP/6-1846, NARG 59.

36. See Frank Costigliola, *Awkward Dominion: American Political, Economic, and Cultural Relations with Europe, 1919–1933* (Ithaca, N.Y.: Cornell University Press, 1984), 176–78.

37. "Present Treatment of American and Other Motion Picture Films in France Particularly with Reference to the Franco-American Trade Agreement," 11 January 1945, 551.4064MP/2-1045, NARG 59; Carl Milliken to Francis Colt de Wolf, 26 December 1945, 851.4061MP/12-2645, NARG 59.

38. Harold Smith to Henry Labouisse, 17 August 1945, 851.4061MP/8-1745, NARG 59.

39. Acheson to American Embassy in Paris, 15 September 1945, 851.4061MP/9-645, NARG 59.

40. *Le Monde*, 17 June 1946.

41. Sheldon B. Vance to Secretary of State, 20 January 1948, 851.4061MP/1-2048, NARG 59.

42. Caffery to Secretary of State, 16 February 1948, 851.4061MP/2-1448, NARG 59.

43. Caffery to Secretary of State, 15 April 1948, 851.4061MP/4-948, NARG 59; Irwin M. Wall, *The United States and the Making of Postwar France, 1945–1954* (New York: Cambridge University Press, 1991), 114–121; Jacques Portes, "Les origines de la légende noire des accords Blum-Byrnes sur le cinéma," *Revue d'histoire moderne et contemporaine* 33 (April–June 1986): 314–28.

44. *FRUS 1946* 5:469. See also Department of State, "France: Policy and Information Statement"; Gimbel, *Origins of the Marshall Plan* 154–58; Milward, *Reconstruction of Western Europe*, 15.

45. *FRUS 1947* 3:230–31 (emphasis in original).

46. Richard J. Barnet, *The Alliance* (New York: Simon and Schuster, 1983), 116.

47. *FRUS 1947* 3:203–49; George Kennan, *Memoirs, 1925–1950* (Boston: Little, Brown, 1967), 325–53; Scott Jackson, "Prologue to the Marshall Plan: The Origins of the American Commitment for a European Recovery Program," *Journal of American History* 65 (March 1979): 1043–68; Michael J. Hogan, "The Search for a 'Creative Peace' : The United States, European Unity, and the Origins of the Marshall Plan," *Diplomatic History* 6 (Summer 1982): 267–85; Richard M. Freeland, *The Truman Doctrine and the Origins of McCarthyism* (New York: Schocken, 1985), 70–114, 151–66; Charles S. Maier, "The Two Postwar Eras and the Conditions for Stability," *American Historical Review* 86 (April 1981): 343; Milward, *Reconstruction of Western Europe*, 466–67.

48. Caffery to Secretary of State, 11 June 1947, 751.61/6-1147, NARG 59.

49. Memorandum by James Reston, March 1947, Arthur Krock Papers, box 1, Mudd Library, Princeton University.

50. Keith to Secretary of State, 7 May 1947, 751.61/5-747, NARG 59. See also Young, *France, the Cold War and the Western Alliance*, 142–50.

51. Vincent Auriol, *Journal du septennat, 1947–1954* (Paris: Colin, 1970), 1:219–24; Schreiner, *Bidault*, 134–47; Grosser, *Affaires extérieures*, 49–54; Elgey, *La république des illusions*, 277–93; Wilfried Loth, "Frankreichs Kommunisten und der Beginn des kalten Krieges," *Vierteljahrshefte für Zeitgeschichte* 26 (1978): 9–65; Marcou, *Le Kominform* 39–72; Daniel Yergin, *Shattered Peace* (Boston: Houghton Mifflin, 1977), 326; *Le Monde*, 13–14, 26 April 1947; 16 May 1947.

52. *FRUS 1947* 3:711–12.

53. Ibid., 3:220–36; see also Michael J. Hogan, *The Marshall Plan: America, Britain, and the Reconstruction of Western Europe, 1947–1952* (New York: Cambridge University Press, 1987), 69–76.

54. *FRUS 1947* 3:237–39.

55. Ibid., 3:301–51; Alan S. Milward, "The Reconstruction of Western Europe," in *The Cold War in Europe*, ed. Charles S. Maier (New York: Markus Wiener, 1991), 241–67; Hogan, *Marshall Plan*, 54–188; Maier, "Two Postwar Eras," 342; Peter Weiler, "The United States, International Labor, and the Cold War: The Breakup of the World Federation of Trade Unions," *Diplomatic History* 5 (Winter 1981): 13; *Le Monde*, 7, 18 June, 13–14, 17 July 1947; Frank, "The French Dilemma," 263–80. For the productivity missions, see Anthony Rowley, "Les missions de productivité aux Etats-Unis" (Paper delivered at colloquium, "La France en voie de modernisation, 1944–1952," 4–5 December 1981).

56. Imanuel Wexler, *The Marshall Plan Revisited* (Westport, Conn.: Greenwood Press, 1983), 106.

57. Hogan, *Marshall Plan*, 152; see also ibid., 206–7.

58. Walter Lippmann Diary, 30 November 1948, Walter Lippmann Papers, box 237, Yale University Library. François Bloch-Lainé, *Profession: Fonctionnaire* (Paris: Edition du Seuil, 1976), 111–12; Monnet, *Memoirs*, 269–70; Economic Cooperation Administration, *European Recovery Program in France, 1948* (Paris: Economic Cooperation Administration, 1948), 105–7; James Edward Miller, *The United States and Italy, 1940–1950* (Chapel Hill: University of North Carolina Press, 1986), 253–54; Harry Bayard Price, *The Marshall Plan and Its Meaning* (Ithaca, N.Y.: Cornell University Press, 1955), 67, 104–5; Wexler, *Marshall Plan Revisited*, 97–117; Chiarella Esposito, "The Marshall Plan in France and Italy, 1948–1950: The Counterpart Fund Negotiations," (Ph.D. diss., State University of New York at Stony Brook, 1985), 47–202; Young, *France, the Cold War and the Western Alliance*, 201–2.

59. Walter Lippmann, "The New Power of the House," *New York Herald Tribune*, European ed., 4 January 1948.

60. *FRUS 1947* 3:792.

61. *FRUS 1948* 3:667.

62. *FRUS 1947* 3:721.

63. Ibid., 3:750.

64. Ronald Radosh, *American Labor and United States Foreign Policy* (New York: Random House, 1969), 321; Roy Godson, "Non-Governmental Organizations in International Politics: The American Federation of Labor, the International Labor Movement, and French Politics, 1945–1952," (Ph.D. diss., Columbia University, 1972), 100.

65. Brown quotations in *Time*, 17 March 1952, 23. See also Godson, "Non-Governmental Organizations," 162–98; Weiler, "United States, International Labor, and the Cold War," 1–22; Alain Bergougnoux, *Force ouvrière* (Paris: Edition du Seuil, 1975), 90–104; Anthony Carew, "Labour and the Marshall Plan," in Maier, *Cold War in Europe*, 314–30.

66. Thomas W. Braden, "I'm Glad the CIA is Immoral," *Saturday Evening Post*, 20 May 1967, 9–13. See also Weiler, "United States, International Labor, and the Cold War," 1–22; Joseph C. Goulden, *Meany* (New York: Atheneum, 1972), 130–37, 310–25.

67. *Time*, 17 March 1952, 23.

68. René Girault, "The French Decision-Makers and their Perception of French Power in 1948," in Becker and Knipping, *Power in Europe?*, 59.

69. Ibid.

70. *FRUS 1948* 3:620; see also ibid., 617–22, 645, 648–49, 666, 675–78.

71. Lawrence S. Kaplan, *NATO and the United States* (Boston: Twayne, 1988), 29.

72. Escott Reid, *Time of Fear and Hope: The Making of the North Atlantic Treaty, 1947–1949* (Toronto: McClelland and Stewart, 1977), 124.

73. Girault, "The French Decision-Makers," 61.

74. Young, *France, the Cold War and the Western Alliance*, 205.

75. Pierre Mélandri and Maurice Vaïsse, "France: From Powerlessness to the Search for Influence," in Becker and Knipping, *Power in Europe?*, 465.

76. Reid, *Time of Fear and Hope*, 117–21. See also Young, *France, the Cold War and the Western Alliance*, 175–221; Wall, *United States and the Making of Postwar France*, 127–142.

77. Barnet, *Alliance*, 130.

78. Yergin, *Shattered Peace*, 363.

79. Walter LaFeber, *America, Russia, and the Cold War, 1945–1975* (New York: Wiley, 1976), 85.

80. Lawrence S. Kaplan, *The United States and NATO: The Formative Years* (Lexington: University of Kentucky Press, 1984), 49–120; Pierre Mélandri, *Les Etats-Unis face à l'unification de l'Europe, 1945–54* (Paris: Pedone, 1980), 171–87.

81. Monnet, *Memoirs*, 292; see also ibid., 288–335.

82. *FRUS 1950* 3:817.

83. See Milward, *Reconstruction of Western Europe*, 362–420; John W. Young, *Britain, France, and the Unity of Europe, 1945–51* (Leicester: Leicester University Press, 1984), 145–65. Mélandri, *Les Etats-Unis*, 229–87; William Diebold, Jr., *The Schuman Plan* (New York: Praeger, 1959), 1–112.

84. *FRUS 1950* 3:722.

85. Hogan, *Marshall Plan*, 223.

86. *FRUS 1949* 4:485.

87. Acheson to Perkins, 19 October 1949, 840.00/11-549, NARG 59.

88. Ibid.

89. *FRUS 1949* 4:638.

90. Serge Guilbaut, *How New York Stole the Idea of Modern Art: Abstract Expressionism, Freedom, and the Cold War* (Chicago: University of Chicago Press, 1983), 153.

91. Ibid., 172. See also ibid., 49–194.

92. Frank Ninkovich, "The Currents of Cultural Diplomacy: Art and the State Department, 1938–47," *Diplomatic History* 1 (Summer 1977): 220.

93. Julian Robinson, *Fashion in the 40s* (New York: St. Martin's Press, 1980), 70.

94. Charles Bricker, "Looking Back at the New Look," *Connoisseur,* April 1987, 137 (emphasis in original).

95. Kurt Lang and Gladys Engel Lang, *Collective Dynamics* (New York: Crowell, 1968), 466–87.

96. J. C. Louis and Harvey Z. Yazijian, *The Cola Wars* (New York: Everest House, 1980), 75.

97. Ibid., 78. See also ibid., 56–77.

98. *Témoignage chrétien,* 3 March 1950. See also Richard Kuisel, "Coca-Cola au pays des buveurs de vin," *L'histoire* 94 (1986): 22–28 Wall, *United States and Making of Postwar France,* 121–125.

99. *Le Monde,* 23, 24 September, 30 December 1949, 2, 3, 4, 5–6, 29 March 1950. See also *New York Times,* 1, 2, 3, 5 March 1950.

100. *Time,* 13 March 1950, 30.

101. Walter Smith to Department of State, 9 March 1950, 451.116/3-950, Bruce to Secretary of State, 19 April 1950, 451.116/4-1950, Bruce to Secretary of State, 5 May 1950, 451.116/5-550, NARG 59.

102. *Sondages: Revue française de l'opinion publique* 1951, no. 1: 26.

103. Thomas A. Bailey, *The Marshall Plan Summer* (Stanford, Calif.: Stanford University Press, 1977), 47.

CHAPTER 3

1. C. Douglas Dillon to Secretary of State, "The Decline of French Confidence in US Leadership," 4 August 1953, 611.51/8-453, NARG 59.

2. Robert B. Glynn, "L'Affaire Rosenberg in France," *Political Science Quarterly* 70 (December 1955): 518.

3. Benjamin C. Bradlee to Mr. Koren, 3 June 1953, U.S. Information Agency (USIA) Files, box 5, Paris Embassy, NARG 84.

4. "L'exécution des Rosenbergs," *Esprit,* July 1953, 58–60.

5. *FRUS 1952–54* 6:1406.

6. Bradlee to Koren, 3 June 1953, USIA Files, box 5, Paris Embassy, NARG 84.

7. Dillon to Secretary of State, 4 August 1953, 611.51/8-453, General Records of the Dept. of State, NARG 59. See also Ronald Radosh and Joyce Milton, *The Rosenberg File: A Search for the Truth* (New York: Holt, Rinehart, and Winston, 1983), 376–78; *Le Monde,* 17 January, 23 February, 21–22 June 1953.

8. *FRUS 1952–54* 6:1406.

9. Dillon to Secretary of State, 31 August 1954, 611.51/8-3154, NARG 59.

10. Dulles to Merchant and Bowie, 15 May 1954, White House Memoranda Series, box 8, John Foster Dulles Papers, Eisenhower Library, copies in Mudd Library, Princeton University, Princeton, N.J. (hereafter cited as Dulles/Eisenhower, Princeton).

11. John H. Holmes to Senator Lester Hill, 18 February 1952, 611.51/2-2352, NARG 59.

12. *Le Monde,* 23, 28, 29 April, 30 April–2 May 1950.

13. *Le Monde,* 20 July, 18 December 1950.

14. *Le Monde,* 22 November 1950.

15. "Digest of Discussion," 31 October 1950, Study Group on France Today, records of groups, vol. 36, Council on Foreign Relations Archives. See also Raymond Aron, "French Public Opinion and the Atlantic Treaty," *International Affairs* 28 (January 1952): 1–8.

16. *Le Figaro,* 8 January 1951.

17. Dillon to Secretary of State, 4 August 1953, 611.51/8-453, NARG 59.

18. *New York Times,* 8 April 1954. See also Claude Mauriac, *The Other de Gaulle Diaries, 1944–1954* (New York: John Day, 1975), 338–40; Philip M. Williams, *Crisis and Compromise: Politics in the Fourth Republic* (Hamden, Conn.: Archon Books, 1964), 132–47; John T. Marcus, *Neutralism and Nationalism in France* (New York: Bookman Associates, 1958), 85–107.

19. Richard L. Merritt and Donald J. Puchala, eds., *Western European Perspectives on International Affairs* (New York: Praeger, 1968), 220–22, 195–96, 252, 254–55; "Summary of Poll on French Attitudes toward U.S.," 3 July 1953, 611.51/7-353, NARG 59.

20. W. R. Tyler, "Report from France on our International Information Activities," 1 May 1950, USIA Files, Paris Embassy, box 4, NARG 84.

21. Gladwyn Jebb to Selwyn Lloyd, 27 September 1956, WF 10345/6, F.O.371/124436, Public Record Office, London.

22. Richard M. Bissell to Paul H. Nitze and enclosure, 23 April 1951, Lot 55 D105, box 2, NARG 59.

23. Tyler, "Report from France," 1 May 1950, USIA Files, Paris Embassy, box 4, NARG 84.

24. Acheson to Paris Embassy, 29 August 1950, USIA Files, Paris Embassy, box 28, NARG 84.

25. Wall, *The United States and the Making of Postwar France*, 213–214.

26. Tyler, "Report from France," 1 May 1950, USIA Files, Paris Embassy, box 4, NARG 84.

27. [DOH], "Psychological Offensive," 3 October 1950, USIA Files, Paris Embassy, box 28, NARG 84.

28. "Prepared by Mr. Harold Kaplan, Restricted-Security Information," n.d. [prob. 1952], USIA Files, Paris Embassy, box 32, NARG 84.

29. W. R. Tyler, "Notes on French Opinion," 11 May 1953, USIA Files, Paris Embassy, box 5, NARG 84.

30. Draft Annex II "Cultural Affairs Policy for France," n.d. [1953], USIA Files, Paris Embassy, box 5, NARG 84. This document fitted the Paris Embassy's emphasis on intensified cultural contacts. See Ambassador James Clement Dunn, "The Foreign Information Activities of the Department of State," 10 February 1953, ibid.

31. Ibid.

32. Dillon to Secretary of State, 4 August 1953, 611.51/8-453, NARG 59.

33. Draft Annex II "Cultural Affairs Policy for France," n.d. [1953], USIA Files, Paris Embassy, box 10, NARG 84.

34. Discussion Meeting Report, 12 December 1950, Study Group on Problems of Strengthening Democratic Leadership Abroad, records of groups, vol. 38, pp. 10–11, Council on Foreign Relations Archives.

35. James Dunn to Secretary of State, 9 September 1952, 511.51/9-852, NARG 59.

36. Horatio Mooers to Dept. of State, 8 November 1950, 511.515/11-850, NARG 59.

37. William R. Tyler to Dept. of State, 27 November 1950, 511.515/11-2750, NARG 59.

38. Joyce to Moffly, 10 April 1953, USIA Files, Paris Embassy, box 5, NARG 84.

39. Charles K. Moffly to Department of State, 25 September 1953, 611.51/9-2553, NARG 59.

40. Dunn to Department of State and enclosure, 10 February 1953, USIA Files, Paris Embassy, box 10, NARG 84.

41. Trevor Barnes, "The Secret Cold War: The C.I.A. and American Foreign Policy in Europe, 1946–1956," *The Historical Journal* 25 (1982): 660.

42. Peter Coleman, *The Liberal Conspiracy: The Congress for Cultural Freedom and the Struggle for the Mind of Postwar Europe* (New York: Free Press, 1989), 50.

43. Ibid., 141.

44. *Le Combat*, 15–17 May 1952.

45. Barnes, "The Secret Cold War," 667.

46. Anita C. Lauve to Department of State, 6 February 1951, 511.512/2-651, NARG 59.

47. De Vandenay Tharand to M. Houghton, 24 July 1951, 511.512/10-2551, NARG 59.

48. Wall, *The United States and the Making of Postwar France*, 149–151.

49. *FRUS 1952–54* 6:1406.

50. Gladwyn Jebb to Selwyn Lloyd, 27 September 1956, WF 10345/6, F.O.371/124436, Public Record Office.

51. John Foster Dulles, telephone conversation with Admiral Radford, 24 March 1954, #266, Reel two, Minutes of Telephone Conversations of John Foster Dulles.

52. *FRUS 1952–54* 13:1688.

53. *FRUS 1952–54* 6:1149.

54. *FRUS 1952–54* 5:713–14.

55. U.S. Congress, Senate Foreign Relations Committee, *Executive Sessions, 1951* (Washington, D.C.: GPO, 1976), 19.

56. *FRUS 1952–54* 5:1783–84.

57. U.S. Congress, Senate Foreign Relations Committee, *Executive Sessions, 1954,* (Washington, D.C.: GPO, 1977), 11.

58. Edward Fursdon, *The European Defense Community* (New York: St. Martin's Press, 1980), 150–88.

59. U.S. Congress, Senate Foreign Relations Committee, *Executive Sessions, 1951,* 468.

60. *FRUS 1952–54* 5:938.

61. *FRUS 1950* 3:54–58.

62. Monnet, *Memoirs*, 345.

63. Wall, *The United States and the Making of Postwar France*, 199. See also Raymond Poidevin, *Robert Schuman, homme d'état* (Paris: Imprimerie nationale, 1986), 313–30.

64. Susan Mary Alsop, *To Marietta from Paris* (London: Weidenfeld and Nicolson, 1974), 168.

65. *FRUS 1952–54* 6:1198.

66. Fursdon, *EDC*, 207–9, 217.

67. C. A. E. Shuckburgh, "The European Defence Community," 28 January 1954, C. (54) 31, Cab 129/65, Public Record Office; Denise Artaud, "France between the Indochina War and the European Defense Community," in *Dien Bien Phu and the Crisis in Franco-American Relations, 1954–1955,* ed. Lawrence S. Kaplan, Denise Artaud, and Mark R. Rubin (Wilmington, Del.: Scholarly Resources, 1990), 255.

68. *FRUS 1952–54* 6:655.

69. *New York Times*, 11 November 1953.

70. *FRUS 1952–54* 5:1522.

71. *Sondages* 1951, no. 1:19, 1954, no. 4:16.

72. Walter Lippmann Diary, 19 May 1952, box 238, Lippmann Papers, Yale University.

73. Townsend Hoopes, *The Devil and John Foster Dulles* (Boston: Little, Brown, 1973), 180 (emphasis in original).

74. Wall, *The United States and the Making of Postwar France*, 188.

75. *FRUS 1952–54* 6:1435.

76. Alsop, *To Marietta from Paris*, 253–54; Jean Lacouture, *Pierre Mendès France* (New York: Holmes and Meier, 1984), 268.

77. "Minutes of Meeting of Secretary Dulles and Mr. Stassen with Foreign Minister Bidault, 2 February 1953," 611.51/2-753, NARG 59.

78. U.S. Congress, Senate Foreign Relations Committee, *Executive Sessions, 1954*, 649.

79. Ibid., 304–5.

80. Ibid., 671.

81. Ibid., 616.

82. Ibid., 590–91, 595.

83. *FRUS 1952–54* 5:870, 949.

84. *New York Times*, 16 December 1953. See also "U.S.-French Political Talks, March 1953," 611.51/4-653, Bonbright to Smith, 18 March 1953, 611.51/3-1853, Dillon to Secretary of State, 22 March 1953, 611.51/3-2153, NARG 59; "Bermuda Conference, December 4–8, 1953," 10 December 1953, no. 1980/117A, Declassified Documents Reference Service (hereafter cited as DDRS).

85. *FRUS 1952–54* 5:889.

86. *New York Times*, 8 April 1954.

87. *FRUS 1952–54* 5:1086.

88. *FRUS 1952–54* 6:1501.

89. Ibid., 6:1333.

90. Ibid., 6:1334.

91. Ibid., 6:1309.

92. Ibid., 5:903–4.

93. Ibid., 5:877.

93. Ibid., 5:877.

94. Ibid., 6:1259–60.

95. Bruce in Fursdon, *European Defense Community*, 267. See also Alsop, *To Marietta from Paris*, 250. For Mendès France's program, see Lacouture, *Mendès France*, 211–341; Pierre Mendès France, *Oeuvres completes* (Paris: Gallimard, 1985), 2:431–557; Pierre Rouanet, *Mendès France au Pouvoir* (Paris: R. Laffont, 1965); Wall, *United States and the Making of Postwar France*, chapter 9.

96. For the rumored deal, see Artaud, "France between the Indochina War and the European Defense Community," 262–64; *FRUS 1952–54* 5:1099, 1030, 1036, 1266; René Girault, "La France dans les rapports Est-Ouest au temps de Pierre Mendès France," in *Pierre Mendès France el le mendésisme*, ed. François Bédarida and Jean-Pierre Rioux (Paris: Fayard, 1985), 251–59.

97. Lacouture, *Mendès France,* 275. See also *FRUS 1952–54* 5:1033–85; Pierre Mélandri, "Les difficiles relations franco-américaines," in Bédarida and Rioux, ed., *Mendès France,* 267–70.

98. *Sondages* 1954, no. 4:16.

99. Barnet, *Alliance,* 161–62; London *Times,* 31 August 1954.

100. Stephen E. Ambrose, *Eisenhower: The President* (New York: Simon and Schuster, 1984), 211.

101. *FRUS 1952–54* 6:1443–45.

102. Dean Acheson, Speech at Johns Hopkins University, 19 March 1959, copy in 611.41/3-1959, NARG 59.

103. Shulman to Dean Acheson, 5 October 1954, Dean Acheson Papers, box 28, Sterling Library, Yale University.

104. *FRUS 1952–54* 5:1175–76, 1266–67, 1270.

105. *FRUS 1952–54* 6:1198.

106. *FRUS 1952–54* 5:1074.

107. Bertrand Goldschmidt, *Atomic Rivals* (New Brunswick, N.J.: Rutgers University Press, 1990), 357.

108. Ibid, 359.

109. Ibid., 354–59; Bertrand Goldschmidt, *L'aventure atomique* (Paris, 1962), 87; Charles Ailleret, *L'aventure atomique française* (Paris: Grasset, 1968), 70–76, 142–78; Lawrence Scheinman, *Atomic Energy Policy in France under the Fourth Republic* (Princeton, N.J.: Princeton University Press, 1965), 41–114.

110. *FRUS 1952–54* 5:1227.

111. Hoopes, *Devil and John Foster Dulles,* 221.

112. *FRUS 1952–54* 5:1200–1542; Mélandri, "Les difficiles relations franco-américaines," 271–76; Rouanet, *Mendès France,* 287–315; Michael M. Harrison, *The Reluctant Ally: France and Atlantic Security* (Baltimore: Johns Hopkins University Press, 1981), 30–32.

113. *FRUS 1952–54* 5:1381–82.

114. Ibid., 5:1520.

115. U.S. Congress, Senate Foreign Relations Committee, *Executive Sessions, 1954,* 280.

116. *FRUS 1952–54* 13:1440.

117. John Foster Dulles, "United States Foreign Policy," 16 May 1954, White House Memoranda Series, box 8 Dulles/Eisenhower, Princeton; Dulles to Merchant and Bowie and enclosed memorandum, 15 May 1954, ibid.

118. *FRUS 1952–54* 13:1259.

119. "Minutes of Meeting of Secretary Dulles and Mr. Stassen with Foreign Minister Bidault at the Quai d'Orsay, Morning of 2 February 1953," 611.51/2-753, NARG 59.

120. Lloyd C. Gardner, *Approaching Vietnam* (New York: Norton, 1988), 59.

121. Gullion, "Political Evolution in Southeast Asia," 30 November 1953, records of meetings, vol. 49, Council on Foreign Relations Archives.

122. Gardner, *Approaching Vietnam*, 104.

123. Ambrose, *Eisenhower: The President*, 173.

124. U.S. Congress, Senate Foreign Relations Committee, *Executive Sessions, 1954*, 52.

125. See George McT. Kahin, *Intervention: How America Became Involved in Vietnam* (New York: Knopf, 1986), 1–65; Philippe Devillers and Jean Lacouture, *Viet Nam: De la guerre française à la guerre américaine* (Paris: Seuil, 1969), 84–337; Michael Schaller, *The American Occupation of Japan: The Origins of the Cold War in Asia* (New York: Oxford University, 1985), 212–45; Andrew Jon Rotter, "The Big Canvas: The United States, Southeast Asia, and the World, 1948–1950" (Ph.D. diss., Stanford University, 1981), 314–86.

126. Gardner, *Approaching Vietnam*, 247.

127. Ibid., 102, 108.

128. George C. Herring, "Franco-American Conflict in Indochina, 1950–1954," in Kaplan, Artaud, and Rubin, *Dien Bien Phu*, 29.

129. Gardner, *Approaching Vietnam*, 119, 138, 247.

130. Ibid., 210; *FRUS 1952–54* 13:1292.

131. Ibid., 13:1549.

132. Gardner, *Approaching Vietnam*, 310.

133. U.S. Congress, Senate Foreign Relations Committee, *Executive Sessions, 1954*, 642–43.

134. Gardner, *Approaching Vietnam*, 318. For Bidault's claim that Dulles offered nuclear weapons, see *FRUS 1952–54* 13:1927–28, 1933.

135. George C. Herring, Gary R. Hess, and Richard H. Immerman, "Passage of Empire: The United States, France, and South Vietnam, 1954–55," in Kaplan, Artaud, and Rubin, *Dien Bien Phu*, 177.

136. *FRUS 1952–54* 6.1473.

137. *FRUS 1952–54* 13:2422.

138. Ibid., 2311–14, 2410–11, 2423.

139. Wall, *United States and the Making of Postwar France*, 290–291.

140. *FRUS 1951* 5:1375, 1392–94.

141. U.S. Congress, Senate Foreign Relations Committee, *Executive Session, 1953* (Washington: GPO, 1976), 156.

142. *FRUS 1951* 5:1382.

143. Acheson quoted in Jim Rowe to Senator Johnson, n.d. [mid-1956], 1980/289A, DDRS. For French resentment, see David Bruce to Department of State, 2 March 1951, 611.51/3-251; John Dorman to Department of State, 26 June 1952, 611.51/6-2652; Dunn to Secretary of State, 3 November 1952, 611.51/11-352; Stephen McClintic to Department of State, 4 September 1952, 611.51/9-452, NARG 59.

144. John Foster Dulles, telephone conversation with Congressman Judd, 24 June 1954, #352, reel 2, Minutes of Telephone Conversations of John Foster Dulles.

145. *FRUS 1952–54* 6:1502–5.

146. Manfred Halpern, speech before Council on Foreign Relations, 20 January 1960, records of meetings, vol. 32, Council on Foreign Relations Archives.

147. *Sondages* 1957, no. 2:41.

148. Gruenther to Admiral Radford, 12 March 1956, no. 1977/184C, DDRS.

149. Murphy to Acting Secretary of State, 3 March 1956, ibid.

150. Amory Houghton Interview, Dulles Oral History, Princeton.

151. Anthony Eden, "Distinction between Large and Tactical Nuclear Weapons," 5 April 1955, C.(55)95, CAB129/74, Public Record Office.

152. Couve de Murville Interview, Dulles Oral History, Princeton.

153. Chester L. Cooper, *The Lion's Last Roar: Suez, 1956* (New York: Harper and Row, 1978), 86. See also Maurice Vaïsse, "France and the Suez Crisis," in *Suez 1956: The Crisis and Its Consequences,* ed. William Roger Louis and Roger Owen (New York: Oxford University Press, 1989), 131–43.

154. Memorandum of Conversation with the President, 4:30 P.M., 30 August 1956; Memorandum of Conversation with the President, 14 August 1956, White House Memoranda Series, box 4, Dulles/Eisenhower, Princeton.

155. Ambrose, *Eisenhower: The President,* 356.

156. Donald Neff, *Warriors at Suez* (New York: Simon and Schuster, 1981), 21.

157. "Discussion at the 302nd Meeting of the National Security Council, Thursday, November 1, 1956," no. 1980/384, DDRS.

158. Andrew Goodpaster, "Memorandum of Conference with the President," 31 October 1956, no. 1978/450C, DDRS.

159. Goodpaster, "Memorandum of Conference with the President," 30 October 1956, no. 1978/450B, ibid.

160. Dillon Interview, 25, Dulles Oral History, Princeton (emphasis in original).

161. Memorandum of Conversation between Eisenhower and Dulles, 7 November 1956, White House Memoranda Series, box 4, Dulles/Eisenhower, Princeton.

162. Maurice Vaïsse, "Post-Suez France," in Louis and Owen, *Suez 1956,* 336; Christian Pineau Interview, 29, Dulles Oral History, Princeton.

163. Dillon Interview, 31, ibid.

164. Memorandum of Talk with American Diplomats, Paris, 9 May 1958, Selected Correspondence, box 137, John Foster Dulles Papers, Princeton.

165. Wilfrid Kohl, *French Nuclear Diplomacy* (Princeton, N.J.: Princeton University Press, 1971), 36. See also ibid. 37–47; Ailleret, *L'aventure atomique française,* 196–314; and Maurice Vaïsse, "Post-Suez France," 336–38.

166. Herbert S. Parmet, *Jack: The Struggles of John F. Kennedy* (New York: Dial, 1980), 401–7. See also Alistair Horne, *A Savage War of Peace* (New York: Viking, 1978), 234–46.

167. Amory Houghton Interview, Dulles Oral History, Princeton.

168. Telephone conversation, 13 November 1957, no. 145; telephone conversation, 11 November 1957, no. 154, reel 10, Minutes of Telephone Coversations of John Foster Dulles.

169. Telephone conversation, 9 February 1958, no. 318, reel 10, Minutes of Telephone Conversations of John Foster Dulles.

170. Memorandum of Talk with American Diplomats, Paris, 9 May 1958, Selected Correspondence, box 137, Dulles Papers, Princeton.

171. Cyrus L. Sulzberger, *The Last of the Giants* (New York: Macmillan, 1970), 456. See also Murphy, *Diplomat among Warriors*, 394–96.

172. Pineau Interview, 29, Dulles Oral History, Princeton.

173. Sulzberger, *Last of the Giants*, 456.

CHAPTER 4

1. John S. D. Eisenhower, Memorandum of Conference with the President, 8 November 1960, 10:30 A.M., no. 1979/336A, DDRS.

2. Andrew Goodpaster, Memorandum of Conversation with the President, 25 August 1959, no. 1987/1713, DDRS.

3. John S. D. Eisenhower, Memorandum of Conference with the President, 8 November 1960, 10:30 A.M., no 1979/336A, DDRS.

4. See Maurice Vaïsse, "Aux origines du mémorandum de septembre 1958," *Relations internationales* 58 (Summer 1989): 253–63.

5. Telephone call to Allen Dulles, 19 May 1958, 5:49 P.M., Telephone Conversations, box 8, Dulles/Eisenhower, Princeton. For de Gaulle's rise to power, see Jean-Pierre Rioux, *The Fourth Republic, 1944–1958* (New York: Cambridge University Press, 1987), 305–13.

6. Sulzberger, *Last of the Giants*, 482 (emphasis in original)

7. Ibid., 483.

8. Bernard Ledwidge, *De Gaulle et les Américains* (Paris: Flammarion, 1984), 14–33.

9. National Security Council, "Operations Coordinating Board Report on U.S. Policy on France," 9 November 1960, NSC Files, National Archives.

10. Keith W. Baum, "Two's Company, Three's a Crowd: The Eisenhower Administration, France, and Nuclear Weapons," *Presidential Studies Quarterly* 20 (Spring 1990): 316; David L. Schalk, "American Opinion of General de Gaulle's Algerian Policy, 1958–1962" (Paper presented at the Conference Celebrating the Centennial of Charles de Gaulle, New York University, 7–8 April 1990).

11. Memorandum, "Anglo-American Relations with General de Gaulle's Government," 9 June 1958, 1987, no. 1987/2777, DDRS.

12. Ledwidge, *De Gaulle et les Américains*, 14–33.

13. "Memorandum of Conversation, Lebanese Crisis," 13 May 1958, White House Meetings with the President, box 6, Dulles/Eisenhower, Princeton. See also Baum, "Two's Company," 321–22; David Schoenbrun, *The Three Lives of Charles de Gaulle* (New York: Atheneum, 1966), 292–93; Ambrose, *Eisenhower: The President,* 464.

14. Adelbert de Segonzac, "De Gaulle," enclosed in McGeorge Bundy to the President, 11 May 1964, Aides Files, box 1, National Security Files, Lyndon B. Johnson Presidential Library (hereafter NSF, LBJL).

15. Schoenbrun, *Three Lives of de Gaulle,* 297; Konrad Adenauer, *Erinnerungen, 1959–1963* (Stuttgart: Deutsche Verlags-Anstalt, 1978), 15–28.

16. De Gaulle letter in Grosser, *Western Alliance,* 187. See also Memorandum, "Anglo-American Relations with General de Gaulle's Government," 9 June 1958, no. 1987/2777, DDRS; Vaïsse, "Aux origines du mémorandum," 253–68.

17. Memorandum of Conference with the President, 9 June 1959, 2:00 P.M., no. 1986/3509, DDRS; see also Harrison, *Reluctant Ally,* 87–88, 95.

18. Grosser, *Western Alliance,* 187.

19. Sulzberger, *Last of the Giants,* 707–8.

20. "Tripartite Consultation between France, the United States and the United Kingdom," 10 March 1961, National Security Files, box 70, John F. Kennedy Presidential Library (hereafter NSF, JFKL).

21. National Security Council, "U.S. Policy on France," 4 November 1959, NSC 5910/1, National Security Council Files, National Archives (emphasis added). Although this policy was crafted during the Eisenhower administration, its analysis persisted into the Kennedy years.

22. John Foster Dulles, Memorandum of Conversation with the President, 13 October 1958, White House Memoranda Series, box 7, Dulles/Eisenhower, Princeton (emphasis in original).

23. Schoenbrun, *Three Lives,* 303.

24. National Security Council, "U.S. Policy on France"; author's interview with Bertrand Goldschmidt, 21 November 1990, Paris. See also Jean Lacouture, *De Gaulle le souverain, 1959–1970* (Paris: Editions du Seuil, 1986), 358–63; Harrison, *Reluctant Ally,* 90–93; Eisenhower to Dulles, 16 December 1958, no. 1982/911, DDRS.

25. John S. D. Eisenhower, Memorandum of Conversation with the President, 9 June 1959, 2:00 P.M., no. 1986/3509, DDRS.

26. Ibid.

27. *Major Addresses, Statements and Press Conferences of General Charles de Gaulle May 19, 1958–January 31, 1964* (New York: French Embassy, 1964), 61.

28. Dulles conversation with the President, 12 November 1959, no. 809, reel 10, Minutes of Telephone Conversations of John Foster Dulles; Eisenhower to General de Gaulle, 17 November 1959, no. 1982/1340, DDRS.

29. John S. D. Eisenhower, Memorandum of Conversation with the President, 9 June 1959, 2:00 P.M., no. 1986/3509, DDRS.

30. Ibid.

31. Eisenhower to de Gaulle, 30 August 1960, no. 1982/1346, DDRS.

32. "Memorandum for Files," 10 August 1960, no. 1982/1344, DDRS.

33. Kennedy to Secretary of State, 21 August 1961, NSF, box 82-98 JFKL.

34. *Washington Post,* 20 December 1962.

35. Dean Acheson Oral History Interview, JFKL.

36. Frank Costigliola, "The Pursuit of Atlantic Community: Nuclear Arms, Dollars, and Berlin," in *Kennedy's Quest for Victory: American Foreign Policy, 1961–1963,* ed. Thomas G. Paterson (New York: Oxford University Press, 1989), 51–52.

37. Harold Macmillan, *At the End of the Day, 1961–1963* (New York: Harper & Row, 1973), 120.

38. Memorandum of Conversation between French Foreign Minister Couve de Murville and Under Secretary Ball, 25 May 1963, NSF, box 72, JFKL.

39. Henry Owen and Harry Rowan, "A New Approach to France," 21 April 1961, NSF, box 70, JFKL.

40. U.S. Congress, Senate Foreign Relations Committee, *Executive Sessions, 1963* (Washington, D.C.: GPO, 1986) 697–98.

41. Memorandum of Conversation in Mr. Nitze's Office, 13 March 1962, NSF, box 71, JFKL.

42. Memorandum for the President, "The U.S. and de Gaulle: The Past and the Future," 30 January 1963, President's Office Files (hereafter POF), box 116A, JFKL.

43. Sulzberger, *Last of the Giants,* 747.

44. William P. Bundy to Secretary McNamara, 6 May 1961, NSF, box 70, JFKL.

45. Arthur Schlesinger, Jr., *A Thousand Days* (Boston: Houghton Mifflin, 1965), 561; see also Christian Plume and Pierre Démaret, *Target de Gaulle* (London: Secker & Warburg, 1974), 55–62.

46. David Nunnerly, *Kennedy and Britain* (London: Bodley Head, 1972), 131. See also ibid., 127–37; Henry Brandon, "Skybolt," London *Times,* 8 December 1963; Richard E. Neustadt, *Alliance Politics* (New York: Columbia University Press, 1970), 30–55; and Neustadt report to Kennedy, "Skybolt and Nassau," 15 November 1963, NSF, box 319-324, JFKL.

47. See Konrad Adenauer, *Erinnerungen, 1959–1963,* 201–2 for de Gaulle's account. See also Lacouture, *De Gaulle,* 333–34.

48. Stuart Symington in U.S. Senate Foreign Relations Committee, *Executive Sessions, 1963,* 622; see also Kennedy to Gavin, 14 June 1962, NSF, box 71, JFKL; "De Gaulle and Great Britain," *espoir* 42 (June 1983): 83–84, 91.

49. Richard E. Neustadt, "Skybolt and Nassau," 15 November 1963, box 319-324, NSF, JFKL. See also Frank Costigliola, "The Failed Design: Kennedy, de Gaulle, and The Struggle for Europe," *Diplomatic History* 8 (Summer 1984): 227–51.

50. Memorandum on de Gaulle, enclosed in Klein to Bundy, 18 April 1963, NSF, box 72, JFKL.

51. *New York Times*, 15 January 1963; for the pressure on Germany, see John J. McCloy to Adenauer, 4 February 1963, POF, box 31, JFKL; George W. Ball, *The Past Has Another Pattern* (New York: Norton, 1982), 272–73.

52. Theodore Sorensen Oral History, 106, JFKL.

53. [John F. Kennedy], "Questions to be settled by the United States in the coming months," 31 January 1963, POF, box 62, JFKL.

54. Remarks of President Kennedy to the National Security Council Meeting of 22 January 1963, no. 1986/2274, DDRS.

55. U.S. Senate Foreign Relations Committee, *Executive Sesssion, 1963*, 334–36.

56. Bundy to the President, 15 June 1963, NSF, box 23, LBJL.

57. U.S. Senate Foreign Relations Committee, *Executive Session, 1963*, 435–436. See also Kennedy to de Gaulle, 24 July 1963, NSF, box 73a, JFKL; David Klein to Bundy, 30 July 1963, ibid.; and Gordon H. Chang, "JFK, China, and the Bomb," *Journal of American History* 74 (1988): 1287–1310.

58. Maurice Couve de Murville Oral History Interview, JFKL; see also Memorandum of Conversation between President Johnson and President de Gaulle, 25 November 1963, no. 1975/94A, DDRS.

59. Theodore Sorensen, *Kennedy* (New York: Harper & Row, 1965), 579.

60. Schlesinger, *Thousand Days*, 356.

61. A. J. Rebeillard to Jacqueline Kennedy, 27 November 1963, Condolence File, box 14, Robert F. Kennedy Papers, JFKL.

62. Paul F. Duvivier to Dept. of State, 29 November 1963, File EX FE 3-1/Kennedy, John F., White House Central Files, LBJL.

63. Bohlen to Secretary of State, 23 November 1963, ibid.

64. George H. Gallup, *The Gallup International Public Opinion Polls: France, 1939, 1944–1975* (New York: Random House, 1976), 402–3, 406.

65. Cyrus L. Sulzberger, *An Age of Mediocrity: Memoirs and Diaries, 1963–1972* (New York: Macmillan, 1973), 185.

66. Memorandum of Conversation between President Johnson and President de Gaulle, 25 November 1963, no. 1975/94A, DDRS; Bohlen to Secretary of State, 25 November 1963, no. 1975/93F, DDRS.

67. Bundy to President, 20 December 1963, Aides Files, box 1, LBJL.

68. Bohlen to Secretary of State, 2 February 1965, no. 1977/327D, DDRS.

69. CIA Memorandum, "Indications of Anti-Americanism," 30 January 1964, NSF, box 169, LBJL. For earlier concern about the CIA's Paris office, see James M. Gavin to Henry M. Jackson, 25 June 1964, Henry M. Jackson Papers, box 74, University of Washington Library, Seattle, Wash.: for the bugging fears, see Sulzberger, *Age of Mediocrity*, 96.

70. Bundy to President, 6 December 1963, Aides Files, box 1, LBJL.

71. Bohlen to Secretary of State, 13 December 1963, no. 1975/95B, DDRS.

72. Ibid.

73. Sulzberger, *Age of Mediocrity*, 54.

74. Bundy to the President with enclosure, 3 January 1966, Aides Files, box 6, LBJL.

75. Sulzberger, *Age of Mediocrity*, 178.

76. Bundy to the President with enclosure, 3 January 1966, Aides Files, box 6, LBJL.

77. Gallup, *Gallup Polls*, 477, 481.

78. Bohlen to Secretary of State, 27 August 1965, no. 1978/276A, DDRS.

79. Sulzberger, *Age of Mediocrity*, 59.

80. Ibid., 61.

81. Bundy to the President with enclosure, 11 May 1964, Aides Files, box 1, LBJL.

82. Richard Helms to Director of Central Intelligence, 10 March 1964, no. 1978/11B, DDRS; see also Bundy to the President, 11 March 1964, Aides Files, box 1, LBJL.

83. Sulzberger, *Age of Mediocrity*, 147.

84. Bundy to the President, 19 February 1965, Aides Files, box 2, LBJL. See also Lacouture, *De Gaulle*, 430–34.

85. Johnson to Bohlen, 25 February 1964, no. 1975/97C.

86. Lodge to the President, 22 February 1964, Aides Files, box 1, LBJL; Rusk to Bohlen, n.d. [February 1964], no. 1975/98A, Bohlen to the President, 26 February 1964, no. 1975/98B, Bohlen to the President, 4 March 1964, no. 1975/99B, Bohlen to Bundy, 12 March 1964, no. 1975/100B, DDRS; Bundy to the President, 15 March 1964, Aides Files, box 1, LBJL; Kahin, *Intervention*, 155, 190–92.

87. Johnson to Ball, 4 June 1964, NSF, box 170, LBJL.

88. Klein to Bundy, 23 July 1964, ibid; see also Marianna P. Sullivan, *France's Vietnam Policy* (Westport, Conn.: Greenwood Press, 1978), 93; Ball, *Past*, 377–78.

89. Bohlen to Secretary of State, 9 February 1965, NSF, box 170, LBJL.

90. Memorandum of Conversation, 19 February 1965, no. 1978/274C, DDRS; Sulzberger, *Age of Mediocrity*, 159.

91. Rusk to Bohlen, 7 March 1965, NSF, box 171, LBJL.

92. Bohlen to Secretary of State, 4 May 1965, no. 1978/74C, DDRS.

93. Richard Funkhouser to Department of State, 12 June 1965, NSF, box 171, LBJL.

94. Gallup, *Gallup Polls*, 461. See also Claude Julien, "La tentation de l'imperialisme," *La nef* 26 (1966): 43–52; Serge Mallet, "Un certain antagonisme," ibid., 139–50.

95. Bohlen to Secretary of State, 4 May 1965, no. 1978/74C, DDRS.

96. Bohlen to President, 20 June 1965, NSF, box 171, LBJL.

97. Bohlen to Secretary of State, 3 June 1965, NSF, box 171, LBJL. See also Bundy to President, 12 June 1965, Aides Files, box 3, LBJL.

98. Henry H. Fowler to Bundy, 5 April 1965, Aides Files, box 15-16 LBJL.

99. Gallup, *Gallup Polls*, 477, 536, 595.

100. Valenti to President with enclosure, 24 May 1965, no. 1976/300F, DDRS.

101. Ernest Goldstein to the President, 23 February 1968, file no. ND19/CO312, White House Central Files, LBJL.

102. Sullivan, *France's Vietnam Policy*, 79, 83, 95.

103. Grosser, *Western Alliance*, 212. See also Zérapha Belooussova, "La visite du général de Gaulle en URSS en juin 1966" (Paper presented at conference, "De Gaulle en son siècle," 19–24 November 1990, Paris).

104. Bohlen to Secretary of State, 27 August 1965, no. 1978/276A, DDRS.

105. *New York Herald Tribune*, 11 June 1965.

106. Cleveland to Secretary of State, 18 December 1965, NSF, box 172, LBJL.

107. Johnson to de Gaulle, 22 March 1966, IT34, White House Central Files, LBJL; Kaplan, *NATO and the United States*, 115–18; Harrison, *Reluctant Ally*, 148–49; Judith Young, "French Defense Policy in the Fifth Republic," (Ph.D. diss., Brandeis University, 1973), 66–70.

108. Thomas J. Schoenbaum, *Waging Peace and War: Dean Rusk in the Truman, Kennedy, and Johnson Years* (New York: Simon and Schuster, 1988), 421.

109. U.S. Congress, Joint Economic Committee, *Soviet Pipeline Sanctions: The European Perspective*, 97th Cong., 2d sess., 22 September 1982, 10.

110. Robert Schaetzel to Dean Acheson, 11 December 1967, Dean Acheson Papers, box 28, Yale University Library.

111. Francis Bator to the President, 18 March 1966 (emphasis added), Johnson to de Gaulle, 22 March 1966, IT34, White House Central Files, LBJL.

112. Charles Ailleret, "Defense in All Directions," *Atlantic Community Quarterly* 4 (Spring 1968): 17–25.

113. Sulzberger, *Age of Mediocrity*, 218.

114. Ibid., 270–71.

115. See Lacouture, *De Gaulle*, 452–85; Grosser, *Affaires extérieures*, 196–205; Kaplan, *NATO and the United States*, 120.

116. Sulzberger, *Age of Mediocrity*, 404.

117. James Chace and Elisabeth Malkin, "The Mischief-Maker: The American Media and de Gaulle, 1964–68" (Paper presented at the Conference Celebrating the Centennial of Charles de Gaulle, New York University, 7–8 April 1990).

118. Bohlen to Secretary of State, 31 March 1965, NSF, box 171, LBJL; Klein to Bundy, 29 April 1965, ibid.

119. Sulzberger, *Age of Mediocrity*, 145. See also Lacouture, *De Gaulle*, 382–405.

120. Sulzberger, *Age of Mediocrity*, 306.

121. McBride to Secretary of State, 11 December 1964, no. 1976/277B, DDRS.

122. Bohlen to Department of State, 2 February 1965, no. 1977/327D, DDRS.

123. Transcript of Senator Church Meeting with President de Gaulle, 4 May 1966, no. 1978/75A, DDRS.

124. "France, the USSR, and European Security," 20 May 1966, no. 1978/11, DDRS.

125. Summary Notes of 566th NSC Meeting, 13 December 1966, Meetings File, box 2, NSF, LBJL.

126. Guy de Carmoy, *The Foreign Policies of France, 1944–1968* (Chicago: University of Chicago Press, 1970), 411.

127. Bundy to the President, 9 February 1965, Aides Files, box 2, LBJL.

128. Transcript of Senator Church Meeting with President de Gaulle, 4 May 1966, no. 1978/75A, DDRS. See also Lacouture, *De Gaulle*, 295–312; Grosser, *Affaires extérieures*, 182–87.

129. McGhee to Secretary of State, 15 January 1965, no. 1978/250C, DDRS.

130. McGhee to Secretary of State, 16 April 1964, no. 1976/70C, DDRS.

131. Bohlen to Secretary of State, 18 February 1964, no. 1976/70B, DDRS.

132. Bohlen to Secretary of State, 8 January 1965, no. 1976/277D, DDRS.

133. U.S. Bureau of the Census, *Statistical Abstract of the United States, 1971* (Washington: GPO, 1971), 766, 753.

134. Grosser, *Western Alliance*, 234–35.

135. Bohlen to Secretary of State, 22 September 1965, NSF, box 172, LBJL.

136. Sulzberger, *Age of Mediocrity*, 152; see also Gordon L. Weil and Ian Davidson, *The Gold War* (New York: Holt, Rinehart and Winston, 1970), 73–100; Marc Alexandre, "Le dollar et la France," *La nef* 26 (1966): 119–38; David P. Calleo, *The Imperious Economy* (Cambridge: Harvard University Press, 1982), 48–53.

137. Grosser, *Western Alliance*, 225.

138. Richard F. Kuisel, "The American Economic Challenge: De Gaulle and the French" (Paper presented at the Conference Celebrating the Centennial of Charles de Gaulle, New York University, 7–8 April 1990).

139. Ibid.

140. Sulzberger, *Age of Mediocrity*, 132; see also Robert B. Dickie, *Foreign Investment: France, A Case Study* (Leyden: A. W. Sijthoff, 1970), 68–71.

141. Jean-Jacques Servan-Schreiber, *The American Challenge* (New York: Atheneum, 1968).

142. Sulzberger, *Age of Mediocrity*, 226.

143. Summary Notes of 569th NSC Meeting, 3 May 1967, no. 1987/1641, DDRS.

144. Fowler to the President, 25 May 1967, Aides Files, box 2, NSF, LBJL.

145. David Caute, *The Year of the Barricades: A Journey through 1968* (New York: Harper & Row, 1988), 25 (emphasis in original).

146. Ibid., 229.

147. Ibid., 221–22.

148. Marianne Debouzy, "The Influence of American Political Dissent on the French New Left," in *Contagious Conflict*, ed. A. N. J. Hollander (Leiden: E. J. Brill, 1973), 63.

149. Caute, *Year of the Barricades*, 87; see also Hervé Hamon and Patrick Rotman, *Generation* (Paris: Editions du Seuil, 1987, 1988); Alain Touraine, *The May Movement*

(New York: Random House, 1971), 22–241; Bernard E. Brown, *Protest in Paris* (Morristown, N.J.: General Learning Press, 1974), 3–60; Gilbert Gantier, "Un certain inspiration," *La nef* 26 (1966): 107–18; Milton Viorst, *Fire in the Streets: America in the 1960s* (New York: Simon and Schuster, 1979), 445; Keith A. Reader, *Intellectuals and the Left in France since 1968* (New York: St. Martin's Press, 1987), 8–9.

150. Caute, *Year of the Barricades*, 220.

151. CIA Intelligence Memorandum, "France's Student-Labor Crisis: Causes and Consequences," 25 May 1968, no. 1987/1217, DDRS.

152. Caute, *Year of the Barricades*, 248. See also ibid., 232–55, and CIA, "France's Student-Labor Crisis: Causes and Consequences."

CHAPTER 5

1. Richard H. Ullman, "The Covert French Connection," *Foreign Policy* 75 (Summer 1989): 8.

2. Sulzberger, *Age of Mediocrity*, 505.

3. Thomas L. Hughes, "De Gaulle's Foreign Policy: 1969 Version," Dept. of State Research Memorandum, 20 December 1968, no. 1986/2659, DDRS.

4. Edward A. Kolodziej, "France Ensnared: French Strategic Policy and Bloc Politics after 1968," *Orbis* 5 (Winter 1972): 1088.

5. Sulzberger, *Age of Mediocrity*, 502.

6. Ibid., 507.

7. Memorandum of Conversation between Charles Lucet and Eugene V. Rostow, 25 November 1968, no. 1986/2660, DDRS.

8. For background on the monetary issue, see Robert Solomon, *The International Monetary System, 1945–1981* (New York: Harper & Row, 1982).

9. Sulzberger, *Age of Mediocrity*, 502.

10. Richard Nixon, *RN: The Memoirs of Richard Nixon* (New York: Grosset & Dunlap, 1978), 370–71.

11. Henry Kissinger, *White House Years* (Boston: Little, Brown, 1979), 108.

12. Nixon, *RN*, 370.

13. Kissinger, *White House Years*, 104, 110. See also Yves-Henri Nouailhat, "Nixon–de Gaulle: Un épisode original des relations franco-américaines," *Revue française d'études américaines* 12 (1987): 309–16, and Joan Hoff-Wilson, "Nixingerism, NATO, and Détente," *Diplomatic History* 13 (Fall 1989): 504.

14. *The Nixon Presidential Press Conferences* (New York: E. M. Coleman Enterprises, 1978), 31–3.

15. Sulzberger, *Age of Mediocrity*, 545.

16. *New York Times*, 1 March 1970.

17. *Washington Post*, 13 March 1970.

18. Sulzberger, *Age of Mediocrity*, 616.

19. *New York Times*, 4 March 1970; see also James O. Goldsborough, "France, the European Crisis, and the Alliance," *Foreign Affairs* 52 (April 1974): 546.

20. *Washington Post*, 28 February 1970.

21. Michel Jobert, *Memoires d'avenir* (Paris: Grasset, 1974), 169. See also Sulzberger, *Age of Mediocrity*, 621–22; *Washington Post*, 22 February 1970; *New York Times*, 4 March 1970; and *Washington Evening Star*, 26 February 1970.

22. *New York Times*, 13 March 1970.

23. *New York Times*, 4 March 1970.

24. *New York Daily News*, 4 March 1970; Kissinger, *White House Years*, 423.

25. *Public Papers of the Presidents: Richard Nixon, 1971* (Washington: GPO, 1972), 802–13.

26. Ibid.

27. Solomon, *International Monetary System*, 176–84; Calleo, *Imperious Economy*, 58–61.

28. William Safire, *Before the Fall* (Garden City, N.Y.: Doubleday, 1975), 497.

29. Ibid., 498.

30. Seymour M. Hersh, *The Price of Power* (New York: Summit Books, 1983), 462.

31. Safire, *Before the Fall*, 514; Susan Strange, *International Economic Relations of the Western World* (Oxford: Oxford University Press, 1976), 2:338–39.

32. *Public Papers: Nixon, 1971*, 886–90.

33. Strange, *International Economic Relations*, 339–40.

34. *New York Times*, 24 September 1971; see also *Le Monde*, 4 September 1971.

35. Kissinger, *White House Years*, 962.

36. Martin Mayer, *The Fate of the Dollar* (New York: Times Books, 1980), 192.

37. *Public Papers: Nixon, 1971*, 1195–96.

38. U.S. Congress, House Subcommittee on Europe and Subcommittee on Foreign Economic Policy, *American Interest in the European Community*, 93rd Cong., 1st and 2d sess., 22 March, 5 April, 7, 8 November, 6 December 1973, 11 June 1974, 81, 04.

39. Schaetzel to Dean Acheson, 8 May 1969, Dean Acheson Papers, box 28, Yale University.

40. Schaetzel to Acheson, 11 August 1969, ibid.

41. Schaetzel to Acheson, 16 September 1969, ibid..

42. Schaetzel to Acheson, 28 April 1970, ibid..

43. Sulzberger, *Age of Mediocrity*, 784.

44. Schaetzel to Acheson, 22 December 1970, ibid.

45. U.S. Congress, *American Interest in the European Community*, 53.

46. Lawrence S. Eagleburger to Dean Acheson, 7 May 1970, Acheson Papers, box 9, Yale University.

47. U.S. Congress, *American Interest in the European Community*, 9.

48. Barnet, *Alliance*, 314.

49. *Department of State Bulletin* 68 (14 May 1973): 593–98.

50. Ibid. See also Schaetzel, "Some European Questions for Dr. Kissinger," *Foreign Policy* 12 (Fall 1973): 74; *Le Monde*, 1 May 1973; U.S. Congress, *American Interest in the European Community*, 121.

51. Schaetzel to Acheson, 15 December 1970, box 28, Acheson Papers.

52. *New York Times*, 9 April 1974. See also ibid., 13, 15 December 1973.

53. Robert Kleiman, "Special Relationships," *New York Times*, 11 December 1973.

54. Goldsborough, "France, the European Crisis, and the Alliance," 541.

55. Ibid., 548.

56. Marvin Kalb and Bernard Kalb, *Kissinger* (Boston: Little, Brown, 1974), 490.

57. Bob Woodward and Carl Bernstein, *The Final Days* (New York: Simon and Schuster, 1976), 70.

58. Henry A. Kissinger, *Years of Upheaval* (Boston: Little, Brown, 1982), 713. See *New York Times*, 21 November 1973; Scott D. Sagan, "Lessons of the Yom Kippur Alert," *Foreign Policy* 36 (Fall 1979): 169.

59. *New York Times*, 13 November 1973.

60. U.S. Congress, House Subcommittee on Europe, *United States–Europe Relations and the 1973 Middle East War*, 93rd Cong., 1st and 2d sess., 1 November 1973, 19 February 1974, 57.

61. Kissinger, *Years of Upheaval*, 721; see also Hoff-Wilson, "Nixingerism," 517.

62. U.S. Congress, *United States-Europe Relations and the 1973 Middle East War*, 34.

63. *Le Monde*, 2 November 1973.

64. James Chace, "American Jingoism," *Harper's*, May 1976, 43.

65. *New York Times*, 31 October 1973.

66. Ibid., 13 November 1973.

67. Grosser, *Western Alliance*, 279–80.

68. Ibid., 277.

69. See Robert J. Lieber, *Oil and the Middle East War: Europe in the Energy Crisis* (Cambridge: Harvard Studies in International Affairs, 1976), 49; *Washington Post*, 19 February 1974; and Edward Malloy, "France, the Alliances, and the Global Energy Crisis: The Politics of Dependence" (Ph.D. diss., George Washington University, 1978), 148–52.

70. *New York Times*, 9 April 1974.

71. Ibid.

72. *Public Papers: Nixon, 1974* (Washington: GPO, 1975), 276.

73. *Time*, 3 June 1974, 20.

74. Arthur Hartman Oral History Interview, 65, Georgetown University Library.

75. Ullman, "Covert French Connection," 9–10.

76. Ibid., 20.

77. Ibid., 11.

78. James O. Goldsborough, "The Franco-German Entente," *Foreign Affairs* 54 (April 1976): 503.

79. *New York Times,* 7 April 1976.

80. Ibid.

81. Ibid.

82. Kissinger, *Years of Upheaval,* 168. See Barnet, *Alliance,* 353–54, and Goldsborough, "Franco-German Entente," 505–6.

83. Ibid.

84. *New York Times,* 6 April 1976.

85. *Washington Post,* 4 February 1980.

86. *New York Times,* 22 May 1980.

87. Michael Meimeth, "Die 'deutschen Ungewissheiten' der siebziger Jahre während der Präsidentschaft Valéry Giscard d'Estaings," *Dokumente* (January 1988): 39–47.

88. Ullman, "Covert French Connection," 18–19.

89. Ibid.

90. Ibid.

91. Arthur Hartman Oral History, 65–66, Georgetown University Library.

92. F. Roy Willis, *The French Paradox* (Stanford, Calif.: Hoover Institution Press, 1982), 59.

CHAPTER 6

1. *New York Times,* 25 April 1988.

2. Ibid., 13 January 1984.

3. Ibid., 19 October 1983.

4. Ibid., 13 January 1984.

5. *Washington Post,* national weekly ed., 10 February 1986.

6. Ibid., 4 March 1985; see also Michel Winock, "La guerre froide," in *L'Amérique dans les têtes,* ed. Denis Lacorne (Paris: Hachette, 1986), 87–96.

7. Richard Burt, Testimony in U.S. Congress, House Committee on Foreign Affairs, Subcommittee on Europe and the Middle East, *Developments in Europe, May 1983,* 98th Cong., 1st sess., 18 May 1983, 20.

8. Michael M. Harrison, "The Successor Generation, Social Change and New Domestic Sources of Foreign Policy in France," in *The Successor Generation: International Perspectives of Postwar Europeans,* ed. Stephen F. Szabo (London: Butterworths, 1983), 37.

9. *Washington Post,* national weekly ed., 4 March 1985.

10. *Time,* 17 September 1977. See Diana Pinto, "La conversion de l'intelligentsia," in Lacorne, *L'Amérique,* 124–36; Reader, *Intellectuals and the Left,* 108–14; Michèle

Lamont, "The Production of Culture in France and the United States since World War II," in *Intellectuals in Liberal Democracies*, ed. Alain G. Gagnon (New York: Praeger, 1987), 167–77.

11. Structuralism involves the effort by anthropologists, literary critics, historians, and other humanists to undertake what they regard as scientific, systematic studies of cultures, texts, and other products of human behavior. Relying heavily on linguistics, structuralists investigate the hidden or implicit hierarchies within language and within other means, such as rituals, by which a given culture expresses its values. The structuralists believe that such analysis can expose the real framework of power within a society and reveal the subtle ways by which words, fashions, customs, and other cultural manifestations produce and preserve those systems of power. Evolving largely out of structuralism, poststructuralism takes even further the emphasis on the hidden hierarchies and ambiguities in language to argue that the investigator's own cultural biases and the unavoidable ambivalences in language, custom, and so on, make it illusory to think that the scientific, systematic study of human culture—or of anything else—is really possible. Appropriately enough, after making this distinction between structuralists and poststructuralists, one must qualify it, since most of these thinkers have themselves evolved along with the ideas, have written from both perspectives and from others in between, and have resisted any categorization of themselves. For a cogent introduction, see Jonathan Culler, *On Deconstruction* (Ithaca, N.Y.: Cornell University Press, 1989), esp. 22–30.

12. Michèle Lamont, "How to Become a Dominant French Philosopher: The Case of Jacques Derrida," *American Journal of Sociology* 93 (November 1987): 610.

13. See ibid., 584–617; Lamont, "The Production of Culture," 167–77; John Sturrock, ed., *Structuralism and Since: From Lévi Strauss to Derrida* (New York: Oxford University Press, 1979), 7–17, 154–78; Reader, *Intellectuals and the Left*; George Ross, "The Decline of the Left Intellectual in Modern France," in Gagnon, *Intellectuals in Liberal Democracies*, 43–64; and Frank Lentricchia, *After the New Criticism* (Chicago: University of Chicago Press, 1980), 157–63.

14. Denis Lacorne and Jacques Rupnik, "France Bewitched by America," in *The Rise and Fall of Anti-Americanism*, ed. Denis Lacorne, Jacques Rupnik, Marie-France Toinet (London: Macmillan, 1990), 3.

15. Ibid., 5–6.

16. *In These Times*, 2–8 October 1985.

17. *Le nouvel observateur*, 3–9 January 1986, 22.

18. Ibid., 21.

19. Lacorne and Rupnik, "France Bewitched by America," 3.

20. Jacques Rupnik and Muriel Humbertjean, "Images of the United States in Public Opinion," in Lacorne, Rupnik, and Toinet, *Rise and Fall of Anti-Americanism*, 79.

21. *Le Monde*, May 1981.

22. *New York Times*, 12 June 1988.

23. *Le nouvel observateur*, 3–9 January 1986, 21.

24. *Le Monde*, May 1981.

25. Chantal Conquin, "President Mitterrand Also Watches *Dallas*: American Mass Media and French National Policy," in *The Americanization of the Global Village: Essays in Contemporary Popular Culture*, ed. Roger Rollins (Bowling Green, Ohio: Bowling Green State University Popular Press, 1989), 16.

26. *New York Times*, 25 June 1990.

27. *New York Times*, 22 September 1985, 25 June 1990; *Washington Post*, national weekly ed., 10 February 1986.

28. *L'Express*, 3–9 April 1987; *Washington Post*, weekly national ed., 3–9 September 1989; *New York Times*, 7 May 1991; *International Herald Tribune*, 1–2 June 1991.

29. *New York Times*, 17 February 1991.

30. Ibid.

31. Ibid.

32. *In These Times*, 1–7 April 1987.

33. *Wall Street Journal*, 25 March 1987.

34. *Washington Post*, national weekly ed., 10–16 April 1989. See also ibid., 10 February 1986; *Le nouvel observateur*, 3–9 January 1986, 21–27; ibid., 13–19 March 1987; *Le nouvel economiste*, 27 March 1987, 40–41; ibid., 3 April 1987, 59; *L'Humanité*, 23, 24 March 1987; and *New York Times*, 22 March 1987.

35. *New York Times*, 2 April 1989. See also ibid., 29–30 March 1989.

36. *Le Monde*, 31 March 1989, 1 April 1989; *L'Express*, 7 April 1989.

37. *In These Times*, 2–8 October 1985.

38. Kevin Devlin, "Eurocommunism: Between East and West," *International Security* 3 (Spring 1979): 95–96.

39. Diana Johnstone, *The Politics of Euromissiles* (London: Verso, 1984), 87–95; Jacques Huntzinger, "La politique extérieure du parti socialiste," *Politique étrangère* 47 (1982): 33–44; Julius W. Friend, *Seven Years in France: François Mitterrand and the Unintended Revolution, 1981–1988* (Boulder, Col.: Westview Press, 1989), 7–80.

40. Daniel Singer, *Is Socialism Doomed? The Meaning of Mitterrand* (New York: Oxford University Press, 1988), 103. See also David Andelman, "Struggle over Western Europe," *Foreign Policy* 49 (Winter 1982–83): 43, and Evan G. Galbraith, *Ambassador in Paris: The Reagan Years* (Washington, D.C.: Regnery Gateway), 115–16.

41. *Libération*, 27 November 1985; *New York Times*, 28 November 1985, 4 December 1985.

42. U.S. Congress, Senate Foreign Relations Committee, *Crisis of Will in the Nato Alliance*, part 4, 19 September 1985, 70. See also Neville Waites, "Defence Policy under Socialist Management," in *Mitterrand's France*, ed. Sonia Mazey and Michael Newman (London: Croom Helm, 1987), 192–217.

43. Poll cited in Stanley Hoffmann, "Gaullism by Any Other Name," *Foreign Policy* 57 (Winter 1984–85): 52.

44. Johnstone, *Euromissiles*, 108.

45. Singer, *Is Socialism Doomed?*, 230.

46. Pierre Lellouche, "The Odd Couple," in *French Security Issues: A Symposium,* ed. Joyce Lasky Shub (Washington, D.C.: American Enterprise Institute, 1983), 9.

47. Robert J. Lieber, *The Oil Decade: Conflict and Cooperation in the West* (Cambridge: Harvard Center for International Affairs, 1983), 139; Antony J. Blinken, *Ally versus Ally: America, Europe, and the Siberian Pipeline Crisis* (New York: Praeger, 1987), 8, 57.

48. Blinken, *Ally versus Ally,* 49.

49. Ibid., 50–59.

50. Mélandri, *Une incertaine alliance,* 322–33; Galbraith, *Ambassador in Paris,* 17–26.

51. Alexander M. Haig, Jr., *Caveat: Realism, Reagan, and Foreign Policy* (New York: Macmillan, 1984), 309. See also ibid., 310–12.

52. *New York Times,* 24 July 1982.

53. Blinken, *Ally versus Ally,* 103.

54. Blinken, *Ally versus Ally,* 3.

55. *New York Times,* 29 August 1982.

56. *Le Monde,* 20 July 1982.

57. *New York Times,* 6 November 1982.

58. *New York Times,* 13 February 1982.

59. U.S. Congress, Joint Economic Committee, *Soviet Pipeline Sanctions: The European Perspective,* 97th Cong., 2d sess., 22 September 1983, 30.

60. *Washington Post,* 11 August 1982.

61. *New York Times,* 31 July 1982.

62. Ibid., 23 July 1982.

63. Ibid., 24 July 1982.

64. Ibid.

65. Ibid., 28 July 1982.

66. U.S. Congress, *Soviet Pipeline Sanctions,* 7.

67. Blinken, *Ally versus Ally,* 125.

68. *New York Times,* 29 August 1982 (emphasis added).

69. Ibid., 18 April 1986.

70. Ibid., 1 May 1986.

71. Ibid.

72. Ibid., 24 April 1986.

73. Ibid., 23 April 1986.

74. Ibid.

75. See Dirk Verheyen, "Eurowimps: European-American Imagery in Historical Context," *Orbis* 31 (Spring 1987): 55–73.

76. U.S. Congress, Senate Committee on Foreign Relations, *Is NATO Still the Centerpiece of U.S. Foreign Policy: Should It Be?,* 99th Cong., 1st sess., part 5, 3 October 1985, 154–55.

77. U.S. Congress, House Subcommittee on Europe and the Middle East, *Roundtable Discussion on United States Policy toward Europe*, 99th Cong., 2d sess., 22 July 1986, 21.

78. NATO expense in U.S. Congress, House Committee on Armed Services, *Defense Burdensharing: The Costs, Benefits, and Future of U.S. Alliances*, 100th Congress, 2d session, 2 February, 1, 2 March 1988, 5.

79. *New York Times*, 2 September 1979.

80. David S. Yost, "Radical Changes in French Defence Policy?" *Survival* 28 (January 1986): 53.

81. Martin Hillenbrand, "American Foreign Policy and the Atlantic Alliance," in *Reagan's Leadership and the Atlantic Alliance*, ed. Walter Goldstein (Washington, D.C.: Pergamon-Brassey's, 1986), 46.

82. *New York Times*, 11 January 1988.

83. U.S. Congress, *Is NATO Still the Centerpiece?*, part 5, 3 October 1985, 10.

84. *New York Times*, 13 November 1983.

85. U.S. Congress, Senate Committee on Armed Services, *NATO Defense and the INF Treaty*, 100th Cong., 2d sess., part 3, 3–4, 16 February 1988, 84. For a general discussion, see Catherine A. Kelleher, "NATO Nuclear Operations," in *Managing Nuclear Operations*, ed. Ashton B. Carter, John D. Steinbruner, and Charles A. Zraket (Washington, D.C.: Brookings Institution, 1987), 445–69.

86. U.S. Congress, *Is NATO Still the Centerpiece?*, part 5, 3 October 1985, 12.

87. Ullman, "Covert French Connection," 17. See also ibid., 13–26.

88. U.S. Congress, *NATO Defense and the INF Treaty*, part 2, 29 January, 1–2 February 1988, 90.

89. Ibid., part 1, 25–27 January 1988, 176.

90. Ibid., part 3, 148. For General Roger's agreement, see ibid., part 2, 29 January 1988, 129.

91. U.S. Congress, *Is NATO Still the Centerpiece?*, part 1, 12 September 1985, 7.

92. U.S. Congress, *Roundtable Discussion*, 2 December 1987, 3.

93. R. James Woolsey, "The Future of NATO's Defense Posture: An American Perspective," *Atlantic Community Quarterly* 26 (Summer 1988): 125.

94. U.S. Congress, *NATO Defense and the INF Treaty*, part 2, 29 January 1988, 241.

95. Thierry de Montbrial, "Security Requires Caution," *Foreign Policy* 71 (Summer 1988): 95; see also *Le Monde*, 9 June 1983; Robert S. Rudney, "Mitterrand's New Atlanticism: Evolving French Attitudes toward NATO," *Orbis* 28 (Spring 1984): 83–96.

96. Robbin F. Laird, *France, the Soviet Union, and the Nuclear Weapons Issue* (Boulder, Colo.: Westview Press, 1985), 79). See also interview with Mitterrand in *Le nouvel observateur*, 18–24 December 1987, 26; Jacques Huntzinger, "Défense de la France, securité de l'Europe," *Politique étrangère* 48 (1983): 395–402; and François Heisbourg, "The British and French Nuclear Forces," *Survival* 31 (July-August 1989): 315.

97. Heisbourg, "British and French Nuclear Forces," 304–15; Laird, *France and Nuclear Weapons*, 45–64; interview with Mitterrand in *Le nouvel observateur*, 18–24 December 1987, 23–26.

98. *In These Times*, 4–10 September 1985.

99. Robert E. Osgood, "The Implications of SDI for U.S.-European Relations," in Robert W. Tucker, *SDI and U.S. Foreign Policy* (Boulder, Col.: Westview Press, 1987), 68–90; David P. Calleo, "SDI, Europe, and the American Strategic Dilemma," in ibid., 101–19, Galbraith, *Ambassador in Paris*, 116–17.

100. U.S. Congress, *Roundtable Discussion*, 2 December 1987, 9.

101. U.S. Congress, NATO *Defense and the INF Treaty*, part 3, 233.

102. *New York Times*, 17 October 1986.

103. Montbrial, "Security Requires Caution," 96.

104. Ibid., 87.

105. U.S. Congress, NATO *Defense and the INF Treaty*, part 1, 9.

106. U.S. Congress, *Roundtable Discussion*, 2 December 1987, 27.

107. U.S. Congress, Senate Foreign Relations Committee, *The INF Treaty*, part 2, 1–5 February 1988, 163. See also ibid., 164–72.

108. U.S. Congress, NATO *Defense and the INF Treaty*, part 2, 240.

109. *New York Times*, 21 January 1988.

110. U.S. Congress, *INF Treaty*, part 2, 186.

111. Ibid., 174.

112. Woolsey, "The Future of NATO's Deterrent Posture," 123. See also Andrew Goldman, "NATO Needs a New Missile," *Orbis* 32 (Fall 1988): 545–50.

113. *New York Times*, 20 July 1990. Genscher made the statement in April 1989.

114. *New York Times*, 9 July 1989.

115. Ibid., 15 July 1989.

116. Ibid.

117. Ibid., 17 July 1989.

CHAPTER 7

1. *Die Zeit*, 24 May 1991.

2. *The Economist* 316 (7 July 1990): 6.

3. U.S. Department of State, *A New Europe, A New Atlanticism: Architecture for a New Era*, 12 December 1989, Current Policy no. 1233.

4. "Address before a Joint Session of the Congress on the State of the Union," 29 January 1991, *Weekly Compilation of Presidential Documents* 27, no. 5 (4 February 1991): 91, 95.

5. U.S. Congress, Senate Foreign Relations Committee, *Nomination of James A. Baker III*, 17, 18 January 1989, 12, 73.

6. *New York Times*, 7 December 1989.

7. U.S. Congress, Senate Committee on Foreign Relations, *Nomination of Lawrence S. Eagleburger*, 101st Cong., 1st sess., 15, 16 March 1989, 50.

8. *New York Times*, 31 August 1990.

9. *International Herald Tribune*, 14 June 1991 (emphasis in original).

10. *International Herald Tribune*, 6 April 1990. See also Frédéric Bozo and Jérôme Paolini, "Trois Allemagnes, deux Europes et la France," *Politique étrangère* 55 (Spring 1990): 119-37; Stanley Hoffmann, "La France dans le nouvel ordre européen," *Politique étrangère* 55 (Fall 1990): 508–12; *Le Monde diplomatique*, February 1990, 8.

11. *New York Times*, 26 February 1989.

12. *International Herald Tribune*, 8 February 1990.

13. *New York Times*, 26 February 1989; *Le Monde diplomatique*, August 1990, 16–17.

14. Walter Schütze, "Frankreich angesichts der deutschen Einheit," *Europa Archiv* 4 (25 February 1990): 133–34; Dominique Moïsi, "The French Answer to the German Question," *European Affairs* 4 (Spring 1990): 30–35.

15. *New York Times*, 15 November 1989; *Le Monde diplomatique*, December 1989, 1, 14–17.

16. Ole Waever, "Three Competing Europes: German, French, Russian," *International Affairs* 66, no. 3 (July 1990): 483.

17. John Newhouse, "Sweeping Change," *The New Yorker* (27 August 1990): 81.

18. *New York Times*, 1 December 1989.

19. Ibid., 2 April 1990. See also Michaël Mertes and Norbert Prill, "L'Allemagne unifiée et l'Europe," *Politique étrangère* 55 (Fall 1990): 563–64; Jean Francois-Poncet, "Ein starkes Gebäude für das Europa der Zwölf," *Dokumente. Zeitschrift der deutsch-französischen Dialog* 47 (January 1991): 23–25.

20. U.S. Congress, House Committee on Foreign Affairs, Subcommittee on Europe and the Middle East, *Developments in Europe, March 1990*, 101st Cong., 2d sess., 22 March 1990, 17.

21. *New York Times*, 7 December 1989.

22. Ibid., 5 December 1989.

23. U.S. Congress, Commission on Security and Cooperation in Europe, *Implementation of the Helsinki Accords*, 101st, Cong., 2d sess., 3 April 1990, 8.

24. Ibid., 8, 18.

25. Ibid., 18; U.S. Congress, Senate Foreign Relations Committee, *The Future of NATO*, 101st Cong., 2d sess., 9 February 1990, 19.

26. U.S. Congress, *Implementation of Helsinki Accords*, 8.

27. U.S. Congress, *Nomination of James A. Baker III*, 104.

28. *International Herald Tribune*, 18 April 1990.

29. Ibid., 6 April 1990.

30. *New York Times*, 6 May 1990.

31. Ibid., 6 April 1990. See also ibid., 20 April 1990, 4 May 1990; *International Herald Tribune*, 18 April 1990; and *Economist Intelligence Unit Country Report: France* 2 (1990): 10; *Le Monde diplomatique*, April 1990, 1, 14–15.

32. Newhouse, "Sweeping Change," 88.

33. *New York Times*, 12 July 1990.

34. *Washington Post*, 6 July 1990.

35. *International Herald Tribune*, 6 April 1990. See also *Le Monde diplomatique*, August 1990, 11; André Giraud, "Construction européenne et la défense," *Politique étrangère* 55 (Fall 1990): 518–20; Michael Brenner, "Une nouvelle optique sur la securité européenne: le regard de Washington," ibid., 555–57.

36. *International Herald Tribune*, 6 April 1990. See also ibid., 12, 16 March, 10 April, 30 May 1990.

37. "London Declaration on a Transformed North Atlantic Alliance, 6 July 1990," *Survival* 32, no. 5 (September-October 1990): 469–72.

38. *Washington Post*, 7 July 1990. See also *Le Monde diplomatique*, August 1990, 1, 16–17.

39. *New York Times*, 28 June 1990.

40. *The Economist* 316 (21 July 1990): 47.

41. *New York Times*, 17 July 1990.

42. Ibid.; *International Herald Tribune*, 17–19 July 1990.

43. *International Herald Tribune*, 22 November 1990; *Le Monde diplomatique*, December 1990, 12.

44. Ibid., 8 October 1990.

45. *Washington Post*, weekly national ed., 1–7 October 1990; Jacques Morizet, "Vingt ans de relations Franco-Irakiennes," *Défense nationale* 46 (December 1990): 53–63.

46. *Washington Post*, 10 August 1990.

47. *New York Times*, 12 February 1991.

48. Ibid, 25 January 1991.

49. Newhouse, "Sweeping Change," 89.

50. *International Herald Tribune*, 18 September 1990.

51. *Washington Post*, national weekly ed., 6–12 May 1990.

52. *New York Times*. 25 September 1990; Daniel Colard, "Frankreichs Diplomatie und die Golfkrise," *Dokumente. Zeitschrift der deutsch-französischen Dialog* 47 (February 1991): 108–13.

53. *International Herald Tribune*, 22 November 1990.

54. *Le Monde diplomatique*, February 1991, 3, 6–7; *Boston Globe*, 15 January 1991; *International Herald Tribune*, 16 January 1991; *New York Times*, 16 January 1991; *Washington Post*, national weekly ed., 4–10 February 1991; Colard, "Frankreichs Diplomatie," 111–13.

55. *Boston Globe*, 15 January 1991; *International Herald Tribune*, 16 January 1991.

56. *Washington Post*, national weekly ed., 4–10 February 1991; *New York Times*, 25 February 1991.

57. *International Herald Tribune*, 15 March 1991.

58. *New York Times*, 15 March 1991.

59. *Le Monde diplomatique*, July 1991, 15; *International Herald Tribune*, 12 June 1991.

60. U.S. Congress, Senate Committee on Finance, *Trip Report on Congressional Delegation: Bentsen*, 101st Cong., 1st sess., (Washington: GPO, 1989), 30.

61. U.S. Congress, *Nomination of Lawrence S. Eagleburger*, 5.

62. *New York Times*, 4 December 1990.

63. *Washington Post*, national weekly ed., 17–23 December 1990.

64. Ibid.

65. *New York Times*, 4 December 1990.

66. *Washington Post*, national weekly ed., 10–16 June 1991.

67. Ibid., 24–30 June 1990.

68. Ibid.

69. Ibid.

70. *New York Times*, 14 July 1991.

71. *Washington Post*, national weekly ed. 17–23 December 1990.

72. U.S. Congress, Joint Economic Committee, *Europe 1992: Long-Term Implications for the U.S. Economy*, 101st Cong., 1st sess., 26 April 1989, 161.

73. Ibid, 158.

74. U.S. Congress, Senate Committee on Finance, *Europe-92 Trade Program*, 101st Cong., 1st sess., 10 May 1989, 14.

75. *New York Times*, 9 June 1991.

76. *International Herald Tribune*, 17 September 1990.

77. Werner Link, "EG/WEU: Eine notwendige Liaison," *Die politische Meinung* 258 (May 1991): 7.

78. Ibid., 4–11; *Frankfurter Allgemeine Zeitung*, 27 May 1991.

79. *International Herald Tribune*, 12 June 1991.

80. *Washington Post*, 12 June 1991; *International Herald Tribune*, 5 June 1991.

81. *New York Times*, 9 June 1991.

82. *Life*, 26 January 1953, 34.

83. *Newsweek*, 27 May 1991. See also *Time*, 27 May 1991.

84. For discussion of "French theory," see chapter 6.

85. *New York Times Book Review*, 5 May 1991.

86. *New York Times*, 15 July 1991.

BIBLIOGRAPHIC ESSAY

Many authors have written on U.S.-French and on U.S.-European relations since 1940. Most of their works deal with relatively short periods of time. Among the important exceptions are Jean-Baptiste Duroselle, *France and the U.S.* (Chicago: University of Chicago Press, 1978); Michael M. Harrison, *The Reluctant Ally: France and Atlantic Security* (Baltimore: Johns Hopkins University Press, 1981); Marvin R. Zahniser, *Uncertain Friendship: American-French Relations through the Cold War* (New York: Wiley, 1975); Crane Brinton, *The Americans and the French* (Cambridge: Harvard University Press, 1968); Henry Blumenthal, *Illusion and Reality in Franco-American Diplomacy, 1919–1945* (Baton Rouge: Louisiana State University Press, 1986); Alfred Grosser, *Affaires extérieures: La politique de la France, 1944–1984* (Paris: Flammarion, 1984); Alfred Grosser, *The Western Alliance: European-American Relations since 1945* (New York: Vintage, 1982); and Richard J. Barnet, *The Alliance* (New York: Simon and Schuster, 1983).

For primary materials, the best sources are the U.S. Department of State's documentary series, *Foreign Relations of the United States* (Washington, D.C., annual volumes), and material in the various presidential libraries, some of which has been reproduced on microfiche by the Declassified Documents Reference Service. See also below for discussion of congressional hearings and manuscript collections.

For discussion of what the Statue of Liberty has meant to the American and French peoples, see Albert Boime, *Hollow Icons: The Politics of Sculpture in Nineteenth-Century France* (Kent, Ohio: Kent State University Press, 1987), and Marvin Trachtenberg, *The Statue of Liberty* (New York: Viking, 1976).

Although they must be used with caution, Charles de Gaulle's memoirs are essential for understanding World War II relations. See Charles de Gaulle, *The War Memoirs of Charles de Gaulle: The Call to Honour, 1940–42* (New York: Viking, 1955), *Unity, 1942–1944* (New York: Simon and Schuster, 1959); and *Salvation, 1944–1946* (New York: Simon and Schuster, 1960). For the U.S. government's perspective, see especially the H. F. Matthews Files in General Records of the Department of State, record

299

group 59, National Archives, Washington, D.C., and the Henry L. Stimson Diary, Henry L. Stimson Papers, Yale University Library (also available on microfilm). For Bullitt, see Will Brownell and Richard N. Billings, *So Close to Greatness: A Biography of William C. Bullitt* (New York: Macmillan, 1987); Gordon Wright, "Ambassador Bullitt and the Fall of France," *World Politics* 10 (October 1957): 63–75; and Orville H. Bullitt, ed., *For the President: Personal and Secret* (Boston: Houghton Mifflin, 1972). The classic work by William L. Langer, *Our Vichy Gamble* (Hamden, Conn.: Archon, 1965), has now been superseded by three excellent studies: Julian G. Hurstfield, *America and the French Nation* (Chapel Hill: University of North Carolina Press, 1986); Robert O. Paxton, *Vichy France: Old Guard and New Order* (New York: Norton, 1973); and André Kaspi, *Franklin D. Roosevelt* (Paris: Fayard, 1988). See also William D. Leahy, *I Was There* (New York: McGraw Hill, 1950); Linda McClain, "The Role of W. D. Leahy in U.S. Foreign Policy," (Ph.D. diss., University of Virginia, 1984); Robert Murphy, *Diplomat among Warriors* (Garden City, N.Y.: Doubleday, 1964); and James J. Dougherty, *The Politics of Wartime Aid: American Economic Assistance to France and French Northwest Africa, 1940–1946* (Westport, Conn.: Greenwood Press, 1978).

Franklin Roosevelt's conflicts with de Gaulle fill many of the pages of Warren F. Kimball, ed., *Churchill and Roosevelt: The Complete Correspondence*, 3 vols. (Princeton, N.J.: Princeton University Press, 1984), and François Kersaudy, *Churchill and De Gaulle* (New York: Atheneum, 1983). See also Douglas S. Anglin, *The St. Pierre and Miquelon Affair of 1941* (Toronto: University of Toronto Press, 1966); Arthur L. Funk, "Negotiating the 'Deal with Darlan,' " *Journal of Contemporary History* 8 (April 1973): 81–117; Paul Victor Joliet II, "French-American Relations and the Political Role of the French Army, 1943–1945," (Ph.D. diss., State University of New York at Binghamton, 1978); and A. W. DePorte, *De Gaulle's Foreign Policy, 1944–1946* (Cambridge: Harvard University Press, 1968). For the U.S. impact on France during the closing years of World War II, see Ronald Schaffer, *Wings of Judgment: American Bombing in World War II* (New York: Oxford University Press, 1985); Martin Blumenson, *Breakout and Pursuit* (Washington, D.C.: Office of the Chief of Military History, 1961); Stephen E. Ambrose, *The Supreme Commander: The War Years of General Dwight D. Eisenhower* (Garden City, N.Y.: Doubleday, 1970); and Henri Michel, *Paris résistant* (Paris: Albin Michel, 1982). The race for Germany's atomic resources can be found in Boris T. Pash, *The Alsos Mission* (New York: Award House, 1969); Michel Bar-Zohar, *The Hunt for German Scientists* (London: Barker, 1967); and Bertrand Goldschmidt, *Atomic Rivals* (New Brunswick, N.J.: Rutgers University Press, 1990).

For France's reluctant involvement in the cold war, see John W. Young's excellent study, *France, the Cold War and the Western Alliance, 1944–49: French Foreign Policy and Post-War Europe* (London: Leicester University Press, 1990). Also useful are Annie Lacroix-Riz, *Le choix de Marianne* (Paris: Messidor, 1985); Reinhard Schreiner, *Bidault, die MRP und die französische Deutschlandpolitik, 1944–1948* (Frankfurt: Lang, 1985); and the essays in Josef Becker and Franz Knipping, ed., *Power in Europe? Great Britain, France, Italy, and Germany in a Postwar World, 1945–1950* (New York: Walter de Gruyter, 1986). Irwin M. Wall offers a first rate account of U.S. influence on France in *The United States and the Making of Postwar France, 1945–1954* (New York: Cambridge University Press, 1991). A superb introduction to overall U.S. policy in this period is Melvyn P. Leffler, "The American Conception of National Security and the Beginning of the Cold War, 1945–48," *American Historical Review* 89 (April 1984): 346–81.

For the economic and political problems of reconstructing postwar France, see Andrew Shennan, *Rethinking France: Plans for Renewal, 1940–1946* (Oxford: Clarendon Press, 1989); Jean Monnet, *Memoirs,* (Garden City, N.Y.: Doubleday, 1978); Michel Margairaz, "Autour des accords Blum-Byrnes: Jean Monnet entre le consensus national et le consensus atlantique," *Histoire, économie, société* 3 (1982): 440–70; George Ross, *Workers and Communists in France* (Berkeley and Los Angeles: University of California Press, 1982); Irwin M. Wall, *French Communism in the Era of Stalin: The Quest for Unity and Integration, 1945–1962* (Westport, Conn.: Greenwood Press, 1983); Lilly Marcou, *Le Kominform: Le communisme de guerre froid* (Paris: Presses de la Fondation Nationale des Sciences Politiques, 1977); Richard F. Kuisel, *Capitalism and the State in Modern France* (New York: Cambridge University Press, 1981); Georgette Elgey, *La république des illusions, 1945–1951* (Paris: Fayard, 1965); and Frances M. B. Lynch, "Resolving the Paradox of the Monnet Plan: National and International Planning in French Reconstruction," *Economic History Review,* 2d. ser., 37 (May 1984): 229–43.

For two excellent analyses of the Marshall Plan, see Alan S. Milward, *The Reconstruction of Western Europe, 1945–1951* (Berkeley and Los Angeles: University of California Press, 1984), which minimizes the plan's economic impact on Europe, and Michael J. Hogan, *The Marshall Plan: America, Britain, and the Reconstruction of Western Europe, 1947–1952* (New York: Cambridge University Press, 1987), which stresses U.S. efforts to remake Western Europe in the American image. See also the Walter Lippmann Diary in the Walter Lippmann Papers, Yale University Library; Chiarella Esposito, "The Marshall Plan in France and Italy, 1948–1950: The Counterpart Fund Negotiations," (Ph.D. diss., State University of New York at Stony Brook, 1985); and Imanuel Wexler, *The Marshall Plan Revisited* (Westport, Conn.: Greenwood Press, 1983). For American influences on French labor unions, see Roy Godson, "Non-Governmental Organizations in International Politics: The American Federation of Labor, the International Labor Movement, and French Politics, 1945–1952," (Ph.D. diss., Columbia University, 1972); Ronald Radosh, *American Labor and United States Foreign Policy* (New York: Random House, 1969); Alain Bergounioux, *Force ouvrière* (Paris: Edition du Seuil, 1975), 90–104; Anthony Carew, "Labour and the Marshall Plan," in *The Cold War in Europe,* ed. Charles S. Maier (New York: Marcus Wiener, 1991), 314–30; "The Most Dangerous Man," *Time,* 17 March 1952, 23; and Thomas W. Braden, "I'm Glad the CIA is Immoral," *Saturday Evening Post,* 20 May 1967, 9–13. On the origins of NATO, see Lawrence S. Kaplan, *NATO and the United States* (Boston: Twayne, 1988); Pierre Mélandri, *Les Etats-Unis face à l'unification de l'Europe, 1945–54* (Paris: Pedone, 1980); and Escott Reid, *Time of Fear and Hope: The Making of the North Atlantic Treaty, 1947–1949* (Toronto: McClelland and Stewart, 1977).

The copies of files from the Dwight D. Eisenhower library and the John Foster Dulles papers, both in the Mudd Library of Princeton University, contain abundant material on U.S.-French relations for the 1953–60 period. The files of record group 59 and the files of the United States Information Agency of the Paris embassy, part of record group 84 of the National Archives, offer rich documentation on the U.S.

psychological offensive. The archive of the Council on Foreign Relations is also helpful. See also Irwin Wall's *The United States and the Making of Postwar France*, cited above; Trevor Barnes, "The Secret Cold War: The C.I.A. and American Foreign Policy in Europe, 1946–1956," *The Historical Journal* 25 (1982): 649–70; and Peter Coleman, *The Liberal Conspiracy: The Congress for Cultural Freedom and the Struggle for the Mind of Postwar Europe* (New York: Free Press, 1989).

For the effect of the Rosenberg trial on France, see Robert B. Glynn, "L'Affaire Rosenberg in France," *Political Science Quarterly* 70 (December 1955): 498–521; Ronald Radosh and Joyce Milton, *The Rosenberg File: A Search for the Truth* (New York: Holt, Rinehart, and Winston, 1983). For the French political and social situation, see Stanley Hoffmann's perceptive *Decline or Renewal: France since the 1930s* (New York: Viking, 1974); Philip M. Williams, *Crisis and Compromise: Politics in the Fourth Republic* (Hamden, Conn.: Archon, 1964); and John T. Marcus, *Neutralism and Nationalism in France* (New York: Bookman Associates, 1958). On the importance of the European Defense Community to U.S. policymakers, see U.S. Congress, Senate Foreign Relations Committee, *Executive Sessions, 1951–54* (Washington, D.C.: GPO, 1976–77), and Townsend Hoopes, *The Devil and John Foster Dulles* (Boston: Little, Brown, 1973). See also Edward Fursdon, *The European Defense Community* (New York: St. Martin's Press, 1980), and Denise Artaud, "France between the Indochina War and the European Defense Community," in *Dien Bien Phu and the Crisis in Franco-American Relations, 1954–1955*, ed. Lawrence S. Kaplan, Denise Artaud, and Mark R. Rubin, (Wilmington, Del.: Scholarly Resources, 1990).

On U.S. relations with Pierre Mendès France, see Wall, *United States and the Making of Postwar France*, cited above; Jean Lacouture, *Pierre Mendès France* (New York: Holmes and Meier, 1984); and René Girault, "La France dans les rapports Est-Ouest au temps de Pierre Mendès France," in *Pierre Mendès France et le mendèsisme*, ed. François Bédarida and Jean-Pierre Rioux, (Paris: Fayard, 1985). For French atomic policy, see Goldschmidt, *Atomic Rivals*, cited above; McGeorge Bundy, *Danger and Survival: Choices about the Bomb in the First Fifty Years* (New York: Random House, 1988); Charles Ailleret, *L'aventure atomique française* (Paris: Grasset, 1968); Wilfrid L. Kohl, *French Nuclear Diplomacy* (Princeton, N.J.: Princeton University Press, 1971); and Lawrence Scheinman, *Atomic Energy Policy in France under the Fourth Republic* (Princeton, N.J.: Princeton University Press, 1965).

Lloyd C. Gardner, *Approaching Vietnam* (New York: Norton, 1988) and George McT. Kahin, *Intervention: How America Became Involved in Vietnam* (New York: Knopf, 1986) are excellent on the origins of U.S. involvement in France's Indochina War. See also Philippe Devillers and Jean Lacouture, *End of a War: Indochina, 1954* (New York: Praeger, 1969); George C. Herring, "Franco-American Conflict in Indochina, 1950–1954," in Kaplan, Artaud, and Rubin, *Dien Bien Phu*, cited above. On the Suez crisis, see the John Foster Dulles Oral History collection in the Mudd Library at Princeton University; Maurice Vaïsse's essays, "France and the Suez Crisis" and "Post-Suez France," in *Suez 1956: The Crisis and Its Consequences* ed. William Roger Louis and Roger Owen (New York: Oxford University Press, 1989); and Chester L. Cooper, *The Lion's Last Roar: Suez, 1956* (New York: Harper and Row, 1978).

On de Gaulle's coming to power in 1958, see Jean-Pierre Rioux, *The Fourth Republic, 1944–1958* (New York: Cambridge University Press, 1987). For the general's relations with Eisenhower and his September 1958 memoranda, see the primary documents cited above; Maurice Vaïsse, "Aux origines du mémorandum de septembre 1958," *Relations internationales* 58 (Summer 1989): 253–63; Jean Lacouture, *De Gaulle le souverain, 1959–1970* (Paris: Editions du Seuil, 1986); Cyrus L. Sulzberger, *The Last of the Giants* (New York: Macmillan, 1970); Keith W. Baum, "Two's Company, Three's a Crowd: The Eisenhower Administration, France, and Nuclear Weapons," *Presidential Studies Quarterly* 20 (Spring 1990) 315–28; and David Schoenbrun, *The Three Lives of Charles de Gaulle* (New York: Atheneum, 1966). Frank Costigliola, "The Pursuit of Atlantic Community: Nuclear Arms, Dollars, and Berlin," in *Kennedy's Quest for Victory: American Foreign Policy, 1961–1963*, ed. Thomas G. Paterson (New York: Oxford University Press, 1989), 24–56, analyzes John F. Kennedy's relations with de Gaulle. The John F. Kennedy Presidential Library has a rich holding of documents pertaining to U.S.-French relations. Two excellent memoirs are Harold Macmillan, *At the End of the Day, 1961–1963* (New York: Harper & Row, 1973), and George W. Ball, *The Past Has Another Pattern* (New York: Norton, 1982), the latter also helpful for the Johnson presidency. See also U.S. Congress, Senate Foreign Relations Committee, *Executive Sessions* 1963 (Washington, D.C.: GPO, 1986), and Arthur Schlesinger, Jr., *A Thousand Days* (Boston: Houghton Mifflin, 1965). For the Johnson years, there is a wealth of primary sources at the Lyndon B. Johnson Presidential Library. See also Cyrus L. Sulzberger, *An Age of Mediocrity: Memoirs and Diaries, 1963–1972* (New York: Macmillan, 1973); Hervé Alphand, *L'etonnement d'etre: Journal, 1933–1973* (Paris: Fayard, 1977); and Guy de Carmoy, *The Foreign Policies of France, 1944–1968* (Chicago: University of Chicago Press, 1970).

For economic relations and for the gold crisis of 1968, see Robert B. Dickie, *Foreign Investment: France, A Case Study* (Leyden: A. W. Sijthoff, 1970), 50–68; Jean-Jacques Servan-Schreiber, *The American Challenge* (New York: Atheneum, 1968); Gordon L. Weil and Ian Davidson, *The Gold War* (New York: Holt, Rinehart, and Winston, 1970); Marc Alexandre, "Le dollar et la France," *La nef* 26 (1966): 119–38; and David P. Calleo, *The Imperious Economy* (Cambridge: Harvard University Press, 1982). On the May 1968 uprising, see David Caute, *The Year of the Barricades: A Journey through 1968* (New York: Harper & Row, 1988); Marianne Debouzy, "The Influence of American Political Dissent on the French New Left," in *Contagious Conflict*, ed. A. N. J. Hollander, (Leiden: E. J. Brill, 1973); Hervé Hamon and Patrick Rotman, *Generation* (Paris: Editions du Seuil, 1987, 1988); Alain Touraine, *The May Movement* (New York: Random House, 1971); Bernard E. Brown, *Protest in Paris* (Morristown, N.J.: General Learning Press, 1974); Gilbert Gantier, "Un certain inspiration," *La nef* 26 (1966): 107–18; and Milton Viorst, *Fire in the Streets: America in the 1960s* (New York: Simon and Schuster, 1979).

The available documentary record for U.S.-French relations thins out for the period after the Johnson administration. In the papers of Dean Acheson at the Yale University library there is a valuable collection of correspondence commenting on Nixon's 1969–71 diplomacy. Among the principal players of the 1970s, the memoirs of Henry A. Kissinger, *White House Years* (Boston: Little, Brown, 1979) and *Years of Upheaval* (Boston: Little, Brown, 1982), are the most useful. Michel Jobert, *Memoires d'avenir* (Paris: Grasset, 1974), and William Safire, *Before the Fall* (Garden City, N.Y.: Doubleday, 1975), are also helpful, while Richard Nixon, *RN: The Memoirs of Richard Nixon* (New York: Grosset & Dunlap, 1978), is much less detailed. A superb study based on

French and American sources is Pierre Mélandri, *Une incertaine alliance: Les Etats-Unis et l'Europe, 1973–1983* (Paris: Sorbonne, 1988). Richard H. Ullman, "The Covert French Connection," *Foreign Policy* 75 (Summer 1989): 3–33, is essential on the development of U.S.-French nuclear cooperation in the 1970s and 1980s. See also Edward A. Kolodziej, "France Ensnared: French Strategic Policy and Bloc Politics after 1968," *Orbis* 5 (Winter 1972) 1085–1108; Yves-Henri Nouailhat, "Nixon-de Gaulle: Un épisode original des relations franco-américaines," *Revue française d'études américaines* 12 (1987): 309–16; Joan Hoff-Wilson, "Nixingerism, NATO, and Détente," *Diplomatic History* 13 (Fall 1989): 501–25; James O. Goldsborough, "France, the European Crisis, and the Alliance," *Foreign Affairs* 52 (April 1974): 538–55; and Seymour M. Hersh, *The Price of Power* (New York: Summit Books, 1983).

On the 1971 monetary crisis, see Robert Solomon, *The International Monetary System, 1945–1981* (New York: Harper & Row, 1982); Susan Strange, *International Economic Relations of the Western World* (Oxford: Oxford University Press, 1976); and Calleo, *Imperious Economy,* cited above. For the economic problems with Europe, see U.S. Congress, House Subcommittee on Europe and Subcommittee on Foreign Economic Policy, *American Interest in the European Community,* 93rd Cong., 1st and 2d sess., 1973–74. On the diplomacy of the Yom Kippur War and the oil embargo, see U.S. Congress, House Subcommittee on Europe, *United States–Europe Relations and the 1973 Middle East War,* 93d Cong., 1st and 2d sess., 1973–74; Robert J. Lieber, *Oil and the Middle East War: Europe in the Energy Crisis* (Cambridge: Harvard Studies in International Affairs, 1976), 49; Edward Malloy, "France, the Alliances, and the Global Energy Crisis: The Politics of Dependence," (Ph.D. diss., George Washington University, 1978); and Scott D. Sagan, "Lessons of the Yom Kippur Alert," *Foreign Policy* 36 (Fall 1979): 160–77.

The memoirs of top officials of the Jimmy Carter administration contain little on U.S.-French relations. See Jimmy Carter, *Keeping Faith: Memoirs of a President* (New York: Bantam Books, 1982); Cyrus Vance, *Hard Choices: Critical Years in American Foreign Policy* (New York: Simon and Schuster, 1983); and Zbigniew Brzezinski, *Power and Principle: Memoirs of the National Security Adviser, 1977–1981* (New York: Farrar, Straus & Giroux, 1983). More useful are F. Roy Willis, *The French Paradox* (Stanford, Calif.: Hoover Institution Press, 1982); Samy Cohen and Marie-Claude Smouts, ed., *La politique extérieure de Valéry Giscard d'Estaing* (Paris: Fondation Nationale, 1985); and Michael Meimeth, *Frankreichs Entspannungspolitik der 70 Jahre. Zwischen Status quo und friedlichen Wandel* (Baden-Baden: Nomos, 1990). See also the oral memoir of Carter's ambassador to France, Arthur Hartman, in the Georgetown University oral history collection.

Although archival documents for U.S.-French relations in the 1980s are largely unavailable, there is a wealth of published material. Congressional hearings, discussed below, and newspaper accounts were particularly useful for this study. For cultural and intellectual relations see the essays in Denis Lacorne, Jacques Rupnik, and Marie-France Toinet, ed., *The Rise and Fall of Anti-Americanism* (London: Macmillan, 1990), published in French as *L'Amérique dans les têtes* (Paris: Hachette, 1986); Michèle Lamont, "The Production of Culture in France and the United States since World War II," in *Intellectuals in Liberal Democracies,* ed. Alain G. Gagnon (New York: Praeger, 1987), 167–77; Michèle Lamont, "How to Become a Dominant French

Philosopher: The Case of Jacques Derrida," *American Journal of Sociology* 93 (November 1987): 584–622; Keith A. Reader, *Intellectuals and the Left in France since 1968* (New York: St. Martin's Press, 1987); John Sturrock, ed., *Structuralism and Since: From Lévi Strauss to Derrida* (New York: Oxford University Press, 1979); George Ross, "The Decline of the Left Intellectual in Modern France," in Gagnon, *Intellectuals in Liberal Democracies*, 43–64; and Frank Lentricchia, *After the New Criticism* (Chicago: University of Chicago Press, 1980).

On the transmutation of the Socialist party, see Jacques Huntzinger, "La politique extérieure du parti socialiste," *Politique étrangère* 47 (1982): 33–44; Julius W. Friend, *Seven Years in France: François Mitterrand and the Unintended Revolution, 1981–1988* (Boulder, Colo.: Westview Press, 1989); and Daniel Singer, *Is Socialism Doomed? The Meaning of Mitterrand* (New York: Oxford University Press, 1988). The Soviet gas pipeline issue is covered well in Antony J. Blinken, *Ally versus Ally: America, Europe, and the Siberian Pipeline Crisis* (New York: Praeger, 1987); U.S. Congress, Joint Economic Committee, *Soviet Pipeline Sanctions: The European Perspective*, 97th Cong., 2d sess., 1983; Alexander M. Haig, Jr., *Caveat: Realism, Reagan, and Foreign Policy* (New York: Macmillan, 1984); and Mélandri, *Une incertaine alliance*, cited above.

For nuclear and strategic issues, see U.S. Congress, Senate Foreign Relations Committee, *Crisis of Will in the Nato Alliance*, 99th Cong., 1st sess., 1985; U.S. Congress, Senate Committee on Foreign Relations, *Is NATO Still the Centerpiece of U.S. Foreign Policy—Should It Be?*, 99th Cong., 1st sess., 1985; U.S. Congress, House Committee on Armed Services, *Defense Burdensharing: The Costs, Benefits, and Future of U.S. Alliances*, 100th Congress, 2d session, 1988; U.S. Congress, Senate Committee on Armed Services, *NATO Defense and the INF Treaty*, 100th Cong., 2d sess., 1988; U.S. Congress, Senate Foreign Relations Committee, *The INF Treaty*, 100th Cong., 2d sess., 1988; Pierre Lellouche, "The Odd Couple," in *French Security Issues: A Symposium*, ed. Joyce Lasky Shub (Washington, D.C.: American Enterprise Institute, 1983); Jacques Huntzinger, "Défense de la France, securité de l'Europe," *Politique étrangère* 48 (1983): 395–402; Robert S. Rudney, "Mitterrand's New Atlanticism: Evolving French Attitudes toward NATO," *Orbis* 28 (Spring 1984): 83–96; Robbin F. Laird, *France, the Soviet Union, and the Nuclear Weapons Issue* (Boulder, Colo.: Westview Press, 1985); David S. Yost, "Radical Changes in French Defence Policy?" *Survival* 28 (January 1986): 53–68; Walter Goldstein, ed., *Reagan's Leadership and the Atlantic Alliance* (Washington, D.C.: Pergamon-Brassey's, 1986); Neville Waites, "Defence Policy under Socialist Management," in *Mitterrand's France*, ed. Sonia Mazey and Michael Newman (London: Croom Helm, 1987), 192–217; R. James Woolsey, "The Future of NATO's Defense Posture: An American Perspective," *Atlantic Community Quarterly* 26 (Summer 1988): 115–29; Thierry de Montbrial, "Security Requires Caution," *Foreign Policy* 71 (Summer 1988): 86–98; François Heisbourg, "The British and French Nuclear Forces," *Survival* 31 (July–August 1989): 304–15; Robert E. Osgood, "The Implications of SDI for U.S.-European Relations" in *SDI and U.S. Foreign Policy*, ed. Robert W. Tucker (Boulder, Colo.: Westview Press, 1987), 68–90; and David P. Calleo, "SDI, Europe, and the American Strategic Dilemma," in ibid., 101–19.

For the dispute over agricultural subsidies, see U.S. Congress, House Subcommittee on Europe and the Middle East, *Roundtable Discussion on United States Policy toward Europe*, 99th Cong., 2d sess., 1986; U.S. Congress, Joint Economic Committee, *Europe 1992: Long-Term Implications for the U.S. Economy*, 101st Cong., 1st sess.,

1989; and U.S. Congress, Senate Committee on Finance, *Europe-92 Trade Program*, 101st Cong., 1st sess., 1989.

This book's analysis of the revolutionary changes of 1989–90 relies largely on newspaper accounts (see endnotes) and on congressional hearings. A good overview of the German aspect in U.S.-French relations is Elizabeth Pond, *After the Wall: American Policy toward Germany* (New York: Priority, 1990). For the policy of the George Bush administration, see U.S. Congress, Senate Foreign Relations Committee, *Nomination of James A. Baker III*, 1989; U.S. Congress, Senate Committee on Foreign Relations, *Nomination of Lawrence S. Eagleburger*, 101st Cong., 1st sess., 1989; U.S Congress, Senate Foreign Relations Committee, *The Future of NATO*, 101st Cong., 2d sess., 1990; U.S. Congress, House Committee on Foreign Affairs, Subcommittee on Europe and the Middle East, *Developments in Europe, March 1990*, 101st Cong., 2d sess., 1990; U.S. Congress, Commission on Security and Cooperation in Europe, *Implementation of the Helsinki Accords*, 101st. Cong., 2d sess., 1990; John Newhouse, "Sweeping Change," *The New Yorker*, 27 August 1990. On French policy toward Germany unity, see Walter Schütze, "Frankreich angesichts der deutschen Einheit," *Europa Archiv* 4 (25 February 1990): 133–34; Frédéric Bozo and Jérôme Paolini, "Trois Allemagnes, deux Europes et la France," *Politique étrangère* 55 (Spring 1990): 119–37; and Davis S. Yost, "France in the New Europe," *Foreign Affairs* 69 (Winter 1990/91): 107–28. For French thinking on future possibilities for NATO, WEU, and European security, see Thierry Mileo, "L'Otan face à son nouvel environnement," *Défense nationale* 46 (March 1990): 11–21; Jean-Pierre Chevènement, "La France et la sécurité de l'Europe," *Politique étrangère* 55 (March 1990): 525–31; and Frédéric Bozo, "La France et l'Otan: Vers une nouvelle alliance," *Défense nationale* 47 (January 1991): 19–33.